For
Sayeed
Best
Ardeshir
Karachi
26/3/20/10

Jinnah and Tilak

Comrades in the Freedom Struggle

Jinnah and Tilak

Comrades in the Freedom Struggle

A.G. Noorani

OXFORD
UNIVERSITY PRESS

Great Clarendon Street, Oxford OX2 6DP

Oxford University Press is a department of the University of Oxford.
It furthers the University's objective of excellence in research, scholarship,
and education by publishing worldwide in

Oxford   New York

Auckland Cape Town Dar es Salaam Hong Kong Karachi
Kuala Lumpur Madrid Melbourne Mexico City Nairobi
New Delhi Shanghai Taipei Toronto

with offices in

Argentina Austria Brazil Chile Czech Republic France Greece
Guatemala Hungary Italy Japan Poland Portugal Singapore
South Korea Switzerland Turkey Ukraine Vietnam

Oxford is a registered trade mark of Oxford University Press
in the UK and in certain other countries

© Oxford University Press 2010

The moral rights of the author have been asserted

First published 2010

All rights reserved. No part of this publication may be reproduced, translated,
stored in a retrieval system, or transmitted, in any form or by any means,
without the prior permission in writing of Oxford University Press.
Enquiries concerning reproduction should be sent to
Oxford University Press at the address below.

This book is sold subject to the condition that it shall not, by way
of trade or otherwise, be lent, re-sold, hired out or otherwise circulated
without the publisher's prior consent in any form of binding or cover
other than that in which it is published and without a similar condition
including this condition being imposed on the subsequent purchaser.

ISBN 978-0-19-547829-7

Typeset in Times
Printed in Pakistan by
Kagzi Printers, Karachi.
Published by
Ameena Saiyid, Oxford University Press
No. 38, Sector 15, Korangi Industrial Area, PO Box 8214
Karachi-74900, Pakistan.

To my friend
Dr G.G. Parikh
a dedicated fighter for freedom,
a committed socialist,
a brilliant physician who cares for the poor,
and, above all, a man of sterling integrity.

'"For all their boasting, practical men do not know either men or the world; they do not even know the reality of their own works". To history is given the task of recovering and placing in context that of which historical figures are "conscious but not self-conscious." If they could return to life, "the geniuses of pure politics, the fatalia monstra recorded in histories, would be astounded to learn what they have done without being aware of it, and they would read of their own past deeds as in a hieroglyph to which they had been offered the keys".'[1]

'.... the depth of evil to which individuals and communities may sink, particularly when they try to play the role of God to history'.[2]

Notes

1. Benedetto Croce, *La Storia come Pensiero e come Azione* (6th edition, Bari, 1954), p. 181. Quoted by Otto Pflanze with his comments in *Bismarck*, Volume III, Princeton University Press, 1990, p. 457.
2. Reinhold Niebuhr, *The Irony of American History*, Charles Scribners' Sons, New York, 1952, p. 173.

Contents

		page
	List of Appendices	xi
	Preface	xiii
1.	A Forgotten Comradeship	1
2.	After Tilak: Jinnah and Gandhi's Congress	57
3.	The Widening Divide	140
4.	Wrecking India's Unity	165
5.	The Gandhi–Cripps Pact	199
6.	Demise of the Cabinet Mission's Plan	211
7.	An Embittered Separation	234
8.	The United Bengal Episode	251
9.	Assessing Jinnah	262
	Appendices	273
	Index	455

List of Appendices

	page
1. Jinnah's Defence of Tilak: The Court Proceedings	275
2. Jinnah's Battles for Press Freedom	351
3. The Lucknow Pact, 1916	360
4. Jinnah's Fourteen Points, 1929	362
5. Jinnah–Rajendra Prasad Pact, 1934	364
6. The Lahore Resolution, 1940	366
7. Stafford Cripps' Offer, 1942	367
8. The C.R. Formula, 1944	369
9. Jinnah's Offer of 12 May 1946	370
10. The Congress' Offer of 12 May 1946	372
11. The Cabinet Mission's Plan of 16 May 1946	375
12. Statement Made by Mr M.A. Jinnah, President of the All-India Muslim League, 22 May 1946	385
13. Resolution Passed by the Congress Working Committee on 24 May 1946	392
14. Statement Issued by the Cabinet Mission in New Delhi, 25 May 1946	395

15. Letter from Viceroy to Mr Jinnah, 4 June 1946 — 397

16. Resolution Passed by the All-India Muslim League Council, 6 June 1946 — 398

17. Letter from Mr Jinnah to Viceroy, 8 June 1946 — 400

18. Resolution of the Congress Working Committee, 25 June 1946 — 402

19. All-India Congress Committee's Resolution of 6 January 1947 — 404

20. All-India Muslim League Council Resolutions adopted at Kaiser Bagh in Bombay on 29 July 1946 — 405

21. The Muslim League Working Committee's Resolution of 31 January 1947 — 409

22. The Partition Plan of 3 June 1947 — 416

23. India Divided: Who is to Blame for Partition? by Sir Chimanlal Setalvad — 422

24. Jinnah's Speech to Pakistan's Constituent Assembly on 11 August 1947 — 426

25. Maulana Hasrat Mohani's Ghazal on Tilak — 429

26. Jinnah and the Muslims of India by A.G. Noorani — 430

27. The Haroon Report by A.G. Noorani — 445

Preface

'The century gave birth to a great epoch; but the great moment found a petty generation'
— Goethe.

A definitive account of India's march towards freedom and its attainment, amidst the carnage and bloodshed that accompanied its partition into two states, yet remains to be written. One is hard put to find, for instance, a thorough analysis of the background to the Cabinet Mission Plan of 16 May 1946—the last chance for preserving the country's unity—and the true causes of its collapse. Little is written of one of its authors Stafford Cripps's role in the collapse.

The festivities of independence could not minimize a sense of tragedy and failure, which Faiz Ahmed Faiz captured in an immortal poem *Subh Azadi* (Dawn of Freedom) in August 1947:

یہ داغ داغ اجالا، یہ شب گزیدہ سحر

وہ انتظار تھا جس کا، یہ وہ سحر تو نہیں

(*This stained daybreak, this night-bitten dawn
This is not the dawn that we had waited for*).

As tragic as the history of this period is, accounts of it produced by the two concerned countries are pathetic. In the sixty years since independence, two generations of what can only be called court historians have dominated academia in India and Pakistan; save for a few honourable exceptions. State control of universities and other institutions of learning is one explanation for this, misdirected patriotism is another. Consequently, the intellectual chasm between the two countries widened as partisanship hardened its grip. This book does no more than mention some facts and indicate some aspects which have been ignored or glossed over.

A study of the relationship between Quaid-i-Azam Mohammad Ali Jinnah and Lokmanya Bal Gangadhar Tilak reveals facets of their personalities which biographers have not cared to explore, and aspects of the freedom movement which have been neglected. This modest effort in that direction will, it is hoped, prod further definitive studies of a most eventful decade in which these two great men fought as comrades in the struggle for freedom. Many a myth deserves to be dispelled. In truth, Jinnah was a participant in mass politics, from the very beginning of his political career. He narrowly escaped deportation from India. Nor was he opposed to non-cooperation in principle. Contrary to the common belief, his relations with Mohandas Karamchand Gandhi, for whom he expressed high regard even at the time of his parting from the Congress, endured till the mid-thirties. None of the Liberals criticized the British as trenchantly as he did. None participated in mass politics. Jinnah's rhetoric reflected fierce patriotism. It bears recalling today and is relevant to any study on the causes of the partition of India at the very moment of its independence. It should rank among the ten greatest tragedies in the history of man; an egregious folly and a blunder of great and lasting consequence.

It is the tallest leaders on both sides who were directly responsible for that tragedy and for the miseries which the people on both sides of the divide suffered in consequence.

Criticism of their policies and conduct is not very welcome; but, it is very necessary if we are to profit by experience. Of this, sadly there is yet little sign. A mature people should have no difficulty in conducting a rigorous scrutiny of their record without denying them the respect that is justly due to them.

Libraries in Britain have whole shelves of critiques of Winston Churchill, though he heroically saved the country from the Nazi invasion. In this, Ghalib must be our guide:

لازم نہیں کہ خضر کی ہم پیروی کریں
جانا کہ اک بزرگ ہمیں ہم سفر ملے

(*It is not necessary for us to follow in the footsteps of Khizr
We know that we met a wise one on our journey*).

Finally, I would urge the reader to accept the advice which Bacon gave in his essay 'Of Studies' written over four centuries ago: 'Read not to contradict and refute, nor to believe and take for granted; nor to find talk and discourse, but to weigh and consider'.

Dr G.G. Parikh, to whom this book is dedicated, will disagree with some of my views; but, not, I hope, disapprove of the work. That G.G. is a friend of forty years' standing is the least of the reasons for the dedication. He is one of the unsung heroes of India. He and his wife Mangla Ben who, sadly, died recently, went to prison during the Quit India Movement and also during the emergency, as did their only child, Sonal Shah.

A heart patient, he is off to village Tara, 64 km from Mumbai, almost every weekend to look after an institution for rural development run by the Yusuf Meherally Centre, which he has taken care of for decades. G.G. knew all the socialist leaders but never hankered after a political career or for publicity. Jayaprakash Narayan respected him greatly. Such persons are very rare. Hence, the dedication.

This book would not have been written but for the encouragement of two friends, Ms Ameena Saiyid, Managing Director, Oxford University Press, Karachi, and Mr Hameed Haroon, Chief

Executive Officer, Pakistan Herald Publications (Pvt.) Ltd., publishers of *Dawn* and *The Herald*.

It grew out of a conversation at a fine dinner in Karachi on 12 October 2008. A year earlier Mr Hameed Haroon had asked me to do a paper on Jinnah and press freedom. It remained unpublished. I took advantage of the presence of both at the dinner to ask if he had any objection to its being published by Oxford University Press. He had none, he said, if due acknowledgment was made. The idea was to publish with the paper the transcript of Tilak's trial in which Jinnah defended him, prefaced by an account of their relationship, which biographers of both had studiously neglected. Tilak died in 1920; but by the time my research reached that crucial year, I was struck by the intense, almost fierce fervour of Jinnah's nationalism, the utter absence of bitterness on his part in the hours of his political defeat, and his participation in mass politics right from the early years of his political career.

Inescapably, 1920 brought the survey to the historic Congress Sessions at Calcutta and Nagpur where Gandhi's programme for civil disobedience was adopted despite Jinnah's solitary protest; especially at Nagpur. None of the myths spread over the years, with reckless disregard for the truth, had the slightest basis: his wife Ruttie's death, the Nehru Report, the Round Table Conference and the rest. He returned to India after a few years' stay in London with a strong desire to achieve a settlement with the Congress; such as the Lucknow Pact of 1916 which he had forged with Tilak. That was not to be. Things went wrong between 1937 and 1939. But there was another opportunity for a rapprochement in 1946. The Congress wrecked it, once again.

Indians and Pakistanis need to come to terms with Jinnah's personality. Indians must acknowledge the wrongs he suffered for long, and Pakistanis, the wrongs he himself went on to

Tilak and Gandhi at Shantaram Chawl.

Shantaram Chawl in Girgaum, Mumbai where Jinnah often spoke with Tilak at mass gatherings.

Bal Gangadhar Tilak.
"Swaraj is my birthright".

Tilak and Gandhi, c. 1919.

Sardar Griha, Mumbai where Tilak lived and died.

Gaikwad Wada, where Tilak started the daily newspaper *Kesari*.

Sardar Vinchurkarwada where Tilak lived till 1905.

P & O S.S. 'Rajputana'.

M.A. Jinnah, c. 1919.

> THIS HALL HAS BEEN RAISED BY THE CITIZENS OF BOMBAY TO COMMEMORATE THEIR HISTORIC TRIUMPH OF THE 11TH DECEMBER 1918 UNDER THE BRAVE AND BRILLIANT LEADERSHIP OF ◊◊ MOHMED ALI JINNAH ◊◊

IN MEMORY OF JINNAH
An honour for a popular leader

In 1918 Jinnah became a popular hero. He and his followers packed the Town Hall on December 10, 1918, to oppose the 'citizens address' to the retiring Governor, Lord Willingdon. The meeting was broken up by the police who assaulted the anti-requisitionists, including Jinnah. A city attorney, B D Lam, suggested the erection of a memorial in Jinnah's honour by raising a public fund. Thus was built the People's Jinnah Hall which stands in the compound of the Congress House in Bombay.

commit. Both must appreciate his splendid record as a dedicated legislator committed to freedom, civil rights, and social reform. As George F. Kennan sagely remarked 'When the ambivalence of one's virtue is recognized, the total iniquity of one's opponent is also irreparably impaired.'

Jinnah has received either uncritical adulation or unrestrained denigration. An informed critical evaluation has been denied to him, one of the most remarkable men of his times.

Even as a person Jinnah has received less than is his due. Yusuf Meherally knew him well. His career as a junior in his chambers ended by his imprisonment for agitating against the Simon Commission. He stoutly opposed Jinnah's later politics but this ardent nationalist bore him no malice unlike another junior, M.C. Chagla, whose nationalism flourished in a sheltered life. As late as on 14 May 1944 Meherally wrote of Jinnah in these warm terms in *Bharat Jyoti*, the Sunday edition of *Free Press Journal*:

> Jinnah's political career has been a study in contrast. But through nearly half a century of active life, two facts stand out prominently. First that he is no friend of the British bureaucracy, second, that he has been a steadfast constitutionalist.
>
> He has a winning presence. A defiant smile hovers over his lips. Above all, he has a captivating personality. After half an hour's conversation with him one returns a devotee. Without doubt, Jinnah is the greatest parliamentarian in India. He has been almost continuously a member of the Central Legislative Assembly from 1910 till today. His great personality, varied experience, intimate knowledge of legal forms and procedure and a gift for withering retort, have made him a formidable opponent of the official benches...

Meherally was a true nationalist who did not feel the need to denounce Muslims or Jinnah. He was no 'Sarkari Musalman'.

A debt of gratitude is due to my friend Mr Kumar Ketkar, Chief Editor, *Loksatta* of the Indian Express Group for his help and encouragement. He helped a lot to secure the priceless photographs of Jinnah and Tilak at the Shantaram Chawl in Mumbai in the second decade of the last century. Jinnah was very much a mass leader even then. The photographs are published in this book courtesy of Kesari Mahratta Library, Pune. I am most grateful to my friend Mr S. Iftikhar Murshed, distinguished diplomat and editor of the prestigious quarterly *Criterion*, for permission to reprint in this book two articles 'Jinnah & Muslims of India' and 'The Haroon Report' which I wrote for the journal. Thanks are due also to Mr Prakash Kumar Sinha and Mr P.M. Mathews, who deciphered my scribblings into a legible typewritten manuscript. Ghousia Ghofran Ali, Managing Editor at the Oxford University Press bore with me patiently and cheerfully, and worked on the manuscript at all its stages. My debt to her is enormous.

Mumbai,
1 January 2010

1

A Forgotten Comradeship

'The two great political centres in Bombay at that time [c. 1916] were Sardar Griha, where Tilak lived and Jinnah's chambers in the High Court. All political roads led to these two places for organization, consultation and decision', their friend and colleague Kanji Dwarkadas testified.[1] Theirs was not what is known as 'drawing room politics'. They plunged deep into mass politics. 'Thousands of leaflets and pamphlets were published week after week. After dinner meetings were held at Kalbadevi and Mandvi and every fortnight big public meetings were held at Shantaram's Chawl, Girgaum, addressed by, among others, Jinnah, Tilak, Khaparde, Khadilkar, N.C. Kelkar and B.G. Horniman', an Englishman who edited the nationalist daily *Bombay Chronicle*. Meetings were also held at places like Mulji Jetha Cloth Market and China Bagh.

Dwarkadas added: 'The Shantaram's Chawl meetings were a bug-bear to Lord Willingdon [Governor of Bombay Presidency which then comprised Sind as well]. For the first time in the history of political agitation, *the masses were approached and were made politically conscious*. ...Omar Sobani, Shankarlal Banker and I met Jinnah daily in his chambers to arrange our day-to-day programme of political propaganda.'[2]

However, biographers of Lokmanya Bal Gangadhar Tilak and Quaid-i-Azam Mohammed Ali Jinnah make at best a passing reference to the comradeship they had forged in the struggle for freedom from British rule and none at all to their personal friendship. The relationship was all the more remarkable given the barriers of age, culture, and political background. Tilak was twenty years older. He was born in Poona (now Pune) on 23 July 1856. Jinnah was born in Karachi on 25 December 1876. They came together in Bombay, as Mumbai was then called, and made the city one of the great centres of the freedom struggle.

But let alone Jinnah, even the great Urdu poet, Maulana Hasrat Mohani's devotion to Tilak is ignored by Tilak's biographers. In India, as in Pakistan, we have not been too far from Stalinist re-writing of history. Hasrat suffered privation and want, and long terms in prison; but he never wavered in his commitment. A biographer records: 'He was an ardent admirer of Tilak since his student days. Once while discussing about their favourites amongst the national leaders, many students named Sir Sayyed Ahmed Khan as their guide and mentor, some named Dadabhai Naoroji or Surendranath Bannerjee. Mohani, however, mentioned Bal Gangadhar Tilak as his mentor and guide'.[3] Hasrat wrote a moving poem on Tilak (see Appendix 16).

The 22nd session of the Indian National Congress, held in Calcutta (now Kolkata) in December 1906, was the first which Jinnah attended. Its President was his mentor, Dadabhai Naoroji. Jinnah, then thirty years old, was no passive observer. Risking criticism from the community, he opposed a resolution urging 'a reservation for the backwardly educated class' in the legislatures and local bodies. He understood that it referred to the Muslims and said that 'they should be treated in the same way as the Hindu community. The foundation, upon which the Indian National Congress is based, is that we are all equal; that there should be no reservation for any class or community'.[4]

At its next session in Surat the Congress suffered a split, between the Extremists led by Tilak, and the moderates.[5] It bears recalling that in those days public figures entered local bodies first. Jinnah was a member of the Bombay Municipal Corporation from 17 February 1904 till his resignation in 1906.[6] Jinnah was the quintessential moderate. But he was also a natural bridge builder, a mediator as well as an advocate for one side. The split in the Congress left both sides unhappy. Jinnah tried to mend the breach as a colleague, M.R. Jayakar, recorded in his autobiography. 'In close contact with Pherozeshah Mehta, leader of the moderates and an occasional visitor to his legal chambers, opposite the Bombay University Gardens, Jinnah made himself very useful in this matter'.[7]

A scholar Hugh F. Owen wrote that 'in later 1915 and 1916 Tilak and Jinnah had worked together for the readmission of the extremists to Congress. And it has been maintained that Tilak played a considerable part in prevailing upon [Pandit Madan Mohan] Malaviya and other participants in the negotiations to acquiesce in the final terms of the [Lucknow] Pact' in 1916.[8]

No Indian leader of his times or later had as many brushes with the law as Tilak did.[9] In 1897 and 1907 Tilak was tried for sedition. He was convicted in both trials. In 1897 he was sentenced to eighteen months' rigorous imprisonment. His counsel Dinshaw D. Davar applied for bail twice but it was refused. On the third occasion he applied to the great judge, Justice Badruddin Tyabji, who granted bail in a reasoned judgment which still ranks as a classic on the subject.[10]

By a quirk of fate the second trial was conducted in the Sessions Court of the Bombay High Court by none other than Davar, now a Judge of the Bombay High Court. On 2 July 1908 Jinnah applied for bail and cited Tyabji's judgment on granting bail. It was rejected. Davar conducted the trial with conspicuous lack of fairness and made offensive remarks on Tilak while pronouncing the sentence. Tilak defended himself, aided by Joseph Baptista. His aim was not to secure an acquittal but, as at any political trial, turn the tables on the state and appeal to public opinion. The jury was split. Eight Europeans who knew not a word of Marathi, in which the articles were written, returned a verdict of 'guilty'. Two Indians, both Parsis, incidentally, returned a verdict of 'not guilty'. The judge accepted the majority verdict and sentenced Tilak to three years' transportation under each of the two charges for which he was tried. The sentences were to run, not concurrently, but consecutively; six years' transportation in all. The government later commuted the sentence to one of simple imprisonment. When Davar asked Tilak if he had anything to say before the sentence was pronounced, he replied 'All I wish to say is that, in spite of the verdict of the jury, I maintain that I am innocent. There are higher powers that rule the destiny of things and it may be the will of Providence that the cause which I represent may prosper more by my suffering than by my remaining free'. Only an inspired man could have spoken thus; so spontaneously. These words are inscribed in marble outside court room no. 46 in the Bombay High Court. The tablet was unveiled by Chief Justice M.C. Chagla in 1956.

Chagla devilled in Jinnah's chambers for six years (1922–8) and was at one point secretary of the Bombay Provincial Muslim League, a position from which he resigned in 1928. He wrote in his memoir:

> It is surprising that there should have been so much in common between Jinnah and Tilak. I understand that the regard Jinnah had for Tilak was reciprocated by Tilak. Jinnah told me that when as a junior he was reading in the chambers of Sir George Lowndes, who afterwards became a member of the Viceroy's Legislative Council, and later still a member of the Privy Council, Lowndes's opinion was once sought regarding some speech that Tilak had delivered. There was going to be a conference and Lowndes asked Jinnah whether he had read the brief and what he thought about it. Jinnah replied that he had not touched the brief and would not look at it as he wanted to keep himself free to criticize the Government for prosecuting a great patriot like Tilak. Jinnah said that Lowndes was amused at the indignation and enthusiasm of his young junior.
>
> Jinnah also told me that after Justice Davar sentenced Tilak to six years' rigorous imprisonment the Government conferred a

knighthood upon Davar and the Bombay Bar Association wanted to give him a dinner. A circular went round asking those who wanted to join the dinner to sign it. When the circular came to Jinnah, he wrote a scathing note that the Bar should be ashamed to want to give a dinner to a judge who had obtained a knighthood by doing what the Government wanted and by sending a great patriot to jail with a savage sentence. It seems that Justice Davar came to know about this and sent for Jinnah in his chambers. He asked Jinnah how he thought Davar had treated Jinnah in his court. Jinnah replied that he had always been very well treated. Davar asked him, next, whether he had any grievance against him [Davar]. Jinnah said he had none. Davar then asked: "Why did you write a note like this against me?" Jinnah replied that he wrote it because he thought it was the truth and however well Davar might have treated him, he could not suppress his strong feeling about the manner in which he had tried Tilak's case.[11]

Chagla's surprise is understandable given the acerbity which overcame him once he broke with Jinnah. But men like Kanji Dwarkadas knew better. Nothing conveys the depth of Jinnah's friendship with Tilak better than the eulogy which the unemotional Jinnah delivered at a meeting to condole Tilak's death on 1 August 1920. It is best set out *in extenso* rather than consigned to the ghetto of an appendix.

> Mr Tilak was a shrewd practical politician. After the split at Surat, where I came to know him first in 1907, Mr Tilak's party in the Indian National Congress had a very small voice and remained in a minority and so far as Mr Tilak was concerned, his conviction by Mr Justice Davar in a case against him for sedition, under Section 124-A of the Indian Penal Code, removed him from the political arena for nearly six years. The sentence passed against him of six years was a savage sentence. I was given a retainer for his defence and was instructed to make an application for bail which was refused by Mr Justice Davar. I am not disclosing any secrets, I hope, with reference to his trial before Mr Justice Davar, when I say that, he was determined not so much to secure his acquittal, but to establish that the Anglo-Indian press was guilty of defaming India and Indian people, which was as much a libel, and the Government

did not take any steps against them. There arose a serious difference of opinion between him and myself as a Counsel, because I refused to adopt any line, as Counsel, except what I considered best for his defence.

After his return from Mandalay, I came in closer contact with him and Mr Tilak, who was known in his earlier days to be communalistic and stood for Maharashtra, developed and showed broader and greater national outlook as he gained experience. I believe, it was at the Bombay Presidency Provincial Conference, over which I had the honour to preside, that the gulf, which was created owing to the Surat Congress split, was bridged over and Mr Tilak and his entire party once more came into the fold of the Indian National Congress in 1915. Since then, Mr Tilak rendered yeoman services to the country and played a very important part in bringing about the Hindu–Moslem unity which ultimately resulted in the Lucknow Pact in 1916. Subsequently, he was one of the pioneers of the Home Rule League movement and established the Indian Home Rule League. In his pursuit to make the Home Rule League movement popular, he delivered a series of lectures all over Maharashtra and again he was convicted by the Magistrate at Poona. The High Court of Bombay acquitted him.

Tilak was for working the Montford Reforms of 1919 and spoke in favour of their acceptance at the Amritsar Congress. Unfortunately soon after the Amritsar Congress, by the cruel hand of Death, Mr Tilak was taken away from us at the most critical moment. I have often wondered what would have been his attitude, had he been alive when the Nagpur Congress sanctioned the policy and programme of Non-cooperation in 1920.[12]

Jinnah not only explained why he did not defend Tilak at the trial in 1908, he also referred to the case in which he did. Tilak returned to India on 16 June 1914 after serving his sentence in Mandalay. The scholar read tomes in prison and wrote his classic *Geeta-Rahasya* in less than six months; from November 1910 to March 1911. Erudite though he was, Tilak could with ease communicate to the masses in the language they understood. Once in the country he plunged into politics. Before long Tilak was involved in yet another court case; just two years after his return from Mandalay. I.A. Guider (Deputy Inspector General of Police, Criminal Investigation Department), moved the district magistrate of Poona on 22 July 1916, alleging that Tilak, 'having previous conviction on charges of sedition' was once again, 'orally disseminating' the crime. He cited three speeches: one delivered at Belgaum on 1 May 1916, and the other two at Ahmednagar, on 31 May and 1 June. He was asked to sign a bond for a sum of Rs20,000, with two sureties each in the sum of Rs10,000, for his 'good behaviour' for a period of one year. This proceedings under Section 108 of the Criminal Procedure Code, 1898, while less than a prosecution, was no less humiliating. Tilak was served with the notice on 23 July, just as he was entertaining friends who had called to congratulate him on his sixty-first birthday.

Jinnah defended Tilak in the court of the district magistrate at Poona, unsuccessfully; but he had the order set aside by the High Court. Proceedings in both the courts (vide Appendix 1). Jinnah was assisted by good lawyers, chiefly by the patriot, Joseph Baptista, popularly known as Uncle Baptista.[13]

In 1958, the government of Bombay published a compilation of police, intelligence and officials' reports on the freedom movement in the province in those days.[14] The records contain a wealth of material on Jinnah's collaboration with Tilak, Baptista, and some others.

Without in any way departing from his professional duties and limits as counsel, as Tilak had desired him to do in the 1908 trial, Jinnah managed to put the government in the dock and enlist public sympathy on behalf of his distinguished client, Tilak. He did not know Marathi; but, properly briefed, he showed a mastery of the nuances of the languages.

M.C. Chagla was present at the High Court when Justices Sir Stanley Batchelor and Lallubhai Shah delivered judgment in November 1916. He wrote:

> I sat in the third row, and a little later, I found Tilak enter and take his seat in the second row. After a while, Jinnah came and sat in the first row reserved for counsel. Judgment was delivered, and the conviction to everyone's relief was set aside. Jinnah then turned round and warmly shook Tilak by the hand. I believe this was the first time that I had seen Jinnah. I might mention here that during my long association with him, I found that Jinnah always showed the greatest respect and regard for Tilak. Even when he was in the process of changing his political stand and becoming more and more communal. I never remember his ever saying anything which was derogatory to Tilak. Two persons in public life for whom Jinnah showed the greatest respect were Gokhale and Tilak. He had hard and harsh things to say about Gandhiji, Nehru and others; but as far as Gokhale and Tilak were concerned, Jinnah had the most profound admiration and respect for them and for their views.[15]

On 27 November 1917 the secretary of state for India, Edwin S. Montagu, wrote in his *Indian Diary* that Tilak had 'the greatest influence of any person in India'.[16] He was a national hero. Even the Lieutenant Governor of the United Provinces was amazed at Tilak's popularity.[17] His group had re-entered Congress as 'an invading body' annexing the Congress. Owen noted that 'in later 1915 and early 1916, Tilak and Jinnah had worked together for the readmission of the extremists to Congress'.[18]

Two of the foremost leaders of the time died in 1915; Gopal Krishna Gokhale on 19 February and Pherozeshah Mehta on 5 November. That was also the year in which Mohandas Karamchand Gandhi returned home. Jinnah presided at a function in his honour organized by the Gurjar Sabha in Bombay on 14 January 1915. Annie Besant presided over the 32nd session of the Congress at Calcutta in 1917. Shortly before that she proposed that an Indian Home Rule League be established. It was discussed at a meeting held in Bombay on 27 December

1915, just before the annual session of the Congress. The idea appealed to Tilak and his followers as a halfway house to re-entry into the Congress. It appealed to the Muslims also. Jinnah had become a household name among the Muslims for his successful piloting of the Mussalman Wakf Validating Act, 1913. He was, besides a national figure, having entered the Viceroy's Imperial Legislative Council in 1910. He had attacked the Aga Khan's deputation to the Viceroy Lord Minto at Simla on 1 October 1906 in a letter published in *Gujarati* of Bombay in the issue of 7 October 1906. *The Times of India* had refused to print it.[19] Jinnah challenged their credentials. 'May I know whoever selected the gentlemen who are supposed to represent Bombay? I know of no meeting of the Mohammedan Community that appointed these worthies [*sic*] to represent Bombay.' He was then a 30-year-old struggling lawyer. He did not join the All-India Muslim League when it was established at Dacca (now Dhaka) on 31 December 1906. He joined, instead, the Indian Mussalman Association which was established at Calcutta on 8 January 1907. Nawab Syed Mohammed was its President with Jinnah as one of the three Vice-Presidents. It was only on 10 October 1913 in London that he was persuaded to join the Muslim League by Maulana Mohammed Ali and Syed Wazir Hasan. He did so on the clear understanding that it would in no way affect his allegiance to the Congress. Within that party he was careful to make clear at its annual session at Allahabad on 28 December 1910 that his opposition to the extension of separate communal electorates to local bodies represented 'my personal views here and nothing more'. He said 'I wish it to be made quite clear that I do not represent the Mohammedan Community here nor have I any mandate from the Mohammedan Community'.[20] As a Congressman Jinnah was not indifferent to Muslim interests. Hence, his introduction of the Wakf Bill in the Imperial Legislative Council on 17 March 1911. As a Muslim Leaguer, he never overlooked the national interest.

The proposal for a Home Rule League was welcomed by all. It was discussed at a meeting held at Bombay on 27 December 1915, just before the annual session of the Congress. Eventually complementary Home Rule Leagues were set up. Joseph Baptista was president and N.C. Kelkar, secretary of Tilak's Home Rule League, which forestalled that of Annie Besant. Motilal Nehru and Tej Bahadur Sapru had one in Allahabad. Jinnah was president of the Home Rule League in Bombay.[21]

Jinnah's explanation for joining this body is noteworthy for its emphasis on mass politics. He had signed a Memorandum which was signed also by eighteen others. This Memorandum of Nineteen, as it came to be called was submitted to the viceroy in September 1916 urging constitutional reforms at the end of the war. Among its signatories were Sir Dinshaw Edulji Wacha, Madan Mohan Malaviya, Ibrahim Rahimtoola, and Mazhar-ul-Haque.

Jinnah said at a meeting of the Home Rule League at Allahabad in October 1917:

> I wish to say why it was that I joined the Home Rule League. When representations were made and resolutions passed, year after year, by the National Congress, when their demands were pressed, last year, in the carefully drafted memorandum of the 19 members of the Imperial Council, it was said that that was the demand of only a few educated agitators and lawyers but that the masses were not ready for any such reform. It was to meet that attack which was made in this country as well as in England, it was to remove that misrepresentation, that they resolved that there should be an educative propaganda and that they should reach the masses and put the verdict of the masses not only before the Bureaucracy but before the Democracy of Great Britain; and I am happy to find not less than 10,000 persons (cries of 'more than 10,000') have come here for the purpose of vindicating their claim, to show that not only a few educated agitators and lawyers *but the masses wanted this reform.*

By pressing their demand, they had brought about a distinct and definite change in the policy of Government. I do not wish to use an expression, which had been used, that the Government had climbed down, but I will say that the Government were convinced that the people of India were not going to tolerate the present state of administration and they demanded a substantial share in the administration of the country, and His Majesty's Government had definitely decided to send Mr Montagu to this country. He was coming here to see what was the force behind the demands that they made in the 19 Members' Memorandum and the Congress–League Scheme.

They had to face three powerful opponents. Firstly, the Bureaucracy:

As Mr Tilak pointed out, the Bureaucracy had enjoyed a monopoly of power in the administration of the country. It was natural that they were unwilling to part with it. The second class of opponents is the members of the Anglo-Indian commercial community who had enjoyed the monopoly of commerce and exploited this country for now over two centuries. What did this community mean when they said that they had a stake in this country? What was their stake? They said that they had invested a large amount of capital in this country. Only the other day, I was trying to find out the total British capital invested all over the world and I found that the total British capital so invested was roughly 1,700 millions. Out of this, only 300 millions were invested in British India, and a large part was invested in countries, where the English people had no voice in the government, such as Russia, Japan, Persia, Argentine, etc. And yet we were told that, so long as the 300 millions remained invested here, they, the sons of the soil, who had got their homes, their property, everything here, should remain under the control of the Bureaucracy for ever. The third element was again, a monopoly, that was the military. I am very glad—I acknowledge freely—that His Majesty's Government had decided to throw open the Commissioned ranks to the sons of the country, but here, again, as Mr Tilak put it, that admission must be a real one and not a shadowy one.[22]

Presiding over the Bombay provincial conference at Ahmedabad on 21 October 1916 he spoke at length on constitutional reform and quoted Prof. Morgan's views on devolution of power in Ireland. He also spoke on curbs on the freedom of press. The Muslim League had, he recalled, adopted the objective of self-government in 1913. Its programme 'has been more and more approximated' to that of the Congress. He touched on the issue of separate electorates. Formerly he was opposed to the idea. But the Muslim community was all for it. Jinnah spoke as a mediator rather than an advocate of separate electorates:

> This question of separate electorates from the top to bottom has been before the country ever since 1909 and rightly or wrongly the Mussalmans community is absolutely determined for the present to insist upon separate electorates. To most of us, the question is no more open to further discussion or argument, as it has become a mandate of the community. As far as I understand, the demand for separate electorates is not a matter of policy but a matter of necessity to the Mohammedans who require to be roused from the coma and torpor into which they had fallen so long. I would, therefore, appeal to my Hindu brethren that, in the present state of position, they should try to win the confidence and trust of the Mohammedans who are, after all, in the minority in the country. If they are determined to have separate electorates, no resistance should be shown to their demand.

What he added revealed the higher stakes for which he was preparing the two communities and the Congress and the Muslims League for a compromise:

> One thing is, however, clear. It is not a question of a few more seats going to the Mohammedans or the Hindus. It is a question, as I have already pointed out, in the first instance, of transfer of the power from the bureaucracy to democracy. ... The Hindus and the Mohammedans should stand united and use every constitutional and legitimate means to affect that transfer as soon as possible. But for a real New India to arise, all petty and small things must be given up.

She is now India irredenta and to be redeemed; all Indians must offer up sacrifice of not their good things, but all those evil things they cling to blindly—their hates and their divisions, their pride in what they should be thoroughly ashamed of, their quarrels and misunderstandings. These are a sacrifice that God would love.

In conclusion, let me tell you that, after all, a great deal depends upon ourselves. Hindus and Mohammedans, united and firm, the voice of the three hundred millions of people, vibrating throughout the length and the breadth of the country, will produce a force which no power on earth can resist. India has, I believe, turned a corner. She has passed through great sufferings and borne them patiently for centuries. There is now a bright and a great future in front of her. We are on a straight road; the promised land is within sight. 'Forward' is the motto and clear course for Young India. But in the onward march, we must be circumspect and never lose sight of the true perspective before us. And Wisdom and Caution should be our watch-words.[23]

Two months later a compromise was finally achieved, in the Lucknow Pact. Hugh F. Owen's essay, cited earlier, meticulously records how it was accomplished. Early in 1916 the issue of separate electorates reared its head in the United Provinces Legislature Council. Motilal Nehru and Tej Bahadur Sapru accepted it as a compromise even if it entailed its extension to local bodies. Madan Mohan Malaviya and C.Y. Chintamani opposed it.[24] Gokhale endorsed separate electorates in 1909; Annie Besant did so in 1915. After his return from Mandalay, Tilak began to reflect afresh on constitutional reforms, on constitutional methods in politics, and on the communal question as only a strong-minded and courageous person would.

His thoughts were recorded in Marathi by Sadashiv Vaman Bapat which M.R. Jayakar translated and quoted in his memoirs:

Tilak wanted the national movement of India to keep entirely free from all contamination with any theological or foreign political questions. He foresaw, as if by prophetic vision, the frightful consequences resulting from accepting the Khilafat dispute and he warned us all against it. To those Hindu nationalists who said that they did not believe a word of this Khilafat but still had agreed to agitate for it only to secure the friendship and active cooperation of the Muslims in our national fight for freedom, Tilak had only one reply that if the Hindus think that they will succeed in deceiving the Muslims, they will soon be disillusioned and will find that they will succeed in deceiving themselves only but not the Muslims, who are very shrewd at the diplomatic table. Let us not, therefore, confound issues. Let us seek Muslim cooperation on the broad national question of Swaraj. In that, by all means, give them special privileges if these will satisfy them and bring them into the Congress fold, but never seek to introduce Theology into our politics.[25]

Writing in his journal *Maratha* on 25 October 1914, Tilak noted that 'a considerable section of the educated Mohammedans have begun to perceive ... the necessity of political agitation on the Congress lines and it would be a fault of the Congress if it does not meet them half way ... suitable concessions [must be] made'. Quoting these remarks Owen wrote, 'And it has been maintained that Tilak played a considerable part in prevailing upon Malaviya and other participants in the negotiations to acquiesce in the final terms of the [Lucknow] Pact.'

The British rulers were alarmed at the prospect of a Congress–Muslim League accord. The commissioner of police did his best to prevent the Muslim League from holding its session in Bombay. Some pro-British members supported him. A meeting was held at the Taj Mahal Hotel in the city on New Year's Day, 1916. On Jinnah's motion it set up a committee 'to frame a scheme of reforms'. Maulana Abul Kalam Azad seconded the motion.

Thirty-four members of the All-India Congress Committee (AICC) met in April 1916 to draw up a draft scheme. It was sent to the Muslim League, which considered it at Mahmudabad

House in Lucknow on 21 August. The Raja of Mahmudabad, a close friend of Jinnah, was progressive in his outlook.

At a joint conference of the Muslim League Reforms Committee and the AICC held at the Indian Association Room at Calcutta on 17 and 18 November 1916 a 'Reform Scheme' was adopted. Surendranath Bannerjee presided over the deliberations. Both, the Congress and the Muslim League held their annual sessions at the Kaisar Bagh in Lucknow on 30–31 December 1916 and endorsed the scheme which became known as the Lucknow Pact. Ambika Charan Mazumdar presided over the Congress session. Jinnah presided over the League session. He delivered his presidential address wearing the Turkish fez cap. The main architects of the Lucknow Pact, of course, were Tilak and Jinnah.[26] The event also marked Tilak's re-entry into the Congress nine years after the split in 1907. Gandhi attended the session.

The resolution adopted by the Congress read *inter alia*:

> That this Congress demands that a definite step should be taken towards Self-Government by granting the reforms contained in the scheme prepared by the All-India Congress Committee in concert with the Reform Committee appointed by the All-India Muslim League. That in the re-construction of the Empire, India shall be lifted from the position of a dependency to that of an equal partner in the Empire and the Self-Governing Dominions.

Hridayanth Kunzru presented the scheme. Its significance was highlighted by Tilak:

> The resolution which I wish to support is the one for which the Congress has been fighting for the last thirty years. The first note of it was heard ten years ago on the banks of the Hoogly and it was sounded by the Grand Old Man of India—Dadabhai Naoroji. Since the note was sounded, differences of opinion arose. Some said that the note ought to be carried on and ought to be followed by a detailed scheme at once, that it should be taken up and made to

resound all over India as soon as possible. There was another party amongst us that said that it could not be done so soon, that the tune of that note required to be a little lower, and that was the cause of dissension ten years ago and I am glad to say that I have lived these ten years to see that we were re-united in this Congress and we are going to put our voices and shoulders together to push on the scheme of Self-Government. Not only have we lived to see these differences closed, but to see the differences of Hindus and Muhammadans closed as well. So we have now united in every way in the United Provinces and we have found that luck in Lucknow.

The resolution is in fact a synthesis of all the Congress resolutions passed during the last thirty years, a synthesis that will help all to proceed to work in a definite and responsible manner. I believe that the Congress has done its work as a deliberative body. The next part is the executive and that will be placed before you afterwards.[27]

The lieutenant governor of United Provinces reported to the viceroy that the Lucknow session 'was a great personal triumph for Tilak, and his enormous popularity was apparent at every turn'.[28]

Jinnah's presidential address listed British objections to India's self-government and systematically demolished them with logic not unmixed with fervour:

1. Democratic institutions cannot thrive in the environment of the East. Why? Were democratic institutions unknown to the Hindu and Mohammedans in the past? What was the village panchayat? What are the history, the traditions, the literature and the precepts of Islam? There are no people in the world who are more democratic, even in their religion, than the Mussalmans.
2. The only form of government suitable to India is autocracy, tempered by English [European] efficiency and character. All nations have had to go through the experience of despotic or autocratic government at one time or the other in the history of the world. Russia was liberated to a certain extent only a few years ago. France and England had to struggle before they conquered the autocracy. Is India to remain under the heel of a

novel form of autocracy in the shape of bureaucracy for all time to come, when Japan and even China have set up constitutional governments on the democratic lines of Great Britain and America?
3. (a) The interests of the educated classes are opposed to those of the Indian masses; and (b) The former would oppress the latter if the strong protecting hand of the British official were withdrawn. This astonishing proposition beats all reason and sense. It is suggested that we who are the very kith and kin of the masses, most of us springing from the middle classes, are likely to oppress the people if more power is conferred; that the masses require protection at the hands of the English officials, between whom and the people there is nothing in common; that our interests are opposed to those of the masses—in what respect, it is never pointed out—and that, therefore, the monopoly of the administrative control should continue in the hands of non-Indian officials. This insidious suggestion, which is so flippantly made, is intended to secure the longest possible lease for the bureaucracy and to enjoy their monopoly. But it can neither stand the light of facts, nor the analysis of truth. One has only to look at the past records of the Congress for more than a quarter of a century, and of the All-India Muslim League, to dismiss this specious plea. The educated people of this country have shown greater anxiety and solicitude for the welfare and advancement of the masses than for any other question during the last quarter of a century.

Mark his strong words on 'the welfare and advancement of the masses'.[29]

The Lucknow Pact had an enormous impact as Owen pointed out:

> The Pact ushered in a period of Hindu–Muslim cooperation culminating in the Khilafat agitation of 1920–21. The Pact was built on very different lines to this later cooperation, which was agitational in style and based on the appeal of Gandhi and the Pan-Islamic leaders, mainly in terms of religious feelings, to large groups of Indians who probably had little concern for the constitutional arrangements of the Pact. Nevertheless, the Pact did provide a basis

for this new cooperation by removing one very important area of public dissension between Congressmen, Hindus and others, and the Muslim League. Members of both organizations—those who believed in a secular state, Hindus in the United Provinces and the other Hindu-majority provinces, and Muslims in the United Provinces, Bengal and the Punjab—had agreed to make sacrifices in varying degrees, for the sake of cooperation for nationalist goals, and so had helped to create an atmosphere of mutual trust in which Hindus and Muslims could combine in the Rowlatt and the Khilafat agitations.[30]

Later events led critics to overlook, with embittered hindsight, some incontrovertible facts. One is that the political and educational backwardness of Muslims persuaded not only Tilak and Gokhale but also Motilal Nehru and Sapru to accept separate electorates. Jinnah did not regard them as a permanent feature at all. In 1927 he said openly from the Muslim League platform: 'I am not wedded to separate electorates; although I must say that the overwhelming majority of the Mussalmans firmly and honestly believe that it is the only method by which they can be secure.' In 1925 he said that the Lucknow Pact 'was never intended to be permanent'.[31] To the United Provinces Muslim conference held at Allahabad on 8 August 1931 he said: 'If a majority is conceded in the Punjab and Bengal, I would personally prefer a settlement on the basis of joint electorates.'[32] The Jinnah–Rajendra Prasad Pact of 1934 envisaged joint electorates and franchise qualifications 'to reflect the population of each community in the voting register'.[33]

Critics ignored, above all, that concessions were made by both sides as the scholar, Uma Kaura, pointed out in her able work which marks a most refreshing departure from the writings of court historians in both countries. She recorded:

> The Congress accepted the demands for separate electorates and also agreed to cooperate with the Muslim League for demanding weightage for Muslims in all those Provinces where the Muslims

were in a minority. Under the Congress–League scheme Muslims got over-representation in the Provincial legislatures in Bihar, Bombay, Madras and Central Provinces. Being aware of the dominant position of the Muslims in UP, they were given 30 per cent of the seats there. The price paid for these concessions was that the principle of weightage for the minority community was also applied to Bengal and the Punjab, *reducing* Muslim representation in the Provincial Legislative Councils from 55 per cent to 50 per cent in the Punjab and to 40 per cent in Bengal.[34]

Throughout his career Jinnah had to balance the claims of Muslims in the provinces in which they were in a minority with those of Muslims in the provinces in which they were in a majority. He was criticized by Muslims in Punjab and Bengal for scaling down their representation. Thirty years later in 1946, despite a convincing victory at the polls, the Nawab of Mamdot could not command a majority in the Punjab Assembly.

The Lucknow Pact signified the increasing eagerness of the Congress to win Muslim cooperation in the nationalist movement. The Hindus of UP and the Punjab had misgivings regarding the Pact as they felt that their interests had been jeopardized to win Muslim cooperation. On the Muslim side, the Punjab and Bengal were the most vociferous provinces in their condemnation of the Pact.

Prof. Ishtiaq Husain Qureshi pointed out that 'weightage in the minority provinces were not of much use' to the Muslims. They remained a minority, 'whereas the loss of majorities in two major provinces resulted in serious handicaps. Its full effect was felt after the elections of 1937 and 1945, when the Muslim League encountered grave difficulties in forming ministries in the Punjab and Bengal.'[35]

A few months after the pact was concluded, Edwin S. Montagu, secretary of state for India, issued a declaration on 20 August 1917 which, while giving an impetus to the nationalists' discourse, created a rift within their ranks by its calculated ambiguities:

> The policy of His Majesty's Government, with which the Government of India are in complete accord, is that of the increasing association of Indians in every branch of the administration and the gradual development of self-governing institutions with a view to the progressive realization of responsible government in India as an integral part of the British Empire. They have decided that substantial steps in this direction should be taken as soon as possible,....

He would visit India and hold talks to elicit opinions. The British alone would 'be judges of the time and measure of each advance'. Thirty years were to elapse before independence was granted.

Montagu toured India in 1917–18, and in conjunction with the viceroy, Lord Chelmsford, produced the *Report on Indian Constitutional Reforms*. It was published on 8 July 1918. An intense debate ensued after the declaration and the report.

Jinnah spoke on the declaration at the Congress's annual session at Calcutta in 1917 and also at the League's session held in the same city on 31 December 1917, more fully at the latter: 'This is the first time in the history of India that the British Government have definitely and clearly stated that the goal of British rule in this country is to establish Responsible Government'. He criticized the government for enacting repressive measures like the Press Act and the Seditions Meetings Act: 'Is it possible for any statute to destroy the soul of the people?'

He replied to the critics of the Lucknow Pact.

> It is said, and I am referring here to what my Mussalman friends say that we are going on at a tremendous speed and that we are in a minority and so might not the government of this country become a Hindu Government? I want to give an answer to it. I wish to address my Mussalman friends on that point. Do you think that in the first instance it is possible that the Government of this country can become a Hindu Government? Do you think that the Government

can be conducted merely by the ballot box? [Cries of No]. Do you think that because the Hindus are in a majority they have therefore to carry a measure in the Legislative Council and there is an end of it? If 70 million Mussalmans do not approve of the measure which is carried by a ballot box, do you think that it could be enforced or administered in this country? [Cries of 'Never'.]

Do you think that the Hindu statesmen with their intellect, with their past history, will ever think of enforcing measures by the ballot box when you get Self-Government? [Cries of 'No'.] Then what is there to fear? [Cries of 'Nothing'.] Therefore I say to my Mussalman friends: Fear not. This is a bogey, which is put before you by your enemies [Hear, hear] to frighten you, to scare you away from cooperation and unity which are essential for the establishment of Self-Government [Cheers]. This country has not to be governed by the Hindus and, let me submit, it has not to be governed by the Mussalmans either, and certainly not by the English [Hear, hear]. It is to be governed by the people and the sons of this country. I, standing here—I believe I am voicing the feeling of whole of India—demand the immediate transfer of a substantial power of the Government of the country.[36]

This was an accurate enunciation of secularism as well as democratic governance.

A month earlier, in November 1917, he said at a meeting in Bombay: 'My message to the Mussalmans is to join hands with your Hindu brethren. My message to Hindus is to lift your backward brother up.'[37]

The Calcutta session of Congress was addressed by Rabindranath Tagore who began by reading an opening invocation. The resolution on self-government urged establishment of responsible government by parliamentary legislation 'within a time limit to be fixed in the Statute itself at an early date'. It also urged that the Lucknow Pact be 'immediately introduced by Statute as the first step in the process'. It was moved by Surendranath Bannerjee and supported by Tilak, Jinnah, C.R. Das, and Bipin

Chandra Pal. Tilak's motto was 'accept what you get and fight for the rest'. He would be happy 'if the first step that we demand is granted to us immediately'.[38]

Strange were the ways of the British Raj. A conciliatory declaration in London was not followed by conciliatory steps in India. It bore a pronounced animus against Tilak. His passport was cancelled to prevent him and his colleagues in the Home Rule League from proceeding to England to represent the League's view before ministers of the British government. As always, a public meeting was held on 8 April 1918 at Shantaram's Chawl at Girgaum in Bombay to protest against the order; Jinnah presided. 'Was it fair', he asked, 'that only one side should be allowed to be heard? Was the case of India to be decided *ex parte*?'

Jinnah referred to the activities in London of a former governor of Bombay, Lord Sydenham: 'A powerful party headed by Lord Sydenham, well-organized, and backed up by wealth and influence, carrying on a campaign of vilification and misrepresentation regarding India's demand for self-government'.[39]

Earlier, Jinnah had attacked him in stronger terms at a public meeting in Shantaram's Chawl in November 1917 which was held under the joint auspices of the two branches of the Home Rule League. The subject was 'The Present European Agitation'. Jinnah said at the outset in his presidential remarks: 'Lord Sydenham, that reactionary who enjoyed the hospitality of this country and earned a fat salary from the coffers of its exchequer, has been carrying on an agitation which is discreditable to any man'.[40]

Jinnah fell foul of successive British governors of Bombay. One of them recommended his deportation. None of the constitutionalists, the Liberals as they were called, incurred such wrath. But, then, none of them espoused the national cause with the intensity and fervour that he did. None used the language he reserved for them, as the record of proceedings show, for the members of the Viceroy's Executive Council.

Indians and Pakistanis alike refer to Jinnah's 'nationalist' past and move on to censure or praise his post-1939 politics. The richness of this phase in his career eludes them. It is of a piece with the Stalinist re-writing of history mentioned earlier, that a hall built in his name by funds contributed, not by a rich donor but by the public, remains ignored and in sorry neglect—the People's Jinnah Hall, as it is aptly called. It was built in the compound of the Congress House and is not very far from Shantaram's Chawl, venue of the battles he fought in Tilak's company.

It was an expression of the public's admiration for Jinnah's strong and successful leadership of a campaign against the governor, Lord Willingdon. The campaign was provoked by Willingdon's insult to his comrade Tilak. In a real sense the People's Jinnah Hall is a memorial to their comradeship and a reminder of a phase in national politics which holds many a lesson for our times.

On 10 June 1918 the governor convened a war conference at the Town Hall in Bombay to enlist popular support for the war effort. It was part of a series that began with the war conference convened by the viceroy on 16 April. Montagu regretted that Chelmsford had not invited Tilak to the conference. 'If I were the Viceroy I would have had him at Delhi at all cost. He is at the moment probably the most powerful man in India, and he has it in his power, if he chooses, to help materially in war effort'.[41]

Tilak, however, had an altogether different approach from Gandhi on the war effort. Gandhi wrote to Pranjivan Mehta on

2 July 1918: 'You must be watching my work of recruitment. Of all my activities, I regard this as the most difficult and the most important. If I succeed in it, genuine swaraj is assured'; an astonishingly unrealistic assessment but reflecting a revealing approach. 'Tilak said he could only encourage recruitment to an army where equal opportunities were open for Indians and Europeans'.[42]

Willingdon made good Chelmsford's lapse by inviting Tilak to his conference in Bombay. Also invited were Jinnah, B.G. Horniman, N.C. Kelkar, Jamnadas Dwarkadas, and S.R. Bomanji. Though the governor's opening speech was critical of the Home Rule League, he prevented Tilak from replying to the criticism. Tilak reiterated his stand that 'home defence was ultimately connected with home rule'. The governor interrupted him to say that 'he could not permit a political discussion' on a resolution pledging loyalty to the King-Emperor. Nor would he permit amendments to the resolution. Tilak left the dais and returned to his place in the hall. N.C. Kelkar followed much the same line and was given the same treatment. Thereupon, Tilak and his colleagues walked out. Jinnah stayed behind and spoke for them and for the Home Rule League. L. Robertson, chief secretary to the government sent a full report of the proceedings to the secretary to home secretary of the government of India. 'I am, however, to invite attention to the objectionable remarks which the Honourable Mr Jinnah thought it fit to make while speaking on Resolution II', on the war effort.[43]

When Jinnah was asked to speak, he rebutted the charge against the League:

> I must say that I was pained, very much pained, that Your Excellency should have thought fit to cast doubts on the sincerity and loyalty of the Home Rule party. I am very sorry, my Lord, but with the utmost respect I must enter my emphatic protest against that view. The Home Rule party is as sincere and as anxious to help the defence of our motherland and the Empire as any one else. I do not

wish to take up the time of this august body at this late hour. But the difference between us and Government is only regarding methods. You want to develop the man-power of this country. You have schemes directed to get recruits, but we say that that is not enough, and that that will not save us from the German menace which is staring us in the face on the frontiers. We say there must be a national army, a citizen army, and not a purely mercenary army. That is the difference ...

If you wish to enable us to help you, to facilitate and stimulate the recruiting, you must make the people feel that they are the citizens of the Empire and the King's equal subjects. But you do not do so. You say that we shall be trusted and made real partners in the Empire. When? We don't want words; we want action and deeds, immediate deeds. I will only give one instance. At the Delhi Conference we unanimously passed a resolution recommending that a substantial number of King's Commissions should be granted to the people of India; but nothing has been done yet.

The Governor: I really must suggest to the Honourable Mr Jinnah that he had better go to the Government at Delhi or Simla and say these things there. I have no power in this particular matter.

Mr Jinnah: I am simply saying this, that I understand that this Government is directed to carry out the proposals approved by the Government of India, and I say that if the Government wants us to cooperate with them and carry out their wishes in this province, then let them trust us. My Lord, I do not wish to detain the Conference longer. But I would say one thing, and that is this. I cannot agree with the method laid down in this resolution. I agree with the first part of the resolution, namely, 'This Conference is of opinion that the man-power and resources of this Presidency should be utilized and developed to the fullest possible extent'. But I do not agree with the latter part, namely, the personnel of the Board. I do not agree with it because I have not been given an opportunity to exercise my judgement upon it. I want to move an amendment but I cannot move an amendment as it has been ruled by Your Excellency that no amendments will be allowed. This is a procedure which is unheard of, not known to my constitution, but since the ruling is given I must bow to it.

The Governor: But the Honourable Gentleman might send any suggestions he wants to be adopted.

The Honourable Mr Jinnah: My Lord, the procedure has already been laid down and I do not wish to challenge anything but I only wish to say that I do not approve of the personnel of the boards. My next point is that I do not approve of the memorandum annexed to the resolution. I have had no opportunity given to me of exercising my judgement upon it and how can I approve of it? I refuse to be a party to the adoption of this memorandum which I have had no opportunity to consider. I hope this Conference would agree and Your Excellency would believe me that to doubt our sincerity, that to doubt our loyalty is an insult to our party and we will not have it.

Towards the end of this conference the governor took exception to the remarks of Jinnah who again spoke: 'I would only request Your Excellency to refer to Your Excellency's speech where Your Excellency has doubted the sincerity of the Home Rule League to help the Government, and if I am wrong I would withdraw my protest.'

Six days later a huge public meeting was held at the hallowed Shantaram's Chawl under Gandhi's chairmanship at which Jinnah moved a resolution embodying the national demands on the war.[44] It was followed by another at China Bagh. It was Home Rule Day.

By now Jinnah had emerged as 'the uncrowned king of Bombay'. He was one of the leaders of the Bar, a leading Congressman, president of the Muslim League as well as the Home Rule League, and chairman of the board of directors of the leading nationalist daily, *Bombay Chronicle*. In the Imperial Legislature Council he was a scourge of the government. K.M. Munshi said that the likes of him, he had never seen before.[45] He was then forty-two and had thirty years of a hectic life ahead of him. Success came to him fairly early in life and his politics, even in the early days, involved mass politics. Men like him were not to be trifled with as Willingdon and, later, others discovered.

As the governor's term of office expired, Sir Stanley Reed, editor of *The Times of India* and some others formed a committee to hold a meeting and vote a memorial on behalf of the city in honour of the departing dignitary. Jinnah and twenty-nine others wrote to him on 8 November warning him that 'should any such meeting be called we shall attend the same for the purpose of opposing' the proposal. On retirement, incidentally, Sir Stanley became a conservative member of parliament and contributed a weekly letter from London to the newspaper, for a good few years after independence. Letters were written to the sheriff of Bombay. B.G. Horniman waged a campaign against the governor.[46] A fiery campaign ensued in the press.

At long last the day for the decisive trial of strength arrived on 11 December 1918.

It was seven o'clock in the morning when the leaders of the anti-requisitionists arrived[47] at the Town Hall and were received with loud cheers by a band of two or three hundred of their supporters, who had arrived on the scene some time previously and were waiting on the roadside in front of the Elphinstone Gardens. Overnight it had been ascertained that no one would be allowed on the Town Hall steps until the doors were opened. The whole place was in charge of a large force of the police and a letter addressed to the commissioner of police had failed to elicit a reply to the questions that were addressed to him in regard to the arrangements. A few hours passed in strange expectation. At ten o'clock the doors were opened, the intention to do so being communicated only a few minutes beforehand to the leaders of the opposition, who immediately took places in the queue which had been kept for them by their supporters. Thus the first persons to enter the Town Hall were Jinnah, Jamnadas, Horniman, Umar Sobhani, K.M. Munshi, Tairsee,

S.G. Banker, P.K. Telang, Mowji Govindji Sheth, Syed Hussain, other leaders, and a large following of supporters. In the meanwhile, Suleman Cassim Mitha had arrived on the steps and assumed command of the operations for packing the meeting with loyalists which had apparently been entrusted to him.

The first victory was gained after the anti-requisitionists secured the front place in the queue and the second when they succeeded in resisting the audacious attempt to thrust them into the back seats. Headed by Jinnah they insisted on their right as the first-comers to take whatever seats they chose and after some argument their claim to occupy the seats in the central part of the Town Hall was conceded. Mrs Ruttie Jinnah was on the steps to the Hall controlling the volunteers.

By five o'clock the Hall was uncomfortably packed. The arrival of the sheriff at this time provoked an extraordinary scene. Those seated on the platform, and standing on it in front, raised vociferous cheers which were immediately drowned by long-continued shouts of 'Shame, Shame'. Other leaders of the requisitionist party received the same demonstration and counter-demonstration from the two parties.

At about 5.30 in the evening, quiet was restored. Immediately after the reading of the notice, convening the meeting, by the sheriff, Horniman rose and addressed the sheriff to make a protest; the latter, however, refused him a hearing and his voice was drowned in the shouts of those on and near the platform supporting the requisitionists. While Horniman was still standing and endeavouring to be heard, Sir Dinshaw Wacha rose and moved that Sir Jamsetjee Jeejeebhoy should take the chair. This was apparently seconded by Sir Fazalbhoy Currimbhoy. Without any attempt to put the motion to the vote, and ignoring Horniman's shouted protest that this party wished to propose amendment that P.K. Telang be elected chairman, Sir Jamsetjee walked to the chair.

From that moment the fate of the meeting was sealed. For about twenty minutes the anti-requisitionists continued their shouts of 'no, no' in protest against this arbitrary procedure and Sir Jamsetjee's taking of the chair while the stewards, volunteers, and other supporters of the platform shrieked and yelled in derision, hurling challenges and epithets at the anti-requisitionists. What was going on the platform, nobody could see or hear. It is said that Sir Jamsetjee put the resolution of appreciation of Lord Willingdon from the chair and declared it carried. The farce came to an end when the commissioner of police appeared on the platform, and backed by a posse of police, ordered the Hall to be cleared. The anti-requisitionists headed by their leaders proceeded to leave the Hall.

Unnecessary violence was used by the police in clearing the Hall and several of the anti-requisitionists were assaulted, including Jinnah, Subedar and others.

When the leaders of the opposition appeared on the steps, after leaving the meeting, they were received with a long continued roar of cheers from a huge crowd. Horniman, while coming down, was seized and carried shoulder-high round the circle amidst a scene of extraordinary enthusiasm, the occupants of the crowded verandahs and balconies also cheering and waving handkerchiefs. The demonstration reached its culmination in Apollo Street where Jinnah, Jamnadas, and Horniman delivered brief speeches from the windows of an insurance company's office. They emphasized the significance of the great victory that had been won for self-determination and declared that never again would flatterers and sycophants dare to flout public opinion. No such popular demonstration had ever been witnessed in Bombay before.

Horniman said that a full account of what happened during the whole day at the Town Hall would be related to them at the meeting that night at Shantaram's Chawl. Amid ringing applause the speaker made way for Jinnah, who in answer to repeated calls from the audience, said, 'Gentlemen, you are the citizens of Bombay. You have today scored a great triumph for democracy. Your triumph today has made it clear that even the combined forces of bureaucracy and autocracy could not overawe you. December the 11th is a Red-Letter Day in the history of Bombay. Gentlemen, go and rejoice over the day that has secured us the triumph of democracy.' A huge demonstration was then staged at Shantaram's Chawl that night.

A police official reported:

> I was asked to clear the Hall. I accordingly entered the Hall with a posse of police and cleared it. Jinnah, Horniman, and one or two others of the anti-requisitionist party were rather roughly handled by some of the stewards while the crowd were being cleared from the Town Hall. Mrs Jinnah made herself conspicuous in the afternoon by appearing in the gallery of the Town Hall and waving greetings to the crowd outside. She later took up a position inside the Town Hall compound and addressed her husband's supporters advising them to stand by their rights and to resist the police. Throughout the day it was very noticeable that the educated Home Rulers adopted a contumacious attitude, refusing to obey the orders of the police, thereby compelling them to execute those orders by force. The 'police' were everywhere greeted by cries of 'shame' and a similar reception was accorded to the members of His Excellency's Executive Council, High Court Judges and other high officials who attended the meeting.

After the Town Hall meeting was over, the anti-requisitionists led by Horniman, Jinnah, and Jamnadas proceeded to Mr V.A. Desai's office at Apollo Street and held an informal meeting.

On the same night at 9.30 p.m. a public meeting was held at Shantaram's Chawl to protest against the management of the meeting at the Town Hall and the conduct of the police. M.A. Jinnah was in the chair. Jamnadas, Horniman, Narsingh Prasad, Bhagwandas Vibhakar, L.G. Khare, M.K. Azad, Mowji Govindji, Dr Erulker, and Mrs Ramibai Kamdar addressed the meeting where 20,000 men were present. An overflow meeting was held at French Bridge at the same time and was addressed by Jamnadas Dwarkadas, N.D. Savarkar, Horniman, and K.M. Munshi.

On the 12th instant at 9.30 p.m. a public meeting was held at Morarji Goculdas Hall when Mr K.M. Munshi, addressed the meeting on the 'Delhi Congress'; Jamnadas Dwarkadas presided. About seventy-five persons attended the meeting. The attorney and pleader friends of Jinnah entertained him at a garden party on the 15th instant at China Bagh in appreciation of his courageous stand for the rights of the citizens of Bombay.

The *Bombay Chronicle*, reported on 12 December 1918:

An overflow meeting was held in Mr Ratansey D. Morarji's compound near French Bridge, Chawpatty, where about fifteen thousand people had gathered. Several speakers, including Dr Savarkar, Mr Jamanadas Dwarkadas, Mr K.M. Munshi and others addressed the meeting.

Mr Jamnadas Dwarkadas, who was received with deafening and continuous cheers, said that Bombay people had shown to the whole world what they were capable of. He the speaker was at first a little diffident about the determination of the people, but he was exceedingly rejoiced to see that they were all made of stern stuff ready to sacrifice everything—even their lives for their principle. [Applause]. That day [11th December] might have been written in blood in the history of Bombay, so many people of their party receiving kicks, boxes and severe injuries at the hands of the police and hired hooligans. ['Shame, shame!']. He could not adequately describe how thankful he was to the people for their courageous stand, and fulfilling the vow they had taken on the eve of the meeting. Up to that time he was their servant, but from that day he swore to be their slave forever, and that he and his colleagues would be ready even to give their lives for the protection of the people's right [Applause].

Continuing Mr Jamnads said by their deeds that day they had abundantly proved that they would never care for self-interest, nor would aim only at the commonweal. [Hear, hear]. They all know what glorious past India had had, but judging from their deeds, he was convinced that if they continued to remain firm in their determination and in asserting their rights, they had a still brighter future for India. [Loud and prolonged cheering].

Mr K.M. Munshi then rose and related in detail all the principal events of the day. They had proved by their deeds that whatever may be the personal qualities of a Governor he would not receive a public memorial if he was not popular. [Hear, hear]. He then eulogized the firmness and sacrifice of the leaders of the counter-requisitionists, particularly the Honourable Mr Jinnah, the likes of whom, the speaker said, he had never seen before.

A Bombay solicitor, B.D. Lam, wrote a letter which the *Bombay Chronicle* published on 14 December. It read:

Sir, I have read with great pride and deep emotion the reports of yesterday's meeting and I cannot withhold my high admiration for the bold and fearless leadership of Mr Jinnah in inaugurating a new era in the public life of Bombay.

The real issues of this fight have been clouded by the excitement caused by the conduct of the Police and the supporters of the Sheriff's meeting. We have, therefore, to look at the result in its proper light, and the true test of the success of Mr Jinnah and his noble band of supporters lies in two great facts. The first is that the supposed public meeting lasted only a few minutes and no speeches could be made by the supporters of Lord Willingdon. To call this a meeting of the citizens of Bombay to vote a memorial is a shame and hypocrisy. The second great truth is that no Sheriff will henceforth make bold to flout public opinion and call a meeting in the name of the citizens of Bombay. That is an achievement of which Mr Jinnah and his followers have reasons to be proud.

If, as a result of the meeting, anybody deserves a memorial it is Mr Jinnah whose fine leadership and fearless courage have marked a great epoch in the public life of Bombay. He has shown the spirit of our late lamented leaders like Dadabhai Naoroji and Gopal Krishna Gokhale.

We should mark our great appreciation of Mr Jinnah's service by raising a fund in which each of his supporters should contribute one rupee. That rupee will come not from a man's pocket but from his heart. If we had our own way we would raise a statue of Mr Jinnah to be placed in the Town Hall of Bombay, for Mr Jinnah has for ever laid low the tyranny of Town Hall meetings held in the name of the public. His name will be cherished forever as the great Indian who stood for the rights of the people. Town Halls in every city are symbols of their true public spirit. That spirit never existed in Bombay, but Mr Jinnah has established it on firm basis in yesterday's proceedings. We ought not to allow this occasion to pass without a fitting tribute to Mr Jinnah. A souvenir ought to be presented to him to mark the everlasting services he has rendered not only to Bombay but to the whole of India.[48]

Each donor contributed a rupee. Within a month 65,000 citizens had raised a fund of Rs65,000. Annie Besant came down specially to inaugurate the People's Jinnah Memorial Hall.[49]

It was in the fitness of things that when, during 'the emergency' in India, the Bombay Committee of Lawyers for Civil Liberties decided to hold a meeting of the city's lawyers to protest against the violation of civil liberties and the rule of law, it was this Hall—the People's Jinnah Hall—that they chose as the venue for the meeting. It was to be a private meeting restricted to invited lawyers since public meetings were banned. It was to be addressed, among others, by M.C. Chagla, former Chief Justice of the High Court, J.C. Shah, former Chief Justice of India and N.P. Nathwani, a former Judge of the High Court. The commissioner of police refused permission to hold the meeting. In a landmark judgment delivered on 16 December 1975, Chief Justice R.M. Kantawala and Justice V.D. Tulzapurkar allowed a writ petition quashing the commissioner's order.[50]

While Willingdon was being given an appropriate farewell, India was rocked by a fierce debate on the reforms recommended in the Montford Report. It was on familiar lines, as in any freedom movement, between those who were prepared to work the concessions that were offered and those who rejected them. At its Calcutta session in December 1917 the Congress had welcomed Montagu's statement of fundamentals.

It had now to respond to detailed proposals that were on offer. A special session of the Congress was held in Bombay from 29 August to 1 September 1918 in a pavilion erected on the Marine Lines *maidan*. Syed Hasan Imam presided. Annie Besant, Tilak, Jinnah, Motilal Nehru, C.R. Das, Malaviya, C. Rajagopalachari, Fazlul Haq, Wazir Hasan, and Abbas Tyabji attended. The Congress–Muslim League *entente* continued. It passed a resolution which appreciated:

> the earnest attempts on the part of Rt. Hon'ble Mr Montagu, the Secretary of State, and His Excellency the Viceroy to inaugurate the system of responsible government in India, and while it recognises that some of the proposals constitute an advance in the present conditions in some directions, it is of opinion that the proposals are disappointing and unsatisfactory and suggests the following modifications as absolutely necessary to constitute a substantive step towards responsible government.

Tilak, in supporting the resolution, recommended the acceptance of the resolution as representing a distilled compromise accepted in the Subjects Committee. He concluded with a warning to the critics of India to remember that unless India is raised to the status of the self-governing colonies, to be an equal member of the Empire, the Empire will lose in strength and will be in danger.[51]

The year 1919 was marred by the massacre in Jallianwala Bagh in Amritsar on 13 April. Hopes generated by Montagu's statement in 1917, and the Montford Report of 1918, were dashed by the Rowlatt Committee's Report and the repressive act based on it. Enactment of the 'Star Chamber Legislation' prompted Jinnah to resign in protest from the Imperial Legislative Council on

28 March 1919. The report was a monumental fraud though one of its recommendations was salutary, namely, detainees should not be lodged in prisons, since they are not criminals, but in 'an asylum ... of a different order from a jail'.[52] However, the report was a virtually *verbatim* reproduction of a report by the head of Department of Criminal Intelligence, James Campbell Ker, as the scholar Mahadeva Prasad discovered.[53]

The Montford Report was discussed by the 34th Congress at Amritsar from 27 December 1919 to New Year's Day 1920. It was a curtain raiser to the fateful year that followed. The year 1920 radically altered the Congress, the Home Rule League, and indeed, the terms of nationalist discourse. It marked a break from the era of constitutional politics to that of non-cooperation with the British and civil disobedience, a conscious violation of the law and cheerful submission to punishment for it.

In a year's time, in two Congress sessions—at Calcutta in September 1920 and Nagpur in December 1920—with a meeting of the Home Rule League in between in October—Gandhi captured the Congress and the League and bent both to his will. His programme was steamrollered in both bodies with a force of personality and tactical skills none had suspected he possessed. It led to Jinnah's resignation from the Congress and the Home Rule League. But, contrary to conventional wisdom, his relations with Gandhi survived the differences; survived even Gandhi's take-over of the League by a coup. They came under strain nearly two decades later in the late thirties. Nor was Jinnah a fundamentalist like Annie Besant in his opposition to civil disobedience. His objection was of a practical nature. In this debate he sorely missed his friend, Tilak, who had died on 1 August 1920, the day Gandhi's programme of non-cooperation began.

There is no better way of understanding the course of politics in that critical phase than by hearkening to the record, the best antidote to myths.

Motilal Nehru presided at the Amritsar session. The resolution on reforms read:

> (1) That this Congress reiterates its declaration of last year that India is fit for full responsible government and repudiates all assumptions and assertions to the contrary wherever made.
> (2) That this Congress adheres to the resolutions passed at the Delhi Congress regarding constitutional reforms and is of opinion that the Reforms Act is inadequate, unsatisfactory, and disappointing.
> (3) That this Congress further urges that Parliament should take early steps to establish full responsible government in India in accordance with the principle of self-determination.

Seconding the resolution Tilak said:

> We will work this Act for the purpose of securing full responsible government. That is our position. That position is enunciated in this resolution that this Congress urges the Parliament to take early steps etc. etc. We are going to use the Act, though we are not satisfied with it. But we are not going to use it in fulsome praise of what is given. There is no difference of opinion as regards using it, but we are going to thank with an *arti* [ceremonial waving of lights] in our hands. Mr Montagu wants us to use it. Well, the question is whether we want to use it or not. We have deliberately omitted from our resolution, because it goes without saying that every Statute of Parliament will be used in this country. We go to Parliament. We ask for legislation. We get it and we shall make it a basis of further agitation. That is our attitude. We get a bit of what we want. We shall use it and always go on agitating for more.

Gandhi's amendment sought to delete the word 'disappointing' and add that the Government of India Act of 1919, based on the Montford Report, was to be worked in a spirit of response to the sentiments expressed in the Royal Proclamation of 24 December 1919 ('let the new era begin'), and warmest thanks were to be offered to Montagu. 'I ask the author of the commentaries of the *Bhagwat Gita* [Tilak], if he accepts the teachings of *Bhagwat Gita*, then let him extend the hand of fellowship to Mr Montagu.'

Jinnah seconded Gandhi's amendment and, said:

> Now Lokamanya Tilak comes on this platform and has told you that we want to use the Act, make the fullest use of it, we will get into the Legislative Councils. We will accept Ministerships, in fact we shall make the fullest possible use of it, but may I know, in the name of Heaven, in the name of everything that is sacred, why does not the Congress say so in its resolution and give a true lead to thousands who are outside waiting to know your opinion? I have no hesitation in saying on this platform that there is a school in this country whose intention is to obstruct and not to work the Reforms. I make bold to say that if you are intending to cooperate, if you wish to take up Ministerships, if the Act which places such opportunities and advantages in your way is worked properly, then I say it will be impossible to resist inquiry being held earlier. I ask you this question: do you object to work the Reforms so as to make the establishment of full Responsible Government as early as possible? [Cries of No, No] Then why not say so? I, therefore, say that Mahatma Gandhi does not propose to do anything more than what this house has expressed over and over again within the last few minutes, that we must work the Reform Act and the only dispute is whether it should form part of the resolution or not.

A compromise was arrived at on the main proposition on the following terms: The first three clauses would remain unaltered but the fourth clause would read: 'pending such introduction this Congress trusts that, so far as may be possible, the people will so work the Reforms as to secure an earlier establishment of full Responsible Government and this Congress offers thanks to the Rt. Hon'ble E.S. Montagu for his labours in connection with the reforms.' This was accepted as a compromise by all except Annie

Besant. Her amendment was therefore put to the vote and declared lost. The compromise resolution was then put to the vote and carried. Thus ended the keen conflict between the views of Das and Tilak, inclusive of 'obstructions when necessary', and Gandhi's and Jinnah's views, that the reforms were to be used for the purpose of obtaining responsible government, and not thrown away.[54]

Jinnah expressed his deep regret at having to differ with 'Lok [sic]' Tilak. 'I speak with the utmost deference for Lok [sic] Tilak. I hope that I shall not be misunderstood in any way'.[55]

The last resolution on a 'Declaration of Rights' has been all but forgotten. It bears reproduction in full here.

> This Congress is emphatically of opinion that in the immediate and imperative interest of this country as well as of the British Empire, a Statute should be forthwith passed by the Imperial Parliament to guarantee the civil rights of His Majesty's Indian subjects and embodying the following provisions:
>
> (1) That British India is one and indivisible and all political power is inherent in the people thereof to the same extent as in any other people or nation of the British Empire.
> (2) That all Indian subjects of His Majesty and all the subjects naturalized or resident in India are equal before the law, and there shall be no penal or administrative law in force in this country, whether substantive or procedural, of a discriminative nature.
> (3) That no Indian subject of His Majesty shall be liable to suffer in liberty, life, property or in respect of free speech or writing or of the right of association except under sentence by an ordinary Court of Justice and as a result of lawful and open trial.
> (4) That every Indian subject shall be entitled to bear arms subject to the purchase of a license as in Great Britain, and that the right shall not be taken away, save by a sentence of an ordinary Court of Justice.

(5) That the press shall be free and that no license or security shall be demanded on the registration of a press or newspaper.
(6) The corporal punishment shall not be inflicted on any subject of His Majesty save under conditions applying equally to all other British subjects.
(7) That all Laws, Ordinances and Regulations now or hereafter brought into existence that are any wise inconsistent with the provisions of this statute shall be void and of no validity whatsoever.

The Congress demanded a Bill of Rights in 1919 even before it did, famously, at Karachi in 1931.[56] As Jayakar remarked: 'The death of Tilak on 1 August 1920 removed from Indian politics the main and principal opponent of Gandhi's non-cooperation movement and it is significant that the scheme of the N.C.O. (non-cooperation) was formally inaugurated on the 1st of August, i.e. the same day as witnessed the death of Tilak'.[57]

On 1 September 1920 the Congress held a special session at Calcutta which Jinnah attended with his wife Ruttie. The most important subject before it was non-cooperation. Gandhi had won the support of the Ali Brothers by espousing the cause of Khilafat. Gandhi's resolution said that, 'it is the duty of every non-Muslim Indian in every legitimate manner to assist his Muslim brother in his attempt to remove the religious calamity that has overtaken him'. That was an onerous task. The 'calamity' had occurred in distant Turkey. It, next, mentioned the Punjab outrages and concluded:

> This Congress is of the opinion that there can be no contentment in India without redress of the two above-mentioned wrongs, and that the only effectual means to vindicate national honour and to prevent a repetition of similar wrongs in future is the establishment of Swarajya. This Congress is further of the opinion that there is no course left open for the people of India but to approve of and to adopt the policy of progressive non-violent Non-cooperation inaugurated by Mahatma Gandhi until the said wrongs are righted and Swarajya is established.

And inasmuch as beginning should be made by the classes who have hitherto moulded and represented public opinion and inasmuch as government consolidates its power through the titles and honours bestowed on the people, through schools controlled by it, its law courts and its legislative councils, and inasmuch as it is desirable in the prosecution of the movement to take the minimum risk and to call for the least sacrifice compatible with the establishment of the desired object, this Congress earnestly advises.

Seven steps were listed: surrender of titles, boycott of durbars, government-aided educational institutions, courts of law, legislatures and foreign goods, and ban on recruitment in the army for service in Mesopotamia (the present day Iraq).

The Subjects Committee adopted the resolution as did the plenary on 8 September. Turning more royalist than the king, Gandhi warned: 'The Mussalmans of India cannot remain as honourable men and followers of the Faith of their Prophet, if they do not vindicate their honour at any cost'. This, of course, was utter nonsense; both as a statement of ethics ('honour') or of the faith. Decades later some Muslim fundamentalists declared that the establishment of the Caliphate was a religious duty.

But, then, Gandhi was not teaching either ethics or theology. He was practicing politics; opportunistic and of baleful consequence. In a month's time he had captured the minds of the people. Bipin Chandra Pal moved an amendment to stave off the movement. Gandhi's resolution was carried by 1,826 votes against 884 for Pal's amendment. Ironically it was Lala Lajpat Rai who presided at the session. He said that though he supported the proposal for non-cooperation he disagreed with several of its details for example, boycott of schools, colleges, law courts and councils.

Jinnah delivered two speeches on the programme. One was on 7 September at the special session of the All-India Muslim League at the Town Hall where he took the chair and the other was on 8 September at the Congress session. These speeches reveal that while he disapproved of the programme he was stoutly opposed to British policies and shared Gandhi's opposition to them fully. He told the League:

> Mr Gandhi has placed his programme of non-cooperation, supported by the authority of the Khilafat Conference, before the country. It is now for you to consider whether or not you approve of its principle; and approving of its principle, whether or not you approve of its details. The operations of this scheme will strike at the individual in each of you, and therefore it rests with you alone to measure your strength and to weigh the pros and the cons of the question before you arrive at a decision. But once you have decided to march, let there be no retreat under any circumstances.
>
> In the meanwhile, there sits in Olympian Simla a self-satisfied Viceroy who alternately offers his sympathies to us unfortunate Mussalmans and regrets Mahatma Gandhi's 'foolish of all foolish schemes', being fortified with a 'character' from His Majesty's Government sent in a recent Despatch from 'Home'—the word Home is in inverted commas. This is the 'changed angle of vision' on which we heard such high-sounding phrases during those critical stages of the war when India's blood and India's gold was sought and unfortunately given—given to break Turkey and buy the fetters of the Rowlatt legislation.
>
> One degrading measure upon another, disappointment upon disappointment, and injury upon injury, can lead a people to only one end. It led Russia to Bolshevism. It has led Ireland to Sinn Feinism. May it lead India to freedom.... And when, in the Punjab, this universal opposition against the Rowlatt Act manifested itself through constitutional methods, it fell to the lot of the Lieutenant-Governor to dishonestly characterize it as 'open rebellion'. Only his administrative genius could have conjured up a vision of 'open rebellion' in a country whose people have been brutally unarmed, and only his cowardly spirit could have requisitioned the application of martial law, secure in his knowledge that weaponless, there could be no retaliation. Martial law was introduced; the manner and circumstances of its proclamation and its administration was calculated to destroy political freedom, political life not only in the

Punjab but throughout India, by striking terror into the hearts of its people.... These are the enormities crying aloud, and we have met today face to face with a dangerous and most unprecedented situation. The solution is not easy and the difficulties are great. But I cannot ask the people to submit to wrong after wrong. Yet I would still ask the government not to drive the people of India to desperation, or else there is no other course left open to the people except to inaugurate the policy of non-cooperation, though not necessarily the programme of Mr Gandhi.[58]

The Times of India reported, on 10 September, his speech at the Congress:

He was convinced the only remedy, the only guarantee and the only security for the non-recurrence of the two great outrages perpetrated in the Khilafat and the Punjab was the attainment of complete self-government. Mr Gandhi had stated that the only way to achieve the object was by non-cooperation and that the time had come for a beginning to be made to put it into actual practice, not merely to offer it as an ideal. Mr Jinnah wanted them to answer a few questions, calmly thinking over them. He asked the audience not to judge in their outraged feelings and with their lacerated hearts or in their desperation, as the audience was charged with that atmosphere. He asked, 'Before you commit the country to your programme, do you believe, are you convinced that Mr Gandhi's programme is practicable?' [Cries of Yes, Yes and No, No]. 'Will you tell me here the day on which I should give up my practice?' [Cries of Today and Tomorrow and laughter]. 'I hear today and tomorrow. The resolution as it is framed runs as follows: "The Congress earnestly advises" O.K., is that a mandate, a command? Why don't you, if you think that this programme of Mr Gandhi is practicable frame the resolution that this Congress issued forth a mandate to every Congressman that he must immediately work the programme? What is the course the Congress adopts? The Congress earnestly advised. I say I am fully convinced of non-cooperation. I see no other way except the policy of non-cooperation. But before I put this policy into practice I want to take stock of the situation to find what are the materials and forces. I want to take stock of my country and my countrymen. Will you not give me time for this? It is no use taking stock in this confusion.... The question for all of us, Hindu and Mohammedans, in this: <u>We are all one</u>. We have got our opponent and we want to make him feel that if he does not behave we will make government impossible. That is the only issue. Don't be driven into side tracks.... Make preparations, have your national schools and a court of arbitration. Find out in what other directions you are able to practice non-cooperation. When you have understood the whole situation you could begin to practice, led by with best brains amongst you'.[59]

Gandhi did not rest on his laurels. He took the battle to Bombay and took over the Home Rule League there. Jayakar's memoirs record in full how that was accomplished.[60] He wrote:

In an evil moment, some of the promoters of this League conceived the idea of asking Gandhi to be its head, in order that the Bombay Branch of the League might assume the same importance as its sister branches, over one of which Tilak presided and, over another, Mrs Annie Besant. When the idea was mooted at a meeting of the Committee of our League, I strongly opposed it ... I opposed his entry into the Home Rule League. *Jinnah, Sobhani, Jamnadas Dwarkadas* and other friends whose opinion was entitled to great respect, *favoured* his entry.

The meeting was adjourned. Gandhi was invited to be present at the next meeting. When Jayakar mentioned his objections, Gandhi gave an explicit assurance. He said that 'the only "fad" on which I would insist...would be a common language for India...and the gospel of *swadeshi* (buy Indian). You need to have no apprehension that any other theories of mine your League will be called to accept.' The pledge was broken.

Once elected president of the League, Gandhi proposed that its name, aims, and objectives be changed. A general meeting was held in Bombay on 3 October 1920 where this was accomplished. Jinnah's amendments were defeated. He raised a point of order. The constitution could not be amended except by a majority of three-fourth. Gandhi overruled him. To an objection by Jamnadas

Dwarkadas he replied, 'it was open to any member, be he life member or otherwise, to resign his membership, if he thought he could not remain a member of the Sabha under its altered constitution.' Dwarkadas was a founding member. The Swarajya Sabha disintegrated. Gandhi himself took little interest in it thereafter. A fund of Rs150,000, an enormous sum then, donated by S.R. Bomanji, remained unclaimed in the High Court.[61]

The object of the coup was clearly to eliminate a rival independent centre as a prelude to the Nagpur session of the Congress two months later. Jinnah and eighteen of his colleagues resigned; including Jayakar, K.M. Munshi, Jamnadas Dwarkadas, Kanji Dwarkadas, and M.K. Azad, a brilliant criminal lawyer.

Their letter of resignation dated 25 October criticized Gandhi's ruling as 'incorrect and arbitrary'. The League was affiliated to the Congress, its aims and objects could not differ from those of the parent body.

Gandhi replied on 25 October to refute the criticism. Jinnah's rejoinder must rank as one of the best letters he wrote. His criticism of the British was sharper than that of Gandhi. He wrote more in pain than in anger:

> I thank you for your kind suggestion offering me 'to take my share in the new life that has opened up before the country.' If by 'new life' you mean your methods and your programme, I am afraid I cannot accept them; for I am fully convinced that it must lead to disaster. But the actual new life that has opened up before the country is that we are faced with a government that pays no heed to the grievances, feelings and sentiments of the people; that our own countrymen are divided; the Moderate Party is still going wrong; that your methods have already caused split and division in almost every institution that you have approached hitherto, and in the public life of the country not only amongst Hindus and Muslims but between Hindus and Hindus and Muslims and Muslims and even between fathers and sons; people generally are desperate all over the country and your extreme programme has for the moment struck

the imagination mostly of the inexperienced youth and the ignorant and the illiterate. All this means complete disorganization and chaos. What the consequence of this may be, I shudder to contemplate; but I, for one, am convinced that the present policy of the government is the primary cause of it all and unless that cause is removed, the effects must continue. I have no voice or power to remove the cause; but at the same time I do not wish my countrymen to be dragged to the brink of a precipice in order to be shattered. The only way for the Nationalists is to unite and work for a programme which is universally acceptable for the early attainment of complete responsible government. *Such a programme cannot be dictated by any single individual*, but must have the approval and support of all the prominent Nationalist leaders in the country; and to achieve this end I am sure my colleagues and myself shall continue to work.[62]

Jayakar found new insights in N.C. Kelkar's *Life of Tilak*.[63] Apparently, Tilak had prepared a manifesto for a new democratic party. It was approved by Gandhi before it was published in Tilak's paper, *Kesari*, on 20 April 1920. It said 'this party proposes to work the Montagu Reforms Act for all it is worth... it will without hesitation offer cooperation or resort to constitutional opposition, whichever may be expedient.' Jayakar's question is pertinent: 'What happened between April and August 1920 which could account for the revolutionary change from cooperation to non-cooperation, except that Tilak, the main opponent of Non-Cooperation, died on 1 August thereby leaving the way clear to Gandhi to unfurl publicly, with the aid of the Ali Brothers, his banner of Non-Cooperation on the very day of Tilak's death'.[64]

When the Congress met at its Nagpur session in December 1920 Gandhi's critics had gone over to swell his ranks. Lajpat Rai, C.R. Das, Malaviya, and Motilal Nehru supported him. Jinnah remained the solitary critic. He began by referring to the goal of Swaraj as complete independence and said:

> Today we have accomplished one thing and that is the majority have the will to make this declaration and I entirely agree that the

majority have the will to make this declaration. But the second proposition is, have we got the means of making this declaration? I say the means which are placed before you by Mr Gandhi are 'legitimate and peaceful' not 'legitimate or peaceful' but 'legitimate and peaceful'. Therefore Mr Gandhi thinks [cries of Mahatma Gandhi],—Yes, Mahatma Gandhi thinks that by peaceful methods, having declared complete Independence for India, he will achieve it. With very great respect for Mahatma Gandhi and those who think with him *I make bold to say in this assembly that you will never get your Independence without bloodshed* [cries of no, no]. If you think that you are going to get your Independence without bloodshed I say that you are making the greatest blunder [cries of no, no—a voice: 'nonsense']. Therefore I say that at this moment you are making a declaration which you have not the means to carry out. On the other hand, you are exposing your hand to your enemies....

You are going to tell your people the moment this resolution is passed that the Indian National Congress has made a bid for Complete Independence, that our Indian National Congress, as Mr Gandhi [cries of Mahatma Gandhi]—as Mahatma Gandhi said, that you want to destroy the British Empire. Then you may have that feeling, you have that wish. But I ask you in the name of reason, have you considered how you are going to destroy the British Empire? If I am right in my opinion that for the moment today it is a mere dream to say that you will destroy the British Empire notwithstanding the fact that we are thirty crores and more; if I am right then I say you are making a declaration and you are committing the Indian National Congress to a programme which you will not be able to carry out. [A voice: 'We will']. What is the reasoning? The only reason that I have been able to get beyond mere sentimental feeling and expression of anger and desperation, and I assure you, I don't feel anything but desperate myself but I may be able to control myself more than others,—[a voice: 'slave mentality']. But what is the reason that is given to us?—The only reason that I have been able to get from the speakers on the Creed was given to me in the Subjects Committee by Mr Mohammad Ali [cries of Maulana]. Mr Mohammad Ali told me [loud cries of Maulana Mohammad Ali]. If you will not allow me the liberty to address you and speak of a man in the language in which I think it is right, I say you are denying me the liberty which you are asking for. I am entitled to say Mr Mohammad Ali [cries of 'Maulana' and cries of 'go on']. I say the only reason that Mr Mohammad Ali gave me was that there are some people who find it impossible to sign the Congress Creed and therefore the Congress Creed must be changed.

Mr Mohammad Ali: That was not the only reason I gave you.

Mr Jinnah: That is the only reason that I gathered; that is the only reason which I understood. I do not say that Mr Mohammad Ali did not give other reasons, but the only reason that I understood after he had made a long speech was this that in order to enable certain people who are not willing to sign the present Congress Creed, it is necessary to change the Creed. Do you think that is a sufficient reason? [A voice: 'No']. You will hear from Mr Mohammad Ali when he comes here what his reasons are beyond mere sentimental talk. I do not say that we should not believe in sentiments nor do I say that sentiment does not play an important part. But remember that you are changing your constitution. Remember this constitution which you change is going to take place in the books of your constitution as a firm, permanent thing which it is not easy to change. You cannot pass a constitution this year and change it next year. The constitution must be sacred to us. ...

If you want complete independence let us not be limited to methods. Why should you be limited to methods? Who is to decide as we go on, what will be the effective methods to achieve the complete Swarajya which we are asking for? I say therefore, I really feel I am unable to agree with it for this reason that it is neither logical nor is it politically sound or wise, not practically capable of being put in execution. I have given you my opinion, gentlemen. Don't for a single moment believe from what I have been saying—[a voice: 'It is your weakness']. I am told it is weakness. I was told in the Subjects Committee it is want of courage. I don't wish to stoop to say that a particular man is weak or dishonest or wanting in courage. If I wish to retort I can say in return that it is your foolhardiness; but these words do not help us [Cries of shame].

I have said what I have to say. In conclusion, to quote the words of our president who is sitting here, he said at the moment the destinies of the country are in the hands of two men and among those two he mentioned Mahatma Gandhi. Therefore standing on this platform, knowing as I do know that he commands the majority in this assembly, I appeal to him to pause, to cry halt before it is too late.[65]

Jinnah was jeered and abused on his train journey back to Bombay with his wife. He was insulted again and again. Maulana Shaukat Ali instigated the crowd at Akola Station to hoot at Jinnah. This drew a letter from a correspondent 'R' which *The Times of India* published on 13 January 1921. Mentioning the incident she wrote 'Sir, this thing is the negation of non-cooperation of which non-violence is the essence'. The correspondent was none other than Jinnah's wife Ruttie.[66]

It was a Faustian bargain which Gandhi had struck with the Ali Brothers. An Australian scholar points out that 'despite his protestations that his support for the Khilafat issue was motivated by the justness of the Muslim cause, Gandhi was also re-establishing himself as a political leader after the failure of the Rowlatt *satyagraha*. By taking up the Khilafat issue he gained substantial Muslim support for his own political programme and undermined the position of Jinnah and the other advocates of constitutional politics. The Khilafatists, for their part, looked to an alliance with Gandhi as a means to gather Hindu support for the Khilafat, and place greater pressure on the government. Gandhi took an active part in the first All-India Khilafat Conference and supported the calls for a Khilafat Day to protest the issue. At the time, Gandhi called for support from India's Hindu population in an attempt to evaluate the level of support for what was essentially a Muslims concern. Impressed by the response to this day of prayers, fasting and *hartal*, Gandhi stepped up his involvement and wrote extensively on the Khilafat issue. When the terms of the Turkish treaty were published in India, Gandhi branded them '*crime against humanity*'. Non-cooperation was the only possible response to these terms. At their meeting at the end of May 1920, the All-India Khilafat Committee endorsed Gandhi's non-cooperation campaign. Despite opposition from Conservative Khilafatists and displeasure over his 'arbitrary manner', the committee accepted Gandhi's views. It called upon the country to withdraw cooperation from the government and continue to do so until justice is done.

> When the question of non-cooperation came before the Congress later in 1920, Muslims formed the core of Gandhi's support. At the Calcutta Special Congress held in September, Gandhi's Non-Cooperation Resolution was accepted by the Congress Subjects Committee 148 votes to 133, with 43 Khilafatists voting in its favour. In the open session the resolution was passed by 1,826 votes to 884 and it was estimated that over 2,000 of the 5,500 delegates who attended were Muslims. Jinnah spoke against the resolution at this meeting and barely escaped being physically attacked by Shaukat Ali, who was restrained by delegates, as Willingdon reported to Montagu on 15 September 1920.[67]

At Nagpur in December, the moderates were again swamped by the Khilafatists and Jinnah had 'no influence' on the proceedings. After a campaign by the Khilafatists to ferry Muslims to the session, in excess of 70 per cent of the delegates were Muslim.

> Given the disparity of Muslims representation at the respective Congress sessions, the importance of the Khilafat issue in regard to the supposedly wider issues of Home Rule and the Punjab atrocities is obvious. Gandhi's programme for non-cooperation initially attracted little support within the Congress itself and it was only through the Khilafat Movement that he gained sufficient support to push through his measures. Although Jinnah emerged as one of the only Congressmen willing to publicly criticize Gandhi's programme as a 'blunder', privately a number of Indian politicians had similar doubts of the wisdom of forcing such a plan on Congress. Similar questions were raised over the representative character of the Congress sessions which accepted non-cooperation.[68]

A work of massive research published this year fortifies this view.[69] Professor Qureshi, a distinguished scholar, writes:

> When the proposition of non-cooperation was brought before the Congress it was debated for three days in the Subjects Committee. The discussion was so heated that at one point 'Shaukat Ali threatened to lay violent hands on Jinnah', the solitary Muslim opposing the motion, and was only prevented from doing so by the physical intervention of other delegates. The opposition, for its part, subjected Gandhi to considerable heckling, but he resisted all pressure to abandon the campaign. When he found that the feeling was running high against him, he threatened to go ahead with the help of the Khilafatists whether or not the Congress accepted it. And the fact is that the Muslim dominance swung the balance in favour of non-cooperation. The proposition was finally accepted by a narrow majority of 144 votes to 132.
>
> When the resolution was moved in the open Congress on 8 September, Lajpat Rai, the president, who understood the political aspect of the Khilafat issue, chose to remain non-committal on non-cooperation. Gandhi refused to admit that non-cooperation would lead to violence or bloodshed, maintaining that if it were adopted and practiced in the manner he had presented it 'you can gain your Swaraj in one year.' B.C. Pal of Bengal tried delaying tactics by proposing that before embarking on non-cooperation they should approach the British prime minister for the redress of their grievances and, in the meantime, re-examine the question of non-cooperation and participate in the elections. Jinnah, Malaviya, C.R. Das and Baptista supported him, but, in the end, his motion was thrown out. Gandhi's resolution, managed by a juggle and toned down with regard to the boycott of schools and courts, was accepted on 9 September 1920 by 1826 votes to 884....
>
> But the determining factor was pressure from the Khilafatists who swayed the opinion in the subjects committee and obtained the verdict in their favour in the open Congress. The Muslim dominance was so visible that at one point Joseph Baptista accused Gandhi of handing over the Congress to Mahomedans. How deeply the Congress was committed to the restoration of the caliphate is not

difficult to discern: the mood ranged from ambivalence to apathy in addition to political opportunism.[70]

During December 1920, the focus of attention was the Congress session at Nagpur, for on its outcome depended the future attitude of the bulk of the Hindu community towards the Khilafat movement. The majority of the moderates, however, chose to stay away from Nagpur and, instead, decided to meet hundreds of miles away in Madras under the maternal wings of Mrs Besant. The extremists among the opponents of non-cooperation, the Bengalis and the Maharashtrians in particular, came determined to reverse the Calcutta Special Congress decision of September 1920. The non-cooperators had not been sitting idle either. They had been concentrating on the opposition, especially the Bengal contingent. The Bengal Provincial Khilafat Committee had even provided a special train for the delegates' trip to Nagpur. Mohamed Ali successfully used his personal influence with a compliant C.R. Das and 'proselytized' him to non-cooperation. A compromise was reached in the subjects committee whereby Das undertook to support non-cooperation not so much as a sell-out to a 'Gujarati Bania', but really as a checkmate to Gandhi from inside by associating himself with his programme. On his part, Gandhi agreed to whittle down the boycott of schools and the surrender of practice by lawyers if it could bring down a powerful adversary. The boycott of the councils was already a dead issue after the elections. On 30 December, Das himself moved the non-cooperation resolution in the open Congress. Other opponents had already been silenced without much difficulty. The moderates of Nagpur were not heard, Malaviya's efforts were nugatory, G.S. Khaparde and Dr B.S. Moonje (b. 1872) were brushed aside and Lajpat Rai wobbled and then became silent.[71]

K.M. Munshi's assessment was fair.

In a sense Jinnah dominated the Congress and the League at the time. He had played the key role in preparing a draft constitution for India and getting it adopted by the sessions both of the Congress and of the League. The historical Lucknow Pact was an integral part of this constitution. The pact, of which the moving spirit was Jinnah, was readily accepted by Annie Besant, Sir Chimanlal Setalvad and other leaders. Malaviya opposed it. Gandhi remained a silent observer.'

Munshi remarked: 'Tilak, while supporting the Pact at the Congress session at Lucknow, said: "It has been said that we, Hindus, have yielded too much to our Muslim brothers. I am sure I represent the sense of the Hindu community all over India when I say that we could not have yielded too much. I would not care if the rights of self-government are granted to the Muslim community only. I would not care if they are granted to the lower classes of the Hindu population. Then the fight will not be triangular, as at present it is".'[72] Munshi's comments on the changes brought about by Gandhi merit notice.

> On 2 October 1920, a general meeting of the Home Rule League was held at the Gokuldas Market Hall in Bombay. Gandhiji presided. Among those present on the occasion were Pandit Motilal Nehru, Jawaharlal Nehru and Rajagopalachari. Jinnah, supported by M.R. Jayakar, moved an amendment to Gandhiji's original resolution, but it was defeated. My amendment, almost to the same effect, supported by Harsiddhbhai Divatia [later Chief Justice of Saurashtra], was defeated by 45 votes to 20. Jinnah then proposed a third amendment, 'Swaraj means responsible government within the Empire'; this was also defeated. The original resolution was passed by a simple majority.
>
> Jinnah then pointed out that, according to the rules, the constitution could not be changed except by a three-fourths majority and without a proper notice being given. But Gandhiji, as President, overruled Jinnah's objection, whereupon we left the meeting.

Munshi added:

> The Nagpur session of the Congress in 1920 switched over to Gandhian aims and means which, we felt sure, would at the end lead the country to terroristic methods. But the bulk of the politically-minded Hindus were with Gandhiji. Even C.R. Das, who had come determined to oppose Gandhiji, surrendered to him. The Congress

session looked less like a political body than a religious gathering celebrating the advent of a Messiah. Jinnah (and, if my memory is right, also Malaviyaji, and Khaparde) stood up in that jeering assembly and opposed the official resolution. After Nagpur, led by Jinnah, about twenty of us left the Congress.

When Gandhiji forced Jinnah and his followers out of the Home Rule League and later the Congress, we all felt, with Jinnah, that a movement of an unconstitutional nature, sponsored by Gandhiji with the tremendous influence he had acquired over the masses, would inevitably result in widespread violence, barring the progressive development of self-governing institutions based on a partnership between educated Hindus and Muslims. To generate coercive power in the masses would only provoke mass conflict between the two communities, as in fact it did. With his keen sense of realities Jinnah firmly set his face against any dialogue with Gandhi on this point.

The record shows however that this is far from accurate. Jinnah disagreed. He did not desert.[73]

Notes

1. Kanji Dwarkadas, *India's Struggle for Freedom 1913–1937: An Eyewitness Story*, Popular Prakashan, Bombay, 1966, p. 59.
2. Ibid., pp. 65–6.
3. Muzaffar Hanafi, *Hasrat Mohaani*, National Book Trust of India, 2004, p. 26. Editor's note: Hanafi's spelling of Mohani.
4. Syed Sharifuddin Pirzada (ed.), *The Collected Works of Quaid-e-Azam Mohammad Ali Jinnah*, Vol. I, 1906–1921, East and West Publishing Company, Karachi, 1984, p. 4.
5. Pattabhi Sitaramayya, *The History of the Indian National Congress*, Vol. I, 1885–1935, Padma Publications Ltd., Bombay, 1935, p. 96.
6. Riaz Ahmad, *Quaid-i-Azam Mohammad Ali Jinnah: The Formative Years 1892–1920*, National Institute of Historical and Cultural Research, Islamabad, 1986, pp. 69–70.
7. M.R. Jayakar, *The Story of My Life*, Vol. I, 1873–1922, Asia Publishing House, 1958, p. 89. Jayakar was Jinnah's associate then but drifted apart and became a leader of the Hindu Mahasabha.
8. Hugh F. Owen, 'Negotiating the Lucknow Pact', *Journal of Asian Studies*, Vol. XXXI, No. 3, May 1972, p. 575, a definitive essay.

9. A.G. Noorani, *Indian Political Trials, 1775–1947*, Oxford University Press, New Delhi, 2005. Chapter 4, 'Tilak's Trials 1897 and 1908', pp. 114–36 and Chapter 6, 'Jinnah Defends Tilak 1916', pp. 163–84.
10. A.G. Noorani, *Badruddin Tyabji*, Publications Division, Government of India, Delhi, 1969, p. 10.
11. M.C. Chagla, *Roses in December: An Autobiography*, Bharatiya Vidya Bhavan, 1973, pp. 14–15.
12. Pirzada, Vol. I, pp. 386–7.
13. K.R. Shirsat, *Kaka Joseph Baptista: Father of Home Rule Movement in India*, Popular Prakashan, Bombay, 1974.
14. Source material for a history of the Freedom Movement in India, collected from Bombay Government Records, Vol. II, 1885–1920, Government Central Press, Bombay.
15. Chagla, *Roses in December*, p. 14.
16. Quoted in Ian Bryant Wells, *Jinnah's Early Politics: Ambassador of Hindu–Muslim Unity*, Permanent Black, Delhi, 2005, p. 107.
17. B.B. Misra, *The Indian Political Parties: A Historical Analysis of Political Behaviour up to 1947*, Oxford University Press, Delhi, 1976, p. 154.
18. Owen, 'Negotiating the Lucknow Pact', p. 575.
19. Pirzada, Vol. I, p. 1.
20. Ibid., p. 17.
21. Misra, *The Indian Political Parties*, pp. 128–9.
22. Pirzada, Vol. I, p. 241.
23. Ibid., pp. 159–60.
24. Owen, 'Negotiating the Lucknow Pact', p. 574.
25. Jayakar, p. 388.
26. Ibid., p. 161.
27. Jayakar, pp. 158–90.
28. Judith Brown, *Gandhi's Rise to Power: Indian Politics 1915–1922*, Cambridge University Press, 1971, p. 26.
29. Pirzada, Vol. I, pp. 192–3.
30. Owen, 'Negotiating the Lucknow Pact', p. 578.
31. Pirzada, Vol. II, 1921–26, p. 251.
32. B.R. Ambedkar, *Pakistan or the Partition of India*, Thacker & Co. Ltd., Bombay, 1946, pp. 314–15.
33. For the text vide, Marguerite Rose Dove, *Forfeited Future: The Conflict over Congress Ministries in British India 1933–1937*, Chanakya Publications, Delhi, 1987, pp. 462–3. An excellent but greatly neglected work of research and rigorous analysis.
34. Uma Kaura, *Muslims and Indian Nationalism: The Emergence of the Demand for India's Partition, 1928–40*, Manohar, New Delhi, 1977, p. 22.

35. A.G. Noorani, 'Jinnah & Muslims of India', *Criterion*, October–December 2008, pp. 47–48, a quarterly published from Islamabad and edited by S. Iftikhar Murshed, a former diplomat.
36. Pirzada, Vol. I, p. 252.
37. Ibid., p. 244.
38. Jayakar, pp. 199–200.
39. Pirzada, Vol. I, p. 274.
40. Ibid., p. 243.
41. Edwin Samuel Montagu, *An Indian Diary*, edited by Venetia Montagu, Heinemann, London, 1930, p. 381.
42. Brown, *Gandhi's Rise to Power*, p. 148.
43. Source material for a history of the Freedom Movement in India, collected from Bombay Government Records, Vol. II, 1885–1920, Government Central Press, Bombay, p. 706.
44. Pirzada, Vol. I, p. 282.
45. *Bombay Chronicle*, 12 December 1918.
46. Matlubul Hasan Saiyid, *Mohammad Ali Jinnah: A Political Study*, Shaikh Mohammad Ashraf, Lahore, 1945, pp. 200–02.
47. We have a full account in M.H. Saiyid's book (pp. 209–14), in the *Bombay Chronicle* of 12 December, and in Vol. II of the Source Material based on police reports published by the Government of Bombay forty years later in 1958 (pp. 720–4).
48. Pirzada, Vol. I, p. 301.
49. Kanji Dwarkadas, p. 79.
50. N.P. Nathwani vs. Commissioner of Police (1976), 78, Bombay Law Reporter, p. 1.
51. Jayakar, p. 20.
52. Para 189, Sedition Committee Report, 1918.
53. J.C. Ker, *Political Trouble in India, 1907–1917*, reprint, Calcutta, Editions Indian, 1973, pp. vi–vii.
54. Jayakar, pp. 307–12.
55. Pirzada, Vol. I, p. 368.
56. For the 1931 text vide Sitaramayya, Vol. I, pp. 463–4.
57. Ibid., p. 388.
58. Pirzada, Vol. I, pp. 389–90.
59. Ibid., pp. 395–6.
60. Ibid., pp. 316–18.
61. Jayakar, p. 319.
62. Pirzada, Vol. I, p. 400.
63. Ibid., Vol. III, Part VI, pp. 59–60.
64. Jayakar, p. 403.
65. Pirzada, Vol. I, pp. 404–6.

66. Syed Sharifuddin Pirzada, *Some Aspect of Quaid-i-Azam's Life*, National Commission on Historical and Cultural Research, Islamabad, 1978, pp. 49–50.
67. Wells, *Jinnah's Early Politics*, pp. 117–19.
68. Ibid.
69. M. Naeem Qureshi, *Pan-Islam in British India: The Politics of the Khilafat Movement, 1918–1924*, Oxford University Press, Karachi, 2009.
70. Ibid., pp. 180–1.
71. Ibid., p.196.
72. D.G. Tendulkar, *Mahatma: Life of Mohandas Karamchand Gandhi*, Vol. I, Publications Division, Ministry of Information and Broadcasting, Government of India, 1988, p. 234.
73. K.M. Munshi, *Pilgrimage to Freedom*, Vol. I, Bharatiya Vidya Bhavan, Bombay, 1967, pp. 7 and 17.

2

After Tilak:
Jinnah and Gandhi's Congress

Jinnah's admiration for Gandhi was not affected. He did not cease to be a member of the Congress either. The coup in the Home Rule League and the jeers at the Nagpur session would have embittered most. They did not affect him. Shortly thereafter, at a meeting in Bombay on 19 February 1921, to mark the sixth anniversary of Gokhale's death, Jinnah commented at length on Gandhi's programme:

> He could tell them honestly and sincerely that he was convinced in his mind that the programme of Mahatma Gandhi for whom he had great respect and admiration was taking them to a wrong channel. Continuing, Mr Jinnah said, if it were not taking them in the wrong channel and if he could be convinced so, he would have been the first man to join it. It was not that he had not the greatest respect and reverence for Mr Gandhi and the men who were working with him because he knew of what noble stuff they were made. He worked with them and was firmly convinced of their noble and sacrificing spirit. He was proud of them and there were many more like them in India now. But he would tell them again—he might be right or he might be wrong—that the programme of Mahatma Gandhi was taking them to a wrong channel. In his opinion what they wanted was a real political movement based on real political principles and based on the fire which burnt in the heart of every man for his motherland. So long as they had not that as the basis, their programme was defective.
>
> Referring to the conditions in Czarist Russia, he asked as to what happened in Russia. The Czar created the Duma and continued in

his despotic attitude and what happened then? He [the Czar] found it impossible to go on with the Duma and had to suspend it. So the Government of India also would have to suspend the Legislative Council if they persisted in going against the will of the country... the people's representatives could make the further work of legislation impossible until the government yielded ... Germany made preparations by mobilizing her forces for forty years before she came out to fight. What was India's mobilization and what was her strength? Mr Gandhi had asked them to come out of the schools and colleges and then to go to villages. But what to do there?

A voice: 'To educate the masses.'

The speaker: 'Young man, take it from me, the villagers know things better than you.'

If they were going to regulate everything in their country by the doctrine of non-violent non-cooperation he was afraid they were forgetting human nature. They were forgetting that they were human beings and not saints. If they really wanted to serve their country at the present moment they must let the political movement go on and their foremost and fundamental work should be to raise the level of the average man of the country [hear, hear]. Mr Gandhi's programme was based on the doctrine of soul-force and it was an essentially spiritual movement. Having for its programme destructive methods which did not take account of human nature and human feelings, non-violent non-cooperation will be a miracle if accomplished. He said, before that it was not a political programme though it had for its object the political goal of the country. Such principles and doctrines as were preached and propagated by Mr Gandhi, were opposed to the nature of an ordinary mortal like the speaker himself. Not one in a million could carry out Mr Gandhi's doctrine which has its sole arbitrator his conscience. The speaker could not contemplate how long the non-violent non-co-operation could last if all the boys were withdrawn from schools and colleges without substituting them by national schools and colleges. He still hoped the government would think less of Mr Gandhi's programme and think more of what the intellectual opinion of the country felt, and he trusted that it would not be very long before a real change of policy was enacted so as to allay and satisfy the feelings of the

AFTER TILAK: JINNAH AND GANDHI'S CONGRESS

people who were in entire accord with the spirit of Mr Gandhi's movement which, however defective, may be picked up and directed in a channel which might make the government and administration of the country impossible.

Concluding, Mr Jinnah said, undoubtedly Mr Gandhi was a great man and he had more regard for him than anybody else. But he did not believe in his programme and he could not support it. He might stand out alone but he would say that in his opinion if the movement were directed in a right channel there was great hope. He did not know what Gokhale would have said or done now but he thought Gokhale would not have endorsed this programme had he been spared to live till now.

This report in the *Bombay Chronicle*[1] puts paid to the notion that it was an embittered parting at Nagpur.

In a letter to *The Times of India* of 10 June 1921, he referred to the governments excesses and wrote:

The answer to this has been a movement of the people led by Mr Gandhi and commonly known as 'non-violent non-cooperation.' History has taught us that repression is the greatest incitement to revolution, and non-cooperation is one of the shapes such a movement would take in India. The intelligentsia of India must be driven towards revolution if things are allowed to drift. Repression is the reply given by the government. Prosecutions and arrest and imprisonment of some of our finest men are matters of daily occurrence all over India. There is a deadlock. Is there a way out? Repression is not the remedy. It will only make the cancer grow and make another Ireland. Conciliation and justice, so often alluded to by Lord Reading, represent the only course. To achieve this, government must give definite proofs—we want deeds, not words.[2]

Even after Nagpur, Jinnah met Gandhi to discuss the state of affairs at Ahmedabad in December 1921, when Gandhi was attending the Congress annual session. Jinnah had resigned from the Congress earlier on 30 September 1921.[3] Jayakar was present with Jinnah when, on 18 December 1921, a message was received from the viceroy proposing that if the agitation against the visit of the Prince of Wales to India was called off he would convene a Round Table Conference. Jinnah and Jayakar pressed him to explore the offer.[4]

After returning from Ahmedabad, Jinnah, Malaviya, Jayakar, Ambalal Sarabhai, Purshottamdas Thakurdas, and K. Natarajan convened a conference. It was Jinnah's idea which he shared with Jayakar. The conference was held at the Cowasji Jehangir Hall in Bombay on 14 January 1922. Jinnah moved a resolution for convening a Round Table Conference. Gandhi and Annie Besant were present. There was not the slightest trace of bitterness in anybody about the happenings in Nagpur. Gandhi sympathized with the conveners; apologized for the use of violence by some non-cooperators, but declined to be party to any resolution which might be passed.

The conference adopted resolutions censuring repressive legislation, imposition of curbs on 'freedom of press and liberty of speech and of association', demanded their withdrawal and requested that 'the civil disobedience contemplated by the Ahmedabad Congress should not be resorted to'. It, next, asked for a convening of a Round Table Conference. A committee of twenty members was set up to parley with the parties. Jinnah, Malaviya, Jayakar, and Dinshaw Petit were among its members. Jinnah, Jayakar, and K. Natarajan were secretaries of this 'Bombay Representative Conference'. Sir Sankaran Nair withdrew from conference.[5]

On 17 January the Congress Working Committee thanked the conference for its pains but demanded 'full settlement of the three claims': Khilafat, the Punjab, and Swaraj. Jinnah and his colleagues persisted with both Gandhi and the Viceroy Lord Reading.[6] They sent a letter to 'Dear Mahatmaji' on 2 February 1922, complaining of his action in writing as he did to the viceroy 'while correspondence was still going on, on the subject of the Round Table Conference'. Gandhi's ultimatum, of which the viceroy took full advantage, ended the matter.[7]

Jinnah doggedly continued his efforts for unity. The 15th session of the Muslim League over which he presided was held at the Globe Theatre in Lahore on 24 May 1924. It was attended by Maulana Mohammed Ali, Dr M.A. Ansari, Asaf Ali, Saifuddin Kitchlew as well as Satyapal, Raisaheb Hans Raj, Lala Goverdhan Das, and Lala Dhuni Chand. After referring to 'mistakes and blunders' Jinnah paid a significant compliment to Gandhi: 'The result of the struggle of last three years has this to our credit that there is an open movement for the achievement of Swaraj for India...the ordinary man in the street has found his political consciousness...'. This was a development which Jinnah warmly welcomed, contrary to Jawaharlal Nehru's charge later.

No less significant was the resolution moved by Jinnah from the chair which the session adopted. It read:

> With a view to better the economic and political conditions of the workers and peasants of India, the All-India Muslim League considers it most essential that the organization of the workers and peasants be taken in hand, and *a movement be immediately started on the lines chalked out by the All-India Congress Committee* in this connection, in order to achieve these objects; the League therefore resolves that a committee of five members be appointed by the Council of the League to meet the committee appointed by the All-India Congress Committee for this purpose to draw up a practical programme for the organizations of workers and peasants of India.[8]

Despite Nagpur, Jinnah was keen on keeping in step with the Congress. It was to be a joint Congress–League exercise cutting across the religious divide. This was hardly surprising; Jinnah was once president of the Postal Union which had 70,000 members.

Maulana Mohammed Ali and Jawaharlal Nehru wrecked the move, as Ian Bryant Wells records:

> The work of this committee was disrupted however by the machinations of Mahomed Ali, who was attempting at this time to rejuvenate his flagging political career. He and his brother Shaukat vehemently opposed the revival of the Muslim League under Jinnah and throughout 1924 Mahomed Ali and Jinnah carried out a heated exchange in the press. In trying to maintain the position of his now almost defunct Khilafat organization, Mahomed Ali attacked both the validity of the Muslim League and that of Jinnah personally. Jinnah returned the criticism in kind and questioned the respectability of the Ali brothers. He spoke disparagingly of Shaukat, suggesting that 'this little Maulana for the last three years has been making an annual attempt to destroy the Muslim League.'
>
> Although Mahomed Ali failed in his attempts to destroy the Muslim League and prevent Jinnah's domination of that organization, he was able to sabotage Jinnah's attempts to negotiate with Congress. As Congress president, he was able to orchestrate the Congress response to Muslim League overtures and subsequently affect the possibility of joint 1924 sessions of the League and Congress. Congress elements that opposed an alliance with the Muslim League were only too willing to use Mahomed Ali as a scapegoat for the breakdown in relations between the two organizations. When the Muslim League official approached Congress, League members were upset by the response they received (as Kidwai wrote to Motilal Nehru): 'Some of the members of the Council were so ruffled by the contemptuous treatment with which the Secretary of the Congress treated the request of the Muslim League Constitution Committee.... That it rejected the suggestions of holding the session at the same place where the Congress is going to he held.' The Congress secretary referred to in this correspondence was Jawaharlal, Gandhi's fervent supporter, who had his own plans for Congress and saw Congress as the leading party in Indian nationalist politics, which precluded equal partnership with the Muslim League.[9]

Jinnah was disheartened but did not give up his search for common ground among nationalists. On 22 May 1925, Jinnah wrote to Jayakar stating that there was an increase in the consensus that the time was ripe for a common understanding between the different political parties with a view to united action. He had informal discussions with several friends on the subject and there was a strong feeling in favour of coordinating their common efforts. He had called a meeting of different leaders at his bungalow to which Jayakar was invited. In the letter was enclosed the following draft statement embodying suggestions which were tentatively made:

> Education, agitation and organization are the essential pre-requisites for the successful prosecution of any national programme that will materially advance the cause of Swarajya. The suspension of the policy and programme of Non-cooperation by the Belgaum Congress, the crystallization of the Swarajists' policy into one of resistance of bureaucracy as it impedes progress to Swarajya, and Das's speech at Faridpur, eliminates the main obstacle to the reunion of all Nationalists on a common platform on the basis of a common programme. The only alternative to a thorough-going programme of non-cooperation is a programme of 'honourable co-operation'. An analysis of the policy of the Swarajists, Independents, and Liberals reveals the existence of much common ground between all the parties in regard to the main principles which will govern the national policy. The Congress has no political programme other than that of the Swaraj Party, while its constructive programme is not open to objection on principle on the part of any of the political parties.... Suggestions have been made that the Nationalists should join either the Swaraj Party or the Liberal Party as a step towards unity. In the view of many, the Congress alone as the greater body, offers a suitable medium for the union of all parties on a common platform. This can, however, be done only with the Congress participating directly in political activities, which function it has now delegated to the Swaraj Party. The yarn franchise also raises difficulties. In the circumstances, the immediate feasible course appears to be for the different parties to retain their individuality and to cooperate with one another to the extent a common programme permits united action, while continuing to make efforts to reunite all progressive sections of the people *on the Congress platform*. This can be done by the Executive Committees of the

different parties acting together or by the creation of a temporary organization in which the progressive elements of all parties can come together.... It is incumbent upon us all to make a beginning in Bombay towards the unity of all progressive sections of the people on a common platform. This can only be done by the temporary creation of a new organization that will pledge itself to pursue common policy enunciated above while working *at the same time for the unit of all parties on the Congress platform.*

Jinnah clearly hoped to rejoin the Congress. One obstacle was the 'yarn franchise', wearing of khadi.

The creed of the new organization shall be: (1) The attainment of Swaraj. (2) The immediate objective is the speedy attainment of full Dominion Status. (3) The membership of the organization shall be open to every adult of either sex over the age of 21, who subscribed to the creed and pays the prescribed subscription.

This exposes the canard that he wished to restrict membership to matriculates which Jawaharlal Nehru later retailed.

The programme shall be: (a) A vigorous prosecution of a broad-based constructive programme through legislative and independent efforts. (2) The co-ordination of activities within the Legislature and public bodies and activities in the country. (3) The pursuit of a policy of 'opposition or support of measures as national interests demand on a consideration of their intrinsic merits' in the Legislatures and public bodies. (4) The organization of the electorates. (5) The organization of an intensive educative political campaign in support of the policy enunciated above. (6) Activities shall be confined to Bombay. (7) The organization shall consist of a President two Vice-Presidents, Secretaries and an Executive Committee.

Jayakar added:

When I got this invitation I had great hopes that at least for the city of Bombay all Nationalists would combine and work the programme sketched out in the letter quoted above. Accordingly, more than one conference was held with Jinnah. I personally supported Jinnah's idea of a new orientation of parties, but I found that *the Swarajists' prejudices against him* and their strict adherence to the very letter of their programme prevented the formation of what Jinnah called a new organization. After several attempts at his residence and mine, ultimately, the attempt was given up. It was revived, as the subsequent pages will show, once more in New Delhi on the advent of the Simon's Commission and there too an attempt to formulate a new inclusive organization failed. The Swarajists' strong faith in their own programme and their unwillingness to make changes in the same interfered with the success of Jinnah's efforts. If this had been accomplished, the country would have been a strong Nationalist Party working for a common programme in which leading Swarajists like Motilal and Das and leading Nationalists like Jinnah would have cooperated, but the thing was not to be and the attempt failed.[10]

Gandhi and Jinnah met in Bombay on 20 November 1924 and agreed on a resolution condemning preventive detention. In December 1929, Jinnah travelled to Gandhi's ashram at Sabarmati to discuss the viceroy's pronouncement on independence. Jinnah and Tej Bahadur Sapru were keen on bringing about a meeting between the Congress leaders and the Viceroy Lord Irwin. On 3 December 1929, Jinnah wrote to Irwin about his meeting with Gandhi and the Patel brothers, Vithalbhai and Vallabhbhai, and said, 'I left with the impression that Mr Gandhi himself is reasonable'.[11] Jinnah and Gandhi differed on the means. They were agreed on the objective and worked together, as best as they could—till 1937.

It is another matter that they disagreed sometimes. The meeting at the Viceroy's House on 23 December 1929 ended in failure. 'Sapru, Jinnah and (Vithalbhai) Patel were frankly disgusted with the attitude adopted by Gandhi', Irwin reported.[12]

During this period Jinnah cooperated actively with Malaviya and Lajpat Rai with both of whom he had close personal relations. What Lajpat Rai's biographer wrote about their relationship might surprise some today:

It was not only for enlisting Hindu support to the Nehru scheme that Motilal had to lean heavily on Lalaji; for, even securing the support of an outstanding Muslim leader like Jinnah, if the relevant date of those days were fully examined, Lalaji's contribution would be found to outweigh that of any other Congress leader. Lalaji strove for a united stand against the Simon Commission, and secured full support from Jinnah. In his last days he was again in touch with Jinnah to secure his support for the All-Parties Conference to consider the Nehru scheme.

Lalaji had generally not much difficulty in working with M.A. Jinnah. They had often worked together in the pre-non-cooperation days and though Jinnah left the Congress when Gandhi came into power, they had once again to work with each other when Lalaji went to the Legislative Assembly—and they were often seen discussing things not on the Assembly agenda but the broader aspects of the Hindu–Muslim relationship. They did not always see eye to eye and sometimes differed sharply and publicly criticized each other with zest and vigour, but it was always possible to know where the differences lay and to what extent they could work together, the boycott of the Simon Commission being an instance in point. During the Assembly session Jinnah would frequently walk into Lalaji's room without an appointment and unannounced. Sometimes he would do so several times in the course of the same day. Lalaji visited him likewise and very often they both would rise from a talk and go together to Malaviyaji to continue the discussion. There were no formalities, and whether or not the talks resulted in agreement there never arose a question as to who should seek whom—the trivial things that in the 'thirties and forties' often hindered pourparlers. Jinnah had no Muslim League Party in the Central Assembly and was the leader of a small group of Independents. The relations between the Swarajist leader and the leader of the Independents were not as smooth as one would have expected between two opposition leaders. Lalaji and Jinnah may not have found a satisfactory formula for a communal settlement, all the same in most Assembly matters, they could wholeheartedly cooperate with each other.[13]

When the Lala returned to India a public meeting was held at Shantaram's Chawl to welcome him, at which Jinnah presided and hailed him as 'one of the greatest sons of India'.[14] Lajpat Rai died on 17 November 1928, from the wounds inflicted on him by police *lathis* on 20 October, while he led a procession at Lahore on the arrival of the Simon Commission. A motion was moved in the Central Legislative Assembly on 15 February 1929, for the appointment of a judicial inquiry. Jinnah delivered a blistering attack on the government.

> The Honourable the Home Member described the tone and the language of the Mover of the Resolution as not compatible with the dignity of this deliberate Assembly. Sir, I listened to the tone and the language of the Home Member and may I state on the floor of this House that it was not compatible with the dignity of the responsible government? ... Really the issue to my mind is, was the assault made by the police on that occasion made on a lawfully assembled gathering of people, or on citizens who were entitled to be there and who gave no cause, reason or provocation to the police for the assault that was made?... Having regard to these serious charges, to these serious allegations which have been made in the Press and at public meetings by responsible men outside and members of this House of the position of Pandit Madan Mohan Malaviya and Lala Hans Raj, is this your answer that a prima facie case has not been made out for the appointment of an independent committee to inquire? Do you wish to shirk such inquiry? ... If you shirk this inquiry, the only conclusion that we on this side of the House will come to is that you dare not face the inquiry.[15]

Lala Lajpat Rai paid Jinnah a tribute for his diligent performance of the duties of a legislator. There was no High Court, let alone a Supreme Court, in Delhi then. Regular attendance in the Central Legislative Assembly entailed considerable disruption in his lucrative practice at the Bar and no small financial sacrifice. Lajpat Rai highlighted Jinnah's 'great sacrifice' in setting aside professional work to attend the vast majority of the sittings of the Assembly.[16]

Above all, he was constructive. If only men like Motilal Nehru and Tej Bahadur Sapru had supported the move, India might have had a Supreme Court in the twenties. When the Central Assembly met in the Assembly Chamber, Imperial Secretariat, Delhi on Saturday 26 March 1921, Dr Hari Singh Gour, an eminent jurist moved a resolution which read: 'This Assembly recommends to the Governor-General in council to be so pleased as to take early steps to establish a Court of Ultimate Appeal in India for the trial of Civil Appeal now determined by the Privy Council in England and as the court of final appeal against convictions for serious offences concerning the failure of justice.'

Sapru moved for circulation of the motion in order 'to collect the opinions of the local governments, the High Courts and other legal authorities and to ascertain public opinion generally' on the subject. The motion was adopted.[17]

After the process ended, the Assembly took up the matter on 17 February 1925. Motilal Nehru opposed any such move till independence was attained. Others used equally spurious arguments such as shortage of accommodation, finance etc. British opinion was uniformly against it. Indian opinion was divided.

Supporting the resolution Jinnah said:

> How is it going to lower the prestige of the provincial High Courts? Then you find in the Privy Council for which I have great respect, although I have no hesitation in saying that the Privy Council have on several occasions absolutely murdered Hindu law, and slaughtered Muhammadan law—with regard to common law, the English law, of which they are the masters, undoubtedly they command the greatest respect of every practitioner and of every Judge in this country.... But apart from that, what is meant of saying that if you have a Supreme Court you will lower the prestige of the provincial High Courts. Who are the members of the Privy Council? Two of

them, or rather three of them at least were Indian Judges who had served in the High Courts here. One is Sir Ameer Ali, another is Sir Lawrence Jenkins, and a third is Sir John Edge. All of them started their career in this country. We trained them up. We raised them to the High Court and then they became Members of the Privy Council, and do you mean to say that it does not lower the prestige of the High Courts in India, when they sit in judgment over them?... Delhi is big enough and long enough. Miles and miles of buildings are cropping up, which are enough to dazzle anybody; and why cannot we locate the Court in a small building?[18]

Constitutional law was not developed then. But in case after case, the Privy Council behaved as an instrument of colonial control, notably in Bhagat Singh's case and in cases in 1942–5.[19]

His range of interests was amazing — the Steel Industry (Protection) Bill, the Currency Bill, the Trade Disputes Bill, the Indian Factories Amendment Bill, the Maternity Benefit Bill and the Trade Union Bill, to mention some. This was apart from his unfailing contribution in debates on amendments to the civil and criminal law. In 1925 Jinnah was president of the Postal Union and ventilated their grievances in the Assembly on 12 February 1925. He was a consistent advocate of social reform and champion of civil liberties.[20]

Jinnah's speech in the Assembly on the Hindu Child Marriage Bill on 11 September 1929 is a fine instance of his commitment to social reform and the independence of an MP.

> I am convinced in my mind that there is nothing in the Quran, there is nothing in Islam which prevents us from destroying this evil. If we can do it today do not wait till tomorrow. I fully recognize the orthodox opinion. I fully appreciate the orthodox sentiments, the orthodox feelings both of the Mussalmans and of the Hindus. Sir, whether certain practices have any sanction, divine or religious or not, usages and customs grow up, and when any social reform is suggested which goes to destroy the usages and the practices to which the people are used and upon they have looked as semi-

religious usages and practices, it is always known all over the world that those people who have got deep sentiments, deep convictions, strong opinions, always resent, and they believe that it is destroying the very root of their social life or religion. Always the social reformer is face to face with this orthodox opinion having behind it this conviction, this sentiment, this feeling which is perfectly understandable and to some extent legitimate. But are we to be dragged down by this section for whom we have respect, whose feeling we appreciate, whose sentiments we regard,—are we to be dragged down and are we to be prevented in the march of progress, in the name of humanity, I ask you? And Sir, as far as my own constituency is concerned, that is, Bombay, I have no mandate from them. This measure has been before this House for a long time, this measure certainly has been discussed in the Press and on the platform; but my constituency has not given me any mandate whatsoever of any kind, and therefore, perhaps I am very happy and perhaps I am in a better position than my Honourable friends who probably are afraid that they may have to face their constituencies in the future, and that they may have some trouble, or some of them may have got some mandates. But, Sir, I make bold to say that if my constituency is so backward as to disapprove of a measure like this then I say, the clearest duty on my part would be to say to my constituency, 'You had better ask somebody else to represent you'. Because, after all, you must remember that public opinion is not so fully developed in this country, and if we are going to allow ourselves to be influenced by the public opinion that can be created in the name of religion when we know that religion has nothing whatever to do with the matter,—I think we must have the courage to say, 'No, we are not going to be frightened by that'.

In the past the government policy was, 'We have enough trouble. We have got the agitators who are making our lives miserable already. Why should we undertake a measure which will make our loyal subjects who always support us, who look upon us as *ma-baps* [mother-father]—the orthodox who are quite content and satisfied—why should we undertake this extra trouble, this extra burden upon our heads to improve your people?' That was their attitude, but I am glad that that policy has been exploded, and I hope for ever, and I hope that government will in future side with us in the matter at any rate concerning social reforms we are working so that we may help

India to take her place among the great nations of the world. We are looking forward to a great India and a great nation.[21]

These words are very relevant today in India and in Pakistan.

Seventeen years earlier he had supported Bhupendranath Basu's Special Marriage Bill in the Imperial Legislative Council on 26 February 1912. That speech also bears recalling in our times when orthodoxy has acquired such virulent forms. The government opposed the Bill supporting, as ever, the reactionary orthodox, its supporters.

Jinnah said:

> Of course, the position of a representative in this council, be he a Hindu or a Muhammadan, is awkward because the orthodox opinion is against it; but that, I submit, is no reason for a representative who owes a duty to his people to refrain from expressing his own convictions fearlessly. It does not necessarily follow that because the majority are against it, they are right. If a representative in this council is convinced in his mind that this is a measure which is good for his country and his people, he ought to support it. Well, now, Sir, let us consider the merits of this Bill. I will deal with the Hon'ble the Law Member first, if I may, as to his points. The Hon'ble the Law member said that so far as Mussalman are concerned, you have a clear authority in the Quran that a Mohammedan cannot marry any one except 'Kitabia'. Well, I will assume that proposition to be correct. May I ask the Hon'ble Member—is this the first time in the history of the legislation of this country that this council has been called upon to override the Mussalman law or modify it to suit the times? This council has overridden and modified the Mussalman law in many respects. For instance, the Mussalman law of contract is not recognized. The Mussalman Criminal Law, which was administered after the advent of British rule, has been abrogated absolutely; the Law of evidence, known to the Moslem law, does not exist any more in this country, and what is more, there is a very recent enactment known as Lex Loci Act, XXI of 1850, or otherwise known as Caste Disabilities Removal Act, to which I may draw the attention of council, and that

is this, that although there is as clear an injunction in the Quran about the forfeiture of inheritance by a Mohammedan in case of apostasy, as the Hon'ble Law Member pointed out in the case of marriage, still it is abrogated by this Act. A Mohammedan now can change his religion, and yet he does not forfeit his right of inheritance, and the law laid down in the Mohammedan texts is to that effect absolutely abrogated, and the same argument applies to the Hindus so far as this Statute is concerned. Well then, Sir, are these not precedents (I do not wish to dispute the Mohammedan Law that the Hon'ble Member has laid down. I assume that it is correct), are these not precedents which stare us in the face? Of course, provided there is a good and a strong case made out, I say these are the precedents, which are ought to follow to keep abreast of times and modern requirements for which there is ample authority in the Mohammedan Law and jurisprudence itself.

No doubt, Sir, as far as I see, the Hindu law or the Mohammedan law, whichever you take (I speak with great diffidence so far as the Hindu law is concerned, and with diffidence so far as the Mohammedan law is concerned because I am not a scholar in Sanskrit or Arabic and I can only go by translations), does create a difficulty in the way of a Hindu marrying a non-Hindu or a Mohammedan marrying anyone who is not 'Kitabia'; but is that difficulty not to be remedied by means of legislation? Is there a case made out or not for the legislature to interfere in this matter? As it has been already pointed out, this is an entirely optional character of legislation and it is not at all compulsory; it does not say that every Mohammedan shall marry a non-Mohammedan or that every Hindu shall marry a non-Hindu. Therefore, if there is a fairly large class of enlightened, educated, advance, Indians, be they Hindus, Mohammedans or Parsis, and if they wish to adopt a system of marriage which is more in accord with modern civilization and ideas of modern times, more in accord with the modern sentiment, why should that class be denied justice unless it is going to do a serious harm to the Hindus or Mussalmans in one way or the other?[22]

Jinnah was as consistent on the role of religion in politics. Speaking at the Central Legislative Assembly on the report of the Joint Parliamentary Committee on Indian constitutional reforms on 7 February 1935, he said: 'I entirely reciprocate every sentiment which the Honourable the Leader of the Opposition expressed, and I agree with him that religion should not be allowed to come into politics.... Religion is merely a matter between man and God.' The issue of safeguards for minorities was 'a political issue'.[23] The proposition was repeated when he addressed the Ismaili College in Bombay on 1 February 1943: 'Religion is strictly a matter between God and man'.[24] When journalists in Srinagar asked him about the Ahmediyas on 24 May 1944, he replied that 'any Muslim could do so, irrespective of his creed or sect, if he wishes to join the All-India Muslim League, provided he accepts the creed, policy, and programme of the All-India Muslim League, and signs the forms of membership, and pays his subscription of two annas. I would appeal to Muslims of Jammu and Kashmir not to raise any sectarian issues.'[25]

He struck a fair balance between respect for religious beliefs and the right to criticize religion in a proper manner in a speech in the Central Assembly:

We in this House wish to make it clear that in future no wanton vilification or attack on any religion shall be permitted—then let us proceed with this Bill. Let us enact a measure which will give us security against these scurrilous writers of the character now described.

... I thoroughly endorse the principle, that while this measure should aim at those undesirable persons who indulge in wanton vilification or attack upon the religion of any particular class or upon the founders and prophets of a religion, we must also secure this very important and fundamental principle that those who are engaged in historical works, those who are engaged in the ascertainment of truth and those who are engaged in bona fide and honest criticisms of a religion shall be protected.[26]

On civil liberties two of his best performances stand out. One was his attack on the order banning Vallabhbhai Patel from speaking for one month at a public meeting. Jinnah's speech on 10 March 1930 was based on considerable research. That remarkable speech retains its relevance:

> What was the emergency, I want to ask, Sir, to pass this order? According to the statement of the Honourable the Home Member, Sardar Vallabhbhai Patel had made several speeches before. Were those speeches against the law? Did he transgress the limits of law or did he not? I have no information. If he was going to make a speech or speeches of the kind which he had already made in regard to which he had already transgressed the limits of law, and if he had already committed offences or infringed the law, then, Sir, your proper course, the proper course on the part of the authorities in that district should have been that Sardar Vallabhbhai Patel ought to have been prosecuted long ago for an offence, but an order should not be passed which goes to the root of the principle of liberty of speech.... What is the real issue before the House? Sir, I will read in the language, which is certainly much better than I can command, a small passage to the House, and I think any one who is a student of history and of political movements in other countries will appreciate this passage and will see the point that I am trying to impress upon the government. 'Liberty of opinion of course is open to abuse....'
>
> Sir Hugh Cocke: What is that book please?
>
> Mr M.A. Jinnah: It is called 'American Government and Politics' by Beard, 4th Edition, Library Edition. It is not mine. It is the Library Edition of the House. Therefore, I think my Honourable friend Sir Hugh Cocke is now thoroughly satisfied.
>
> Sir Hugh Cocke: Quite.
>
> Mr M.A. Jinnah: 'Liberty of opinion, of course, is open to abuse; it is constantly abused; but what is more open to abuse is the right to suppress opinion and far more often, in the long history of humanity, has it been abused. Still all matters of sentiment may be put on one side. It is a hard, cold proposition: by what process are we most

likely to secure orderly and intelligent government, by the process of censorship or that of freedom? On this question a comparison of English and Russian history is illuminating.' Do you want to follow the Russian history or the English history?

When my friend is on the Treasury Benches, we may expect the Russian methods then. Sir, I shall continue to read the passage now. 'Again and again those who have attempted to stop the progress of opinion by the gallows and prison have merely hastened their own destruction by violence.'

I therefore ask the government not to allow, in the first instance, their policy and their programme to deal with this serious situation to be deflected in the slightest degree by the whimsical or fanciful action of a district officer about whom the Honourable the Home Member said that, if he had done anything else, he would have been guilty of a dereliction of duty. The Honourable the Home Member may stand there and support that officer, but let us remember that the Home Member did not know anything about it. He had no idea. I have not heard that the Bombay Government have been consulted. Therefore it comes to this—that there was no emergency and I maintain most emphatically that there was no emergency. Vallabhbhai Patel had made no speech or speeches which came within the purview of the Penal Code.[27]

The other instance was his powerful defence of Bhagat Singh in the Assembly. Ironically, he defended hunger strikes.

You know perfectly well that these men are determined to die. It is not a joke. I ask the Honourable the Law Member to realize that it is not everybody who can go on starving himself to death. Try it for a little while and you will see. Sir, have you heard anywhere in the world, except the American case, which my Honourable friend Mr Jamnadas Mehta pointed out, an accused persons going on hunger-strike? The man who goes on hunger-strike has a soul. He is moved by that soul and he believes in the justice of his cause; he is not an ordinary criminal who is guilty of cold-blooded, sordid, wicked crime.

Mind you, Sir, I do not approve of the action of Bhagat Singh, and I say this on the floor of this House. I regret that rightly or wrongly youth today in India is stirred up, and you cannot, when you have three hundred and odd millions of people, you cannot prevent such crimes being committed, however much you may deplore them and however much you may say that they are misguided. It is the system, this damnable system of government, which is resented by the people. You may be a cold-blooded logician: I am a patient cool-headed man and can calmly go on making speeches here, persuading and influencing the Treasury Bench. But remember, there are thousands of young men outside. This is not the only country, not youths, but grey-bearded men have committed serious offences moved by patriotic impulses. What happened to Mr Cosgrave, the Prime Minister of Ireland? He was under sentence of death a fortnight before he got an invitation from His Majesty's Government to go and settle terms?[28]

Jinnah was as anti-British as any Congressman. The British hated him. Willingdon recommended to his successor as governor of Bombay, Lord Lloyd, Jinnah's deportation to Burma. Lloyd 'was not disposed to begin his career by conferring unnecessary martyrdom'. He changed his mind, however, and discussed the proposal with the Viceroy Lord Chelmsford, who, in turn, reported it to the Secretary of State Edwin S. Montagu on 16 April 1919.[29]

Jinnah was labelled an 'extremist' and even a 'Bolshevik' by the government.[30] Reading saw in him a 'strong anti-British feeling'. Jinnah adopted in the Assembly sharp rhetoric in the manner deployed in the House of Commons. That riled the British members of the Executive Council. Ian Wells accurately perceived, 'What was acceptable from a British politician was clearly not from an Indian'. The British found him 'unapproachable'.[31]

When he gave evidence in London before the British Parliament' Joint Select Committee on the Government of India Bill, the

Secretary of State Edwin S. Montagu began to question him in an offensive manner:

> Q. 3633: How long have you been in public life Mr Jinnah?
> Mr Jinnah: Since I was twenty-one.
>
> Q.3634: Have you ever known any proposal come from any government which met with your approval?
> Mr Jinnah: Oh, yes.
>
> Q. 3635: Can you mention it to me?
> Mr Jinnah: The other day I supported the government's Taxation Bill about the income-tax under the Imperial Council.
>
> Q. 3636: You must have felt very uncomfortable?
> Mr Jinnah: No, I have supported the government on various occasions.

As the questioning proceeded and Montagu became offensive Jinnah tartly retorted that his comments were incorrect 'and you know it, or, at least, you ought to know it' (Q. 3666). Major Ormsby Gore asked:

> Q. 3810: You said you spoke from the point of view of India. You speak really as an Indian Nationalist?
> Mr Jinnah: I do.
>
> Q. 3811: Holding that view, do you contemplate the early disappearance of separate communal representation of the Mohammedan community?
> Mr Jinnah: I think so.
>
> Q. 3812: That is to say, at the earliest possible moment you wish to do away in political life with any distinction between Mohammedans and Hindoos?
> Mr Jinnah: Yes. Nothing will please me more than when that day comes.

In the light of a later malicious smear that Jinnah wanted membership of the Congress to be restricted to matriculates his answers to Lord Islington's questions on franchise are pertinent. 'Even literates might be left out, because it is a property qualification' (Answer to Q. 3883). Islington asked:

> Q. 3884: You would say that there are people in India who, though they be not literate, have a sufficient interest in the welfare of the country to entitle them to vote?
> Mr Jinnah: I think so, and I think they have a great deal of common sense
>
> Q. 3885: People who have that kind of common sense which would justify them having a vote?
> Mr Jinnah: Yes; I was astonished when I attended a meeting of mill hands in Bombay when I heard some of the speeches, and most of them were illiterates.

Reminded of his views on separate electorates, Jinnah was careful to point out that 'at present we are in a minority' in the Muslim Community.[32]

Jinnah was consistently opposed by the toadies among the Muslims and warned them against playing the British game of divide and rule.

> To the Mohammedans the government says: 'Well, we are your friends, we want to do everything we can, but these wicked Hindus are creating all the difficulties'. And the Mohammedans readily believe it and my Honourable friend still has his faith in the government, and he still keeps voting in the government lobby every time.... My Hindu friends have realized and my Mohammedan friends have realized now that this is the old game which is continued with a certain amount of success. But, Sir, do not play this game. The sooner you give it up, the better it is in your interests and in our interests. Let us get to the issue itself. Let us deal with every question on its merits, and we know perfectly well, Sir, that in this country at any rate there are three parties, not to talk about

the fourth party discovered recently by the Home Member, and these three parties which are interested in the future progress and the welfare of this country are the Hindus and the Mohammedans and the British.[33]

Hence his plea for communal unity, 'Swaraj is almost an interchangeable term with Hindu–Muslim unity. If we wish to be free people, let us unite; but if we wish to continue slaves of the bureaucracy, let us fight amongst ourselves and gratify petty vanity over petty matters, an Englishman being our arbiter' he told the Muslim League session on 24 May 1924.[34]

Even in the Central Assembly, Jinnah had to constantly face opposition from the pro-British Muslims. On one such occasion on 7 March 1930, he said:

> I know my friends of the Central Muslim Party are very keen, very zealous in safeguarding the interests of the community to which I have the honour to belong. [Sir Zulfiqar Ali Khan: 'Hear, hear.']. But I cannot understand how you are going to advance the interests of your community by supporting a wrong thing.
>
> Nawab Sir Sahibzada Abdul Qaiyum: We want better masters than the present ones. What is the use of change if we do not get better ones?
>
> Mr M.A. Jinnah: Yes. And let me tell you, Sir, in answer to that, that seventy millions of Mussalmans should not be afraid of facing the issue squarely and fairly no matter what the government do and no matter what the Hindus do. [Hear, hear.] You are seventy millions. What is the good of leaning upon the government? What is the good of your appealing to the Hindus? Do you want concessions? I do not want concessions. [Hear, hear.] What is the good? You are seventy million Mussalmans. Organize yourselves in this country, and you will be a power, and you will be able to dictate not only to the government, but to the Hindus and to every one else your just rights. Show a manly attitude. Why are you going to support a wrong thing? Support this motion if you think it be a right

one. My friend, Mr Anwar-ul-Azim, said, 'Yes, government are to be blamed; but then I do not know whether, if I agree with you and vote with you, I shall incur the displeasure of the Treasury Benches'. [Laughter.]

Nawab Sir Sahibzada Abdul Qaiyum: Not quite so.

Mr M.A. Jinnah: Sir, let the Treasury Benches realize that, whether the Hindus settle with us, or whether they do not, whether they march with us or whether they do not, we mean to march forward, and we want responsible government in this country [hear, hear], with due provisions for the safeguards for Mussalmans and other minorities.

Mian Mohammad Shah Nawaz: Responsible government is the desire of everybody; but, before you march, let the Hindus and Muslims compose their differences.

Mr M.A. Jinnah: Then vote for this motion and prove it by your vote.

Mian Mohammad Shah Nawaz: Hindus and Muslims should settle their differences. Put a united demand for Dominion Status before the Round Table Conference and it will be effective.

Mr M.A. Jinnah: My friend is going much further than I am going. This motion says that we do not approve of the irresponsible nature of the Executive Council. Do you approve of it? You do not. Then why don't you vote for this motion?

Let me explain, Sir, to my friends that this is purely a constitutional issue. That is where my friends do not seem to appreciate the position. This is purely a constitutional issue. We want to record our votes on this constitutional issue, that the present Executive Council is not of a responsible nature; we want to make it clear that Dominion Status is not in action in this country, leave alone the establishment of full Dominion Status and responsible government. That is what we want to make clear....[35]

The British did not spare epithets for him. On 30 March 1936, Willingdon, now viceroy, called Jinnah 'really more Congress than the Congress.' The governor of the United Provinces, Harry Graham Haig, dubbed him 'the arch enemy of the British Raj'.[36]

Given this nationalist stand, reliance on the masses came naturally as the meetings at Shantaram's Chawl showed. His explanation for joining the Home Rule League in 1917 was that he wanted 'to reach the masses'. One test came in 1925 when he proposed to Jayakar and others that a new political party be set up. Its membership was to 'be open to every adult of either sex over the age of 21'. He urged the spread of education precisely so that people become aware of their right. His speech on Gokhale's Elementary Education Bill in the Imperial Legislative Council on 19 March 1912 was a scathing attack on people who sought to perpetuate backwardness.

> Then, it is said: 'Oh! but the people will become too big for their boots', if I may use that expression that 'they will not follow the occupations of their parents, they will demand more rights, there will be more strikes, they will become socialists.' Well, Sir, are you going to keep millions and millions of people under your feet for fear that they may demand more rights; are you going to keep them in ignorance and darkness forever and for all ages to come because they might stand up against you and say we have certain rights and you must give them to us? Is that the feeling of humanity? Is that the spirit of humanity? I say, Sir, that it is the duty of the zamindars and of the landlords to be a little less selfish. I say, Sir, that it is the duty of the educated classes to be a little less selfish. They must not monopolize the pedestals, but they must be prepared to meet their people. They must be brought down from their pedestals if they do not do their duties properly. I say, Sir, that it is the elementary right of every man to say, if he is wronged, that he is wronged and he should be righted.[37]

To Yahya Hashim Bawany goes the credit for unearthing a highly significant document which he published in the compilation he edited.[38] A Gujarati monthly *Vismi Sadi* (Twentieth Century) gave Jinnah a list of eight questions to answer. Jinnah gave the answers in his own handwriting and signed at the end in Gujarati. Asked 'what quality is admirable in a man' he replied 'Independence'. To the question 'What do you believe is the success of [sic] life?' he responded 'To acquire the love of masses'. The document was published in the May 1916 issue of the journal and is reprinted in Bawany's compilation.[39]

The legislature and the public platform are allies in political campaigns. Jinnah was well aware of the Irish Nationalists' use of the House of Commons to promote their cause and the Parnellites' obstructive tactics in the House once. The Muslim League's 1924 session found that he had in mind use of similar techniques in India; not to further Muslim interests but India's cause. He said, 'We ought to be prepared, if the Government do not make a satisfactory response to the national demand for reforms, as a last resort to make the Government by Legislature or through the Legislature impossible and we should, if necessary, adopt for that purpose all means and measures to bring about Parliamentary obstruction and constitutional deadlocks.'[40]

Use the legislature, but if that did not work, obstruct the conduct of the government's business. He did not flinch from the next step, should even obstruction fail to secure redress. Anyone who reads his speeches at the Calcutta and Nagpur sessions of the Congress in 1920 will be struck by the fact that the divide between Jinnah and Gandhi was far narrower than the one between Jinnah and Annie Besant. She was fundamentally opposed to the use of extra-constitutional means. Jinnah was not. He objected to Gandhi's programme because it was unrealistic and impractical. In this, he was proved right as the report of the Congress Civil Disobedience Enquiry Committee established only two years later.[41] It was signed by Hakim Ajmal Khan, Motilal Nehru, Dr M.A. Ansari, C. Rajagopalachari, Vallabhbhai

Patel, and S. Kasturi Ranga Iyengar. Religion was not spared abuse for political ends. Appendix XII of the report reproduced a *muttafiqa* (joint) *fatwa* of the Ulema (clergy) of India 'pronounced in a grand meeting of the Jamiat-ul-Ulema' at Delhi. It enjoined Muslims to forbear from entering the legislatures and warned them that it was 'prohibited, according to the laws of Shariat'. The report itself was at variance with the *fatwa*. Three members were in favour of entry into the councils; namely Ajmal Khan, Motilal Nehru, and Vallabhbhai Patel. Jinnah did not gloat over the report, such as it was. His statement in response to a question by the *Bombay Chronicle* was in the spirit of a colleague who disagreed over the means but hinted that he might well use them himself. It was critical of the British, not of the Congress. It is an historic statement because it was for the first time that Jinnah spoke of 'direct action'.

Q: What is your opinion on the report of the Civil Disobedience Committee as a whole?
Jinnah: In order to understand the report you have to go into the genesis of the Non-cooperation movement. The people of India had sufficient provocation and undoubtedly was driven to desperation by the policy of the Government with regard to what is known as the Punjab, Khilafat and Swarajya questions, but the programme of Non-cooperation adopted at Calcutta Special Congress and confirmed at Nagpur was considered by many as unwise, unsound and not practical. The authors of the movement undoubtedly aimed at paralysing the administration of the Government. The movement in essence was planned for direct political action by the masses. The only restriction placed was non-violence in its methods. It was an organized campaign of peaceful resistance to laws and it was to be carried out by four stages. In my opinion the country was not prepared for any such revolutionary movement and I hold that it is not prepared today for any kind of 'direct action'. Therefore, sooner the triple bar, viz., the boycott of schools and colleges, Law Courts and Councils is removed the better. From this it does not follow that the Government should merely rejoice in its abandonment and continue its policy in defiance of public opinion. The principle of Non-cooperation is very much like the Sinn Fein movement in

Ireland. Arthur Griffith was the pioneer of that movement. The unwise policy pursued by the Government of England only supported the forces of Sinn Fein movement until it took such deep roots in Ireland that the British Cabinet was compelled to settle with the very men who were considered rebels just as the authors of Non-cooperation are now looked upon as law-breakers and criminals. And it is possible that the Non-cooperation movement which has not succeeded as expected by its authors may again take roots—and probably firmer roots—if the Government do not meet the reasonable demands of the people. It is further possible, as was the case in Ireland, that the authors of the Non-cooperation movement may find themselves in exactly the same position as Arthur Griffith did, viz., the very forces which they created were not controllable by them and we have not yet heard the last of opposition as De Valera continues to defy the very men who were the founders of the Sinn Fein movement. The question, therefore, to be considered at the present moment is 'What is the wisest course to adopt'? And it depends not only on what Non-cooperation door may not do but equally on what is going to be the policy and attitude of the Government.

Jinnah wanted to use the legislature to 'appraise the voters' about the political situation. The Bombay Students' Brotherhood organized a debate on the proposition that 'Freedom can best be achieved by constitutional agitations rather than by Direct Action'. Its was held on a Sunday, 4 February 1922 in the Hall of the Servants of India Society founded by Gokhale. D.G. Dalvi spoke in support of the proposition and cited Tilak's experience. Jayakar opposed it. To Dalvi's criticism that Direct Action 'led to the creation of a Dictator', Jayakar replied that the Congress resolution appointed Gandhi as dictator only in the event of the members of the Working Committee being arrested. He requested Jinnah, who was in the Chair, to express his opinion on the proposition.

Reading his comments now, most admirers or detractors would be astonished to discover how wrong their image of Jinnah as an uncompromising constitutionalist was. The report in the *Bombay Chronicle*, 11 February 1922 reads:

> Mr Jinnah replying to the vote of thanks said that he was glad that an opportunity was offered to him to express his views. According to Mr Dalvi freedom could be obtained by constitutional method and therefore it was not necessary to resort to direct action. By freedom they meant Government of the people, by the people and for the people. *He knew of no country which had won freedom by constitutional agitation.* Constitutional method held good when the Government itself was constitutional. But the question arose when the Government itself was not constitutional and did not function according to the will of the people. *His own view which he had pressed before was that no country achieved freedom without bloodshed.* It was true that in India they had a bureaucratic Government and had no freedom. But the question in his opinion was *when the time had come for Direct Action or whether the country was ripe for it?* Speaking for himself he said that the time had not arrived and he was not for Direct Action at present. …He had his sympathy with Direct Action without which freedom was impossible, especially in a land like theirs which was dominated by a foreign rule.[42]

In a speech at the Hindu College in Delhi on 14 March 1924, Jinnah warned that the:

> Government was watching them and knew that there were not many statesmen in India and also the weak points of Indians. The Government will not yield, and they have to attain their object by unity, character and discipline. If the Government persistently continue a policy of indifference and injustice and the constitutional party fails then those who believe in direct action must come into prominence. The Government which has the experience of Ireland, he trusted, will not compel India to resort to direct action.[43]

The theme reappeared years later in a statement he issued on 30 April 1937, to stress that the Muslim League did not differ much from the Congress. But 'in the present circumstances and realities of India, the Muslim League is not prepared to resort to direct action, because it will be suicidal in the present divided condition of India'.[44]

The record explodes myths commonly trotted out to explain the radical change in the policy Jinnah adopted in the late thirties—the disagreement at the Nagpur session of the Congress in December 1920, aversion to mass politics, marginalization, and his wife Ruttie's death on 20 February 1929. He continued to speak of Gandhi with respect long after Nagpur. In a letter published by *The Times of India* on 30 October 1925, he angrily denied the report 'that I denounced the Congress as a "Hindu Institution".' His opposition to civil disobedience—or 'direct action by the masses' as he called it—was based on practical grounds. His wife's death shook him to the core and he withdrew from society and became distant. But his efforts at a settlement did not abate. As for marginalization, Motilal Nehru realized that Jinnah's support was crucial to the success of the Nehru Report as the historian Mushirul Hasan records, based on archival material which he cites:

> Though never ever tied to the Congress, Jinnah's political concerns were no different from many of its leaders. The cause of India's freedom and of communal amity were close to his heart—a passion he shared in equal measure with Azad, Ajmal Khan, and Ansari. No wonder, his leaving India in May 1928 caused anxiety in Congress circles. Jinnah's absence from the country, Motilal told Purshotamdas Thakurdas, 'is most disappointing. I can think of no other responsible Muslim to take his place'. Ansari was equally upset, because Jinnah was, in his judgement, 'the only man to deliver the goods on behalf of the Muslim League'. So, when Jinnah returned to India in October, Motilal was delighted. He confided in Thakurdas again. 'So much depends on Jinnah that I have a mind to go to Bombay to receive him. If I have the necessary funds within the next few days, I hope to create a strong opinion amongst the Mussalmans to greet Jinnah on his arrival. Therefore please lose no time to raise as much money as you can for this great enterprise.

Jinnah did not disappoint. He was unhappy that the Nehru Committee repudiated two of his favourite schemes—the Lucknow Pact and the Delhi Proposals. But he was neither bitter nor indignant. Though troubled by Ruttie's serious illness and by the anti-Nehru Report crusade in UP, Jinnah kept his cool and as always, appeared unruffled. With meticulous care, he took charge of the Muslim League and negotiated with Motilal and other Congress leaders with his usual skill and aplomb.[45]

Jinnah proposed three amendments to the Nehru Report: (1) one-third of the central legislature should consist of Muslims; (2) in the event of adult suffrage not coming into effect, the Bengali and Punjabi Muslims should have reserved seats for ten years; and (3), residuary powers must vest in the provinces.

> The Hindu Mahasabha and Sikh delegates were in no mood to listen to Jinnah at the All-Parties National Convention at Calcutta on 28 December 1928. They refused to accept 33 per cent Muslims representation at the Centre. The Liberals, along with the Hindu communalists, stood firmly against vesting residuary powers in the provinces. Jayakar warned the delegates that, having once restrained his supporters from rebelling against the Nehru report, it would be impossible for him to persuade them to accept further concessions. They listened to his admonition rather than take note of Jinnah's pleading. Jinnah was mocked, rebuffed, and rejected by a hostile gathering. He was never ever going to return to such an unfriendly assembly.[46]

Even this did not deter him from continuing with his efforts for a rapprochement. He was opposed by the Hindu Mahasabha and its allies in the Congress. Mushirul Hasan writes:

> such was the hegemonic influence of the Hindu Mahasabha in the late 1920s that even the secular-oriented Congress leadership often succumbed to its ideological pressures. Notice, for example, how the Malaviya–Lajpat Rai combination used a communal platform as a means of rallying public support from 1922 onwards and made concessions to communal feelings which were already running high. Yet, they and their allies adorned the Swarajist benches and occupied

important positions in the Congress hierarchy. Malaviya represented the Mahasabha point of view at the 1931 Round Table Conference and was immediately rewarded with a presidential chair at the 1932 Congress. In this way, the most communally-minded leader could assume the nationalist garb and freely sail between the Mahasabha and the Congress.[47]

Jinnah had also to place opposition from the reactionaries and pro-British leaders amongst the Muslims. 'Unfortunately his Muslim compatriots were not prepared to go as far as he', he told the Muslim League session on 30 December 1924.[48] In 1927 he openly told the League 'I am not wedded to separate electorates' though 'the overwhelming majority of Muslims demanded it'.[49]

M.C. Chagla, who had devilled in Jinnah's chambers in the High Court, resigned as secretary of the Bombay Provincial Muslim League when it rejected the Nehru Report.[50] Chagla urged Jinnah to abandon his 'rigid neutrality' on the Nehru Report.[51] He little realized that Jinnah's circumspection was inspired by a desire to keep the League's factions together and to arrive at an accord with the Congress. It is now conventional wisdom that his amendments did not ask for too much and the Congress leaders' role was, to say the least, unwise.

That Jinnah was not angry with Chagla is evident from the letter he wrote to Chagla on 5 August 1929, which is being published here for the first time. It begins with a compliment to Chagla and not only reflects Jinnah's secular approach but his position as a mediator between the Muslims and the Hindus.

> Dear Chagla, I received your letter of the 28th July 1929, and many thanks for it. You know that I shall always welcome a frank opinion from anyone, especially from one, who gives his thought to these problems which are facing us. The situation is not so easy as you think. Of course, I cannot discuss in detail, but let me tell you that Pandit Motilal Nehru's statement was far from satisfactory. Besides,

immediately after the statement it was suggested that Mr Gandhi and I should meet on the 10th of this month in Bombay. In view of the fact that Mr Gandhi is going to meet me I have refrained from issuing any statement for the present.

I fear that the Hindu–Moslem question as it is generally called—is not likely to be settled unless we all, who are working for the freedom of India come to recognize it as a national problem and not a communal dispute. Unless the majority community and their leaders grasp that elementary principle and deal with it in that spirit it will not be possible to get the minority community into line with any national programme. However, we will discuss this further when we meet but I assure you that I fully realize the vital importance of it and nobody wishes more heartily than I do to help the two great communities to come together and work in a friendly spirit for the advancement of India. But these wishes cannot be realized unless the Hindu leaders and the Moslem leaders get into the right frame of mind and adopt the right spirit and tackle in a practical manner what is one of the greatest problem for which there is no parallel in the world.[52]

That was the even-handed mediator in Jinnah. He tried, on the one hand, to bring Muslims closer to the nationalist movement for India's freedom, and on the other, to urge the leaders of that movement to reckon with Muslims' insecurities and their demands for proper safeguards. This was brought out most strikingly in his impassioned reply to the debate on the Nehru Report at the All-Parties' National Convention in Calcutta on 28 December 1928.

In his opening remarks, Jinnah had said:

No country has succeeded in either wresting a democratic constitution from the domination of another nation or establishing representative institutions from within without giving guarantees for the securities of the minorities wherever such a problem has arisen. Majorities are apt to be oppressive and tyrannical and minorities always dread and fear that their interests and rights, unless clearly and definitely safeguarded by statutory provisions, would suffer and be prejudiced, but this apprehension is enhanced all the more when we have to deal with a communal majority.

Jayakar, now a Hindu Mahasabhaite, spoke on 'the rights and status of Hindus', challenged Jinnah's representative credentials which he lived to regret ('advocate of the small minority of Muhammadans') and made offensive remarks.

Replying to the debate Jinnah said:

> The offensive remarks or insinuations served no good purpose and I will not follow the style or the manner of the speech delivered by my friend, Mr Jayakar.... But I think it cannot be denied and I hope that Mr Jayakar and others will agree with me, that every country struggling for freedom and desirous of establishing a democratic system of Government has had to face the problem of minorities wherever they existed and no constitution, however idealistic it may be, and however perfect from the theoretical point of view it may seem, will ever receive the support of the minorities unless they can feel that they, as an entity, are secured under the proposed constitution and government and whether a constitution will succeed or not must necessarily depend as a matter of acid test whether the minorities are in fact secure.

He went on to remind the Convention:

> We are here, as I understand, for the purpose of entering into solemn contract and all parties who enter into it will have to work for it and fight for it together. What we want is that Hindus and Mussalmans should march together until our object is obtained. Therefore, it is essential that you must get not only the Muslim League but the Mussalmans of India and here I am not speaking as a Mussalman but as an Indian. And it is my desire to see that we get 7 crores of Mussalmans to march along with us in the struggle for freedom. Would you be content with a few? Would you be content if I were to say, I am with you? Do you want or do you not want the Muslim India to go along with you? ...

> It is up to the majority, and majority alone can give. I am asking you for this adjustment because I think it is the best, and fair, to the Mussalmans. Look at the constitutional history of Canada and Egypt. The minorities are always afraid of majorities. The majorities are apt to be tyrannical and oppressive and particularly religious majorities, and the minorities, therefore, have a right to be absolutely secured. Was the adjustment between French Canadians and British arrived at on population basis or on the ground of pure equity? Was the adjustment between the Copts Christians and Mussalmans in Egypt regulated by such considerations? We are dealing in politics. We are not in a Court of Law and therefore it is no use resorting to hair-splitting and petty squabbles. These are big questions and they can be settled only by the exercise of the highest order of statesmanship and political wisdom.[53]

Only a year before, in 1927, the Punjab Muslim League led by Sir Mohammad Shafi split the League and formed a faction of reactionaries at once pro-British and communal.

Prof. Reginald Coupland well described Jinnah's transformation from a rebuffed mediator to an ardent advocate.

> Always in the forefront of Indian politics, he had hitherto failed to command the confidence of his community as a whole. He had been a sectional rather than a communal leader, an outspoken anti-British nationalist, who had seemed to conservative-minded Moslems too 'Congress-minded' to be regarded as a whole-hearted champion of Islam. But now he was no longer only one of several leaders. Hailed by vociferous Moslem crowds as the personification of the communal pride and pugnacity awakened by Congress policy, he was fast becoming the leader.[54]

The breach did not occur at the Round Table Conference in London in 1930–1, either. It occurred in 1937–8 when the Congress, having formed ministries in several provinces, after the first general election under the Government of India Act, 1935, refused to share power with the Muslim League. Worse still, it denied that a minority problem existed or that the Muslim League was an ally to parley with on an equal footing.

Jinnah returned to India in 1934, after a long stay in London, and soon set about reorganizing the Muslim League and renewing efforts for a settlement with the Congress. In 1934 Jinnah and Rajendra Prasad concluded a pact on the basis of joint elections.[55] The Hindu Mahasabha opposed it, as did some Congressmen.

He did not return to India to promote his political career. He returned with hope. A letter to Sir Mohammad Yakub, dated 29 December 1932, reflected robust optimism:

> Of course I agree that there is the greatest need of unity amongst the Mussalmans and that there should be only one organization. I cannot follow the efforts and results so far produced by Allahabad and of Malaviya's new unity move. Of course my views are that the Mussalmans should stand solid by 14 points. But if a satisfactory scheme can be suggested by the Hindus on the basis of Joint Electorates we should not bar settlement on that account provided however that all other points are accepted. Well, but now there does not remain very much to settle. One-third in the Centre and separation of Sindh is announced. *So the Mussalmans have secured practically all they wanted,* except the Residuary power and 51 per cent in Bengal.
>
> Of course my heart is in India but at present there is no chance of my going to India. Do write to me and keep me in touch with things. If I can do anything here please do not hesitate to write and of course I shall do all I can.

Once in India, he began bridge-building.

It is well known that Jinnah returned to India, on the persuasion of Liaquat Ali Khan and his wife in April 1934, after a stay of over three years in England. He went back a month later only to sail for India in January 1935 after his election as an Independent member of the Central Legislature from Bombay. Jinnah attended the first session of the new Assembly, but, in April, he returned to his West Heath House in London, where he remained until October 1935.

News of his plans to return was received warmly. Dr M.A. Ansari's letter to Jinnah dated 30 December 1934 reflects the sentiments:

> My dear Jinnah, I must begin by welcoming you home and hope that you are fully restored to health. Now that you have been returned to the Assembly again at a very critical juncture in the history of constitutional changes, your usual patriotic outlook and political foresight would prove a great asset to the opposition. With the divergent elements with which you will have to deal, you will have a strenuous time until the summer recess. It is more than obvious that a very great deal would depend on the attitude the Muslim members may adopt at this time, and it is equally clear that yours will be the greatest share in shaping their outlook and views. On more than one occasion you have made your own point of view perfectly clear. We all remember that you characterized the White Paper Scheme as 'treacherous' and now comes the JPC [Joint Parliamentary Committee] Report which is in most respects much worse than the White Paper Scheme. Your recent interview since your return as published in the Press laying stress on unity of purpose has paved the way for a definite move in the right direction. Keeping that in view I am anxious for an interchange of views and I particularly want to know what in your view can be the basis of co-operation between the majority of the elected members of the Assembly.... It is, therefore, essential that the majority of the members should come to some agreement regarding the course of action they should adopt and if the government does not propose any resolution of that nature, there ought to be an agreement regarding the phrasing of the resolution which the majority of the members should support. I am therefore, anxious to know how you would like to phrase such a resolution.... I wonder if it would be possible for you to come to Delhi for consultation along these lines.[56]

Iqbal's letter to Ansari, written soon thereafter on New Year's Day, 1935, informed him:

> I received a letter from Mr Jinnah this morning. I think the time has come for Hindus and Muslims to work together. I have no doubt that you will do your best to bring about a national pact which will form a basis for future co-operation. If this opportunity is lost present tensions will only stiffen more and more making co-operation impossible.

A prophecy which came true.[57]

Syed Abdullah Brelvi, editor of *Bombay Chronicle* formed the same impression, which he reported to Ansari on 2 January 1935:

> I have had some talks with him [Jinnah] and, so far as I can gather from the conversation, he is prepared to go to any length to agree to an acceptable compromise on the question of the Communal Award on the basis of the Joint Electorate without any change in the number of seats allocated to them under the Communal Award. I personally think this would be a good compromise provided the Muslims and the Hindus agree to it.[58]

Jinnah's reply to Ansari dated 3 January 1935 deserves to be reproduced in full:

> My dear Ansari, Thank you so much for your very kind and encouraging letter. I appreciate it all the more as it comes from a sincere and old friend. I shall be glad to meet the Congress leaders and the Congress Party members of the Assembly and will try my best to run up to Delhi as requested by you for the purpose stated in your letter, but I have heard that you are coming to Bombay. If that is so please let me know and we can have a talk during your stay in Bombay. More when we meet.

Those were times when he was prepared to 'run up to Delhi' to meet the Congress leaders.[59] If three years later that ardour of thirty years was gone, the cause lay not in his 'ambition' but in the snubs he had received for three years from 1937 to 1939. They proved to be the proverbial last straw after the snubs on the Nehru Report and at the Round Table Conference in London.

On 9 January, Jinnah wired to Ansari: 'RECD NO REPLY MY LETTER ARE YOU COMING BOMBAY DO YOU STILL DESIRE MY MEETING CONGRESS LEADERS WIRE DATE MEETING'.[60]

Syed Abdullah Brelvi pressed Ansari on 19 January:

> I hope by the time this reaches you, you must have had discussions with Jinnah and that a satisfactory understanding between his party and the Congress Party will have been arrived at. If it is possible to come to a definite settlement of the Hindu–Muslim question more than half of our work will be accomplished. From my conversation with him, I found him to be ready to accept any honourable compromise.[61]

Sadly, as we shall see, Gandhi had other ideas. So, did Nehru. Jinnah consistently sought a Congress–League accord on a sharing of power. 'It does not require political wisdom to realize that all safeguards and settlements would be a scrap of paper, unless they are backed by power', Jinnah told the Lucknow session of the Muslim League in October 1937. The theme was repeated in a speech at the Muslim University Union at Aligarh on 5 February 1938: 'The only hope for minorities is to organize themselves and secure a definite share in power to safeguard their rights and interests. Without such power no constitution can work successfully in India'.[62] The Congress, as consistently, set its face against that.

When he addressed the Dayal Singh College in Lahore on 5 March 1936, he said: 'I feel myself among kindred spirits. This College does not believe in any creed and I, too, feel that the salvation of India lies in the non-sectarian feelings. It was this creed which I had in the past, and I have at present, and which I will have in future clearest to my heart'. He feelingly referred to Gokhale and said 'Give me more Gokhales' adding 'India has everything God has given her everything but man has not served her well'.[63]

He appealed to the All-India Students' Conference at Lucknow on 13 August 1936, not to think of the problems that were facing the country in terms of religion but teach a lesson to their elders who were spoiling the national life by their communalism. 'I am not at all afraid of a revolution, if that is necessary for the country, I will say "yes".'[64]

Jinnah addressed a crowded meeting of students of the postgraduate department of the Calcutta University at the Ashutosh Hall on 21 August 1936. The Vice-Chancellor, Shyama Prasad Mukherjee presided. Jinnah exhorted them to shun communalism:

> It is up to you all, whether as Hindus and Muslims or Parsees or Christians, it is up to you, neither as a Hindu nor as a Muslim but as an Indian to find this solution because this question must be solved and without a complete solution of this question India cannot make any appreciable progress in the direction of freedom.... So long as you look to a third party, so long as you depend upon a third party, you stand condemned and are unfit for self-government. If there are differences and disputes between yourselves, you know to rise to the occasion and settle them amongst yourselves, as friends, as partners and as countrymen.

Shyama Prasad Mukherjee welcomed Jinnah on behalf of the university and on behalf of every one of those present. It was, indeed, very kind of him, he said to have agreed to come and visit the university and address a few words to the students of the postgraduate department. This university in the past had had the opportunity of inviting distinguished Indians irrespective of caste or creed. 'You can ask what is the reason why Mr Jinnah's personality appeals so strongly to the youth of India,' he said, 'I would not refer to his undoubted position as a lawyer of brilliance and as a keen debater, as these are well-known facts, but over and above these we claim him to be an Indian nationalist [hear, hear]. Besides we claim him to be one of those fighters who know how to fight stubbornly for the attainment of the ideal which they have made their own.'[65]

As late as on 20 September 1937, Jinnah spoke in the very terms which he had used since 1906:

> There is no difference between the ideal of the Muslim League and that of the Congress or any other recognized political organization in the country, the ideal being complete freedom for India. There cannot be any self-respecting Indian who favours foreign domination or does not desire complete freedom and self-government for his country. I, therefore, appeal to every patriotic Indian that, instead of fighting for a distant ideal to mould the whole of India into mere citizens when the Hindus will cease to be Hindus and Mussalmans, Mussalmans politically, let us first solve this problem of the minorities.
>
> I have repeatedly been asked why there should be a Muslim League.... The election manifesto speeches of prominent Muslim League members would test the testimony that we wanted to send in the legislature men who were patriotic nationalists and independent.... But the freedom of our country does not mean freedom for the majority and the rule of the majority. I may assert that even the ordinary majority can be extremely oppressive and tyrannical. It, therefore, stands to reason that the majority, with a fundamentally different culture, traditions, social life, and outlook always tries to force its ideals on the minorities.... It was pure and simple a question of the minorities which had to be faced by statesmen in other countries and was to be solved. In conclusion, I may state that none desires a settlement with majority community more than myself. I want unity. I want a united front.[66]

He was going to fight the elections as a nationalist who was also concerned with Muslims' rights. 'Ours must be a party of progressive, patriotic and independent men who will not only serve Mussalmans but India as a whole.'[67] He was not organizing the League as a rival to the Congress but as an interlocutor with the aim of forging a partnership. But the sands of time were running out. Jinnah yearned for a partner like Tilak, with whom he could conclude a 'pact' settling the communal question finally unlike the Lucknow Pact of 1916 which was avowedly an interim solution. 'It was never intended to be permanent' he told an All-Parties' Conference on 24 January 1925. In 1934, he gave up separate electorates which he had stipulated in his famous Fourteen Points of 1929.

The atmosphere in the country was charged with communal feeling and intolerance. He aspired to 'produce a patriotic and liberal-minded nationalist bloc, who will be able to march hand in hand with the progressive elements in other communities'.[68] But there were no takers for the offer. On 12 August 1936, Jinnah and Nehru addressed a meeting of the All-India Students' Federation. Jinnah found, he complained on 27 December 1937, that Muslim students were excluded from the posts of office bearers. 'I am sorry to say that I have failed so far' he admitted while wishing the Muslim Students' Federation all success. That was a vivid reflection of the change.

Any assertion of the rights of the Muslim minority was branded as 'Communalism'. Jinnah was provoked to remark: 'The worst today on earth, the most wicked communalist today amongst Muslims, when he surrenders unconditionally to the Congress and abuses his own community, becomes the nationalist of nationalists tomorrow. These terms and words and abuses are intended to create an inferiority complex amongst the Mussalmans and to demoralize them'.[69]

Jinnah himself had come under attack as a 'communalist'. He sensed the change and it hurt him.

> I have lived all my life,—it cannot be said that I have ever thought otherwise than to fight, and, if necessary, to die for the freedom of my country. Two year ago, I was the same Mr Jinnah as I am today. Two years ago, I was also president of the Muslim League. Since 1913, I have always stood for what is the creed of the Muslim League, namely, that the rights and interests of the Muslims and other minorities must be safeguarded. I have not changed. Yet two years ago, I was the hero of nationalism. If you look up the papers— the same papers which are now abusing me and vilifying me,—you will see that they were all holding me up as the hero of heroes of the nation.
>
> What have I done since? During the last two years one important event has happened. A new constitution has been framed and introduced in India. Under that circumstance my community was hopelessly placed. Numerically in a minority, educationally backward, economically nowhere, and financially almost bankrupt, we had to run the election under the new constitution on the basis of separate electorates.... You will find it in the report of the Round Table Conferences that I and the Muslim delegates stood for joint electorates over and over again, but that it was rejected.... I ask my Hindu friends to read the League resolutions over and above again. They will then find that the policy of the Muslim League is one of full-blooded nationalism.[70]

This was said on 27 October 1937. On 12 April 1939, Jinnah first propounded the Two-Nation Theory, followed by the Pakistan Resolution on 23 March 1940. Whatever led to so radical, unexpected, and unpredictable a change in less than two years? The answer is to be found in a close analysis of the actual events in this brief period from 1937 to 1939—and in none of the four or other escapist myths. They are hugged because the truths, which an analysis of this brief phase yields, are unflattering to both, Jinnah's detractors and admirers. What is it that drove a man of sterling qualities, with a deep commitment to Indian nationalism, as speech after speech records, to advocate the Two-Nation Theory and demand India's partition? Neither denunciation nor apologias provide any help in understanding the change; least of all the myths of old.

Related to the political transformation was the transformation of Jinnah's personality. He was very much a Committee man whose participation colleagues valued a lot. A Committee man must be a good listener and a constructive speaker. He was both. The self-image in those times was accurate. Jinnah told the Central Assembly on 12 September 1929: 'I am a patient cool-headed man'.[71] A decade later that ceased to be true, he was a changed man. What brought about the change, and who was responsible for it? Also, need he have gone as far as he did after the Congress repeatedly spurned his overtures? As we shall see, the Congress' stance did not change even in 1946 when there was a real chance of averting the partition.

What follows is not a definitive essay on the causes of the partition of India but an indication of some important landmarks on the route to what, in this writer's opinion, deserves to rank as one of the ten greatest tragedies in the history of man.

Jinnah was right to draw attention to the Muslim League's election manifesto and its resolutions during this period. Professor Reginald Coupland noted in his classic study—which deserves to rank with Lord Durham's famous report on Canada —that the election manifestoes of the Congress and the Muslim League differed little: 'To all appearances the social policy it [the League's manifesto] advocated was much the same as the Congress policy'. There were 'only two points' on which they differed—the language question and separate electorates. Both were susceptible to compromise. The language pointedly recalled the Lucknow Pact: 'Whatever its precise implications, the League manifesto was clearly an offer of cooperation, and ... the whole constitutional controversy would have been different if the Congress leaders had accepted the offer'.[72]

The Muslim League's leaders had agreed to fight the elections in the United Provinces on a more or less common platform. It was understood that they expected, in the event of a joint victory, to be allotted two places in the ministry. But, when the results were known, there was a hitch. The League, it appeared, would be admitted to the ministry only on terms, and, after lengthy discussion behind the scenes and in the Press. These terms were communicated to the Provincial League leader, Chaudhry Khaliquzzaman, not by the presumptive Premier, Pandit G.B. Pant, but by Maulana A.K. Azad, a Bengali Muslim member of the Congress Parliamentary Sub-Committee. They were as follows:

> The Moslem League group in the United Provinces legislature shall cease to function as a separate group.

> The existing members of the Moslem League Party in the United Provinces Assembly shall become part of the Congress Party, and will fully share with other members of the Party their privileges and obligations as members of the Congress Party. They will similarly be empowered to participate in the deliberations of the Party. They will likewise be subject to the control and discipline of the Congress Party in an equal measure with other members, and the decisions of the Congress Party as regards work in the legislature and general behaviour of its members shall be binding on them. All matters shall be decided by a majority vote of the Party; each individual member having one vote.

> The policy laid down by the Congress Working Committee for their members in the legislatures along with the instructions issued by the competent Congress bodies pertaining to their work in such legislatures shall be faithfully carried out by all members of the Congress Party including these members.

The Moslem League Parliamentary Board in the United Provinces will be dissolved, and no candidates will thereafter be set up by the said Board at any by-election. All members of the Party shall actively support any candidate that may be nominated by the Congress to fill up a vacancy occurring hereafter.

All members of the Congress Party shall abide by the rules of the Congress Party and offer their full and genuine co-operation with a view to promoting the interests and prestige of the Congress.

In the event of the Congress Party deciding on resignation from the ministry or from the legislature the members of the above mentioned group will also be bound by that decision.

To the published statement of these terms, Maulana Azad appended a short note. 'It was hoped that, if these terms were agreed to and the Moslem League group of members joined the Congress Party as full members, that group would cease to exist as a separate group. In the formation of the provincial Cabinet it was considered proper that they should have representatives.'

These documents speak for themselves. They show that in the first action taken by the Congress leaders under the new constitution, in their first move in the field of parliamentary politics, there was nothing of that spirit of compromise without which parliamentary government cannot be expected to work successfully or long. The logic of 'majority rule' was to be strictly enforced. The Congress would form no coalition with a minority party. If League politicians wanted a share in government, they must join the Congress and submit to the control of Congress bodies in all of which the Muslim members would be in a minority. If this ultimatum were accepted, it was frankly hoped, and with good reason, that the League would cease to exist. It is not surprising that Chaudhry Khaliquzzaman, backed by Mr Jinnah, rejected it.[73]

In a letter to Rajendra Prasad on 21 July 1937, Nehru acknowledged that:

> During the general elections in the UP there was not much conflict between the Congress and the Muslim League. It was the desire of both parties to avoid a conflict as much as possible and to accommodate each other. In the early stages of the election campaign, a number of Muslims who were more or less Congressmen were doubtful if they would stand on behalf of the Congress or the League. If they had been pressed to do so they would have probably stood on the Congress ticket. But as there was no such pressure they drifted gradually to the League side under the vague impression that it was much the same thing.[74]

The results of the elections showed that while the Muslim League's performance was unimpressive, the Congress' performance in Muslim constituencies was no better. Nehru drew a wrong lesson from the results—the Congress' neglect of the Muslim masses—and set about correcting the mistake with disastrous results. He had little time for the League even at the best of times. Even during the election campaign, he had declared on 16 January 1937 at Ambala that 'all those people who talk in terms of Hindu rights and Muslim interests are job hunters, pure and simple, and fight for the loaves and fishes of office. How long are we going to tolerate this nonsense, this absurdity?' He proceeded to add famously, 'There are only two forces in the country, the Congress and the government. Those who are standing midway shall have to choose between the two'.[75] This, apparently, was a repetition of a theme he had propounded earlier in Calcutta. They were fateful words. In one fell swoop, Nehru not only discarded the entire two decades' record of conciliation between the Congress and the League since 1916, including the Jinnah–Prasad Pact of 1934, but also rejected the League's locus standi as a party in the negotiations. He did so in a language calculated to offend. There were Muslims in the Congress 'who could provide inspiration to a thousand Jinnahs'.[76]

Jinnah retorted on 3 January: 'There is a third party, namely, Mussalmans. We are not going to be dictated by anybody'. However, mindful of the stakes involved he added, 'We are willing to cooperate with any group of a progressive character, provided its programme and policy correspond with our own. We are not going to be the camp followers of any party. We are ready to work as equal partners with [sic] a settlement for the welfare of India'.[77]

Gandhi fully shared Nehru's views. He wrote in *Harijan* of 6 August 1938: 'If a fight is to be avoided, Governors must recognize the Congress as the one national organization that is bound one day or other to replace the British Government'.[78] The Muslim League did not count. None of the Congress leaders realized, apparently, that over time the League would only improve on its pathetic performance in the 1937 elections.

Nehru's approach was at variance with the trend of conciliation efforts. He brushed aside Jinnah's concerns and took a position which rendered a settlement impossible. The communal question became impossible to solve if the very existence of the question was denied, as Nehru did on 10 January 1937. 'His [Jinnah's] reference to a third party is also far from happy or complimentary to the Muslims. Between British imperialism and Indian nationalism he would have them remain as a political group apart, apparently playing off one against the other, and seeking communal advantage even at the cost of the larger public good.'[79] This implied that Congress alone represented 'Indian nationalism'. From this it was a short step to claiming power exclusively. Indeed, he said as much: 'The Congress represents Indian nationalism ... there are only two forces in India today—British imperialism and the Congress representing Indian Nationalism'.[80]

The tragedy was that there was much in common between the two secularists Nehru and Jinnah. Nehru amplified:

Religion is both a personal matter and a bond of faith, but to stress religion in matters political and economic is obscurantism and leads to the avoidance of real issues. In what way are the interests of the Muslim peasant different from those of the Hindu peasant? Or those of a Muslim labourer or artisan or merchant or landlord or manufacturer different from those of his Hindu prototype? The ties that bind people are common economic interests, and, in the case of a subject country especially, a common national interest. Religious questions may arise and religious conflicts may take place, and they should be faced and settled. But the right way to deal with them is to limit their sphere of action and influence, and to prevent them from encroaching on politics and economics. To encourage a communal consideration of political and economic problems is to encourage reaction and go back to the Middle Ages.[81]

Tilak, Gokhale, Motilal Nehru, and the rest were no less guilty when they went about tackling the communal question. How?

Having convinced himself that it was the Congress' neglect of Muslims that led to its poor showing in Muslim constituencies he launched the Muslim mass contact movement with quixotic zeal. James E. Dillard raised the following question in his essay: 'How grave a miscalculation was it for Congress to marginalize and bypass the Muslim League in mobilizing a campaign to integrate Muslim voters into their political fold?'[82]

It was doomed to failure because the basic assumption underlying was false; as false as the assumption of socialists on the eve of the First World War that the working class would unite across national boundaries to prevent war. The working class proved to be as nationalistic, if not chauvinistic, as any. Once communal distinctions are regarded as being unreal, there was no incentive to offer anything to Muslims as a community. As we shall see the Congress offered no concession to Muslim sentiments and left Congress Muslims destitute and forlorn. Nehru's self-absorption rendered him insensitive. 'I came into greater touch with the Muslim masses than most of the members of the Muslim

League. I have had vast Muslim audiences in the Punjab and elsewhere. They did not ask me about the communal problem or percentages or separate electorates'.[83]

Mooted first in the Congress Working Committee on 27–28 February 1937, it fizzled out by the end of 1938. Dillard explains why:

> The success of the Muslim Mass Contacts campaign depended on the active support of provincial and district Congress committees. That this support was often not present can be attributed to a couple of factors. One reason was that these bodies were often controlled by men with anti-Muslim proclivities who had close links with the Hindu Mahasabha and other overtly communal organizations.[84]

J.B. Kripalani, general secretary, wrote to the secretary of the Bengal Provincial Congress Committee granting permission for dual membership of both the Congress and the Hindu Mahasabha. This was the stance of some in the Congress in 1938 before the Two-Nation Theory was propounded.

The confirmed secularist and socialist, Jawaharlal Nehru, believed fervently but erroneously that there was no such thing as a minorities' problem. India was one; as a progressive nation that shed communal barriers. After independence, Nehru emerged as the foremost champion of the rights of the minorities, of Muslims in particular. That is a measure of the poignancy of the tragedy this secularist perpetrated in the late thirties; not exclusively though, as we shall see.

Basically, Nehru had nothing to offer to the Muslims while his colleagues in the Congress were restive even about any approach to the Muslims. The Muslim Mass Contacts movement was doomed to failure. Dillard pinpoints the flaws: 'First, it was based on a series of fresh assumptions that questioned the very efficiency of negotiating with a handful of Muslim politicians for short-term political gains. As Nehru observed, "We have too long thought in terms of pacts and compromises with communal leaders, and neglected the people behind them". He even called it a "discredited policy" and hoped that Congress would not revert to it.'

The Muslim League was none too strong then.

> The Muslim University at Aligarh, a premier educational centre and focus of intense intellectual and political activity, mirrored trends among the Muslims intelligentsia. The University remained in the forefront of the nationalist struggle all through the 1920s and 1930s. Many students, including leaders of the influential Students Union, voiced support for Congress. Pro-Congress students spearheaded the 1936 students' strike against the University's representation of nationalist activities and opposition to a move by the Students Union to initiate an All-India Muslim Students Federation. *The Mass Contacts campaign also struck a favourable chord in wider Aligarh circles.*

The political climate in the country in general, and UP in particular, remained highly conducive to the success of the Mass Contacts campaign. 'Despite mounting communal pressures and increased Hindu–Muslim strife, Congress could still count on the support of powerful Muslim groups in NWFP, UP and Bihar. Indeed, the progress of the Mass Contacts campaign in 1937 and 1938 caused veritable panic in Muslim League circles and led Jinnah to launch a counter offensive to turn the tide.'[85]

The other flaw lay at the root of the problem. It was to foil Nehru's policies right till the end:

> Within two years after Nehru launched the Mass Contacts campaign, it ran into trouble—not so much due to the Muslim League's opposition or the lack of Muslim support but because of *Congress' own reluctance to pursue it with any sense of purpose....* One critical failing was that the idea for the campaign was Nehru's, *and he alone,* along with a handful of trusted comrades, pressed it

relentlessly until it formed part of the Congress platform. *Relatively few Congress members shared Nehru's enthusiasm.*[86]

The success of the Muslim Mass contacts campaign depended on the active support of provincial and district Congress Committees. That this support was often not present can be attributed to a couple of factors. One reason was that these bodies were often controlled by men with anti-Muslim proclivities who had close links with the Hindu Mahasabha and other overtly communal organizations.[87]

In a press statement on 25 April 1937, Nehru told the Muslims 'Only a lunatic can think that the Muslims can be dominated and coerced by any religious majority in India'.[88] This, of course, was small comfort to them.

He added:

> Those who talk of the Congress entering into a pact or alliance with Muslims or others, fail to understand that Congress or the new forces that are moving our people. We have already made a great pact among our people, a great pact among ourselves, among all who desire national and economic freedom, to work together to this common end. The Muslims are in this pact just as the Hindus and Sikhs and so many Christians. They are there as Indians, and if they have problems inter se, as they must have occasionally, they will discuss them and decide them democratically, they will discuss them and decide them democratically within the great organization which has come to represent to such a remarkable degree the will of the Indian people.[89]

This implied *one* national organization representing all. Differences could be sorted out within it. Pacts with others were ruled out.

Chaudhry Khaliquzzaman was told off sharply in a letter on 1 July 1937:

> Is the League a democratic organization or is it not just a close preserve of certain individuals? Why should I accept it as the

representative of the Muslims of India when I know it represents the handful of Muslims at the top who deliberately seek refuge in the name of religion to avoid discussing mass problems? I have a certain measure of intelligence and I have studied political, economic and allied problems. Am I to insult my intelligence by talking baby-talk of an age gone by? You know what has happened in the Muslim countries of the West, in Turkey and Iran and Egypt and Palestine and Syria. You know also what Muslims there think of communalism and all its work. Do you not see that this communal policy which the Muslim League here has fathered is a policy more injurious to the Muslims of India than anything that a majority could do would be? It is a doomed policy both from the point of view of the community and the larger world, but unhappily people get wrapped up in little things, in the affairs of the moment, and to not see whither the world is going. It is quite possible that the Muslim League may win a few elections, may rouse up some of the Muslim masses in the name of Islam and the Koran. But is that the way to build up the strength of the Muslim minority in the country or make it play an effective part in the shaping of India's destiny?[90]

But he was even-handed. Nehru noted in his *Autobiography* (1936): 'Many a Congressman was a communalist under his national cloak'.[91] The Hindu Mahasabha's communalism 'masquerades under a nationalistic cloak'.[92]

Sadly, there was another and unworthy factor that governed his behaviour. It was an intense, irrational dislike of Jinnah, bordering on hate. It existed even in the early thirties when Jinnah was universally hailed as an Indian nationalist. It drove Nehru repeatedly to say of Jinnah things which he knew were not true. His *Autobiography*, published in 1937 contained this passage:

A few old leaders, however, dropped out of the Congress after Calcutta, and among these a popular and well-known figure was that of Mr M.A. Jinnah. Sarojini Naidu had called him the 'Ambassador of Hindu–Muslim unity', and he had been largely responsible in the past for bringing the Muslim League nearer to the Congress. But the new developments in the Congress non-cooperation and the new constitution which made it more of a popular and mass organization — were thoroughly disapproved of by him. He disagreed on political grounds, but it was not politics in the main that kept him away. There were still many people in the Congress who were politically even less advanced than he was. But temperamentally he did not fit in at all with the new Congress. He felt completely out of his element in the khadi-clad crowd demanding speeches in Hindustani. The enthusiasm of the people outside struck him as mob-hysteria. There was as much difference between him and the Indian masses as between Savile Row and Bond Street and the Indian village with its mud-huts. He suggested once privately that only matriculates should be taken into the Congress. I do not know if he was serious in making this remarkable suggestion, but it was in harmony with his general outlook.[93]

In writing this, Nehru drew on his imagination rather than his memory. It is incredible that Jinnah would have made such an absurd suggestion. Nehru, surely, knew the qualifications Jinnah prescribed for members of the political party he hoped to launch. His evidence before the Parliamentary Committee as far back as 1919 belied the charges. But they stuck. Nehru's biographer Sarvepalli Gopal wrote even as late as in 1976: 'Jinnah had no use for mass politics'.[94]

Nehru wrote to K.T. Shah on 12 July 1929: 'I do not see exactly how Jinnah will fit in. I find there is not very much in common between him and me so far as our outlooks are concerned'.[95] In 1929 Jinnah was an acclaimed national figure.

On 27 October 1928, less than a month before Nehru's letter to K.T. Shah, the *Bombay Chronicle*, edited by a staunch Congressman, S.A. Brelvi, wrote: 'Mr Jinnah's position in Indian politics is, indeed, very unique. Standing as he does *in the rank of the greatest politicians* of the day, as President of the All-India Muslim League and a trusted friend of Hindus, Mr Jinnah exercises a great influence over his countrymen'.

AFTER TILAK: JINNAH AND GANDHI'S CONGRESS

Jinnah did not change his stand at the Round Table Conference in London and he refused to support Muslim extremists or accept the Congress line. This is what *The Manchester Guardian* wrote:

> Mr Jinnah's position at the Round Table Conference was unique. The Hindus thought he was a Muslim communalist, the Muslims took him to be a pro-Hindu, the Princes deemed him to be too democratic. The Britishers considered him a rabid extremist with the result that he was everywhere but nowhere. None wanted him.

Jinnah himself referred to this in a public speech at Lahore in March 1936:

> I displeased the Muslims. I displeased my Hindu friends because of the "famous" 14 points. I displeased the Princes because I was deadly against their underhand activities and I displeased the British Parliament because I felt right from the beginning and I rebelled against it and said that it was all fraud. Within a few weeks I did not have a friend left there.[96]

He attended only the first two sessions of the conference, but not the third, Jinnah spent the major part of the years 1932–4 in political wilderness in England.[97]

Ian Bryant Well's research brings out Nehru's feelings, expressed in private, which came to the fore in 1937 with astonishing virulence. Wells records:

> Throughout the Round Table Conference, Jawaharlal kept up a steady stream of correspondence with Gandhi hostile to Muslim concerns, and particularly critical of Jinnah. Jawaharlal's reaction was sharp when Jinnah had informed the conference on 5 September 1931 that: 'The new constitution should provide for reasonable guarantees to Muslims and if they are not provided, the new constitution is sure to break down.' Jawaharlal branded this 'an amazing farrago of nonsense and narrow-minded communalism'. He was even more scathing in his condemnation of 'Jinnah's ridiculous

14 points'. By the end of September, Jinnah's continued demand that his Fourteen Points be accepted in their entirety had brought Jawaharlal's biting sarcasm to the surface: 'I wonder if any purgatory would be more dreadful for me than to carry on in this way. If I had to listen to my dear friend Mohammad Ali Jinnah talking the most unmitigated nonsense about his 14 points for any length of time I would consider the desirability of retiring to the South Sea Islands where there would be some hope of meeting with some people who were intelligent enough or ignorant enough not to talk of the 14 points'.[98]

It is not the die-hard Muslim leaders who earned Nehru's wrath, but the nationalist Jinnah and years before Jinnah propounded the Two-Nation Theory or demanded Pakistan.

The frenzy grew thereafter. In his prison diary Nehru wrote on 28 December 1943: 'Jinnah ... offers an obvious example of an utter lack of the civilized mind'. He lacked 'even the capacity to understand this world and its problems'. What he went on to add would have convinced Jinnah that one of the basics on which his strategy rested was wrong. The Congress would prefer partition to sharing power with the League. It would not accept his terms for a union as the price for averting a 'vivisection' of India. 'Instinctively I think that it is better to have Pakistan or almost anything if only to keep Jinnah far away and not allow his muddled and arrogant head from [*sic*] interfering continually in India's progress'.[99]

On 22 January 1945 he wrote: 'We have all been rather upset by a speech delivered by Sarojini (Naidu) at a Press Conference in Madras. An excessively foolish speech'. The provocation was her description of Jinnah on 18 January as the one incorruptible person in India: 'I may not agree with [Jinnah]; but if there is one who cannot be bought by title, honour or position, it is Mr Mohammad Ali Jinnah.'[100]

Later in the year, after his release from prison Nehru made a demand of the kind unheard of in politics. It was insolent and unrealistic, besides. He asserted in a speech at Bombay on 11 November 1945 that, 'the Congress cannot go in for any compromise with the Muslim League until it changes its present policy *and its leadership* and joins hands with the forces in the country which are fighting for independence' — that is, the Congress.[101]

At the All-India Congress Committee (AICC) session on 23 September 1945, Nehru revived his idea of Muslim mass contact and said: 'the Congress should keep as far away from the Muslim League as possible'.[102] He rejected the plea put forward by Mian Iftikharuddin, a leftist and president of the Punjab Pradesh Congress Committee and Dr K.M. Ashraf, a Congress member of the Communist Party of India (CPI), for a settlement with the League. In 1946, Ashraf wrote a well-documented thesis on the genesis of Pakistan for discussion within the CPI. That did not take place. It was published by his son sixty years later in two volumes.[103] Nehru said at the AICC: 'As far as going to the Muslim League — Never. This is war. We shall face the Muslim League and fight it'. Vallabhbhai Patel said: 'The methods of negotiation and conciliation, which is the keynote of peaceful policy, can never be abandoned by the Congress'. Ashraf remarked: 'In other words, the Congress declared war on the League while at the same time, it adopted a policy of surrender towards British imperialism'.[104]

Even the prospect of compromise did not diminish Nehru's antipathy towards Jinnah. It was bad enough that he repeated to Viceroy Lord Wavell on 3 November 1945 what he said publicly: 'The Congress could make no terms whatever with the Muslim League under its present leadership and policy, that it was a reactionary body with entirely unacceptable ideas with which there could be no settlement'.[105]

But what was inexplicable was his assessment of Jinnah even after he had accepted the British Cabinet Mission's Plan of 16 May 1946. It rejected Pakistan and provided for a centre vested with powers in respect of defence, foreign affairs, and communications presiding over three groups of provinces. They could secede from the group in which they were placed after the first general election; but not from the Union. Nehru told the members of the Mission on 10 June 1946, even before he became Congress president:

> The Congress were going to work for a strong Centre and to break the Group system and they would succeed. They did not think that Mr Jinnah had any real place in the country. The Muslim League and the Congress each represented entirely different outlooks on the work of the Constitution-making Body and they were bound to have strong differences in the Interim Government.[106]

At his very first meeting with the new viceroy, Lord Mountbatten, on 25 March 1947, Nehru described Jinnah as 'a financially successful though mediocre lawyer, Jinnah had found success later in life. He had not been politically successful until after the age of 60.'[107]

Jinnah turned sixty on 25 December 1936. As it happened Nehru and he had shared a platform on 12 August 1936, when Nehru recalled their first meeting 'about a quarter of a century ago'. It was in Europe, and 'at that time I was a student at Cambridge while you had already achieved distinction in the political service of the country'.[108] Jinnah was a national figure well before that in 1916. He was forty then. The comments on his professional competence as a lawyer do not flatter Nehru.

Asaf Ali, Nehru's close friend had parted company with Jinnah. He was appalled by the antipathy which Nehru bore towards Jinnah which he expressed freely to his friend. Asaf Ali's memoirs[109] consist of the diary he wrote in prison. He disagreed with the Congress' Quit India resolution of 8 August 1942. 'A bad gambler's throw has produced this situation ... Gandhiji expected that a compromise would follow the adoption of the Quit India resolution'. In July 1944 he noted:

> Certain persons [read: Jinnah] and policies are like the red rag to him [Nehru] and the very mention of them sends him into an unreasonable outburst of passion, expressed more in his tense face ... the impression of a proud and unreasoning victim of volcanic emotions'.

Asaf Ali asked Nehru what was the solution to the communal issue 'if not the one proposed by Jinnah? Could any progress be made without solving this question? ... He was frankly not hopeful of any deal with Jinnah, who he thought was not aware of the world forces and economic developments....'

There must be few precedents where a front rank leader, as Nehru undoubtedly was, to nurse for two decades antipathy towards another leader of a similar rank. An antipathy so irrational, almost violent, as to drive him repeatedly to belittle him to all and sundry, and in effect, to rule him out as an interlocutor during a crucial phase in the struggle for freedom. His entire record was obliterated. In despair, Jinnah turned to Gandhi. S. Gopal's characterization of the response is accurate. He was 'firmly rebuffed'.[110]

B.G. Kher was a respected solicitor in Bombay whom Jinnah knew well, professionally and personally. He sent Kher with a special message to Gandhi about Hindu–Muslim unity. Kher met him at Tithal. Gandhi's letter to Jinnah from Tithal on 22 May 1937 read: 'Kher has given me your message. I wish I could do something but I am utterly helpless. My faith in Unity is as bright as ever; only I see no daylight out of the impenetrable darkness, and in such distress I cry out to God for light.'

The correspondence continued, however, desultorily. On 15 February 1938, Jinnah suggested:

As regards the formulation of proposals which would form the basis of unity, do you think that this can be done by correspondence. Surely you know as much as I do what are the fundamental points in dispute. In my opinion, it is as much up to you to suggest ways and means of tackling the problem. If you genuinely and sincerely desire and feel that the moment has come for you to step in and with your position and influence you are prepared to take the matter up earnestly, I will not fail to render all the assistance I can.

Gandhi's reply on 24 February 1938 was, to say the least, odd.

I have read your letter to Jawaharlal also. I observe that both the letters invite not written replies but a personal discussion, I do not know whether it will take place in the first instance between you and Jawaharlal or, now that Subhas Bose succeeds him, between you and the latter. If you desire that before this there should be a talk between you and me, I would be delighted to see you in Segaon any time which is convenient to you before March 10, after which, if health permits, I might have to go to Bengal. So far as I am concerned, just as on the Hindu–Muslim question I was guided by Dr Ansari, now that he is no more in our midst, I have accepted Maulana Abul Kalam Azad as my guide. My suggestion, therefore to you is that conversation should be opened in the first instance as between you and the Maulana Sahib. But in every case regard me as at your disposal.[111]

In 1938 the hopes of 1937 were being dispelled. The Jinnah–Nehru correspondence registered little progress. Jinnah's remarks in a letter of 17 March 1938 showed that he still hoped for such a pact: 'I consider it is the duty of every true nationalist, to whichever party or community he may belong, to make it his business and examine the situation and bring about a pact between the Mussalmans and Hindus and create a real united form'.[112]

In this phase Gandhi's personality and his relationship with Nehru must not be overlooked. Gandhi had emerged as the supreme leader after the Nagpur session. The Gandhi–Nehru relationship was brilliantly analysed by Nirad C. Chaudhuri in a review article in the first volume of Gopal's biography. It was entitled 'India's Ineffectual Angel'.[113] Gandhi could control him with ease. In prison Nehru delivered himself of his accumulated anger. On 14 July 1943, he confided his feeling to his diary:

> With all his very great qualities he has proved a poor and weak leader, uncertain and changing his mind frequently. How many times he has changed during these last four years since the war began? It is very very sad, this deterioration of a very great man. The greatness remains in many ways, but the sagacity and intuitive doing of the right thing are no longer in evidence.[114]

A few months later a row broke out among the leaders in prison on the policy they should adopt towards the government.

'To criticize any step taken by Bapu is *lese majeste*'. Such was the hold Gandhi had acquired over Congressmen and others. Nehru would bristle and even break but only to submit. On 5 August 1944 his mind went back to the past.

> That revealing incident after the Calcutta AICC in 1937 [October] when Bapu completely lost control over himself over the Mysore resolution and cursed us as mischief-makers — the Rajkot incident when he fasted and then made a mess of everything — that 'inner voice' business — the conflicts over non-violence — the breaks with Bapu and subsequent reconciliations ... another of Bapu's amazing series of articles in *Harijan* — the passion which seemed to envelop him — and so on to August 8, 1942.

> And now? All these explanations without end and toning down of everything — this grovelling before the Viceroy and Jinnah — This may be the satyagraha technique. If so, I fear I do not fit in at all — It does not even possess the saving grace of dignity — Tall talk and then excuses and explanations and humility.

> What I may do outside after our release, I do not know. But I feel that I must break with this woolly thinking and undignified action —

> which really means breaking with Gandhi. I have at present no desire even to go to him on release and discuss matters with him— What do such discussions lead to? I suppose I shall see him anyhow....[115]

As before he followed the Mahatma. However, the resentment which Nehru had contained within himself, he could contain no longer in prison. The companions in jail were the very men with whom he had disagreed in the Working Committee besides the select band of faithfuls who had supported him. Like him none of them thought of resigning on a question of principle. The rows in prison were a repeat of the debates in the party executive. Over both, the shadow of the Mahatma dominated. This time Nehru found his judgment vindicated. Every fibre in his being loathed Nazism. Here he was a mute witness, powerless to shape the events in his own country and embarrassed that in some eyes, the 'Quit India' movement harmed the cause of the Allies and, at one remove, helped the Axis powers.

As ever, ambiguity marked his judgment. B. Shiva Rao reported to Tej Bahadur Sapru a talk he had with Nehru in January 1942. 'He asked with whom we were going to negotiate—an Empire which is crumbling to dust?'[116] The fall of Singapore to Japanese arms on 15 February and of Rangoon on 7 March must have confirmed him in this assessment.

It was a shallow view. On 22 June 1941, Hitler had attacked the Soviet Union. On 7 December 1941, Japan attacked Pearl Harbour bringing the 'unsinkable air-craft carrier', the United States, into the war. Historians are agreed that by mid-June 1942 'the limit of Japanese power [was] reached'. Nirad C. Chaudhuri had a poor opinion of Nehru's and Subhas Chandra Bose's understanding of international affairs. He analysed the 1942 episode in detail in an article in *The Times of India* of 28 February 1982, aptly entitled, 'They were Ignorant of International Politics'. This was a reference to 'the two Cambridge men' in the Congress, Nehru and Subhas Chandra Bose, 'who were always talking about the international situation. They were also regarded by their political colleagues as expert authorities on international affairs ... (but) their ideas on international politics were only a projection of their nationalism, which prevented their seeing any international situation for what it was'.

The failing persists, still. South Asia has produced world-class economists, historians, scientists, and diplomats. It has not produced a single world-class scholar on international affairs. Nationalist self-absorption is no help in scholarly pursuits.

The myopic outlook on world affairs was laid bare in all its unreality at an historic meeting of the Congress Working Committee in Allahabad from 27 April to 1 May 1942. By then the Congress as well as the Muslim League had rejected the British governments proposals for a long-term solution to the political problem as well as for an interim government during the war. They were presented by a Cabinet Minister, Sir Stafford Cripps when he came to India and became known as the Cripps Proposals of 30 March 1942. They envisaged an independent Indian Union with the right of any province not to accede to the Union; the first ever hint of the partition of India in an official document. On 11 April 1942, the Congress Working Committee said that it 'cannot think in terms of compelling the people in any territorial unit to remain in India against their declared and established will'. It was swiftly countermanded on 29 April by a resolution of the general body, the All-India Congress Committee which opposed the grant of 'liberty to any component State or territorial unit to secede from the Indian Union'. This was known as the Jagat Narain resolution.[117]

Failure of the Cripps Mission inflamed public opinion, Gandhi was not present at the Congress executive meeting on 27 April but sent through Miraben (Madeleine Slade) a draft resolution for its consideration. It triggered off a vigorous debate. The split in the Working Committee on this draft foreshadowed the rows in prison. The fault lines were stark and deep. One man alone had the courage of his convictions—C. Rajagopalachari, C.R. or Rajaji as he was fondly called. The former premier of Madras (1937–9) got the Madras Congress Legislature Party to adopt a resolution on 23 April 1942 to 'acknowledge the Muslim League's claim for separation' and 'invite' it to forge an accord on 'a National Government' to fight the war against the Axis Powers—Germany, Italy, and Japan. A week later on 30 April C.R. resigned from the Working Committee.[118] His logic was impeccable. If the principle of partition was accepted, the Muslim League's fears of compulsion would vanish and it might accept an All-India Agency, however loose; a prospect that was never far from Jinnah's calculations. C.R. was present at Working Committee's meeting on 27 April.

Gandhi's draft declared that 'Britain is incapable of defending India ... Japan's quarrel is not with India. She is warring with the British Empire.... If India were freed her first step would probably be to negotiate with Japan'. Nehru spoke first. He said:

> Gandhiji's draft is an approach which needs careful consideration. Independence means, among other things, the withdrawal of British troops. It is proper; but has it any meaning, our demanding withdrawal? Nor can they reasonably do it even if they recognize independence. Withdrawal of troops and the whole apparatus of civil administration will create a vacuum which cannot be filled up immediately.
>
> If we said to Japan that her fight was with British imperialism and not us she would say, 'We are glad the British army is withdrawn; we recognize your independence. But we want certain facilities now. We shall defend you against aggression. We want aerodromes, freedom to pass our troops through your country. This is necessary in self-defence'. They might seize strategic points and proceed to Iraq, etc. The masses won't be touched if only the strategic points are captured. Japan is an imperialist country. Conquest of India is in their plan. If Bapu's approach is accepted we become passive

partners of the Axis Powers. This approach is contrary to the Congress policy for the last two years and a half. The Allied countries will have a feeling that we are their enemies.... A draft like this weakens their [the British government's] position. They will treat India as an enemy country and reduce it to dust and ashes. They will do here what they did in Rangoon.... The whole background of the draft is one which will inevitably make the world think that we are passively lining up with the Axis Powers. The British are asked to withdraw. After the withdrawal we are to negotiate with Japan and possibly come to some terms with her. These terms may include a large measure of civil control by us, a certain measure of military control by them, passage of armies through India, etc. ... Whether you will like it or not, the exigencies of the war situation will compel them to make India a battleground. In sheer self-defence they cannot afford to keep out. They will walk through the country. You can't stop it by non-violent non-cooperation. Most of the population will not be affected by the march. Individuals may resist in a symbolic way. The Japanese armies will go to Iraq, Persia, etc. throttle China and make the Russian situation more difficult.... So far as the main action is concerned there is no difficulty about Bapu's draft. But the whole thought and background of the draft is one of favouring Japan. It may not be conscious. Three factors influence our decisions in the present emergency: (i) Indian freedom, (ii) sympathy for certain larger causes, (iii) probable outcome of the war; who is going to win? It is Gandhiji's feeling that Japan and Germany will win. This feeling unconsciously governs his decision. The approach in the draft is different from mine.

Rajendra Prasad tabled a draft amendment. Nehru said:

It [Babu Rajendra Prasad's amendment] retains the approach in Bapu's original draft. The approach is a variation from the attitude we have taken up about the Allies. At least I have committed myself to that sympathy 100 per cent. It would be dishonourable for me to resile from that position. There is no reason why that choice should arise. But it has arisen somewhat in this approach. The portion of the draft about resistance has some substance.

Vallabhbhai Patel said:

> I see that there are two distinct opinions in the Committee. We have ever since the outbreak of war tried to pull together. But it may not be possible on this occasion. Gandhiji has taken a definite stand. If his background is unsuitable to some members of the Committee there is the other background which is unsuitable to us. ... I am not in favour of making any approach to Jinnah. We have made repeated attempts and courted many insults. The Congress today is reeling under two blows, one Cripps and the other Rajaji's resolution which have done us enormous harm. I have placed myself in the hands of Gandhiji. I feel that he is instinctively right, the lead he gives in all critical situations.

Since the draft presented by Rajendra Prasad was not acceptable to Nehru and a few other members of the Committee, the president asked him to prepare a draft on his own. Nehru presented a draft in the next sitting of the Committee. It sought to cover the points contained in Prasad's draft but the approach was different. The discussions showed that the division of opinion revealed in the earlier discussions persisted.

> Jawaharlalji modified his draft with a view to accommodating better the other group, but the difference in approach remained. The draft was not acceptable to the whole Committee. Thereupon the President put the two drafts to the vote. Those who voted for Gandhiji's draft as modified by Rajendra Babu were Sardar Vallabhbhai, Rajendra Babu, J.B. Kripalani, Shankar Rao Deo, Sarojini Naidu, and Prafulla Chandra Ghosh. Those who voted for Jawaharlalji's draft were Jawaharlal Nehru, Govind Ballabh Pant, Bhulabhai Desai, and Asaf Ali. Among the invitees Shri Jairamdas Daulatram, Acharya Narendra Deo, Achyut Patwardhan, Bardoloi, and Biswanath Das voted for Rajendra Babu's draft and Shri Satyamurti and Mrs R.S. Pandit voted for Jawaharlalji's draft.

> Rajendra Prasad's draft was passed by the Committee in the morning sitting on May 1. The subject was however re-opened by the president Maulana Azad in the afternoon sitting. He pleaded with those who supported Rajendra Babu's draft to accept Jawaharlalji's

draft and make it a unanimous resolution. It was the President's opinion that there was practically no difference between the two drafts though the protagonists of both the drafts held that a vital difference in approach persisted. Supporters of Rajendra Babu's draft yielded to the wish of the President and accepted Jawaharlalji's draft.[119]

Thus, even a strong-minded man like Vallabhbhai Patel surrendered his independent judgment to Gandhi's. But Nehru was not ready to break with him either, even on a question of life and death for the country. He papered over fundamental differences with a compromise draft—the drift in favour of Gandhi's stand was unmistakable. Nehru went along with it—and rued the day he had so hopelessly compromised himself. The Working Committee passed the Quit India resolution with his support on 14 July. The AICC endorsed it on 8 August. Gandhi did not view the Quit India movement on 8 August 1942 as an irrevocable breach with the British. He expected them to negotiate. Arrest was farthest from his mind. He took the precaution of sending Mira Ben 'to explain to [the Viceroy] Linlithgow the purport [sic] of the Working Committee's resolution. Linlithgow refused to meet her'.[120]

Munshi recalled that as early as in 1940 'Sardar Patel felt convinced that the Allies were going to lose the war'.[121] Gandhi felt the same way, as Azad noted:

> There was another point on which my reading of the situation differed from Gandhiji's. Gandhiji by now inclined more and more to the view that the Allies could not win the war. He feared that it might end in the triumph of Germany and Japan, or that at the best there might be a stalemate. Gandhiji did not express this opinion about the outcome of the war in clear-cut terms but in discussions with him, I felt that he was becoming more and more doubtful about an Allied victory. I also saw the Subhas Bose's escape to Germany had made a great impression on Gandhiji. He had not formerly approved many of Bose's actions, but now I found a change in his outlook.[122]

Gandhi was not deterred. On the morning, after the AICC session had ended, he told his devoted secretary, Mahadev Desai: 'After my last night's speech, they will never arrest me'.[123] He was arrested a few hours later.

Azad's memoir published posthumously in 1959, disclosed for the first time the gross miscalculations in rich detail. To be sure, like Nehru, he, too, did not resign from the party's executives, as C.R. did.

Azad wrote:

> I could not believe that with the enemy on the Indian frontier, the British would tolerate an organized movement of resistance. Gandhiji seemed to have a strange belief that they would. He held that the British would allow him to develop his movement in his own way. When I pressed him to tell us what exactly would be the programme of resistance, he had no clear idea ... I was sceptical of the Japanese attitude and held that we could not place any trust in Japanese professions. It seemed to me most unlikely that they would stop their victorious march when they saw the British withdraw. To me it seemed that instead of stopping them, such a step might encourage them in their march to India. Would they not regard the British withdrawal as the most favourable opportunity for occupying India? I could not give categorical answers to these questions and I therefore hesitated to adopt Gandhiji's line.
>
> Gandhiji held that the British would regard his move for an organized mass movement as a warning and not take any precipitate action. He would therefore have time to work out the details of the movement and develop its tempo according to his plans. I was convinced that this would not be the case. The Government would not wait but arrest Gandhiji and other Congress leaders as soon as Congress passed any resolution for launching a mass movement....
>
> Among members of the Working Committee only Jawaharlal supported me and then only up to a point. The other members would not oppose Gandhiji even when they were not fully convinced. This

was not a new experience for me. Apart from Jawaharlal, who often agreed with me, the other members were generally content to follow Gandhiji's lead. Sardar Patel, Dr Rajendra Prasad and Acharya Kripalani had no clear idea about the war. They rarely tried to judge things on their own, and in any case they were accustomed to subordinate their judgment to Gandhiji. As such, discussion with them was almost useless. After all our discussions, the only thing they could say was that we must have faith in Gandhiji. They held that if we trusted him he would find some way out. They cited the example of the Salt Satyagraha Movement in 1930. When this had begun, nobody knew what was going to happen. The Government themselves were contemptuous of the move and had openly ridiculed it. In the end however, the Salt Satyagraha Movement had proved a great success and compelled the British to come to terms. Sardar Patel and his colleagues held that this time also Gandhiji would have the same success. I confess that this kind of reasoning did not satisfy me.

Gandhiji's idea seemed to be that since the war was on the Indian frontier, the British would come to terms with the Congress as soon as the movement was launched. Even if this did not take place, he believed that the British would hesitate to take any drastic steps with the Japanese knocking at India's doors. He thought that this would give the Congress the time and the opportunity to organize an effective movement. My own reading was completely different. I was convinced that in this critical stage of the war, the Government would not tolerate any mass movement. It was a question of life and death for the British. They would therefore act swiftly and drastically....

I had on earlier occasions also differed from Gandhiji on some points but never before had our difference been so complete. Things reached a climax when he sent me a letter to the effect that my stand was so different from his that we could not work together. If Congress wanted Gandhiji to lead the movement, *I must resign from the Presidentship and also withdraw from the Working Committee.* Jawaharlal must do the same. I immediately sent for Jawaharlal and showed him Gandhjiji's letter. Sardar Patel had also dropped in and he was shocked when he read the letter. He immediately went to Gandhiji and protested strongly against his action.[124]

Gandhi withdrew his letter.

Azad's fears came true. The Congress leaders were arrested on 9 August and put on a train to Ahmednagar.

> Ours was a corridor train, Mrs Sarojini Naidu now came to our compartment and said that Gandhiji wanted to meet us. We walked down the corridor to his compartment which was some distance away. *Gandhiji was looking very depressed.* I had never seen him looking so dejected. *I understood that he had not expected this sudden arrest. His reading of the situation had been that the Government would take no drastic action.* I had of course warned him again and again that he was taking too optimistic a view but obviously he had placed greater faith in his own judgment. Now that his calculations had proved wrong, he was uncertain as to what he should do.

In an article 'Rediscovery of Achyut Patwardhan' in *Janata* (a Bombay weekly) of 13 February 2005, a veteran Socialist, Madhu Dandavate, agreed with Azad. Gandhiji's 'calculation was that some time will be given by the Government to Gandhiji for talks ... Gandhiji's conjecture was that he will have the opportunity to discuss with Viceroy the implications of the Quit India resolution'.

The dissenters were not a house united. If in 1942 C.R. and S. Satyamurthi, a brilliant parliamentarian, were all for negotiations with Jinnah, Nehru and Azad were totally opposed to it. Not so Asaf Ali, though he supported Nehru in the Working Committee. His prison diary was as critical of Gandhi as Nehru's prison diary was. Jinnah could not have improved on Asaf Ali's review of 'Congress politics of the last 23 years under Gandhiji'. He painted 'a depressing picture' as he traced the course of events. He concluded

> In my opinion 1942 was a wrong decision ... Gandhiji and his group precipitated a crisis prematurely, and Jawaharlal simply abdicated his reason. And now we are in a quandary. A bad gambler's throw

has produced this situation ... Gandhiji meant well, and expected that a compromise would follow the adoption of the Quit India resolution,

that is, the British would capitulate in the face of their certain defeat by Japan. Both the assumptions were utterly unrealistic.

Asaf Ali respected Gandhi 'for his saintly life' but like Nehru, he decided on 9 August 1943: 'I can no longer follow him in politics'. On 25 May 1944, he returned to the 1942 decision: 'Were only Jawaharlal adamant, the disaster could have been staved off. But Jawaharlal succumbed, and Maulana was knocked on the head. The rest of us after that did not count.' If outside the Congress only Jinnah could stand up to a dictatorial Gandhi, within it, only Nehru could. But Nehru, as Nirad C. Chaudhuri correctly judged, lacked the mettle. Also, he thought perhaps that he did not enjoy enough popular support to challenge the Mahatma.[125] With Congress leaders behind bars, Jinnah could consolidate his strength organizationally while the communists had a field day.

Two questions brook no evasion. If Gandhi's aim was to settle with the British what place had he in mind for the Muslim League in the new set up. Secondly, if the British had indeed cooperated in this move, what would have been the form and shape of the new Constitution that would have been framed? This was the very strategy which the Congress leaders followed after their release from prison in 1945, that is, bypass the League and settle with the British.

In prison Nehru and Azad were greatly exercised over Gandhi's talks with Jinnah in September 1944 and his endorsement of Rajagopalachari's formula which he offered to Jinnah. There was no cause for alarm though.

Ambedkar correctly understood what was afoot.

> This Quit India Resolution was primarily a challenge to the British Government. But it was also an attempt to do away with the intervention of the British Government in the discussion of the minority question and thereby securing for the Congress a free hand to settle it on its own terms and according to its own lights. It was in effect, if not in intention, an attempt to win independence by bypassing the Muslims and the other minorities. The Quit India Campaign turned out to be a complete failure. It was a mad venture and took the most diabolical form. It was a scorch-earth campaign in which the victims of looting, arson, and murder were Indians and the perpetrators were the Congressmen....
>
> On coming out of gaol, he found that he [Gandhi] and the Congress had not only missed the bus but had also lost the road. To retrieve the position and win for the Congress the respect of the British Government as a premier party in the country which it had lost by reason of the failure of the campaign that followed up the Quit India Resolution, and the violence which accompanied it, he started negotiating with the Viceroy. Thwarted in that attempt, Mr Gandhi turned to Mr Jinnah. These talks failed, predictably. The C.R. formula was a non-starter. By consenting to the establishment of a Provisional Government, the League would have executed its promise to help the Congress to win independence. But the promise of the Congress to bring about Pakistan would remain executory. Mr Jinnah who insists, and quite rightly, that the promises should be concurrent could never be expected to agree to place himself in such a position. ... To make the Provisional Government the agency for forging a new Constitution, for bringing about Pakistan, nobody will accept. It is a snare and not a solution.[126]

Ambedkar does not confine himself to tearing the C.R. formula to shreds. He is singular in criticizing Gandhi for missing an excellent opportunity for subjecting the Lahore Resolution to the kind of scrutiny which Jinnah would have undertaken if he were in Gandhi's place. None asked Jinnah directly and pointedly to explain the calculated ambiguities in the Resolution.[127] Rajagopalachari's formula envisaged a commission 'for demarcating contiguous *districts*' in which the Muslims were 'in absolute majority' and for a plebiscite thereafter. All this was to be done by a provisional interim government, run by the Congress, no doubt, *after* the British had transferred power to that government.

In total contrast, Tilak would not have accepted Gandhi as a supreme leader or even leader. After his death G.S. Khaparde, a life-long friend, remained loyal to his 'political gospel' as Jayakar noted: 'He stoutly maintained his opposition to Gandhi's doctrine, poured contempt on it whenever possible, and ended his eventful life without yielding by hair's breadth, in his opposition to the Non-cooperation Movement in any shape or form.'

He sent Jayakar 'A Proposal' in which he remembered the events since the Amritsar Congress and wrote:

> The Congress itself has become a one-man show. Its foreign propaganda and London office have been abolished. The social and industrial conferences have fallen into the background and the Taluq, District, and Provincial Conferences meet merely to spread the use of Khaddar and further the movement of Non-cooperation. The reforms have been condemned, root and branch, and anybody and everybody trying to work them is hated as the enemy of his country. Schools, Colleges, Courts, and Councils are boycotted, and any kind of association with Government, whether honorary or stipendiary, is held up to public ridicule. Public life, so far as Congress goes, is soiled by vituperation such as has never been witnessed before, and all wisdom regarded as the monopoly of the followers of Mr Gandhi. *Young India* is their official Gazette, and the fulminations in it, taken together, constitute their gospel. There is no distinction observed between democracy and mobocracy. A dictatorship, contingent on certain events, has been established and what appears contemplated is a jump from the partially democratized institutions of the country back into the autocracy of a single individual.... Much admits of being added but it is believed that enough has been said to show the injurious character of the new

cult; and those that share the view above indicated are requested to communicate with the undersigned with a view to meet, consult and determine a line of action which will be consonant with the lessons of history and will further the progress of India to her political salvation.

It was signed by Khaparde and bore the date 15 August 1922.[128]

Among the Liberals, Sir Chimanlal Setalvad stood out for his refusal to be too deferential to Gandhi. Tej Bahadur Sapru would address him as 'Mahatmaji' but criticize him severely in private. In a revealing letter to B. Shiva Rao dated 16 November 1940, Sapru poured out his heart. He described himself as one 'lacking in that faith in the Mahatma, which is at the present moment a necessary condition for a public man in India to claim audience.'

He proceeded to opine:

> Indeed my view all along has been that for a long time to come the British or Western type of majority rule in India will not do and we shall have to come to some arrangement by which we may take along with us the minorities in matters of general interest. All this is possible if there is the goodwill behind. You at Delhi where there has been no responsible government probably cannot have any idea of the experience we have had of party dictatorship or of Congress Ministries wherever they have existed and particularly in the UP and Bihar. I shall not dilate upon this subject as that will be going into controversial matter, but one thing I shall say that so long as these people were in power they treated everybody else with undisguised contempt and asserted the weight of their majority in a most unfortunate manner. You say in your letter that the Congress is agreeable to waiving its demand for a party majority in the executive. I wish they would say so in so many words. My experience has been that they say one thing today and then try to explain it or explain it away the next day.[129]

Sapru had begun to lose patience much earlier, as his letter to Sachidanand Sinha revealed:

> Don't you think that the Mahatma's statement which has appeared in the press is a perfect piece of special pleading muddle-headedness... I cannot for the life of me see why poor Francis Wylie should come in for all this abuse. This is what is meant by drawing the shrewd herring across the trail to divert attention from your own mistakes and misdeeds by blaming others... Whether British Imperialism survives or dies is not the question but if it should die it will be succeeded by the rule of dictatorship the more intolerable because politics will be mixed up with religious sanctions. Unbelievers like me who have never believed in surrendering their conscience or independence of judgment to leaders whose claim to obedience is based more upon the sanctity attaching to them rather than upon their wisdom or judgment will have seriously to ask themselves whether they can live in this country under the new systems. Frankly I am in a state of revolt and if I should speak out my mind I think it may lead to very serious trouble. I know far more of what has been happening behind the scenes than I can tell you...
>
> Mirza Ismail is a great friend of mine but I do not share his weakness for the Congress or his optimism about the situation... I should be very interested to know what Jinnah thinks about it all. Frankly with all my horror of Jinnah's latter day politics I think he is the only man in India left who can accept the challenge.[130]

That Jinnah did, eventually, but not before uttering in remarkable candour a *crie de coeur* which few have noted. He recalled his efforts for a settlement at the Muslim University Union on 5 February 1938 and said:

> At that time, there was no pride in me and I used to beg from the Congress. I worked so incessantly to bring about a rapprochement that a newspaper remarked that Mr Jinnah is never tired of Hindu–Muslim unity.... *The Mussalmans were like the No Man's Land; they were led by either the flunkeys of the British Government or the camp-followers of the Congress. Whenever attempts were made to*

organize the Muslims, toadies and flunkeys on the one hand and traitors in the Congress camp on the other frustrated the efforts. I began to feel that neither could I help India, nor change the Hindu mentality, nor could make the Mussalmans realize their precarious positions. I felt so disappointed and so depressed that I decided to settle down in London. Not that I did not love India; but I felt utterly helpless. I kept in touch with India. At the end of four years, I found that the Mussalmans were in the greatest danger. I made up my mind to come back to India, as I could not do any good from London. Having no sanction behind me I was in the position of a beggar and received the treatment that a beggar deserves.... Political language is woolly and misleading. I shall speak plainly. What is the attitude of the Congress? It may be summed up thus: 'The Muslim League is composed of toadies; it is a reactionary body, it is in alliance with imperialistic power.' ... The Congress did not have patience with the League which had adopted a full-blooded nationalistic programme. We were trying to make the Muslim League completely representative of the Muslim community. I was misrepresented and maligned in the Congress press. I was dubbed a communalist ... there is an essential difference between the body-politic of the country and that of Britain. The majority and minority parties in Britain are alterable, their complexion and strength often change. Today it is Conservative Government, tomorrow Liberal and the day after Labour. But such is not the case with India. Here we have a permanent Hindu majority and the rest are minorities which cannot within any conceivable period of time hope to become majorities. The majority can afford to assume a non-communal label, but it remains exclusively Hindu in its spirit and action. The only hope for minorities is to organize themselves and secure *a definite share in power* to safeguard their rights and interests. Without such power no constitution can work successfully in India. ...

What the League has done is to set you free from the reactionary elements of Muslims and to create the opinion that those who play their selfish game are traitors. It has certainly freed you from that undesirable element of Maulvis and Maulanas. I am not speaking of Maulvis as a whole class. There are some of them who are as patriotic and sincere as any other; but there is a section of them which is undesirable. Having freed ourselves from the clutches of the British Government, the Congress, the reactionaries and so-called Maulvis, may I appeal to the youth to emancipate our women.

It was a progressive party he sought to build. Jinnah had long been patient with Gandhi's use of religious symbols in politics. Lala Lajpat Rai had criticized him even in the twenties. 'The introduction of religion in the Non-Cooperation Movement was in my judgment a great blunder'.[131] To this was allied Gandhi's assertion of authority to dictate the Congress' politics according to the promptings of his 'inner voice'. The Congress leaders accepted that, most notably in 1942, without demur.

Jinnah went his own way rather than submit to Gandhi's dictatorship. Tilak assuredly would have done the same if he had lived longer. Jinnah attacked Gandhi publicly on both the grounds—dictatorial authority and injection of religion in politics—both of which he loathed, only *after* the breach in 1938. Even Gandhi's unfortunate stand on the Nehru Report and his attitude at the Round Table Conference in London were criticized *after* the breach. The only explanation for this circumspection is that he wished to keep open the lines of communication with the Congress' mentor. Nehru's uneasiness with Gandhi's religiosity is well known. Gandhi himself told Richard G. Casey, governor of Bengal, when they met on 6 December 1945 that 'Jinnah had told him that he [Gandhi] had ruined politics in India by dragging up [*sic*] a lot of unwholesome elements in Indian life and giving them political prominence— that it was a crime to mix up politics and religion the way he had done'.[132] This was a reference to the flotsam and jetsam that entered politics in the Khilafat days.

Estrangement of Muslims from Congress, which religious cries and symbols effected, is a twice-told tale. Ignored is its baleful consequence on the Muslims themselves. The Khilafat Movement brought to the fore some of the most reactionary elements among

Muslims as Iqbal complained in a letter to Akbar Shah Mujibabadi.

> The influence of the professional Maulvis had greatly decreased owing to Sir Syed Ahmad Khan's movement. But the Khilafat Committee for the sake of political *fatwas* had restored their influence among Indian Muslims. This was a very big mistake [the effect of] which has probably, not yet been realized by anyone. I have had an experience of this recently. I had written an English essay on Ijtihad, which was read in a meeting here and, God willing, will be published, but some people called me Kafir. We shall talk at length about this affair, when you come to Lahore. In these days, particularly in India, one must move with very great circumspection.[133]

Jinnah released his pent up resentment only on 26 December 1938, in his presidential address to the annual session of the Muslim League at Patna. 'I have no hesitation in saying that it is Mr Gandhi who is destroying the ideal with which the Congress was started'.[134]

In his presidential address to the annual session of the Muslim League, on 24 April 1943, in Delhi, Jinnah gave the bill of particulars to his charge with all the precision of an accomplished advocate.

> It was in 1916–17, while this was going on, that Mr Gandhi came on the horizon. Let us see what happened. Mr Gandhi puts his declaration in *Young India* on May 12, 1920 — You will remember that in this same auspicious month of May Mr B.C. Pall made his declaration seven years ago — and what does Mr Gandhi say? 'It will be seen that for me there are not politics but religion. They sub-serve religion.' You will see later what Mr Gandhi has done in pursuance of his declaration. He says further ... 'The politician in me has never dominated a single decision of mine, and if I take part in politics, it is only because politics encircle us today like the coils of a snake, from which one cannot get out, no matter how much one tries. In order to wrestle with this snake, I have been experimenting with

myself and my friends in politics by introducing religion into politics.'

Let me tell you, ladies and gentlemen, he has done that with a vengeance, as you will perceive when I go further. In 1921, after he captured the Congress at Nagpur, he said in *Young India* on October 21, 1921: 'I call myself a Sanatani [orthodox] Hindu because, firstly, I believe in the Vedas, the Upanishad the Puranas and all that goes by the name of Hindu scriptures and therefore in Avatars and rebirth. Secondly, I believe in the Varnashrama Dharma [the law of the Caste system] in its Vedic form. Thirdly, I believe in the protection of the cow as an article of faith, and fourthly, I do not disbelieve in idol worship.' In spite of these declarations, which are so clear and unequivocal, the Hindu Nationalists got a little nervous about it. 'It has been whispered that by being so much with Mussalman friends, I make myself unfit to know the Hindu mind. The Hindu mind is myself. Surely, I do not live amidst Hindus to know the Hindu mind when every fibre of my being is Hindu. My Hinduism must be a very poor thing if it cannot flourish under influences the most adverse.'[135]

Notes

1. K.M. Munshi, *Pilgrimage to Freedom*, Vol. I, Bharatiya Vidya Bhavan, Bombay, 1967, pp. 408–11.
2. Ibid., p. 413.
3. Pirzada, Vol. I, p. ix.
4. M.R. Jayakar, *The Story of My Life*, Asia Publishing House, 1958, p. 504.
5. Ibid., pp. 519–28.
6. Ibid., pp. 541–6.
7. Ibid., p. 553.
8. Pirzada, *Foundations of Pakistan*, pp. 581–2.
9. Ian Bryant Wells, *Jinnah's Early Politics: Ambassador of Hindu–Muslim Unity*, Permanent Black, Delhi, 2005, pp. 143–4.
10. Jayakar, Vol. II, pp. 558–61.
11. Waheed Ahmad, *Jinnah-Irwin Correspondence 1927-1930*, Research Society of Pakistan, University of Punjab, Lahore, 1969, p. 30.
12. Ibid., p. 16.

13. Feroz Chand, *Lajpat Rai: Life and Work*, Publications Division, Ministry of Information & Broadcasting, Government of India, 1978, pp. 496–8.
14. *Collected Works of Lajpat Rai*, Vol. VIII, p. 151, fn.1.
15. Pirzada, Vol. I, pp. 329–31.
16. Wells, p. 146.
17. The opinions are collected in *Papers on Dr H.S. Gour's Resolution in the Legislative Assembly regarding the establishment of an ultimate Court of Appeal in India*, Simla, Superintendent Government Central Press, 1922.
18. Pirzada, Vol. II, pp. 308–10.
19. A.G. Noorani, *The Trial of Bhagat Singh*, Oxford University Press, Karachi, 2001.
20. A.G. Noorani, 'Jinnah and Civil Liberties', in *The Jinnah Anthology*, 2nd edition, edited and compiled by Liaquat Merchant and Sharif al Mujahid, Oxford University Press, Karachi, 2009, pp. 66–9.
21. Pirzada, Vol. III, pp. 382–4.
22. Pirzada, Vol. I, pp. 35–7.
23. Jamiluddin Ahmad (ed.), *Speeches and Writings of Mr Jinnah*, Shaikh Muhammad Ashraf, Lahore, Vol. I, p. 5.
24. Ibid., p. 469.
25. Jamiluddin Ahmad (ed.), Vol. II, p. 148.
26. Pirzada, Vol. III, pp. 207–8.
27. Pirzada, Vol. III, pp. 457–9.
28. A.G. Noorani, *The Trial of Bhagat Singh: Politics of Justice*, Oxford University Press, Karachi, 2001, p. 84, Chapter 6 'When Jinnah Defended Bhagat Singh'.
29. Wells, pp. 88 and 107, based on Chelmsford and Montagu Papers.
30. Ibid., p. 107.
31. Wells, p. 213.
32. Joint Select Committee on the Government of India Bill, Vol. II, Minutes of Evidence, HMSO, London, 1919, pp. 218–29.
33. Pirzada, Vol. III, pp. 299–300.
34. Ibid., Vol. II, p. 99.
35. Pirzada, Vol. III, pp. 439–40.
36. Dove, pp. 382 and 397 respectively.
37. Pirzada, Vol. I, pp. 45–6.
38. Yahya Hashim Bawany, *Rare Speeches and Documents of Quaid-i-Azam*, Arif Mukati, Karachi, 1987.
39. Ibid., pp. 39–40. Vide also, Khwaja Razi Haider, *Ruttie Jinnah: The Story, Told and Untold*, Pakistan Study Centre, Karachi, 2004, p. 89.
40. Pirzada, Vol. II, p. 101.
41. Report of the Civil Disobedience Enquiry Committee appointed by the All-India Congress Committee, 1922, published by M. Hayat, Secretary, Enquiry Committee, Allahabad.

42. Reproduced in Riaz Ahmad, pp. 141–4.
43. Documents on Khilafat Movement, Non-cooperation and Khilafat Movement in Delhi, p. 52.
44. Waheed Ahmad (ed.), *Quaid-i-Azam Mohammed Ali Jinnah: The Nation's Voice, Speeches and Statements March 1935–March 1940*, Quaid-i-Azam Academy, Vol. I, 1992, p. 143.
45. Mushirul Hasan, *Nationalism and Communal Politics in India, 1885–1930*, Manohar, New Delhi, 1991, pp. 272–3.
46. Ibid., pp. 273–4.
47. Ibid., p. 280.
48. B.R. Ambedkar, *Pakistan or the Partition of India*, Thacker & Co., Ltd., Bombay, 1946, p. 314.
49. Ibid., p. 314.
50. *Bombay Chronicle*, 29 November 1928.
51. *Bombay Chronicle*, 29 August 1929.
52. Chagla Papers, Nehru Museum and Memorial Library [NMML], New Delhi.
53. Ravinder Kumar and Hari Dev Sharma, *Selected Works of Motilal Nehru*, Vol. VI, NMML, Vikas, pp. 582 and 590–1 respectively.
54. Reginald Coupland, *India: A Restatement*, Oxford University Press, 1945, pp. 183–4.
55. Marguerite Rose Dove, *Forfeited Future: The Conflict over Congress Ministries in British India 1933–1937*, Chanakya Publications, Delhi, 1987, pp. 462–3.
56. Mushirul Hasan (ed.), *Muslims and the Congress: Select Correspondence of Dr M.A. Ansari, 1912–1935*, Manohar, 1979, pp. 231–2.
57. Ibid., p. 233.
58. Ibid., p. 234.
59. Ibid., p. 235.
60. Ibid., p. 236.
61. Ibid., p. 250.
62. Jamiluddin Ahmad, Vol. I, pp. 30 and 43, respectively.
63. Waheed Ahmad, Vol. I, pp. 29–30.
64. Ibid., p. 63.
65. Ibid., p. 79.
66. Ibid., pp. 172–3.
67. Ibid., p. 81, 28 August 1936.
68. Ibid., p. 99, 19 October 1936.
69. Jamiluddin Ahmad, Vol. I, p. 31, October 1937.
70. Ibid., pp. 188–9.
71. Pirzada, Vol. III, p. 390.
72. Reginald Coupland, *The Indian Problem: Report on the Constitutional Problem in India*, Oxford University Press, New York, London, 1944, pp. 14–15.

73. Ibid., pp. 111–12.
74. S. Gopal (ed.), *Selected Works of Jawaharlal Nehru*, [henceforth SWJN], Orient Longman, New Delhi, 1976, Vol. VIII, p. 165.
75. Ibid., p. 7.
76. *Bombay Chronicle*, 10 February 1937.
77. Waheed Ahmad, Vol. I, p. 108.
78. Quoted in Lionel Carter (ed.), *United Provinces' Politics, 1938, Governors' Fortnightly Reports and Other Key Documents*, Manohar, Delhi, 2009, p. 259.
79. SWJN, Vol. VIII, p. 120.
80. Ibid., p. 121.
81. Ibid., p. 120.
82. James E. Dillard, 'The Failure of Nehru's Mass Contacts Campaign and the Rise of Muslim Separatism', *Journal of South Asia and Middle Eastern Studies*, Vol. XXXI, No. 2, Winter 2008, pp. 43–69.
83. Ibid., p. 121.
84. Ibid., p. 65.
85. Ibid., p. 63.
86. Ibid.
87. Ibid., pp. 65–6.
88. SWJN, Vol. VIII, p. 127.
89. Ibid., p. 128.
90. Ibid., p. 143.
91. Jawaharlal Nehru, *An Autobiography*, Oxford University Press, 1989, p. 136.
92. Ibid., p. 467.
93. Ibid., pp. 67–8.
94. Sarvepalli Gopal, *Jawaharlal Nehru: A Biography*, Vol. I, 1889–1947, Oxford University Press, 2004, p. 223.
95. SWJN, Vol. IV, 1972–4, pp. 563–4.
96. *Civil & Military Gazette*, 3 March 1936.
97. Waheed Ahmad, *Jinnah–Irwin Correspondence 1927–1930*, Research Society of Pakistan, University of the Punjab, Lahore, 1969, pp. 18–19.
98. Wells, pp. 232–3. These letters were published in 1972 in SWJN, Vol. V, pp. 31–32, 137 and 46.
99. SWJN, Vol. XIII, 1980; p. 324.
100. Ibid., p. 546.
101. SWJN, Vol. XIV, p. 311.
102. Ibid., p. 91.
103. K.M. Ashraf, *Hindu–Muslim Question and Our Freedom Struggle, 1857–1935*, Sunrise Publications, New Delhi, 2005, Vols. I and II.
104. Ibid., Vol. II, pp. 209–10.
105. Penderel Moon (ed.), *Wavell: The Viceroy's Journal*, Oxford University Press, Karachi, 1998, p. 180.

106. N. Mansergh, E.W.R. Lumbey, and Penderel Moon (eds.), *Constitutional Relations between Britain and India: The Transfer of Power*, 1942–7, 1970–82, Vol. VII, p. 855 [henceforth ToP].
107. ToP, Vol. X, p. 12.
108. SWJN, Vol. VII, p. 336.
109. M. Asaf Ali, *Memoirs: The Emergence of Modern India*, edited by G.N.S. Raghavan, Ajanta, 1994.
110. S. Gopal, *Jawaharlal Nehru: A Biography*, Vol. I, p. 223.
111. Pirzada, *Quaid-e-Azam Jinnah's Correspondence*, 1977, pp. 88–92.
112. Ibid., p. 254.
113. *The Times Literary Supplement*, 14 November 1975.
114. SWJN, Vol. XIII, pp. 185–6.
115. Ibid., pp. 456–7.
116. Rima Hooja, p. 360.
117. Ambedkar, op. cit., p. 396.
118. *The Indian Annual Register*, 1942, Vols. I and II, p. 289.
119. *Congress Responsibility for the Disturbances 1042–43*, Manager of Publications, Delhi, vide pp. 42–9 for the texts of the minutes and the rival drafts.
120. Munshi, op. cit., p. 82.
121. Ibid., p. 75.
122. Maulana Abul Kalam Azad, *India Wins Freedom: An Autobiographical Narrative*, Orient Longman, Bombay, 1959, p. 41.
123. D.G. Tendulkar, *Mahatma—Life of Mohandas Karamchand Gandhi*, Vol. VI, Publications Division Ministry of Information and Broadcasting, 1988, p. 216. Vide M.C. Setalvad, *Bhulabhai Desai*, Publications Division, Government of India, New Delhi, 1968, p. 236.
124. Azad, op. cit., pp. 74–85.
125. M. Asaf Ali, op. cit., p. 260.
126. Ambedkar, op. cit., pp. 407–10.
127. Ibid., p. 411.
128. M.R. Jayakar, *The Story of My Life*, Vol. II, pp. 32–3.
129. Rima Hooja (ed.), *Crusader for Self-Rule: Tej Bahadur Sapru and the Indian National Movement*, Rawat Publications, Jaipur and New Delhi, 1999, pp. 281–2.
130. Ibid., pp. 272–3.
131. *The People*, 26 July 1925.
132. ToP, Vol. VI, p. 613.
133. Muhammad Sadiq, *A History of Urdu Literature*, Oxford University Press, 1984, p. 460.
134. Jamiluddin Ahmad, op. cit., p. 73.
135. Ibid., pp. 481–3.

3

The Widening Divide

In the discourse about the transformation which Gandhi brought about in the Congress, the aspects of religiosity and dictatorial authority are overlooked. Gandhi raised the level of political consciousness in the masses and heightened their self-respect. He was one of the century's greatest communicators, beyond a doubt. But the transformation he ushered in had its harmful consequences. Tilak, Lajpat Rai, and Gokhale—Titans all—would never have submitted to this. Nor did Jinnah.

In 1938 Jinnah went on to build the Muslim League with a single-minded zeal. But the rhetoric he deployed was abusive. Those who disagreed were 'traitors'.[1] There was no stopping him as he went about the task of political mobilization with a view to establishing his credentials as a third party. In seven years that was fully achieved. In 1945 he felt himself confident to recall his retort to Nehru in 1939 and admitted that he, 'like a lamb, bleated that there was also a third party', the Muslim League.[2] But the campaign was carried out with great acerbity.

Phillips Talbott, who became US assistant secretary of state for Near Eastern and South Asian affairs in the Kennedy administration, was in India then as correspondent for the *Chicago Daily News*. He was present at the Lahore session of the Muslim League on 23 March 1940, when the Pakistan Resolution was adopted. His description of Jinnah was not unfair.

He has never accepted an honour from the British government; the prospect of personal gain or favour seems hardly to have affected his policy. Yet he is undoubtedly a megalomaniac (and a shrewd one). That is his driving power.... Mr Jinnah stands as the mouthpiece, protector and defender of the Muslim peoples of India. In that capacity he castigates Gandhi, Nehru and what lesser Congress lights he designs to notice. No man in Indian public life today uses such intemperate language in published references to other leaders.

This was written as early as on 20 September 1941.[3] The tone and quality of political discussion were lowered. Let alone opponents, even colleagues were not spared. His use of the word 'go-between' to Sir Sikandar Hayat Khan drove the urbane and proud prime minister of Punjab to write to Jinnah on 8 July 1940 in these words:

I am writing this letter to convey my protest and indignation on the tone and wording of your reply as also against the most unusual and objectionable step of releasing the correspondence to the press without my permission. Believe me that it has caused me immense pain to find that a person of your position and experience should have stooped to take such an unmannerly and undignified step.... Your telegram, to put it mildly, shows an utter lack of decency and sense of proportion. I never had any intention of acting as an intermediary between Mr Savarkar and yourself. You have reserved to yourself the privilege of acting 'go-between' between the Hindus and the Working Committee and this is as it should be as after all it is primarily the function of the office-bearers of the League to play this delicate role.

It is for me, and for that matter, it is the inherent right of every individual member of the League to decide whom to see, and where and when.... You say 'Hindu leaders welcome to see me regarding Hindu–Muslim question'. I only wish they could be made to reciprocate this desire. It appears they are shy of going near you because they are not sure of the kind of welcome they would receive if they were to see you.

My recent talks with a lady, who is held in great esteem throughout India and who claims to have known you 'for years' as a fellow-worker in the political field, would help you in appreciating the nature and depth of the feeling which seems to be prevalent among Congressmen and others. She said, 'Oh, why don't you try to bring Jinnah and Congress leaders together and get this tangle solved. He was such a nice man—I do not know what has happened to him.' I suggested in reply that she should herself see you and try to find a solution of the difficulties. She immediately retorted: 'But he would bite my head off.' I said, 'Surely an old friend like you need have no such fears.' She said 'Yes I know Jinnah, he is very nice, but everybody does not understand him. He puts on a brusque and bullying attitude merely to hide his lack of self-confidence. He does not mean it; he suffers from an inferiority complex and adopts a haughty and superior attitude to conceal this shortcoming.'

She may or may not be correct. But even Quaid-i-Azam is after all a human being and it would do no harm, even if the description given by this lady is not true, to do a little heart-searching and see whether there is no room for self-correction or self-improvement if for no other reason but [sic] to remove this erroneous impression regarding the accredited order of the Muslims.

Jinnah's reply of 1 August 1940, showed how far he had travelled to become 'the Supreme Leader':

I must say that I find your letter to be a bundle of contradictions and self-condemnatory...your talks were reported to be in connection with the Hindu-Muslim question.... I am really amused when you say that it appears that the Hindu Congress leaders are shy of coming near me because they are not sure of the kind of welcome they would receive if they came to see me. Do you really, seriously believe this? You know that they have come to see me before on more than one occasion, and they were welcomed....

I am really astonished that you are impressed by what that famous old woman told you about me. I wish you would use your own independent judgment.

That was a rude reference to Sarojini Naidu by her former friend.[4]

Jinnah knew well enough Pakistan could be established only through an accord among all the three parties—the Congress, the Muslim League, and the British. To speak derisively of the leaders of a party is to render conciliation that much more difficult. Of the three the League was the weakest party and Jinnah very well knew that also.

The style sprang from a change in the substance of the policy he adopted that was as radical as the style of rhetoric Jinnah had adopted. On 13 August 1938 he said haltingly, 'India is not a nation state; it is a state of *nationalities.*' A few months later he said on 12 April 1939, 'I make no secret of the fact that Muslims and Hindus are two *nations*'.[5]

In 1937 Nehru broke the settled basis of Indian political discourse by rejecting the concept of religious minorities and by rejecting the Muslim League altogether as a participant in the discourse. In 1939 Jinnah destroyed the basis by denying that India constituted a nation; contradicting flatly his assertion to the *Daily Telegraph* in 1929 that India formed 'a homogeneous nation'. Jinnah discarded the Two-Nation Theory in his celebrated address to Pakistan's constituent assembly on 11 August 1947, when he referred to 'a nation of 400 million'. By then the Two-Nation Theory had had its baleful effects to the full. They continue still to affect relations between the two communities in howsoever a small degree; thanks now to the advocates of Hindutva. It was propounded first by V.D. Savarkar in 1924 in his essay *Hindutva* published in 1923. Jinnah brought it to the fore as a political credo of a major political party.

The Muslim League was transformed. The Quaid-i-Azam acquired the same authority as the Mahatma did in the Congress. Dissent was not tolerated by either. The Lucknow Pact itself was based on the concept of India as one nation; a plural society in which the two major communities agreed to settle their differences. Jinnah departed from the fundamentals on which he had agreed with Tilak, his partner in 1916. In Sri Lanka, the Cleghorn Minute on Tamil 'homelands' played havoc. To Jinnah only the Muslim majority provinces were the Muslims' homelands. By implication, Muslims in non-Muslim majority provinces were not in their homelands.

He departed also from Tilak's style which he had publicly admired. Invited to speak on the second anniversary of Tilak's death on 13 August 1922, Jinnah said that:

> Tilak was always ready to discuss with him various political problems confronting his Motherland. He had to deal with various leaders in the country but nobody excelled Mr Tilak in the liberality of his views. He remembered when he was at Lucknow in 1916 when Mr Tilak stood at the front not as a Hindu but as a Nationalist. He was as the friend of Young India and the colleague and counsellor of India. In spite of all that he was very humble, he never hesitated to go to men who were far humbler than himself. He had often come to the speaker's chamber very willingly when he found that it would be convenient for him to do so. That was exactly the sort of man Mr Tilak was. In Mr Tilak they had lost a leader at a critical moment in the political history of India. The Non-cooperation movement was launched at that time by a man for whom he had great respect [Gandhi]. They felt that the only answer was the launching of the Non-cooperation movement.[6]

Jinnah himself had lived up to his words. He bore no bitterness after the Nagpur session and twice travelled to Ahmedabad to hold talks with Gandhi in 1921 and 1929. Rebuffs in 1937 and 1938 had embittered him. The political situation drove him to despair. Having rejected federation, he acquired the onus of suggesting an alternative. We now find the problem of a 'permanent majority' in most plural societies; not only in the Third World but also in Europe. The parties either share power or partition the country. Arend Lijphart's seminal work

Democracy in Plural Societies, published in 1982, propounded the concept of 'consociational democracy'. This would have been unacceptable to the Congress. The Lucknow Pact was a step in that direction. In 1939 Jinnah desperately sought a way out.

On 4 December 1938, the Muslim League's Council set up the Foreign Committee with Sir Abdullah Haroon as chairperson. Its objective was propagation of the League's policies and programme in India and abroad. Later in the month, the League's 26th session at Patna authorized the president 'to adopt such a course as may be necessary with a view to exploring the possibility of suitable alternative' to the federation set up by the Government of India Act, 1935.

But if not the Act, 'precisely what alternative did Jinnah propose', the viceroy, Lord Linlithgow, kept asking. Lord Linlithgow reported to the secretary of state, Lord Zetland, on 28 February 1939 on his meeting with Jinnah:

> a couple of days ago ... I asked him what suggestions he had to make, to which he replied that, while he did not reject the federal idea, it must be a federation which would ensure an adequate equipoise between Muslim and Hindu votes, and in which there should be an appropriate balance between the communities. I asked him how he contemplated securing this, to which he replied that he had in his mind the manipulation of territorial votes and the adjustments of territorial divisions as to bring it about. He blushed a little as I pressed the implication of these suggestions upon him, but in the end maintained that at any rate his project for the carving up of this country was a better one than Sikandar's.[7]

In plain words, a sharing of power on the basis of equality.

The League's Working Committee set up another committee when it met at Castle Mustafa in Meerut on 26 March 1939. Recalling the Patna resolution, it said:

the President with the concurrence of the Working Committee hereby appoints a Committee of the following gentlemen to examine various schemes already propounded by those who are fully versed in the Constitutional developments of India and other countries and those may be submitted hereafter to the President and report to the Committee their conclusions at an early date.

The members were Jinnah, as president, Sir Sikandar Hayat Khan, Nawab Mohammed Ismail Khan, Sir Abdullah Haroon, Khwaja Nazimuddin, and three others, Liaquat Ali Khan was appointed its convenor. Only the day before, on 25 March 1939, when Liaquat Ali Khan spoke of 'dividing the country in a suitable manner' he added, 'if this is done, a limited and specific Federation would not only be easy but desirable.'

The League's historic session was held at Lahore on 21–24 March 1940. It appointed a committee to draft the main resolution on 22 March. It discussed a preliminary draft based on Sir Sikandar's draft. He had proposed:

(e) That the regions may, in turn, delegate to a Central Agency, which for the convenience may be designated the Grand Council of the United Dominions of India, and on such terms as may be agreed upon, provided that such functions shall be administered through a Committee on which all regions (dominions) and interests will be duly represented and their actual administration will be entrusted to the Units. (f) That no decision of this Central Agency will be effective or operative unless it is carried by at least a two-third majority. (g) That in the absence of agreement with regard to the constitution, functions and scope of the grand Council of the United Dominions of India, cited above, the regions (dominions) shall have the right to refrain from or refuse to participate in the proposed Central structure. (h) That adequate, effective and mandatory safeguards will be specifically provided in the Centre for minorities in the Units, in the regions and in the Centre, in regard to the religious, cultural, economical, political, administration and other spheres.

This did not affect sovereignty. It only provided for coordination. The Subjects Committee dropped these provisions for a centre. They do not figure in the Lahore Resolution as adopted by the session. Jinnah obviously did not wish to commit himself to any central agency ahead of negotiations.

The Nawab of Chhatari, wrote to Jinnah on 16 October 1940: 'even the Lahore resolution will not solve the problem because the Muslims in the minority provinces will suffer in any case.' Jinnah assured him on 22 October: 'the resolution made it quite clear that we cannot leave the Muslims in the Hindu provinces to their fate' and asked him to come out 'with a definite scheme of his own' which he promised to consider before making a final decision in this regard. Chaudhry Khaliquzzaman was also restive despite his support to the Lahore resolution.[8]

The Constitution Committee set up in March 1939 apparently went into hibernation. The Foreign Committee did all the running. Finally on 23 December 1940, Haroon submitted his report to Jinnah as 'Chairman, Foreign Sub-Committee' of the League.

The report contained a precious nugget in paragraph 16 which read:

> The Lahore resolution of the League does not look forward to the proposed regional states assuming immediately as they are formed, powers of defence, external affairs, customs etc. This argues that there should be a transitional stage during which these powers should be exercised by some agency common to them all. Such a common coordinating agency would be necessary even independent of the above consideration, for under the third principle of the resolution, it will be impossible to implement effectively the provision of safeguards for minorities without some organic relationship subsisting between the states under the Hindu influence. A federation is not to the taste of the Muslims, because they fear that the Hindus will, on the strength of their majority, dominate the

Muslims. But since some common arrangement is essential to the fulfilment of the provisions of the resolution, an agreed formula has to be devised whereby the Muslims shall have the control at the Centre on terms of perfect equality with the Non-Muslims.[9]

This agency would have solved Jinnah's dilemma of old. On relations between the two parts of India, the report said that 'the subjects to be assigned to this central machinery shall be (a) External relations, (b) Defence, (c) Communications, (d) Customs, (e) Safeguards for minorities and voluntary inter migration etc. subject to the following provision in respect of defence and intermigration.' It went too far and cast an unfortunate gloss on para 16. Each State would have its own Army but 'the Navy will be entirely under the Centre'.

There is every reason to believe that Jinnah, the hard-headed lawyer, would have separated the wheat from the chaff and used the nugget in Para 16 of the report constructively—if only it had been kept under wraps so as not to tie his hands. It was to be discussed by the Working Committee on 22 February 1941. On 18 February *The Statesman* reported the contents—an obvious leak by a scheming member. The meeting was postponed. Jinnah disowned the committee and its report.[10]

Sir Sikandar Hayat Khan publicly repudiated the charge that he was the author of the Lahore Resolution. It was a speech bold and prophetic, which he delivered in the Punjab Legislative Assembly on 11 March 1941.

> It has been said that I am the author of the Lahore Resolution. I have no hesitation in admitting that I was responsible for drafting the original resolution. But let me make it clear that the resolution which I drafted was radically amended by the Working Committee, and there is a wide divergence in the resolution I drafted and the one that was finally passed. The main difference between the two resolutions is that the latter part of my resolution which related to the centre and co-ordination of the activities of the various units,

was eliminated. It is, therefore, a travesty of fact to describe the League resolution as it was finally passed as my resolution. It must be taken as the official resolution of the Muslim League which was ratified by the Muslim League.

My Hon'ble friends can call it Pakistan or by whatever name they like. They dubbed it Pakistan, and it is now popularly known as Pakistan. The ignorant masses have now adopted the slogan provided by the short-sighted bigotry of the Hindu and Sikh press. If I may venture a word of protest and advice, I consider it a fatal mistake on the part of the Hindus and Sikhs to raise this hare. ...I am almost certain that the average Muslim himself does not realize the implications of Pakistan or even know which particular scheme he is supporting.... The Hindus and Sikhs started the cry of Pakistan and now the Muslims have taken it up. Both sides are now responsible for popularizing the Pakistan bogey which did not exist until it was created by the opponents of the League and is now being utilized by both to exploit the masses.... It is a great mistake to give the Lahore Resolution a name, which from the Hindu and Sikh points of view is provocative, and is undesirable even from the Muslim point of view, as it has already created a great deal of confusion among the Muslims.

...Moreover, the Muslims fear that if the provinces are not free and autonomous, there will always be a danger of undue and unwarranted interference from the centre, which will be dominated by Hindus. They argue that so far as the seven Hindu-majority provinces are concerned, they will be 'on velvet' the whole time because they will have a Hindu government in the provinces and Hindu majority at the centre.... The facts are that in seven provinces Hindus are in a majority. In those provinces let Muslims accept that majority and co-operate with them. In four provinces the Muslims are in a majority. In these provinces Hindus and Sikhs should accept that position and co-operate as honourable partners. After all, we have to live together—as we have been living together for the last thousand years or more...

Here is my recipe for what it is worth; I say, give complete autonomy and freedom to the units, and let them be demarcated into regions or zones on a territorial basis. Representatives of the units within each zone should represent their respective units as also the region at the centre. The centre thus constituted will not be a domineering, hostile centre looking for opportunities to interfere with the work of provincial governments, but a sympathetic agency enjoying the confidence and support of the provinces—a body set up by the units to control and supervise the central administrative machinery and to see that the work entrusted to it by the provinces is carried on efficiently, amicably and justly. You can call it the central government or a co-ordination committee, or call it by any other name you like. ...Once the idea of domination and interference is abandoned the problem becomes quite simple. Then Muslims would not be justified in asking for a complete severance from the rest of India. I am sure they will not. If they still persist, then I think that they would be worthy of being sent to a lunatic asylum. All they can reasonably ask for is that there shall not be a domineering centre which may undermine their power and authority in the Muslim-majority provinces.

The centre will be elastic in the sense that except for subjects entrusted to it by prior agreement, e.g. defence, maritime customs, currency and coinage and external affairs, only such other matters or powers will be delegated to the centre as the units may by agreement decide to transfer, and for such period as may be specified in the instrument of delegation. As regards actual administration of these subjects, they can be administered by committees on whichever region must be represented, or in the alternative by a representative executive. Again, the decisions need not be on a bare majority basis. Once the basic issues are settled it should not be difficult to devise means whereby an adequate and effective voice is assured to the representatives of every region, and the danger of any section being overwhelmed by a sheer communal majority is completely eliminated. You can lay down a two-thirds or even a three-fourths majority for any administrative act to be effective. I am merely giving you an idea; it will be for the experts to devise a suitable scheme. My point is that once there is agreement on the basic principles, it should not be difficult to secure agreement in matters of detail....

So far as we in the Punjab are concerned, let me assure you that we will not countenance or accept any proposal which does not secure freedom for all [cheers]. We do not desire that Muslims should domineer here, just as we do not want the Hindus to domineer where Muslims are in a minority. Nor would we allow anybody or section to thwart us because Muslims happen to be in a majority in this province. We do not ask for freedom, that there may be Muslim Raj here and Hindu Raj elsewhere. If that is what Pakistan means I will have nothing to do with it. If Pakistan means unalloyed Muslim Raj in the Punjab then I will have nothing to do with it.... Supposing the Hindus of the seven provinces in which they are in a majority suggest that we must accept a particular type of constitution for the Punjab and India, and if we do not consider it to be suitable I will say to them: 'Thank you very much for your suggestions and advice, but I am sorry I cannot accept it because it does not suit the Punjab.' Similarly, if the Muslims from those very provinces try to press on us their point of view and we find that their proposals or suggestions are against the interests of the Punjab, we cannot but give them the same reply as to the Hindus. We should make it clear to them that matters pertaining to the proposed new constitution can only be settled by discussion and in consultation with our Hindu and Sikh friends. That seems to me to be the rational position, one which we can reasonably adopt and should adopt. Any other course would lead to further confusion and might eventually result in bloodshed; and if unfortunately it comes to that, the responsibility will be of those who exploit the unsophisticated masses by catchwords and slogans. I have given this warning before and I repeat it today in the hope that it will bring home to all concerned the danger of rousing the passion of the ignorant masses and disseminating bitterness by word of mouth.

To be sure, the partition of India had been mooted before by several politicians and publicists, Lala Lajpat Rai proposed partition in *The Tribune* of 14 December 1924:

Under my scheme the Muslims will have four Muslim states: (1) The Pathan Province or the North-West Frontier; (2) Western Punjab; (3) Sindh; and (4) Eastern Bengal. If there are compact Muslim communities in any other part of India, sufficiently large to form a province, they should be similarly constituted. But it should be distinctly understood that this is not a united India. It means a clear partition of India into a Muslim India and a non-Muslim India.

Nearly three quarters of a century later, the paradox of a member of the majority community, demanding the country's break up, was explained by a politician with a record of selfless service to the socialist movement and a publicist of rare perspicacity, Prem Bhasin. Writing in the annual number, 1998, of *Janata*, a weekly founded by Jayaprakash Narayan, under the article titled 'The Congress–BJP Duo', he analysed:

> The ease with which a large number of Congressmen and women — small, big and bigger still have walked into the RSS–BJP boat and sailed with it is not a matter of surprise. For, there has always been a certain affinity between the two. A large and influential section in the Congress sincerely believed even during the freedom struggle that the interests of Hindu Indians could not be sacrificed at the altar of a united Independent India. Pandit Madan Mohan Malaviya and Lala Lajpat Rai had, for instance, actually broken away from the Congress and founded the Nationalist Party which contested elections against the Congress in the mid-twenties.

But how could the partition of India suit the interests of the Muslim minority in India? Ambedkar was no detractor of Jinnah. In his magnum opus *Pakistan or the Partition of India*, Ambedkar wrote:

> Mr Jinnah, who represents this ideological transformation, can never be suspected of being a tool in the hands of the British even by the worst of his enemies. He may be too self-opinionated, an egotist without the mask and has perhaps a degree of arrogance which is not compensated by any extra-ordinary intellect or equipment. It may on that account he is unable to reconcile himself to a second place and work with others in that capacity for a public cause. He may not be overflowing with ideas although he is not, as his critics make him out to be, an empty-headed dandy living upon the ideas of others. It may be that his fame is built up more upon art and less on substance. At the same time, it is doubtful if there is a politician

in India to whom the adjective incorruptible can be more fittingly applied. Anyone who knows what his relations with the British Government have been, will admit that he has always been their critic, if indeed, he has not been their adversary. No one can buy him. For it must be said to his credit that he has never been a soldier of fortune.[11]

His critique of the Lahore Resolution, therefore, cannot be brushed aside as being partisan.

> Will Pakistan obviate the establishment of Hindu Raj in Provinces in which the Mussalmans are in a minority? Obviously it cannot. This is what would happen in the Muslim-minority provinces if Pakistan came. Take an all-India view. Can Pakistan prevent the establishment of Hindu Raj at the centre over Muslim minorities that will remain in Hindustan? It is plain that it cannot. What good is Pakistan then? Only to prevent Hindu Raj in Provinces in which the Muslims are in a majority and in which there could never be Hindu Raj! To put it differently Pakistan is unnecessary to Muslims where they are in a majority because there, there is no fear of Hindu Raj. It is worse than useless to Muslims where they are in a minority, because Pakistan or no Pakistan they will have to face a Hindu Raj. Can politics be more futile than the politics of the Muslim League? The Muslim League started to help minority Muslims and has ended by espousing the cause of majority Muslims. What a perversion in the original aim of the Muslim League! What a fall from the sublime to the ridiculous! Partition as a remedy against Hindu Raj is worse than useless.[12]

Far from succeeding in its avowal objective—'solve the communal question'—the Lahore Resolution could only aggravate it. Especially since it was sought strenuously to be justified on the basis of the spurious Two-Nation Theory which owed seeds of alienation and communal distrust. Its territorial application was based on the preposterous 'homelands' theory.

The Muslim majority provinces were the Muslims' 'homelands', not the entire country. In fact, Islam came to South India before it reached the North as Prof. Roland Miller and Maulana Syed Suleman Nadvi point out.

> Islam in India in all probability began in Kerala, and the Mappilas are the descendants of the first Indian Muslims. Although there are hints of Muslim piratical activity on the north-west coast of India already at the time of Caliph Umar, the first recorded instance of a permanent Muslim presence in India is Muhammad ibn Qasim's conquest of Sind (711–715). There is, however, a strong basis for Nadvi's assertion: 'It is an open fact that long before the Muslims settled in northern India, there were colonies in southern India'.[13]

In Sri Lanka 'the Cleghorn Minute' on the Tamils' 'homelands' darkened counsel. In India it wreaked havoc. The theory belied, both, history and geography. No wonder Muslims felt demoralized and disoriented after the partition; specially the Muslims in Delhi and UP.

Nehru was very much alive to the presence of Hindu communalists within the Congress. 'Many a Congressman was a communalist under his national cloak. But the Congress leadership stood firm and, on the whole, refused to side with either communal party....'[14] He was very candid in a talk with the Communist leader Dr Z.A. Ahmed on 27 and 28 June 1945. If the Congress were to accept the demand for Pakistan, 'there is a strong anti-Pakistan Hindu opinion inside the Congress which would go over to the *Hindu Sabhas*'.[15]

Judging by his statements on Muslims in the Hindu-majority provinces, one wonders if Jinnah had thought out the impact of Pakistan on their lives. He made contradictory statements on exchange of population—a heinous idea. There were times when he held forth the 'hostages' idea. While on 12 April 1946, he cited as 'fortunate that there would be a corresponding minority of 25,000,000 Hindus in Pakistan' (to Norman Cliff of the *News Chronicle*), a year later the hostages idea acquired a dangerous but revealing variant after the establishment of Pakistan. On

25 August 1947, *Colliers'* weekly reported Jinnah's remarks to Weldon James: 'The minorities are in effect hostages to the requirements of mutual cooperation and good neighbouring between the Government of Pakistan and the Indian Union'. This implies that success of Pakistan as a solution to the communal problem depended on good relations between the two States—a questionable assumption at the best of times. In a speech at Kanpur on 30 March 1941, he said that 'in order to liberate seven crores of Muslims where they were in a majority he was willing to perform the last ceremony of martyrdom if necessary and let two crores of Muslims be smashed'.[16] It is not given to any leader to 'let' fellow humans be 'smashed'.[17]

In an interview to Donald Edwards of the BBC in New Delhi as late as on 3 April 1946—almost on the eve of the partition— Jinnah was asked what he proposed for those areas where the Muslims were in a minority. Jinnah replied: 'They may accept citizenship in the State in which they are. They can remain there as foreigners; or they can come to Pakistan. I will welcome them. There is plenty of room. But it is for them to decide.'

No state is bound to accept 'foreigners' on its territory. It has the right to expel them and Pakistan was hardly in a position to accept even a large fraction of the two crores he had led. The only charitable explanation for this bizarre scenario he pointed, is that he did not intend to insist on Pakistan but would have accepted something less. Opinion on this is divided. Evidence however does suggest a readiness to accept less. The League's Working Committee's draft of 22 October 1939 spoke of a 'confederation of free states'.[18] In an article in *Time and Tide* (London) of 19 January 1940, two months before the Pakistan Resolution, Jinnah asserted that 'there are in India two nations, who both must share the governance of their *common motherland*'. This implied sharing power in a united India.

The last para of the Lahore Resolution itself envisaged an interim centre. It authorized the Working Committee 'to frame a scheme of Constitution in accordance with these basic principles, providing for the assumption by the respective regions of all powers such as defence, external affairs, communications, customs and such other matters as may be necessary.'

Ayesha Jalal cites documents in the Quaid-i-Azam Papers besides the testimony of the Reforms Commissioner, H.V. Hodson. He wrote in a report on his tour (8 November–7 December 1941) that:

> ...orthodox supporters of Pakistan...from Jinnah downwards', were thinking in terms of the British staying on, with defence in British hands for an undefined 'transitional period'. The real point was that 'every Muslim Leaguer...interpreted Pakistan as consistent with a confederation of India for common purposes like defence, provided the Hindu and Muslim element therein stood on equal terms'.

Pakistan, as this intelligent observer realized, was in essence a 'revolt' against the notion of minority status with safeguards. At best, such a status relegated Muslims to being 'a Cinderella with trade-union rights and a radio in the kitchen but still below-stairs.'

The Reforms Commissioner was looking at the Pakistan demand from the outside. But the insiders' view confirms his analysis. I.I. Chundrigar from Bombay, a Leaguer of pelf and persuasion, told the men down the line that the object of the Lahore resolution was not to create 'Ulsters', but to achieve 'two nations...welded into united India on the basis of equality'. 'Bold departure' though it seemed to be, the resolution was hunting for an alternative to majority rule, not seeking to destroy the unity of India.

As he [Jinnah] told Nawab Ismail in November 1941, he could not openly and forcibly come out with these truths 'because it is likely to be misunderstood especially at present'. In a line which reveals more than a thousand pages of research and propaganda, Jinnah admitted: 'I think Mr Hodson finally understands as to what our demand is.'[19]

Jalal adds:

> Interviews with two of the most important leaders from the Punjab in the A.I.M.L. Council provide interesting insight into Jinnah's strategy. According to Mian Mumtaz Daultana, Jinnah never wanted a Pakistan which involved the partition of India and was all in favour of accepting the Cabinet Mission's proposals. The ten-year trial period was the bait Jinnah offered to the separatists in the League Council. Daultana said that this was enough time to ensure a Hindu–Muslim accommodation, and as far as this Punjabi Leaguer was concerned these 'ten years would be forever'. (My interview with Mian Mumtaz Daultana, 10 February 1980). Shaukat Hayat claimed responsibility for bringing Jinnah round to accept the Mission's 16 May statement. According to Shaukat it was he who told the Great Leader: 'let us wait for ten years'. (Interview with Shaukat Hayat, 5 February 1980, Islamabad).[20]

Prof. R.J. Moore found evidence which is baffling: 'The Cripps Mission file (802) in the Quaid-i-Azam Papers contains correspondence between Jinnah and Cripps regarding *the creation of a new Indian Union* but it is "embargoed".' That is significant. One hopes the embargo will be lifted now, six decades later. What he proceeded to add, however, conflicts with the readiness to accept 'a new Indian Union'. It suggests a readiness, instead, to accept a 'truncated' Pakistan as Jinnah put it 'On 17 January 1942 Jinnah had disclosed to Coupland his readiness for Punjab to cede Ambala Division to UP and for Bengal to cede its Hindu western districts to Bihar provided it acquired Assam'—which, as he knew, had a Hindu majority except for the Sylhet District.[21]

This shows that Jinnah *knew* that Pakistan *inescapably* entailed the partition of the Punjab and Bengal. The Lahore Resolution's reference to 'such territorial adjustments as may be necessary' could have had no other meaning. As we shall see, that prospect did not attract him. He would have conceded *some* areas but fears of loss of huge chunks of Punjab and Bengal haunted him though they were an inevitable consequence of the Lahore Resolution. Besides, once the establishment of a separate Muslim state was demanded, on the basis of the Two-Nation Theory, it was not only unrealistic but presumptuous to expect Hindus of those areas to accept citizenship of an avowedly Muslim state when geography and their numbers, in compact, contiguous areas, offered an alternative — split the provinces.

Jinnah gambled twice over; first in imagining that the Congress would share power and *thus* avert partition — oblivious to the fact that the Two-Nation Theory and the Pakistan demand served only to harden the attitude of a Congress that had little taste for power sharing — and next, in not reckoning with the predictable consequences of the partition of India. Partition of Punjab and Bengal was one but by no means the only consequence. In this, Jinnah came increasingly to resemble Gandhi for whom Asaf Ali used an identical word apropos the Quit India resolution. Neither was too candid with his followers. Or, indeed, with most colleagues. Both had an inordinately high opinion of their tactical skills. They would 'pull it off'. Asaf Ali wrote:

> Gandhiji and his group precipitated a crisis prematurely, and Jawaharlal simply abdicated his reason. And now we are in a quandary. A bad gambler's throw has produced this situation... Gandhiji meant well, and expected that a compromise would follow the adoption of the Quit India resolution.... After the failure of the Cripps Mission, Gandhiji committed himself to a course which, in spite of resistance of some — Maulana and Jawahar and in a humble way, myself — culminated in the July and August resolutions of 1942.[22]

Before Gandhi and Jinnah came to dominate the Congress and the Muslim League, respectively in 1920 and 1937, these parties were run on democratic norms. They fostered the personality cult — the leader alone knew what was good for the people.

Ambedkar gave them their just deserts—if a trifle too harshly—in a lecture he delivered in the Gokhale Memorial Hall, Poona on 18 January 1943. It was published under the title 'Ranade, Gandhi, and Jinnah'.

We have on the horizon of India two Great Men, so big that they could be identified without being named—Gandhi and Jinnah. What sort of a history they will make may be a matter for posterity to tell. For us it is enough that they do indisputably make headlines for the Press. They hold leading strings. One leads the Hindus, the other leads the Muslims. They are the idols and heroes of the hour.

... it would be difficult to find two persons who would rival them for their colossal egotism, to whom personal ascendancy is everything and the cause of the country a mere counter on the table. They have made Indian politics a matter of personal feud. Consequences have no terror for them; indeed they do not occur to them until they happen. When they do happen they either forget the cause, or if they remember it, they overlook it with a complacency which saves them from any remorse. They choose to stand on a pedestal of splendid isolation. They wall themselves off from their equals. They prefer to open themselves to their inferiors. They are very unhappy at and impatient of criticism, but are very happy to be fawned upon by flunkeys. Both have developed a wonderful stage-craft and arrange things in such a way that they are always in the limelight wherever they go. Each of course claims to be supreme. If supremacy was their only claim, it would be a small wonder.

In addition to supremacy each claims infallibility for himself. Pius IX during whose sacred regime as Pope the issue of infallibility was raging and—'Before I was Pope I believed in Papal infallibility, now I feel it.' This is exactly the attitude of the two leaders whom Providence may I say in his unguarded moments—has appointed to lead us. This feeling of supremacy and infallibility is strengthened by the Press.... accept a hero and worship him has become its principal duty. Under it, news gives place to sensation, reasoned opinion to unreasoning passion, appeal to the minds of responsible people to appeal to the emotions of the irresponsible.... Never has the interest of the country been sacrificed so senselessly for the propagation of hero-worship. Never has hero-worship become so blind as we see it in India today. There are, I am glad to say, honourable exceptions. But they are too few and their voice is never heard.

Entrenched behind the plaudits of the Press, the spirit of domination exhibited by these two great men has transgressed all limits. By their domination they have demoralized their followers and demoralized politics. By their domination they have made half their followers fools and the other half hypocrites. In establishing their supremacy they have taken the aid of 'big business' and money magnates. For the first time in our country money is taking the field as an organized power...Politics in the hands of these two Great Men have become a competition in extravaganza. If Mr Gandhi is known as Mahatma, Mr Jinnah must be known as Quaid-i-Azam.... When is all this to end? When is there to be a settlement? There are no near prospects.[23]

These two titans bequeathed to their respective peoples a political culture based on the personality cult which holds them in its stifling grip to this day. Personal antipathies were obscenely pronounced.

We have noted the Gandhi–Nehru equation and also Nehru's marked dislike of Jinnah. In the sneering remarks on Gandhi which Jinnah began to make from 1938 or so, his dislike of Gandhi was expressed clearly. Only with later disclosures do we learn that the Mahatma was also a man of intense dislikes. The Governor of Bengal, Richard C. Casey, reported to Viceroy Wavell on 2 and 3 December 1945 his talks with Gandhi, when the visitor said that 'he believed Jinnah to be a very ambitious man and that he had visions of linking up the Moslems of India with the Moslems in the Middle East and elsewhere and that he did not believe that he could be ridden off his dreams'.[24] That prospect was farthest from Jinnah's mind. The charge was a bit too much from an ardent Khilafatist of former years in respect of a known sceptic.

A few months later, on 17 July 1946 Gandhi told Louis Fischer that 'Jinnah is an evil genius. He believes he is a prophet...he was a maniac'.[25] Gandhi yearned for the day when Jinnah would sit submissively before him, like the others. He told a prayer meeting on 31 May 1947: 'God willing, Jinnah Saheb too will come and sit here one day and say that he is not, and never has been, our enemy'.[26] It was a very revealing remark. Jinnah had become an obsession. Even his finances interested Gandhi. 'Being the son of a merchant he knew how to multiply his earnings as a lawyer by wise investments'.[27]

Another target of his intense dislike was Ambedkar. Just when the parleys with the Cabinet Mission began, Gandhi, presented the Secretary of State Pethick-Lawrence with three demands on 30 March 1946: 'Release of all detenus; abolition of salt tax; and dismissal of Ambedkar' [from the Governor-General's Executive Council]. A few months later, this is what Gandhi wrote in a letter in Gujarati to Vallabhbhai Patel from Pune on 1 August 1946, only a year before Independence:

> The main problem is about Ambedkar. I see a risk in coming to any sort of understanding with him, for he has told me in so many words that for him there is no distinction between truth or untruth or between violence and non-violence. He follows one single principle, viz. to adopt any means which will serve his purpose. One has to be very careful indeed when dealing with a man who would become a Christian, a Muslim or Sikh and then be reconverted according to his convenience. There is much more I could write in the same strain.[28]

It is incredible that Ambedkar would have said any such thing and that too to a political adversary. Ambedkar himself was unsparing in his public attacks on Gandhi, but Gandhi's antipathy was expressed in private. Azad was not neglected, either. If Gandhi had had his way, a man who had borne the brunt of his community's attack and followed Gandhi and the Congress loyally would have been excluded from membership of the first cabinet of independent India. One is shocked to read Gandhi's letter to Nehru dated 24 July 1947:

> I did not say anything yesterday about the Maulana Saheb. But my objection stands. His retiring from the cabinet should not affect our connection with him. There are many positions which he can occupy in public life without any harm to any cause. Sardar is decidedly against his membership in the cabinet and so is Rajkumari. Your cabinet must be strong and effective at the present juncture. It should not be difficult to name another Muslim for the cabinet.[29]

Add Subhas Chandra Bose to the list and the pattern becomes clear. He was forced to resign as Congress president not long after his election. Gandhi could not tolerate dissenters like Azad and Bose and intensely disliked adversaries like Jinnah and Ambedkar.

Jinnah was as intolerant of open dissent within the League and treated opponents with scant courtesy. It was a grave misfortune that at a critical moment, when India's future as a unified country was being decided, there were at the helm of its affairs, in the two major political parties, men of sterling qualities and deep antipathies—Gandhi, Jinnah, and Nehru.

Tilak, the idol of the masses, was a total contrast in his humility as Jayakar wrote,

> One evening, I returned to my chamber in the High Court at half-past seven after finishing the work of the day. I then found Tilak had been waiting in my chamber for nearly three hours. When I taxed my office boy for his failure to inform me of the visit of this great leader, he apologized and said, 'I did not know that it was the Lokmanya; from his dress I took him to be one of your upcountry clients, come to offer you a brief.' When Tilak heard this he replied, 'Why do you blame your servant? I am really an upcountry client come to offer you a brief to accompany me to England to plead our cause.' These words were said with such grace and humour that I agreed to consider his request. Eventually, however, neither Jinnah

nor I found it possible owing to difficulties, to join any of the three Deputations.[30]

Dissent from the hero's views is denounced in India and Pakistan even now. Azad is criticized in India; Liaquat Ali Khan in Pakistan. His crime? He was prepared to consider alternatives, as indeed, were other Muslim Leaguers more discreetly. On 19 April 1947 Liaquat left the viceroy in no doubt that he was more realistic than Jinnah. 'If your staff will work out exactly what partition means and then if you present the full difficulties to Mr Jinnah, he will of course understand them *even though he has not worked them out for himself.*'[31]

Notes

1. Jamiluddin Ahmad, Vol. I, pp. 39–44.
2. Ibid., Vol. II, p. 254.
3. Phillips Talbott, *An American Witness to India's Partition*, Sage Publications, 2007, p. 164.
4. Jinnah Papers, Third Series, Vol. XV.
5. Waheed Ahmad (ed.), *Quaid-i-Azam Mohammed Ali Jinnah: The Nation's Voice, Speeches and Statements March 1935–March 1940*, Quaid-i-Azam Academy, Vol. I, 1992, pp. 267 and 368, respectively.
6. *Bombay Chronicle*, 14 August 1922; Riaz Ahmad, pp. 160–1.
7. Mushirul Hasan (ed.), *Documents on the Movement for Independence of India*, 1939, Part 2, Indian Council on Historical Research, Oxford University Press, New Delhi, 2008, p. 1760.
8. Muhammad Aslam Malik, *The Making of the Pakistan Resolution*, Oxford University Press, Karachi, 2001, pp. 199–200, 224–5, and 228–9. This is based on Quaid-i-Azam Papers, File 242, pp. 33–5. The texts merit close study. Vide Malik, p. 199.
9. Ibid., pp. 73–92 for the text.
10. Vide A.G. Noorani, 'The Haroon Report', *Criterion*, Vol. III, No. 4, pp. 64–75.
11. B.R. Ambedkar, *Pakistan or the Partition of India*, Thacker & Co., Ltd., Bombay, 1946, p. 323.
12. Ibid., p. 358.
13. S.S. Nadvi, 'The Muslim Colonies in India before the Muslim Conquests,' *Islamic Culture*, VIII 1934, p. 478; Roland Miller, *Mappila Muslims of Kerala: A Study in Islamic Trends*, Orient Longman, 1976, p. 39.

14. Jawaharlal Nehru, *An Autobiography*, Oxford University Press, 1989, p. 136.
15. K.M. Ashraf, *Hindu–Muslim Question and Our Freedom Struggle, 1857–1935*, Sunrise Publications, New Delhi, Vol. II, 2005, p. 305.
16. Jamiluddin Ahmad (ed.), *Speeches and Writings of Mr Jinnah*, Shaikh Muhammad Ashraf, Lahore, Vol. I, p. 246.
17. Vide A.G. Noorani, 'Jinnah and Muslims of India', *Criterion*, Islamabad, October–December 2008, Vol. III, No. 4, pp. 43–63.
18. Ayesha Jalal, *The Sole Spokesman: Jinnah, the Muslim League and the Demand for Pakistan*, Cambridge University Press, 1994, p. 57, fn. 48.
19. Ibid., pp. 70–1.
20. Ibid., p. 202, fn. 81.
21. R.J. Moore, *Escape from Empire: The Attlee Government and the Indian Problem*, Clarendon Press, Oxford, 1983, p. 54, fn. 117.
22. M. Asaf Ali, *Memoirs: The Emergence of Modern India*, edited by G.N.S. Raghavan, Ajanta, 1994, pp. 260–1.
23. Dr Babasaheb Ambedkar, *Writings and Speeches*, Education Department, Government of Maharashtra, 1979, Vol. I, pp. 226–7.
24. Mansergh, ToP, Vol. VI, p. 591.
25. *Collected Works of Mahatma Gandhi*, Vol. 85, p. 514.
26. Ibid., Vol. 88, p. 45.
27. Ibid., Vol. 89, p. 97. This at a prayer meeting on 27 August 1947.
28. Ibid., Vol. 85, p. 102.
29. Ibid., Vol. 88, p. 408.
30. M.R. Jayakar, *The Story of My Life*, Vol. I, 1873–1922, Asia Publishing House, 1958, p. 210.
31. ToP, Vol. X, p. 332.

4
Wrecking India's Unity

> I assert this with confidence that not even at the end of 1946 did anybody in India believe in the possibility of a partition of the country. Yet within six months it was announced as a policy, and accepted as a proposal, and in less than three months from the announcement of the plan the monstrous and unnatural partition of India became a fact.

Nirad C. Chaudhuri's confidence was hopelessly misplaced.[1] Well before that year, leaders of all the three sides, the British, the Congress and the Muslim League knew that partition of India was highly probable. None cared to educate the people, though.

As far back as 1924, Lala Lajpat Rai expressed his willingness to accept the partition of India. In 1930 the great poet-philosopher Iqbal proposed that 'the Punjab, the North-West Frontier Province, Sind and Baluchistan (be) amalgamated into a single State' with 'the exclusion of Ambala Division, and perhaps of some districts where non-Muslims predominate. For India, it means security and peace resulting from an internal balance of power; for Islam, an opportunity to rid itself of the stamp that Arabian Imperialism was forced to give it, to mobilize its laws, its education, its culture, and to bring them into closer contact with its own original spirit and with the spirit of modern times'.[2]

But, it was to be a state within India. He omitted Bengal. In a letter to Jinnah on 21 June 1937, he went further, 'Why should not the Muslims of North-West India and Bengal be considered as nations entitled to self-determination just as other nations in India and outside India are? Personally, I think that the Muslims of North-West India and Bengal ought at present to ignore Muslim minority provinces'. That came to pass a decade later. Note that while his Muslim 'nations' were confined to the two regions, Jinnah extended the concept to the entire country with the regions dubbed as the 'homelands', an historical falsehood to support a spurious theory.[3]

The cry for partition gathered strength, from 1937, significantly, most stressing institutional links with the rest of India.[4] The trend culminated in the Muslim League's Lahore Resolution of 23 March 1940.

The truth is that while India's independence was inevitable, an Indian federation was not. The great constitutional lawyer, A.V. Dicey, neatly summed up the prerequisite, namely, 'the existence of a very peculiar state of sentiment among the inhabitants of the countries which it is proposed to unite. They must desire union, and must not desire unity. If there be no desire to unite, there is clearly no basis for federalism'.[5]

This puts paid to the intellectual escapism, which shunning the historical record, glibly asserts that the partition was inevitable. The sentiment for 'union' was palpable as late as 1938. It began to wane in stages, but the tide was reversible — even as late as 1946. After 1940, Indian unity thrived on honoured time. There was no effort to defuse the bomb that was ticking away, loud and clear.

The realist that he was, the Reforms Commissioner, V.P. Menon, accurately stated the reason for the change in a letter to Evan Jenkins, the viceroy's private Secretary on 7 July 1945:

Up to 1935, Muslims, generally speaking, were under the impression that their interests would be safeguarded if they could get adequate representation in the legislatures. Thanks to the Congress policy of excluding all the other parties from the Provincial Executive, the minorities learnt that the majority party in the legislature could set at naught the wishes of the minorities and that representation in the legislatures would not alone be a sufficient safeguard. This was the real motive power behind Jinnah's cry of Pakistan. Exclusion from a share in the power was the real foundation on which the present position of the Muslim League was built up. It is therefore not surprising that the cry of Pakistan is more vociferous in the Provinces in which the Muslims are in a minority than in the majority Muslim Provinces.[6]

In 1938, Nehru visited Stafford Cripps at Filkins, his country home, with Krishna Menon in tow. Present at the dinner were Clement Attlee, Aneurin Bevan, Richard Crossman, Leonard Barnes and Harold Laski. They discussed how a Labour Government could transfer power to India. In December 1939, Cripps came to India and learnt a lot. He met Liaquat Ali Khan and G.D. Birla in Delhi on 11 December 1939. Professor R.J. Moore, perhaps the foremost authority on India's partition, a scholar who combines thorough archival research with rigorous analysis, recorded what Cripps heard:

> Birla admitted that Congress may have been seriously at fault in excluding non-Congress Muslims from provincial cabinets in 1937. In consequence talented Muslims, such as Liaquat in Uttar Pradesh, felt themselves consigned to permanent opposition. Now they wanted not merely cultural safeguards but an equal voice in politics, with power to veto legislation inimical to them. Congress would not entertain such a dereliction of democratic responsible government. Birla saw only one solution: separate Hindu and Muslim nations, with the cession of districts and appropriate population movements, followed, perhaps, by a loose federation holding the minimum powers necessary.

> Liaquat corroborated Birla's gloomy analysis. The time for safeguards had passed. The Muslims now wanted a settlement of the

communal question on constitutional lines prior to the settlement of the imperial issue. The experience of Congress provincial government had convinced Muslims that western democracy was unsuitable to India. It was necessary to find a constitution that rendered government by the majority community impossible *without a defined measure of minority support*. Liaquat sketched three possible constitutional solutions: partition; free sovereign states, with Hindu and Muslim federations, and a confederation; and Dominion status for each province, with a federal government exercising such powers as they chose to cede, subject to their right to opt out. The implication of the Muslim position for Cripps scheme was that the League would not attend a constituent assembly free to devise a constitution by a three-fifths majority vote.

On 11 December Cripps took the overnight train for Lahore pondering a new thought: 'There emerges a picture of a rather loose federation of provinces with few reserved subjects and with the right of the provinces to withdraw if they wish and new boundaries to make provinces either predominantly Muslim or Hindu—as the sort of lines of a possible settlement, with a constituent assembly to work out the scheme. It might be necessary to agree the basis of the outcome of the constituent assembly in *advance*.

Discussions with the premier, Sikandar Hayat Khan, corroborated the trend of Cripps's thoughts of a settlement in terms of a loose federation as a prior condition of detailed constitution-making. Cripps met Jinnah at his house in Malabar Hill, Bombay, on Friday, 15 December, where Jinnah underlined the impossibility of western democracy in India, *with its inevitable permanent entrenchment of the majority community....* The difficulty of making progress was apparent the next day, when Cripps suggested to Nehru that he should meet Jinnah. Nehru insisted upon the prior cancellation of the deliverance celebrations. It was clear to Cripps that 'Congress are anxious not to do anything to build up Jinnah's power'.[7]

The options were narrowing. The choice lay between a loose federation based on power sharing and the partition of India, entailing the partition of Punjab and Bengal as well. In a sense, Jinnah had won the game less than six months after the Lahore Resolution. The British government's declaration of 8 August 1940 pledged: 'It goes without saying that they [the government] could not contemplate the transfer of their present responsibilities for the peace and welfare of India to any system of government whose authority is directly denied by large and powerful elements in India's national life'. Jinnah had only to mobilize the Muslims' support for Pakistan to fill the bill. Nehru or the Congress could not 'build up Jinnah's power' by treating with him. Their patronage of Congress Muslims did not enhance the credibility of either, especially since the Congress had nothing to offer them.

Jinnah derived his strength and representative status from the support of the Muslim masses, not the Congress' recognition. If he could establish that at the polls, he would acquire a strong position at the negotiating table. Beneath Nehru's charge of obstruction of freedom lay the demand that the British should transfer power to the Congress alone. The League did not matter, nor, by implication, the people it represented. The League was in no position to fight. As late as on 5 December 1946, Nehru assured Cripps that 'the Muslims would come in anyhow, sooner or later, provided that they felt that the Constituent Assembly was going ahead in any case'.[8] The implication was obvious. The British need not take any notice of the League's protests. It would come in anyway.

As B.R. Ambedkar recalled, British policy towards India worked in three stages. In the first, the policy was proclaimed by Lawrence whose statue in Calcutta bore the motto, 'The British conquered India by the sword and they will hold it by the sword'. In the second, the Indians' incapacity for parliamentary institutions was cited as the reason for denial of India's demands. The Montford Declaration of 1917 marked the transition from the first to the second stage and the Cripps Mission of 1942 marked the change from the second to the last, when the British declared their acceptance of India's demand for independence if only Indians would produce an accord on the future set up which enjoyed the concurrence of all the important elements in the national life. The boycott of the legislatures impeded the progress in the second stage; failure to compromise, in the last. Obstructionists on the road to freedom were those who obstructed a Congress–League accord.

All the three sides accepted the fundamental principle of consent embodied in the August 1940 Declaration. The Congress' Election Manifesto published on 11 December 1945, pledged that 'the federation of India must be a willing union of its various parts'.[9]

There was, thus, common ground on the fundamental. Unknown to the public, chinks developed in the armour of both adversaries. In his prison diary, Nehru had resigned himself to partition and thus 'get rid' of Jinnah. On 10 January 1947, he told Major Woodrow Wyatt, a member of the visiting British Parliamentary Delegation, that 'granted, however, (a) plebiscite, and (b) territorial readjustments so that solid blocks of Hindu territory were not included, he accepted Pakistan'. Wyatt reported to the Viceroy Lord Wavell, 'possibly Congress hopes that a truncated Pakistan would be unacceptable. Anyhow, Nehru seems to realize that the Congress must give up its claim to represent the Muslims'.[10] Nehru, significantly, did not propose a loose union of any power-sharing scheme.

Jinnah met Wyatt, who was soon to become a favoured interlocutor, on 8 January. 'He did not envisage predominantly non-Muslim areas like the Ambala Division remaining in Pakistan, but insisted that Pakistan must be "a living state economically and culturally".'[11]

Less than a month later, in two long talks with Wyatt, spread over 2, 3 and 4 February, Jinnah conceded much more, provided the 'principle of Pakistan' was first accepted, as the Viceroy's Private Secretary, George Abell, recorded in a note on 5 February:

> But (a) he agreed without hesitation that the Burdwan Division of Bengal could not be included in Pakistan; (Ambala Division had previously been written off to Coupland); (b) he said that once the 'principle of Pakistan' was admitted he would gladly cooperate in an interim executive council; (c) he said he envisaged a sort of centre—there would be a British Crown Representative who would 'coordinate' the policies of the two federations in such matters as Defence and Foreign Affairs. This item (c) related to the final (not the interim) set-up. It was not clear that there would be any central legislature—presumably not.

All these three points (a), (b) and (c) seem to me to indicate that Jinnah is prepared to concede a lot more than might appear at first sight. Mr Jinnah did however tell Major Wyatt that he must at all costs have Calcutta. He also said that if HMG refused to admit the Muslims' claim to a separate state, the Muslims would make serious trouble and were quite as capable of causing bloodshed as the Congress; he himself would welcome two years' rest in the Aga Khan's palace.[12] A copy was sent to V.P. Menon, the Reforms Commissioner.

Not surprisingly, Jinnah's associates were more forthcoming with the governors and the viceroy in private. The Leagues' leaders seemed fearful of the consequences of Pakistan. Aurangzeb Khan, chief minister of the Frontier Province, gave Governor Cunningham to understand that he was not in favour of 'dismemberment from the rest of India'.[13] The governor of UP reported to the viceroy on 1 January 1946, a discussion with Chaudhry Khaliquzzaman—who made a desperate attempt in his memoirs to belittle Jinnah:

but the strong impression that I got when I was talking to him was that he did not believe in Pakistan any more than I do. If there are to be separate Muslims States, however, they must according to him, have plenty of Hindus in them to provide an insurance against the Muslims of Oudh being maltreated by the majority community here. He was very naïve about this and almost smacked his lips at the thought of the fun the Pakistan Government(s) [*sic*] would have in protecting—vicariously—the interests of their co-religionists in Hindustan.[14]

The governor of Bengal, Richard Casey, interrogated Khwaja Nazimuddin on 12 September 1945 who swore that Pakistan was not a bargaining counter. Casey warned that:

> they would have a bitterly hostile Hindustan on their flank.... I believe that they relied too implicitly on their leader, Mr Jinnah—and that apart from whatever thought he may have given on the subject, I did not believe that any other Muslim had really applied himself to the study of the many problems involved—and the many alternatives—and had compared their potential position under Pakistan with what could be achieved by adequate safeguards.[15]

Casey noted, perceptively, that 'Jinnah apparently takes the view that if he puts up any concrete proposals at this stage they will merely be torn to pieces'.[16] His fear was perfectly justified, as events were to establish. 'He [Liaquat Ali Khan] admits that it would be difficult to include the Burdwan Division in Bengal–Pakistan'.[17] When the governor asked Ispahani if the Muslim League was still absolutely intent on Pakistan and nothing else, Ispahani said, 'as for himself, he was not'.[18] The governor of Assam's impression of Saadulla, which he conveyed to the viceroy on 5 February 1946 was, 'I am sure that he is not, at heart, a believer in Pakistan—few Assam Muslims are—but he has to support the idea publicly'.[19] Khaliquzzaman conceded more when he met Governor Wylie:

> The Muslim League waive full Pakistan demand (a) if predominantly Muslim areas were formed into separate federal units with ports (sic.

for facts) not subject control by Federal Government and (b) if they were allowed to retain their Armed Forces for subsidiary events, major defence of the country to be responsibility of federal Government.[20]

Penderel Moon was one of the most cerebral civilians who served in India. He was close to Sikandar Hayat Khan and his books reflect much understanding. He wrote a brilliant memorandum which Sir William Croft, deputy under-secretary of state in the India Office, sent to his civilian chief, Sir David Monteath, on 11 January 1946. He pointed out that realistically, partition had become irresistible and the Congress would accept it, if properly defined:

> Congress leaders are avid of power. Not a single one of them belongs to the Pakistan areas; therefore not a single one of them will be personally affected adversely by the creation of Pakistan. On the other hand, non-acceptance of Pakistan, by prolonging the Hindu–Muslim deadlock, will inevitably delay their obtaining the power which they so ardently desire.[21]

Croft also circulated another memo. It was by 'FM' who was Ms Freda Martin, later wife of Guy Wint, a journalist attached to the External Affairs Department and a member of the Foreign Secretary Sir Olaf Caroe's 'Brains Trust', also known as the 'Viceroy's Study Group'. No civil servant reflected more intensely on India's strategic problems than Caroe did.[22]

The significance of FM's memo lies in the fact that it was written at the suggestion of Cripps on FM's return from India. 'Congress now want power', she noted. 'Pakistan in some form was inevitable', if the Hindu majority areas in Punjab and Bengal were excluded. It was not a prospect that Jinnah welcomed. But nor could he confide to his colleagues, bar Liaquat Ali Khan and Nawab Mohammed Ismail Khan of Meerut, whom Jinnah respected for his integrity and independence. He remains a neglected figure in Indo–Pak writings. FM astutely noted

Jinnah's problem with his colleagues, which explains his loneliness, and the failings loneliness breeds—distrust and arrogance:

> Jinnah observing the behaviour of his elder henchmen in the provincial governments, is said to have concluded that they are not to be trusted. He judges that they cannot be relied on to disregard the lure of office and high salaries when the only price they need to pay to retain them is compromise. The result has been a tightening up of party discipline (the increased 'totalitarianism' on which many people have commented, and at which the party leaders themselves complain).[23]

Jinnah came more and more to rely on the younger leaders. They were 'fanatically obedient', whether out of conviction or calculation. Jinnah had few he could trust and only a few to advise him fearlessly and realistically. He played with his cards close to his chest. It was a weak hand, despite his strengths. Nor did he have anyone, like his partner Tilak, to negotiate with. Torn between a 'truncated' Pakistan, he abhorred, and a strong centre, which he detested, a ray of light appeared in Professor Sir Reginald Coupland's grouping formula; provinces grouped together but under a centre of limited powers.

Coupland was a member of Cripps's team in 1942. His report, the 'Constitutional Problem' (1942–3) submitted to Nuffield College at Oxford was followed in 1945 by his book, *India: A Restatement*, in which he proposed an '"Agency Centre" ... something between a normal federation and a mere Confederacy or League ... (and) the establishment of Regional Governments between the Central and provincial Governments ... a triple system'.[24] The loose centre as a sop to the Congress and the regional groups as a sop to the League. It is unlikely that Cripps did not hear of the idea. It was the basis for the Cabinet Mission's Plan.

The British did not watch the show idly from the sidelines. From 1945 they were busy preparing contingency plans. Since V.P. Menon was at the centre of their deliberations, Vallabhbhai Patel must have got wind of the plans. Every major document pronounced against Pakistan, even while reckoning with the force which the movement had acquired.

A particularly constructive contribution was made by K.M. Panikkar, prime minister of Bikaner, in a memorandum dated 10 October 1945, entitled 'The Next Step in India' sent through Guy Wint. Characteristically, he proposed the appointment of a constitutional adviser to the viceroy with a faint hint that he was most qualified for the post. (Sir B.N. Rau was on special duty in the governor-general's secretariat [reforms]). But he sensibly pointed out the absurdity of any constituent assembly functioning without an accord on the fundamentals between its leaders. The constituent assembly of India was guided by proposals adopted by the Congress, a fact that the chairperson of its Drafting Committee, B.R. Ambedkar, acknowledged at the end on 25 November 1949. Without such an accord the Congress' cry for a constituent assembly, rightly aroused fears of majority rule.

Panikkar creditably proposed that 'unless a procedure of bringing the parties together on some minimum basis of agreement is evolved *before* the constituent assembly meets there is some danger of the whole plan proving abortive'. To anticipate, this is precisely what the British Cabinet Mission's Plan of 16 May 1946 sought to accomplish. The Congress sought to enter the constituent assembly it set up, discard the basis on which it was set up as fetters on a 'sovereign' body—limited centre over three groups of provinces—and proceed to do what it pleased, leaving the League high and dry. The game depended on British acquiescence in the sabotage of British proposals. It all but succeeded. It failed because, as mentioned earlier, contrary to Nehru's confidence, Jinnah did not acquiesce. 'The Muslims would come in any how, sooner or later, provided that they felt that the Constituent Assembly was going ahead in any case'.[25]

But this left Jinnah no alternative but a truncated Pakistan. The British were prepared for it, despite reservations. It was a cruel irony. The Unionists were set on the course of partition; the separatists were striving secretly to have a limited union based on groups and thus save the Muslims from a terrible tragedy; saving the League's face in the bargain.

Panikkar advised that 'the principle of a Muslim homeland should be accepted subject to territorial adjustments' in Punjab and Bengal.[26] The Viceroy Lord Wavell began his exercises no sooner the war ended. His first essay was sent to London on 21 August 1945. It was entitled 'Pakistan and the Punjab' and was backed by facts and population figures. There were, he wrote, two possibilities, namely 'a loose form of Federation' and 'a Federation of a tighter kind', leaving the provinces free to secede.[27]

London wanted to know what the boundaries of Pakistan could possibly be. V.P. Menon and B.N. Rau drew up a 'Note on Demarcation of "Pakistan Areas"' on 23 January 1946.[28] The Secretary of State for India, Lord Pethick–Lawrence, pressed Wavell for his considered views. Wavell's reply of 6 February 1946 was a definitive document:

> If compelled to indicate demarcation of genuinely Muslim areas I recommend that we should include: (a) Sind, N.W.F.P, British Baluchistan, and the Rawalpindi, Multan and Lahore divisions of the Punjab less Amritsar and Gurdaspur districts; (b) in Bengal, the Chittagong and Dacca divisions, the Rajshahi division (less Jalpaiguri and Darjeeling), the Nadia, Murshidabad and Jessore districts of the Presidency division, and in Assam the Sylhet district. In the Punjab the only Muslim majority district that would not go into Pakistan under the demarcation is Gurdaspur (51% Muslim). Gurdaspur must go with Amritsar for geographical reasons.[29]

The Cabinet Mission comprising Pethick-Lawrence, Cripps and A.V. Alexander arrived in India on 24 March 1946. By 11 April, these men along with the viceroy had met all the interested parties and informed Prime Minister Clement Attlee that:

> In our directive we are enjoined to see that any scheme which we accept makes adequate provision for the Defence of India and the adjoining areas.
>
> There appear to us to be two possible bases of agreement, the first a unitary India with a loose federation at the Centre charged primarily with control of Defence and Foreign Affairs (Scheme A). The second based upon a divided India, the Pakistan element consisting only of the majority Muslim Districts that is roughly Baluchistan, Sind, North-West Frontier Province and Western Punjab in the North-West and Eastern Bengal without Calcutta but with the Sylhet District of Assam in the North-East. The two dividend parts would have a Treaty of alliance offensive and defensive but nothing in the way of an actual executive centre (Scheme B). They mentioned its defects at length. For an accord is the first requirement towards any effective Defence. We hope, therefore, that you will agree to our working for an agreement on the basis of Scheme B if this seems to us to be the only chance of agreed settlement. We should of course ourselves prefer something on lines of Scheme A but this may prove impossible of attainment.[30]

Attlee replied promptly:

> Cabinet agreed that, while Scheme A is preferable, you may work for an agreement on basis of Scheme B if it seems to be the only chance of an agreed settlement. I send you...the views of the Chiefs of Staff for your information and for use in the discussion.... An agreement involving a loose all-India federation is far better than Scheme B. We recognize, however, that this may be impossible of achievement. The alternative of Scheme B, in spite of the disadvantages listed below, is better than no agreement at all as this would lead to widespread chaos.

Attlee set out the strains partition would impose on India's defence but concluded:

> Scheme B will have to be accepted if the only alternative is complete failure to reach agreement and consequent chaos. But India will be confronted by grave dangers as a result of this partition; and, if Scheme B has to be adopted, every effort should be made to obtain agreement for some form of central defence council to be set up which will include not only Pakistan, Hindustan and the Indian States, but also Burma and Ceylon.[31]

Cripps, the Mission's draftsman and driving force, prepared a memorandum on 18 April. It envisaged 'a three-tier' arrangement with the group in the middle.[32] It was the first draft of the Mission's Plan.

More notable was his success in persuading Jinnah to accept an Indian Union. Neither liked the other, each had a professional's respect for the other's forensic skills. The record of Jinnah's talks with the Cabinet Mission clearly establish that he preferred a loose federation to Pakistan. When the Mission met him on 6 April 1946, they proposed two alternatives. One was:

> a separate State of Pakistan consisting of, say, Sind, North-West Frontier Province, Baluchistan, the Muslim-majority districts of the Punjab, except perhaps Gurdaspur, Eastern Bengal and the Sylhet District of Assam.

The other was:

> a Union Centre for the essential subjects, say, defence, foreign affairs and communications, it might then be possible to include in one Federation the whole of the provinces of Sind, Baluchistan, North-West Frontier Province, the Punjab and Bengal plus perhaps the Sylhet district of Assam. In such a Union the two parts might have equal representation.... There might be provision that any party to it could secede after a certain period, say 15 years.....

Mr Jinnah asked how, if there were equal representation, decisions were to be reached and Sir S. Cripps said that there would be no Union Parliament. The responsibility would go back to the two Federations if agreement could not be reached and differences could only be decided by inter-Governmental agreement. *Mr Jinnah expressed doubts as to whether this arrangement would work in practice.*

On the second alternative, Jinnah said 'the question of the territory of Pakistan could be discussed'. He voiced his fears clearly enough. '*If he made a concession he would have lost it before the negotiations began.* It was Congress who should make a proposal'. If the League's demand for the provinces entire was not acceptable, 'they should say what they considered he ought to have. He was not prepared to say what he was willing to give up'.[33]

However, when Cripps met Jinnah on 25 April he 'thought that he had made some progress with Jinnah'. He had, indeed, reversed his position completely, for Jinnah was now prepared. He was now prepared to accept a loose centre rather than a diminished Pakistan, having realized that Pakistan, as he demanded, was not achievable. Cripps 'put to Mr Jinnah again the two plans which the Delegation had put to Mr Jinnah when they saw him formally, i.e., Plan A for a three-tier Federal Union and Plan B for minimum sovereign Pakistan. He had also referred again to the plan which he had put to Mr Jinnah on the previous day. *Mr Jinnah had said that Plan B was definitely unacceptable*'. That, remember, was the Pakistan he was forced to accept on 3 June 1947.

'He was prepared, however, to consider Plan A if the Congress were prepared to consider it and if he could be assured of that he would put it to the Muslim League Working Committee.'[34] He was right. He could hardly be expected to offer a Union, retreating radically from his demand, only to have the offer turned down. But that is precisely what happened. He had altered his position between 16 and 25 April after careful deliberation.

This will surprise many today, hence this quotation from the official record of the meeting of the cabinet delegation and the viceroy of 26 April:

> He [Jinnah] had assured Sir Stafford that he would do this [put it to the Muslim League Working Committee] not with a recommendation for its [Plan A] rejection but as a proposal that they should consider, though of course at some stage in the proceedings he would give his own views on the subject.
>
> Sir Stafford had seen Pandit Nehru as regards the third plan but had been told that it had no chance of acceptance by the Congress.
>
> The Secretary of State, Pethick-Lawrence, said that the immediate point for decision was whether an approach should now be made to the Congress as to the acceptability of Plan A. This had already been considered by the Working Committee and rejected. There was a risk in raising it again that it might be rejected once more and this would make it more difficult to use the three-tier plan as the basis of the ultimate award. On the other hand, Mr Gandhi's main objection to Pakistan was to it having sovereignty and it now appeared that Mr Jinnah was for the first time prepared to consider something less than a sovereign Pakistan.

It was after these talks that on the next day, 27 April, the Mission invited both parties to a conference to discuss the possibility of an agreement upon a scheme based on the following fundamental principles. Basically 'a Union Government dealing with Foreign Affairs, Defence and Communications'. There would be two groups of provinces: one of the predominantly Muslim areas and the other of the rest.[35]

Jinnah had ceased to be a problem, for he had accepted a union based on groups only the day before. The only hurdle was the Congress' consent to such a union and to the groups. Thus, before Jinnah walked into the Conference Hall at the Viceregal Lodge in Simla with three colleagues, on 5 May, he had in private all but given up the demand for Pakistan, formulated once again in a more explicit form in a resolution by the Muslim League Legislators' Convention on 9 April, a copy of which he sent to the Mission for the record. It is anyone's guess whether the Reforms Commissioner, V.P. Menon, knew of the Jinnah–Cripps talks on 26 April. If he did, it is unlikely that he did not share so vital a development with Patel.

There were three main items on the conference agenda 'Groups of Provinces' was the first, followed by 'Union' and 'Constitution-making machinery', each of which had ancillary items. The conference never really took off. It reflected a political culture of talking to each other through a third party. Many would say that this culture prevails, still. The Congress President, Maulana Abul Kalam Azad, wrote to Pethick-Lawrence on 6 May rejecting the group, 'a sub-federation', claiming, 'we are not aware of any such arrangement in any country'. The Congress was 'entirely opposed' to such groups with a separate executive and legislature.[36] This was unfortunate.

Partition had ceased to be an issue. The sole issue now was a limited union based on groups of provinces. The Mission, in a last minute effort, attempted to bridge a divide, which had narrowed considerably. On 8 May, it sent to the Congress and the League 'Suggested Points for Agreement' between them at the conference. They envisaged parity at the centre between the Muslim-majority provinces and the rest, in the legislature as well as in the executive. The Constitutions of the union and the groups will provide liberty to any province to call 'for a reconsideration of the terms of the Constitution after an initial period of 10 years and at 10 yearly intervals thereafter'.

More to the point, after a preliminary meeting, the constituent assembly 'will divide into three sections', two for British India and one for the princely states. In view of the later controversy, it is important to note the procedure that was prescribed. 'The first two sections will then meet separately to decide the Provincial Constitutions for their group, and, if they wish, a group Constitution'. When these are settled, it will be open to any province to opt out of its original group.[37] Opting out of the group comes <u>after</u> the province has seen the proceedings. The Mission and the viceroy were in constant touch with Attlee on the proposals and proceedings. Gandhi was present at Simla and met the Mission's team. He wrote to Cripps on 8 May rightly rejecting the parity clause, inherently unworkable as it was, but ominous was his stand that the constituent assembly 'would be free to throw out any of the items' and the parties were also free to 'amend the suggestions'.[38]

Jinnah told Woodrow Wyatt that he felt that the Mission had revised its 27 April formula on 8 May in favour of the Congress. 'He is prepared to stick to the Union Government which he regards as a great concession'. He conceded that 'any province in that (Muslim) group which does not like the Constitution *can opt out of the Muslim group*'.[39]

What is overlooked in most analyses of these negotiations is that when the Mission asked both parties to send 'a precise written statement' of their position, the memorandum which Jinnah sent on 12 May embodying 'principles to be agreed to as our offer', envisaged a confederation, not partition.[40] This was in keeping with his compulsions, which he had confided in the Mission on 16 April and with the basic approach of this astute negotiator. 'If you start by asking for sixteen annas in a rupee, there is room for bargaining', Jinnah had said at a press conference in New Delhi on 13 September 1942.[41] There would be a 'Constitution of the Union' (Para 10) with the powers in respect of foreign affairs, defence and 'communications necessary for defence' (Para 1).

If the advocate of partition himself offered a confederation, he had brought the federation into the realm of the possible. The Congress' proposals, also of 12 May 1946 and its note on the League's offer, made little effort to meet the League even half way.[42]

The Congress' note provided provocatively for power to the union 'to take remedial action in cases of breakdown of the Constitution and in grave public emergencies'. It envisaged dissenting provinces keeping out of the group initially rather than opting out later.[43] Its comment on 'a reconsideration of the terms of the Constitution' proposed by the Mission on 8 May went far. 'Though it is implied, we would avoid reference to secession as we do not wish to encourage secession'.[44] As a matter of fact, 'reconsideration of the terms of the Constitution' do not necessarily imply secession which is so drastic a step as to require explicit mention. Reconsideration of 'the terms' mean just that, a review of the terms, not a rejection of the polity itself.

The Cabinet Mission's Plan, published on 16 May 1946, moved beyond its suggestions of 27 April or 8 May to meet the Congress' concerns. It provided for a union confined to defence, foreign affairs and communications. As a sop to the League, there were to be three groups of provinces: Group B of Punjab, NWFP, Baluchistan and Sind; Group C of Bengal and Assam; and Group A of the rest. Provinces could secede from a group *but not from the Union.* There was no way in which Bengal could have fettered Assam's choice. Group C had a total of 70 seats, 36 Muslims, 34 general. The League had won only 35 seats. It would have had to provide a chairperson to run the group, reducing its strength to 34. Moreover, in the entire constituent assembly, the Congress had 201 members against the League's 78. The Congress contended that the provinces had the right, at the outset, not to go into the section that was to frame the group's constitution, though the plan gave them the right to opt out only after the first general election. The language used for the reviews differed significantly.

Para 15(6) provided for a 'reconsideration of the terms of the Constitution and the Groups'. But Para 19(viii) enabled 'any province to elect to come out of any group in which it has been placed', by a vote of its legislature 'after the first general election under the new Constitution'. In contrast, no such liberty was allowed 'to come out' of the union.

An initial draft was sent to the governors for their opinion. Frederick Burrows of Bengal was a member of the Labour Party and president of the National Union of Railwaymen. He liked to tell visitors that while his predecessors enjoyed hunting and shooting, he relished shunting and hooting. The draft read, 'Once the Provincial and group constitutions have been settled by the group Constituent Assemblies *and their content is known to it*, it will be open for any Province *to change its group* by a decision of its Provincial Legislative assembly'.[45] This was a reference to *change* of its group, not to the province's opting out.

Burrows' suggestion on 9 May, on this point (Para 2 [b]) also related to 'the power to contract out of original group into another', and suggested deletion of those lines.[46] The Mission also regarded it as such when it met the next day. It decided thus, 'Para 19(vi) amended. It was agreed that the decision to opt out of a Group must be taken by the new Legislature under the new Constitution and that it was not necessary to specify that a Province could opt into another Group. This should be left for negotiation'.[47]

The liberty to opt out was retained. It was surely more appropriate that the right should be exercised by an assembly elected after the constitution was finalized, than one elected on a restricted franchise in 1946 in an altogether different situation. The League's 35 members in the C Group of 70 could hardly have rigged the franchise to debar Assam from exercising its right to opt out. It would have been a breach of faith. The League's 78 members faced in the Union Constituent Assembly a Congress monolith of 201.

Conventional wisdom on both sides of the Radcliffe Line ordains the scheme to be unworkable. Pakistanis disclaim its federal bit and Indians, its 'loose Union' and the groups. Pakistani reaction is mixed, however, with bitter reproach at the Congress' double talk. Was Pakistan, then, an achievement or a reluctant necessity? Indians are as disingenuous. There was nothing to prevent Group A (the India of today, mainly) from establishing a centralized polity as the Constitution of India does. The leaders of Group A would have belonged to the same political party which ran the union. Any minister or civil servant can walk the distance between the north and south blocks on the Raisina Hill in New Delhi in two minutes; a clerk probably in five, the *chaprasi* in fifteen. The union would have had army cantonments in Karachi, Rawalpindi, Peshawar, Quetta, and Calcutta. Unions notoriously amass power, over time.

In Groups B and C, educationally advanced and economically prosperous powerful Hindu and Sikh communities would have faced the majority with confidence. In Group B, the League had 21 members in a House of 35 (Sir Muzaffar Ali Qizilbash, a non-Leaguer who won a seat thanks to the Unionists). There was no way that separate electorates could have been continued. Jinnah abandoned them in 1934 in a pact with Rajendra Prasad. The League's unity would have frayed, as Jinnah always feared. Once a union was accepted, provincial claims would have come to the fore. In the new set up, Muslim candidates would have vied with one another to solicit non-Muslim votes. The subcontinent would have been spared the carnage, massive transfers of population, bitter strife, the wars, and Great Power intrigues, which have played havoc with the lives of the people. The forces of bigotry and violence, which arose in both countries, would have been denied the breeding ground of hate and official patronage.

It was an enormous concession which Jinnah made, a big climb-down for a haughty man. The Muslim League Council, which accepted the Plan on 6 June, met *in camera* uniquely. Jinnah was not wrong when on 9 May he impressed on the Mission and the viceroy the measure of the concession. The minutes record, 'Mr Jinnah had emphasized that he was trying to be reasonable but the acceptance of a Union of any kind was a great concession from his point of view and that he was already the subject of criticism from his supporters for having yielded on this'. Also, 'he agreed that Assam was not a Muslim-majority Province'. He needed its initial presence in the group as a sop, clearly. With so candid an admission, he would not have tried to rig its option to quit; indeed he could not have even if he had tried. Jinnah has received less than his due for his statesmanship, which was of as high an order as was his partnership with Tilak thirty years earlier in forging the Lucknow Pact of 1916.[48]

Many would be surprised when reminded that Prof. D.R. Gadgil, one of the most respected figures in India, accorded his approval on 30 September 1946. This and much else was recorded by a highly literate Congressman in Bombay, P.R. Lele, in an excellent essay entitled 'Constituent Assembly'.[49] It provides a fund of information. Referring to Azad's remark, on 6 May, 'we are not aware of any such arrangement in any country', Lele proceeded to list a host of constitutional provisions unique to India and wrote:

> Politics is a human affair. If you want a compromise, you have to pay a price. Ever since the Lahore Session held in 1940 the Muslim League has demanded Pakistan. Is it possible that the League would give up that demand except for some substantial return? The League Resolution of June 6, 1946, has mentioned the compulsory grouping of Muslim Provinces in two sections viz. B and C as the quid pro quo for accepting a Union. In assessing the outcome of the three

months' negotiations, Maulana Abul Kalam Azad has enumerated it as a triumph that—'All schemes of partition of India have been rejected once and for all.' Could a triumph like this come without a price, without some sacrifice? Lord Pethick-Lawrence and Sir Stafford Cripps would appear to have specified the price and offered the same.

The Working Committee of the Congress appointed an Experts Committee to prepare the raw material for the Constituent Assembly. One of the members of that Committee is Dr D.R. Gadgil. He spoke on the Constituent Assembly on September 26 and said: 'The proposals of the Cabinet Delegation provided a compromise between the position taken by the Congress and that of the Muslim League. Any position which questioned the fundamentals of that compromise would make the working of the Constituent Assembly impossible.'

The three-tier constitution involving the compulsory grouping of Provinces is not the brainwave of the Cabinet Mission. It has been suggested by Prof. Coupland in his Report on the constitutional problem in India published in March 1944. With reference to this problem Dr Gadgil avers a group government of some type or another is an absolute necessity in the future Indian Government.[50]

The Cripps offer of 1942 permitted the provinces to secede from the union. The Mission's Plan of 1946 barred it. Vallabhbhai Patel's reaction was no different from his *bete noire* Azad's reaction. He wrote to K.M. Munshi, jubilantly on 17 May, immediately after the Plan was published. Munshi's comments on the letter are apt:

Sardar wrote to me displaying vivid emotion of pleasure which, with him, was very rare: 'Thank God, we have successfully avoided a catastrophe which threatened our country. Since many years for the first time an authoritative pronouncement in clear terms has been made against the possibility of Pakistan in any shape or form. The continuous threat of obstruction to progress and the power of veto from obstructionist elements has been once for all removed. The withdrawal of the British Power in India is no more in doubt and we are now free to shape our own destiny without hindrance or interference from outside.

Munshi realized what that implied, 'It was evident that Sardar was prepared to pay a price for averting the partition of the country, and was willing to share power with the Muslim League'.[51] This was the heart of the plan—sharing power.

However, nine days later, on 26 May, Sardar Patel wrote to Gopichand Bhargava:

> The Cabinet Delegation has made certain recommendations for the consideration of the Constituent Assembly. It is open to the Constituent Assembly to accept or reject them. These proposals may not be acceptable to the Sikhs; and, therefore, it is for them to approach the Cabinet Delegation for necessary changes. There is only one Constituent Assembly for the whole of India. The idea of Pakistan has been reservedly condemned and rejected. The group assemblies are not constituent assemblies in any shape or form. The provinces are free to do whatever they like; and, therefore, there is no reason to be afraid of.

On 15 June, Sardar Patel wrote to Thakurdas Bhargava, 'We do not accept the groupings as proposed in the Scheme *nor do we accept the interpretation of the Cabinet Mission* in this respect'.[52]

Patel's fundamentally false stand in these proceedings emerges very clearly from his contradictory letter to Dr B.R. Ambedkar on 1 September 1946. The Scheduled Castes leader had written to him on 12 August, enclosing a memorandum of demands on behalf of the Scheduled Castes. To fob him off, Patel cited the correct interpretation of the plan, as indicated by the Mission itself and pleaded his helplessness:

> Many points in the memorandum depend upon the nature of the constitution and the distribution of powers, functions and finances between the various sections, for instance, the Provincial

constitutions will be settled by the sections and the Congress will not be in a majority in Sections B and C. The formation of Group governments may restrict the scope of the Union Centre to very narrow limits and it may have no power to interfere with the provincial and Group governments with reference to the Scheduled Castes.[53]

Sardar Patel has received much acclaim for realism; not unjustly. He has received less criticism than is deserved for allowing, on matters that touched him deeply, emotions to get the better of his pragmatic realism, for example in 1942.

As he joined Gandhi and Nehru in a demolition squad to reduce the Mission Plan to rubble, did it not occur to him or to them that its alternative was partition. It is unthinkable that news of the hectic deliberations in British circles in London and New Delhi did not reach their ears. V.P. Menon, in particular, could not have failed to alert them of the danger. The responsibility and the guilt were collective.

A myth grew up that after his election as president of the Congress, in succession to Maulana Azad, Nehru delivered an outburst which killed the plan. What he declared at his press conference on 10 July 1946, achieved that result. Earlier on 7 July he had told the All-India Congress Committee (AICC), 'We are not bound by a single thing except that we have decided to go into the Constituent Assembly'. Three days later, he rejected the provisions for grouping. Nehru said:

> The big probability is that from any approach to the question, there will be no grouping. Obviously, Section A will decide against grouping. Speaking in betting language, there was 4 to 1 chance of the North-West Frontier Province deciding against grouping. Then Group B collapses. It is highly likely that Assam will decide against grouping with Bengal, although I would not like to say what the initial decision may be, since it is evenly balanced. But I can say with every assurance and conviction that there is going to be finally no grouping there, because Assam will not tolerate it under any

circumstances whatever. Thus you see this grouping business approached from any point of view does not get on at all.[54]

In short, the Congress would seize the Constituent Assembly, set up under the plan, not as an agreed mechanism as envisaged by the plan itself, but to impose its own diktat while professing to accept it in its 'entirety' or 'as a whole', i.e. not every part of it.

However, such an assertion of the right to interpret, and impliedly to ignore unacceptable parts of the plan, was made by Gandhi at the very outset. He maintained his stand even after the British government declared on 6 December 1946 that the Congress' interpretation was wrong. Gandhi declared his stand at the very outset and maintained it consistently until the very last. As in 1942, he led from the front.

Volumes 84, 85, and 86, the *Collected Works of Mahatma Gandhi*,[55] provide a full record of his statements on the Mission's Plan. On 17 May 1946, the very day after it was published, Gandhi pointedly said, 'it was not an award'. The Mission had 'recommended to the country what in their opinion was worthy of acceptance by the Constituent Assembly'. The assembly was set up as part of the plan with all its provisions regarding the groups. Gandhi delinked it from the plan so the assembly could freely enforce the wishes of the Congress majority untrammelled by the plan. 'The provinces were free to reject the very idea of grouping'. He proceeded to laud the plan, but 'subject to the above interpretation, which he held was right.[56] This set the policy for the Congress to follow. It was this policy which wrecked the plan. Nehru's famous outburst came nearly two months later, on 10 July 1946.

Gandhi's strong intellectual powers were fully reflected in a detailed and lucid 'Analysis' he wrote in *Harijan* on 20 May. It was published five days later after an advance copy was sent to Cripps. Gandhi made no secret of the fact that the sole attraction of the plan was the Constituent Assembly. The Mission's Plan, which created it, could be ignored. In truth, the plan was neither a judicial verdict nor an arbitral award. Like the Cripps offer of 1942, it was a mediator's recommendation to the contesting parties. If accepted, it became an agreement between the two. The mediator had every right to clarify what was meant by the recommendations, especially since the British were to implement them by legislation. It was open to either side to reject his recommendation or clarification. What neither side could do, however, was to profess to accept it but subject to its own unilateral interpretation. The accord collapses then. If the Congress with its majority in the constituent assembly asserted such a right, it could override the provisions regulating its procedure to ensure protection against the majority diktat. Moreover, if it challenged the only concession to the Muslim League—the grouping of provinces.

Gandhi wrote, 'It is the best document the British government could have produced in the circumstances', but only to add:

> It is an appeal and an advice. It has no compulsion in it. Thus the Provincial Assemblies may or may not elect the delegates. The delegates, having been elected, may or may not join the Constituent Assembly. The Assembly having met, may lay down a procedure different from the one laid down in the Statement.... Are the Sikhs, for whom the Punjab is the only home in India, to consider themselves against their will, as part of the section which takes in Sindh, Baluchistan and the Frontier province? Or is the Frontier Province also against its will to belong to the Punjab, called 'B' in the Statement, or Assam to 'C' although it is a predominantly non-Muslim province? In my opinion, the voluntary character of the Statement demands that the liberty of the individual unit should be unimpaired. Any member of the sections is free to join it. The freedom to opt out is an additional safeguard.... It presupposes that the Chairman of the Constituent Assembly at its first meeting will ask the delegates of the Provinces whether they would accept the group principle and if they do, whether they (would) accept the assignment given to their Province. This freedom inherent in every

province and that given by 15(5) will remain intact. There appears to me to be no other way of avoiding the apparent conflict between the two paragraphs as also charge of compulsion which would immediately alter the noble character of the document.[57]

The Congress President Maulana Azad wrote to the Mission on 20 May criticizing the plan and asserting that the constituent assembly would 'be a sovereign body', which could 'vary in any way it likes the recommendations and procedures suggested by the Cabinet Delegation...its final decisions will automatically take effect'.[58] Pethick-Lawrence pointed out the obvious in his reply on 22 May, 'The scheme stands as a whole and can only succeed if it is accepted and worked in a spirit of compromise and cooperation. You are aware of the reasons for the grouping of the Provinces, and this is an essential feature of the scheme *which can only be modified by agreement between the parties*'.[59]

On 24 May, the Congress Working Committee passed a resolution on the same lines as its president's letter. 'The Assembly would be sovereign...in their view it would be open to the Constituent Assembly itself at any stage to make changes and variations, with the proviso that in regard to certain major communal matters a majority decision of both the major communities will be necessary'—impliedly not in regard to changes in the Mission's Plan itself.[60]

Meanwhile on 22 May, Jinnah issued a long statement which the leading dailies published in full. Few dailies care for the text today. Jinnah concluded an elaborate survey of the proceedings with the observation that the decision lay with the League's Working Committee. But one remark deserves note, 'Our proposal that Pakistan Group should have a right to secede from the Union after an initial period of ten years, although the Congress had no serious objection to it, has been *omitted* and now we are only *limited* to *a reconsideration of terms of the Union Constitution* after an initial period of ten years'. Jinnah was too good a lawyer not to appreciate the difference between the two formulations. He accepted the plan with full knowledge of the fact that it did not provide for secession from the union.⁶¹

The Cabinet Mission repeatedly clarified the true position. On 17 May, the secretary of state, in reply to the question regarding the choice of a particular province to opt out of a particular group, replied:

> The Provinces automatically came into the sections 'A', 'B' and 'C' which are set out in the Statement. Initially they are in a particular section to which they are allocated in the Statement and that particular section will decide whether a group shall be formed and what should be the constitution. The right to opt out of the group formed by that section arises after the constitution has been framed and the first election to the Legislature has taken place. It does not arise before that.⁶²

On 25 May, the Mission issued an authoritative statement which said:

> The interpretation put by the Congress resolution on paragraph 15 of the statement, to the effect that the Provinces can in the first instance make the choice whether or not to belong to the Section in which they are placed, does not accord with the Delegation's intentions. The reasons for the grouping of the Provinces are well known and this is an essential feature of the scheme and can only be modified by agreement between the parties. The right to opt out of the groups after the constitution making has been completed will be exercised by the people themselves, since at the first election under the new provincial Constitutions this question of opting out will obviously be a major issue and all those entitled to vote under the new franchise will be able to take their share in a truly democratic decision.⁶³

There was another reason for this, which Cripps mentioned in his press conference on 16 May. The existing provincial assemblies were elected on a limited suffrage, not adult suffrage, and 'are not truly representative of the whole population because of the effect of the communal award, with its weightages'. Hence the opting out after fresh elections.[64]

Since both Gandhi and Nehru made pointed references to the North-Western Province, more than once, it is important to note that the Congress government, headed by Dr Khan Saheb, won a majority of seats in the 1946 general elections but on a minority vote. What legitimacy could the assembly or government have commanded if it had decided to keep away from the sections that were to frame the group and provincial constitutions, instead of waiting till the next general elections on the basis of adult suffrage? Besides, the people would have had the advantage of judging the new constitution for themselves instead of the Khan Saheb ministry and its superiors in Delhi, usurping their right to decide.

Prof. Sho Kuwajima of the Osaka University of Foreign Affairs, wrote a definitive work *Muslims, Nationalism and the Partition: 1946 Provincial Elections in India*. He pointed out that 'the elections of 1946 were held under a very limited franchise system. Most women, and people of lower classes, were deprived of their right to vote'.[65]

While the Congress won 19 seats in Muslim constituencies, the Muslim League won 17. The Congress had a total of 30 seats plus 2 of the Jamiat-ul-Ulema and 1 of the Akalis. But the Congress secured 139,975 votes, a percentage of 39.24; the League secured 147,880, a percentage of 41.46. Kuwajima records:

> The North-West Frontier Province was the only province where the Congress could win the majority of the Muslim seats. It got the support of 22.2 per cent of the urban voters and 41.1 per cent of the rural voters in the Muslim constituencies, while the League got the support of 43.6 per cent of the urban voters and 40.7 per cent of the rural voters in the same constituencies including the dual

constituency of Peshawar city. The Muslim seats were predominantly rural, and the Congress won 18 out of the total of 33 rural seats, while the League won 13 seats. At this stage, the League in the NWFP still remained 'the party of the towns and of the non-Pathan Hazara districts'. But, it is also to be noted that the League got a slightly larger percentage of the total Muslim votes.[66]

Such an assembly could legislate. It could not settle the future of the province. Only a new poll could.

Since the talks had collapsed on 16 June, the Mission and the viceroy issued a statement on an interim 'Coalition Government' of the two major parties.[67]

On 21 June, George Abell, private secretary to the viceroy, sent to Azad, in strict confidence, a copy of the instructions to governors about the elections to the constituent assembly for transmission to the speakers of the provincial assemblies. The document had been adopted as early as on 23 May by the Cabinet Mission and the viceroy, and was communicated to the governors the next day. Cripps was absent since he was unwell. Para 2 provided that any person was eligible for election provided that he was duly proposed and seconded by another member of the constituent assembly 'and (b) that the nomination is accompanied by declaration that he has not been proposed for candidature to represent any other province *and* that he is willing to serve as representative of the province *for the purpose of paragraph 19 of the Statement*'.[68]

Para 19(iv) and (v) bound members to 'divide up into the three sections' which would then proceed to settle the provincial and group constitutions with liberty to every province 'to elect to come out of any Group in which it has been placed' after the next general elections. Bengal used a vaguer formulation, however ('for the purpose of framing a new Constitution of India'). The pledge left no room for any ambiguity or fudge. A decision could no longer be postponed.

Notes

1. Nirad C. Chaudhuri, *The Continent of Circe*, Jaico Publishing, India, 1965, p. 291.
2. Syed Sharifuddin Pirzada (ed.), 'Presidential address to the 21st Session of the Muslim League at Allahabad on 29 December, 1930', *Foundations of Pakistan*, Vol. II, National Publishing House Ltd., Karachi, pp. 159–60.
3. Sheikh Muhammad Ashraf, *Letters of Iqbal to Jinnah*, n.p., Lahore, 1942, p. 24.
4. Sikandar Hayat Khan and Syed Abdul Latif, 'Confederacy of India' by A. Punjabi, a nom de plume of Mian Kafayat Ali. Vide Uma Kaura, *Muslims and Indian Nationalism*, n.p., Manohar, 1977, pp. 151–62, for a brisk survey; and Pirzada (ed.), *Evolution of Pakistan*, Royal Book Company, Karachi, 1995, for extracts from the texts.
5. A.V. Dicey, *An Introduction to the Study of the Law of the Constitution*, Macmillan, London, 1967, p. 141.
6. ToP, Vol. XII, Appendix I, HMSO, London, p. 790.
7. R.J. Moore, *Churchill, Cripps and India: 1939–1945*, Clarendon Press, Oxford, 1979, pp. 11–13.
8. Peter Clarke, *The Cripps Version: The Life of Sir Stafford Cripps*, The Penguin Press, Allen Lane, 2002, p. 464.
9. Pattabhi Sitaramayya, *The History of the Indian National Congress*, Vol. II, Appendix I, Padma Publications Ltd., Bombay, 1947, p. ii.
10. ToP, Vol. VI, p. 796.
11. Ibid., p. 799.
12. Z.H. Zaidi (ed.), *Jinnah Papers*, First Series, Vol. I, Part II, National Archives of Pakistan, 1993, p. 561.
13. ToP, Vol. VI, p. 112.
14. Ibid., p. 45
15. Ibid., pp. 246–7.
16. Ibid., p. 194.
17. Ibid., p. 195.
18. Ibid., p. 732.
19. Ibid., p. 881.
20. Zaidi, p. 575.
21. Ibid., p. 774.
22. Peter John Brobst, *The Future of The Great Game: Sir Olaf Caroe, India's Independence, and the Defence of Asia*, University of Akron Press, Akron, 2005.
23. Ibid., p. 767.
24. Sir Reginald Coupland, *India: A Re-Statement*, Oxford University Press, n.p., 1975, pp. 272–3.
25. Clarke, p. 464.

26. Zaidi, pp. 520–1.
27. Ibid., pp. 504–10.
28. Ibid., p. 542.
29. Ibid., pp. 567–8; ToP, Vol. VI, pp. 912–13.
30. ToP, Vol. VII, pp. 220–1.
31. Ibid., pp. 260–1.
32. Ibid., p. 303–10.
33. Ibid., pp. 281–5.
34. Ibid., p. 342.
35. *Papers Relating to the Cabinet Mission to India, 1946*, Manager of Publication, Delhi, 1946, p. 9. Henceforth referred to as Cabinet Mission Papers.
36. Ibid., p. 13.
37. Ibid., p. 15.
38. ToP, Vol. VII, p. 465.
39. Ibid., p. 475, italics by Wyatt.
40. Ibid., p. 516.
41. Jamiluddin Ahmad (ed.), *Speeches and Writings of Mr Jinnah*, Vol. I, Shaikh Muhammad Ashraf, Lahore, 1960, p. 415.
42. Vide appendix for the text of these historic but neglected documents.
43. Cabinet Mission Papers, p. 21.
44. Ibid., p. 23.
45. ToP, Vol. VII, p. 424.
46. Ibid., p. 482.
47. Ibid., p. 496.
48. Ibid., Vol. VII, p. 480 for the minutes.
49. P.R. Lele, 'Constituent Assembly', Phoenix Publications, Bombay, 1946.
50. Ibid., pp. 62–3.
51. Munshi, p. 103.
52. G.M. Nandurkar (ed.), *Sardar's Letters Mostly Unknown*, Vol. IV, Sardar Vallabhbhai Patel Smarak Bhavan, Ahmedabad, 1977, pp. 201 and 206 respectively.
53. Sumit Sarkar (ed.), *Towards Freedom Documents on the Movement for Independence in India 1946*, ICHR, Oxford University Press, New Delhi, 2007, p. 908.
54. *Indian Annual Register*, Vol. II, 1946, pp. 145–7.
55. *Collected Works of Mahatma Gandhi*, New Delhi, Publications Division, Government of India.
56. Ibid., Vol. 84, p. 162.
57. Ibid., Vol. 84, pp. 169–72.
58. Cabinet Mission Papers, pp. 33–4.
59. Ibid., p. 34.
60. Ibid., pp. 29–30.
61. Ibid., p. 287.

62. *The Statesman*, 18 May. *Political History of Assam*, Vol. III, Publication Board Assam, Guwahati, 1999, p. 346.
63. Cabinet Mission Papers, p. 24.
64. ToP, Vol. VII, p. 597.
65. Sho Kuwajima, *Muslims, Nationalism and the Partition: 1946 Provincial Elections in India*, Manohar, New Delhi, 1998, p. 212.
66. Ibid., p. 189.
67. Cabinet Mission Papers, pp. 43–4, for the text. The controversy that ensued on it is advisedly not discussed here. The focus is on the long-term solution.
68. ToP, Vol. VII, p. 1027, fn. 1; Sitaramayya, Vol. II, Appendix IV, pp. ccvi–vii for the text.

5

The Gandhi–Cripps Pact

It was Gandhi who resolved the Congress' dilemma by a decisive intervention as soon as he learnt of the undertaking. An historic understanding he reached with Stafford Cripps enabled the Congress to accept the Mission's Plan with its reservations intact. Sudhir Ghosh, a Tata employee, was the go-between. Gandhi and Patel liked him; Cripps used him; Nehru disliked and distrusted him. Prof. Clarke, Cripps' biographer, described him accurately—'oleaginous'.[1]

From the very beginning, Cripps was set on winning Gandhi's confidence. His diary entry of May 14 explains why he behaved as he did:

> I think that more than ever he [Gandhi] holds the key to the situation. It is very doubtful whether Congress will very acquiesce in our statement and its suggestions. Gandhi alone can persuade them to do it and I believe we could have got his support if we had trusted him and consulted him first. I see the dangers but I would have taken the risk… The really critical situation has been reached because if Congress turns it down and refuses to come into an interim Government, it will be impossible for us to carry on in the existing state of tension without wholesale suppression which will in effect mean war. My own view is that we must at all costs come to an accommodation with Congress. We can get through I believe without the League if we have Congress with us but not without Congress even if we have the League.[2]

Ghosh's memoirs tell part of the story;[3] while Pyarelal's book records more truthfully, albeit with some inaccuracies.[4] One must consult also 'The Transfer of Power' documents and *Wavell: The Viceroy's Journal* edited by Penderel Moon.

On 22 June, Ghosh advised Cripps and Pethick–Lawrence to talk to Sardar Patel. It was decided that the next day, Sunday morning, Ghosh would take Pethick-Lawrence from a Quaker prayer meeting at the YMCA in New Delhi to meet Patel:

> The search for Vallabhbhai Patel next morning, Sunday 23rd June, was quite an experience.... After the prayer meeting the Secretary of State asked me to get into his car and we asked the chauffeur to drive down to Mr Birla's house in Albuquerque Road [now called Tees January Marg]...where Vallabhbhai Patel was staying. But the Secretary of State did not wish to go into Mr Birla's house. So he asked the chauffeur to stop the car under the jamun trees outside on the road and I walked in to look for Vallabhbhai; it was almost like two schoolboys on an escapade! But Vallabhbhai was not to be found there; I was told that Vallabhbhai had gone to see Gandhiji at the Bhangi Colony on Reading Road. So the Secretary of State and I proceeded towards Reading Road. As we approached the Roman Catholic Cathedral on Irwin Road we saw Vallabhbhai and his daughter, Maniben, coming from the opposite side in another car. I raised my hand and the car stopped. I walked over to Vallabhbhai and told him that the Secretary of State was anxious to talk with him; would he join us in the other car. We had a few words and decided that we had better go to No. 2 Willingdon Crescent where the Secretary of State was staying, instead of settling the future of India standing there on the road in front of the Gole Post Office. The half an hour's discussion that followed at 2 Willingdon Crescent, made history.
>
> Sir Stafford Cripps and Mr A.V. Alexander joined us.... The Secretary of State said that he had seen reports in the newspapers that the Congress Working Committee had decided to reject the Viceroy's proposals announced on 16th June, for the formation of an Interim Government, and it had already indicated its dissatisfaction with the long-term proposal for constitution-making, as announced by the Mission on 16th May, although the Mission had not yet received the formal letter of rejection. After the Congress Party had

sent in their rejection of both, which seemed imminent, the position officially would be that the Muslim League had accepted the long-term plan of constitution-making, and was only too willing to come into the Interim Government while Congress had rejected both and, logically, it would become necessary for the Viceroy to ask the Muslim League to form a Government because the announcement on this subject: 'In the event of the two major parties or either of them proving unwilling to join in the setting up of a Coalition Government, it is the intention of the Viceroy to proceed with the formation of an Interim Government which will be as representative as possible of those willing to accept the statement of May 16' (Para 8).

At this stage, Ghosh intervened *inter alia* to say:

> Surely his misgivings with regard to paragraph 19 of the 16th May statement dealing with the grouping of provinces could be removed by the Mission.... Vallabhbhai liked this argument and pointed out to the Mission that if they could scrap the whole discussion that had taken place with all the parties on the subject of forming an Interim Government, and if the Mission would give Gandhiji satisfactory assurances about the two points I had raised, then he thought he could persuade the Congress Working Committee to accept the long-term proposals for constitution-making and the matter of forming an Interim Government could be settled on a clean slate at a later date. This threw a new light on the atmosphere of darkness.

> Sir Stafford Cripps quickly drafted a sentence on a piece of paper and showed it to Sardar: Read 'for the purposes of the declaration of May 16' in place of 'for the purposes of para 19 of the declaration of May 16'.[5]

Gandhi had been much exercised over the matter. To the Working Committee, he said, 'if the worst came to the worst, it [the constituent assembly] could be turned into a rebel body'. Just then Rajendra Prasad received a wire from Assam complaining of the proposed undertaking whereupon Gandhi exclaimed 'Even the Constituent Assembly plan now stinks I am afraid, we cannot touch it'.[6]

Cripps met Gandhi the same evening. Pyarelal records:

> In the morning today when Sudhir came to see Bapu he said that last night he had seen Cripps. The latter had told him that they had decided that if Congress accepted the long-term plan and rejected the short-term proposal, all that the Cabinet Mission had done under the 16th June declaration for the formation of an Interim Government would be scrapped and an attempt made de novo for the same. They invited Bapu and Sardar to meet them. They seem to have made up their minds to clear up the mess created by the assurances given to Jinnah by Lord Wavell. At seven a.m. Bapu accompanied by Sardar and Sudhir went to meet the Cabinet Mission.[7]

The next day, 24 June, was a hectic one. At 7 a.m. Gandhi, Patel, and Ghosh met the Mission minus the viceroy. Since it was Gandhi's day of silence, he scribbled on short slips:

> 'I understood from Sudhir something quite different. I understood that you proposed to scrap the whole plan of Interim Government as it has gone on up to now and consider the situation de novo....'

> Cripps explained at some length that what they meant was that if Congress accepted the long-term plan of Constitution-making, even if it was unable to accept the short-term plan of an Interim Coalition Government, then what would remain was the acceptance by both Congress and the Muslim League, of the Constitution-making plan and, in terms of the commitment made by them, a Government representative of both would be got together—at a suitable date; if Congress rejected both then Mr Jinnah could ask them to go ahead with a Government representing those who had accepted the 16th May [Constitution-making]) proposal, i.e. only the Muslim League.

After listening to this explanation, Gandhi wrote down on his bits of paper:

> 'I was quite clear up to yesterday afternoon that the Congress should work the Constituent Assembly to the best of its ability. But the rules I read yesterday have revolutionized my mentality. There is a serious

flaw. I accuse nobody. But a flaw is a flaw. The three parties must not work with three minds and hope for success.'

The flaw that Gandhiji was talking about was the flaw in the instructions issued by the Government to the Speakers of the State Legislatures that candidates for election to the Constituent Assembly were to sign a pledge that they were to frame a Constitution in terms of Paragraph 19 of the 16th May State paper (which provided for the grouping of provinces). The meaning of the State paper was that they were free to form groups of provinces but they were not necessarily meeting for that specific purpose.

Sir Stafford Cripps explained that it was the Mission's intention to rectify the 'flaw' as Gandhiji called it. Thereafter Gandhiji wrote: 'Then you should not isolate a particular section from the whole. Why not say 'under the state paper as a whole?'

Sir Stafford Cripps said that that clarification could certainly be made. Gandhiji scribbled his last remark: 'However, I would gladly discuss this question also with you in the evening. I am sorry to cause you all this trouble. I only hope that you perceive my object in all this effort.'

It seemed clear that Gandhiji had relented. Gandhiji and the British Ministers along with the Viceroy arranged to get together again in the evening at the Viceroy's House in a formal meeting of the Mission.[8]

At 10 a.m., the cabinet ministers recounted to the viceroy their talks with Gandhi and Patel. It was agreed to see Gandhi 'in a full meeting at 8 p.m. that evening and have a note taken'.[9]

In the afternoon at the Congress Working Committee, Gandhi demanded statutory backing for the constituent assembly.[10] It received statutory sanction only with the Indian Independence Act, 1947. At 8 p.m., Gandhi and Patel met the Mission and the viceroy.[11] Gandhi raised the issue of the instructions to the speaker and produced the telegram from Assam. Cripps and

Pethick-Lawrence cited the anaemic Bengal declaration. Neither faced the issue which Gandhi had squarely raised—members would not be bound by Para 19 of the Mission's Plan.

At 10 p.m., Cripps received a letter from Gandhi which warned, 'The instructions to the Governors, innocuous as they have proved to be, have opened up a dreadful vista. I, therefore, propose to advise the Working Committee not to accept the long-term proposition without its being connected with the Interim Government'.[12]

Meanwhile, the Associated Press of India carried a news report, obviously officially inspired, to suggest that the Bengal formulation held the field.[13]

The next morning on 25 June, the Congress Working Committee met and decided to accept the Mission Plan. Its resolution mentioned its reservations and stated, 'They felt, however, taking the proposals as a whole, that there was sufficient scope for enlarging and strengthening the Central authority and for fully ensuring the right of a Province to act according to its own choice in regard to grouping....'[14]

The entry of 25 June in Wavell's *Journal* summed up his feelings:

> The worst day yet I think. Congress has accepted the statement of May 16 though with reservations on its interpretation. They did not intend to do so, having always said that they would not accept the long-term policy unless they accepted the short-term one—Interim Government. Now Cripps having assured me categorically that Congress would never accept the statement of May 16 instigated the Congress to do so by pointing out what tactical advantage they will gain as regards the Interim Government. So did the Secretary of State. When I tackled him on this, he defended it on the ground that to get the Congress into the Constituent Assembly was such a gain

that he considered it justified. It has left me in an impossible position *vis-à-vis* Jinnah.[15]

Wavell wrote a 'Note for the Cabinet Mission', setting out the facts. The papers had reported the Mission's concessions. Either there was a reversal of policy or 'the assurance given to Mr Gandhi is not entirely an honest one'. 'I take it that this [the Congress' proposed acceptance] cannot regarded as an acceptance of the Statement of May the 16th and that the Delegation will say so clearly'.[16] The Mission and the viceroy met twice that day to consider the Congress' reply. The ministers argued that they knew where they stood. Pethick-Lawrence said, 'If we had pressed the matter it might have kept the Congress from agreeing to the long-term plan, and that he could not feel that that would have been a better outcome. The Viceroy said that he thought an acceptance by the Congress which they meant to break was worse than a refusal'.[17]

They met again at 3.30 p.m., this time to consider how to face Jinnah. Their meeting with him two hours later was a stormy one. When Jinnah alleged that they had resiled from the statement of 16 June on the interim government because the Congress had rejected it, Pethick-Lawrence, stung to the quick, retorted that they 'were not asking for Mr Jinnah's opinion of their conduct'.[18] A.V. Alexander was later sent to offer apologies to Jinnah.

Why did the Mission behave as it did? Pethick-Lawrence's explanation in a 'Note for Attlee', submitted on 13 September, as the Congress belied hopes of conciliation, expressed the truth. 'It is only fair to the Viceroy to admit that the difficulties in which we now find ourselves result from the failure to get clear satisfaction on this point (grouping). But our judgment at the time was that to press it to a final conclusion would result in the Congress not accepting the Statement of 16 May'.[19]

Colin Reid of *The Daily Telegraph* told Wavell on 3 August that 'Jinnah knew all about Cripps interviews with Gandhi and Patel and the way in which the Congress acceptance of the May 16 Statement was obtained'.[20]

Cripps' biographer has a feeble explanation:

> Cripps knew perfectly well that Congress's acceptance of his constitutional scheme (the Statement of 16 May) had been hedged about with potentially disabling reservations, notably over grouping of provinces. Gandhi's susceptibilities had been appeased on this point. Cripps and Pethick-Lawrence—and Alexander too, it should not be forgotten—had refrained from exposing this ambiguity, treating it as a practical problem to be resolved by the increasing momentum of an actual transfer of power.[21]

The honest course for both the Cabinet Mission and the Congress was to face the fact that the Congress did not, and would not, accept the Mission's Plan. That became all too evident seven months later. In June 1946, Plan B could have been revived and the partition planned with greater efficiency than it was between 3 June and 15 August 1947. Much bloodshed would have been spared, but that required facing the truth honestly, which was apparent since at least 1945—the Congress preferred partition to sharing power with the Muslims League in a united India. It could not risk the odium of rejecting openly a federation Jinnah had accepted. Hence its double-talk.

The irony was that on 23 June, Cripps wrote a careful note on the 'Legal Aspects of the Grouping Question'. It read thus:

> It is to be noted—(i) that these are recommendations only; (ii) that 15 (5) only states that it is permissible for Provinces to form groups. It does not purport to lay down that they shall do so, nor how they shall set about so doing.
> 2. There is, however, a sanction for the above provisions in paragraph 19(vii). There it is stated that any resolution in the

Union Constituent Assembly varying the provisions of paragraph 15 shall require a special form of majority vote.
3. This means that if anyone desires to make it impossible for the provinces to form groups with executives and legislatures, he would have to obtain the support of a majority of both the major communities.
4. If therefore a resolution were to be proposed that the provinces do not meet in Sections A, B, and C as laid down in 19(i) this would (in my view) be a denial of the permission granted in paragraph 15(5) and it would therefore require a majority of each of the two major communities.
5. The actual setting-up of the Sections is prefaced by the terms of Section 17 of the document which states, 'We now indicate the constitution-making machinery which we propose should be brought into being forthwith'.
6. It is this proposal, which forms the substance of the Statement and an acceptance of the Statement must be taken to mean an acceptance of the proposals which follow Section 17. For the present purpose, these consist of paragraphs 19(i), (iii), (iv) and (v).
7. From these it is clear that the Provincial constitutions are to be settled in the Sections and that each Section is to decide 'whether any Group constitution shall be set up and if so with what provincial subjects the Group shall deal'.
8. There is therefore no other means of arriving at the Provincial constitutions than by the Sectional meetings and it is also clear that the option to set up groups recommended by paragraph 15 can only be exercised by these Sections.

Any other method of carrying out these essential steps in the constitution-making would be contrary to the provisions of the proposals.

Therefore on the proper interpretation of the document, paragraphs 19 (iv) and (v) are not (in my view) overridden by the provision of paragraph 15 (5).

The note was endorsed by the Mission and the viceroy as the 'Office Note on the Legal Aspects of the Grouping Question'.[22]

The very next day, 23 June, if not indeed the day on which he wrote the note, Cripps watered down the undertaking with full knowledge of Gandhi's intentions, which he did not conceal from Cripps or any one else, namely that the Cabinet Mission's Plan was not binding on the constituent assembly or the Congress which was in a majority there. That included the grouping provisions. This rendered the Congress' professed acceptance of planning a dishonest tactic. Gandhi felt 'a moral difficulty' in that 'by signing the declaration required by the electoral rules a member of the Constituent Assembly might be bound morally to accept the Delegation's interpretation'.[23] Surely the moral obligation would be as real, as binding if a party professed to accept the plan and enter the assembly it set up. Prof. R.J. Moore agrees with Wavell's censure. 'At this point Pethick-Lawrence and Cripps gave Gandhi what Wavell justly described as a "dishonest assurance" that delegates to the Constituent Assembly were not required to undertake to meet in the sections'.[24]

The Mission would not honestly admit failure. Gandhi and the Congress would not honestly reject a plan providing for an Indian Union which Pakistan's advocate, Jinnah, had publicly accepted at the outset, on 6 June. When Gandhi said on 17 May at his prayer meeting that the plan 'contained the seed to convert this land of sorrow into one without sorrow and suffering', it was 'subject to the above interpretation' on grouping and the rest.[25]

In the thirties, the Congress demanded a constituent assembly which it knew it would dominate. Panikkar, among others, pointed out that the differences with the League had to be resolved first if the assembly was to succeed. This, the Mission Plan sought to do. It recommended a scheme as a basis for the accord and a constituent assembly to implement it. Gandhi rejected that accord, as did the Congress and seized on the assembly. It could be made a 'rebel body' and 'I regard the Constituent Assembly as the substitute of satyagraha'.[26] It was not to be a forum for conciliation and compromise with Jinnah.

Neither Cripps nor Gandhi nor his associates gave any thought to conciliation with Jinnah, or, where their stratagem left him when confronted with a *fait accompli*.

The Cabinet Mission's Plan was officially pronounced dead in April 1947, by the Viceroy Lord Mountbatten, rejecting Sardar Patel's false assertions of its acceptance. It died a slow death from the wounds inflicted by Gandhi and Cripps jointly in June 1946.

Notes

1. Peter Clarke, *The Cripps Version: The Life of Sir Stafford Cripps*, The Penguin Press, Allen Lane, 2002, p. 467.
2. Ibid., p. 431.
3. Sudhir Ghosh, *Gandhi's Emissary*, Houghton Mifflin, Boston, 1967.
4. Pyarelal Nayar, *Mahatma Gandhi: The Last Phase*, Vol. I, Navajivan Publishing House, Ahmedabad, 1956.
5. Ibid., pp. 168–70.
6. Ibid., pp. 234–5.
7. Ibid., p. 235.
8. Ibid., p. 236; Ghosh paper, pp. 72–3.
9. ToP, Vol. VII, p. 1024.
10. Nayar, p. 237.
11. ToP, Vol. VII, pp. 1026–9.
12. Ibid., pp. 1029–130.
13. *The Hindustan Times*, 25 June 1946.
14. Cabinet Mission Papers, pp. 51–3.
15. Penderel Moon (ed.), *Wavell: The Viceroy's Journal*, Oxford University Press, Karachi, 1998, p. 305.
16. ToP, Vol. VII, pp. 131–2.
17. Ibid., Vol. VII, p. 1042.
18. Ibid., p. 1047.
19. Ibid., Vol. VIII, p. 321.
20. Moon, p. 328.
21. Clarke, p. 459.
22. ToP, Vol. VII, pp. 1018–21.
23. Ibid., Vol. VII, p. 598.

24. R.J. Moore, *Escape from Empire: The Atlee Government and then Indian Problem*, Oxford University Press, 1983, p. 138.
25. *Harijan*, 26 May. *Collected Works of Mahatma Gandhi*, Vol. 84, p. 162.
26. *Collected Works of Mahatma Gandhi*, Vol. 84, p. 425.

6

Demise of the Cabinet Mission's Plan

To Cripps, an accord with the Congress was a necessity; an accord with the League a desirable option. The entry in his diary made that clear. Nehru reflected the Congress view when he told Cripps that the League had no stomach for a fight. Jinnah proved them wrong. But his options had narrowed precariously between acquiescence in the *fait accompli*; a constituent assembly dominated by the Congress without the checks and balances of the Mission's Plan or a truncated Pakistan. Even after the bitter clash with the Mission on 25 June and the Congress' equivocation the same day, he tried to revive the Mission's Plan until December 1946. He had a weak hand to play. He could have given up Assam, but how could he give up the NWFP without undermining the entire group? But the Congress was determined to wrest NWFP and to wreck the group completely. Gandhi did not conceal his views from the Mission. He rejected not only Para 19 but also the basics in Para 15. He wrote to Pethick-Lawrence on 19 May:

> Even the basis in para 15 of the State Paper is a recommendation. Do you regard a recommendation as obligatory on any member of the contemplated Constituent Assembly? There is such a ring about the quotation. Can those who enthusiastically welcome the Paper but are discerning enough to repudiate, for instance, grouping, honourably seek to educate the country and the Constituent Assembly against the grouping clause? If your answer is 'yes' does it not follow that the Frontier and Assam province delegates would be free to abstain from joining the sections to which they are arbitrarily assigned? I know the legal position. My question has reference to the honourableness of opposition to grouping.

The All-India Congress Committee met in Bombay on 6 July to ratify its executive's resolution of 25 June, Nehru taking over as president in succession to Azad. Jinnah convened a meeting of the Muslim League Council in Bombay to withdraw the League's acceptance of the Mission's Plan. On the same day, 29 July 1946, it passed another resolution which said *inter alia*:

> The Council of the All-India Muslim League is convinced that now the time has come for the Muslim Nation to resort to direct action to achieve Pakistan to assert their just rights, to vindicate their honour and to get rid of the present British slavery and the contemplated future Caste-Hindu domination.... This Council directs the Working Committee to prepare forthwith a programme of direct action to carry out the policy enunciated above and to organize the Muslims for the coming struggle to be launched as and when necessary. As a protest against and in token of their deep resentment of the attitude of the British, this Council calls upon the Mussulmans to renounce forthwith the titles conferred upon them by the alien Government.[1]

Like the scheme it was directed to prepare in the last para of the Lahore Resolution, the Working Committee did not meet 'to prepare forthwith a programme for direct action' — the two words Jinnah had often used in the twenties.

Jinnah's speech to the Muslim League Council contained a candid admission which is of poignant significance after the partition only a year later. Speaking on 29 July 1946, at the very end of the session, after the council had passed the resolutions withdrawing its acceptance of the Cabinet Mission's Plan and for 'direct action', Jinnah said that:

> The Muslim League was moved by higher and greater considerations than any other party in India... (It had) sacrificed the full sovereignty of Pakistan at the altar of the Congress for securing the whole of India. They voluntarily delegated three subjects to the Union and by doing so did not commit a mistake. It was the highest order of statesmanship that the League displayed by making concessions...

we were moved by a desire not to allow the situation to develop into bloodshed and civil war.... We made this sacrifice of giving three subjects to the Centre and accepted a limited Pakistan. We offered this unequivocal sacrifice at the altar of the Congress.[2]

Gandhi told Nehru on 17 July, 'We have given it [Mission's Plan] our own interpretation. But if the federal Court gives a different interpretation, we shall have to be firm'.[3] The plan provided for a reference to the court (para 19[vii]) by the president of the assembly, 'if so requested by a majority of either of the major communities'. But this was confined to the issue whether a matter raised 'any major communal issue', not whether it violated the plan. For that, all that was provided was that a resolution varying the basics in para 15 would require a majority of the representatives of both the communities. It was silent on a violation of the procedure prescribed in para 19 concerning the sequence of the proceedings—preliminaries, sections for group constitutions and reunion to settle the union constitution. In a press statement on 26 August, regarding the viceroy's broadcast on 24 August in which he said that the Congress agreed to refer to the court 'any dispute of interpretation'. Jinnah reminded him of the Congress stand on the plan and asked if: 'on the very threshold parties fundamentally differ in their interpretation regarding the basic terms. Are we going to commence the proceedings of the Constituent Assembly with litigation and law suits in the Federal Court? Is this the spirit in which the future Constitution can be framed for 400 million people of this subcontinent?'[4]

This was the heart of the matter. Before long, Wavell discovered it again. The occasion for Wavell's broadcast was his decision to induct a fresh team as members of his Executive Council in an interim government. Representatives of the Congress were sworn in on 2 September but not before a major clash with him. Wavell was shaken by what he saw in Calcutta after the riots on 16 August. When he met Gandhi and Nehru, he pleaded with them to allay Jinnah's fears so that he could enter both the constituent assembly and the interim government. He asked them to issue a declaration in these terms:

> The Congress are prepared in the interests of communal harmony to accept the intention of the Statement of May 16th that provinces cannot exercise any option affecting their membership of the sections or of the groups if formed, until the decision contemplated in paragraph 19(viii) of the Statement of 16th May is taken by the new legislature after the new constitutional arrangements have come into operation and the first general elections have been held.

He intimated that he would not undertake the responsibility of summoning the constituent assembly till the point was settled. The offer was rejected.

Leonard Mosley's detailed account of this stormy meeting based on 'Government of India Records' reads:

> Give me a simple guarantee that you accept the Cabinet Mission Plan, asked Wavell. We have already said that we accept it, replied Gandhi, but we are not prepared to guarantee that we accept it in the way that the Cabinet Mission set out. We have our own interpretations of what they propose.
>
> Said Wavell: Even if those interpretations differ from what the Cabinet Mission intended?
>
> Replied Gandhi: But of course. In any case, what the Cabinet Mission Plan really means is not what the Cabinet Mission thinks but what the *interim Government thinks* it means. (This was a new suggestion made, no doubt because now the Congress was in the Government).
>
> Wavell pointed out that the interim Government's opinion, as things were at the moment, would almost inevitably be pro-Congress and anti-Muslim League, since the League was boycotting the Government. How could it be unbiased?

Gandhi replied that he was not concerned with bias. He was simply concerned with the legal basis of the discussion. Legally, this was a matter for the interim Government to decide. Once the interim Government was in power, such matters as the Muslim League's ambitions and artificial anxieties could be voted upon; but not before.

But don't you see, exploded Wavell, in an unusual burst of temper, it will be a Congress Government. They are bound to be lacking in impartiality.... Will the Congress commit itself to a declaration, a declaration which will satisfy the Muslim League and assure the continuation of a stable and unitary government? He reached into his drawer and pulled out a paper. This is what I have in mind.... Gandhi handed it over to Nehru, who read it through and said: 'To accept this is tantamount to asking Congress to put itself in fetters.'

Wavell replied: So far as the Cabinet Mission Plan is concerned, that is what I feel you should do. When Congress accepted the Cabinet Mission Plan in the first place, I cannot believe that you did so not knowing its implications. If so, why did you accept it at all? The plan for dividing the country into groups was implicit. You cannot now turn round and say that you did not realize that is what was intended.

Gandhi: What the Cabinet Mission intended and the way we interpret what they intended may not necessarily be the same.... If Congress will give me the guarantee for which I ask, I think I can persuade Mr Jinnah and the Muslim League to reconsider their refusal to join the interim Government. We need them in the Government; India needs them, and, if you are seriously concerned over the dangers of civil war—and you must know as well as I that the danger is great—then you need them too. ... As a result of the killings in Calcutta, India is on the verge of civil war. It is my duty to prevent it.[5]

Jinnah profited by the experience of 1939 when the Congress ministries in the provinces resigned and left the field open to him. His nominees joined the interim government on 15 October on terms far worse than were available earlier. But he had made his point. When asked to rescind the withdrawal of acceptance of the Mission's Plan, the basis of the government, he argued that the Congress had still to accept it. The deadlock was complete.

On 14 November, Gandhi instructed Sudhir Ghosh, now in London, the line he should take when he spoke to Cripps and Pethick-Lawrence, 'What they can and must do is to transfer the whole power to the willing and capable party at the earliest moment, to withdraw the British part of the army and disband the rest.... This is the royal road to peaceful transfer and no other'.[6] This was a consistent refrain and an objective which was pursued unflinchingly. G.D. Birla was told on 26 November 1946, 'I believe the State Paper of May 16 will probably have to be changed'.[7]

In an effort to resolve the deadlock, the British government invited Jinnah, Nehru, Liaquat Ali Khan, and Baldev Singh to London for discussions. The statement it issued on 6 December 1946, at the end of the exercise, was fair warning to anyone who cared to read it. It carried the authority of the Lord Chancellor Lord Jowitt:

> His Majesty's Government have had legal advice which confirms that the statement of May 16 means what the Cabinet Mission have always stated was their intention. This part of the statement, as so interpreted, must, therefore, be considered an essential part of the Scheme of May 16 for enabling the Indian people to formulate a constitution which His Majesty's Government would be prepared to submit to Parliament. It should, therefore, be accepted by all parties in the Constituent Assembly...

Jowitt's opinion reads:

> The proposals contained in paragraph 19(iv), which are part of the proposals for the constitution-making machine, are clear; after the

preliminary meeting the provincials representatives are to form themselves into certain designated sections, and it is for these sections—and not for the individual provinces—to settle provincial constitutions.

The sections may also decide whether—and if so to what extent—a group constitution shall be set up for any provinces.

I do not agree that it is any part of the recommendations for the constitution-making machinery that the provinces shall in the first instance make their choice as to whether or not to belong to the section in which they are placed.

No such conclusion can possibly be arrived at without disregarding the perfectly clear words of 19(iv) of the Statement.

The Resolution of the Congress Working Committee of the 24th May 1946 attempts to justify this construction by the necessity of making paragraph 15 consistent with paragraph 19.

But there is no such necessity for the two paragraphs are dealing with different concepts; the former containing recommendations as to the basic form of the constitutions to be evolved as a result of the functioning of the constitution-making machine, the latter containing recommendations as to the construction of that machine itself.

In any event, even if there were such a necessity it would be wholly illegitimate to construct an implication therefrom to negative an express term.

I therefore conclude that the recommendation involves that it is for the majority of the representatives in each section taken as a whole to decide how provincial constitutions shall be framed and to what extent, if any, they shall be grouped.

I should add that I come to the above conclusion solely on the terms of the statement (Cmd. 6821) itself; if it were legitimate to pray in aid the doctrine of 'contemporanea exposition' kit is obvious that my conclusion is reinforced.[8]

The British government's statement concluded on this ominous note:

> There has never been any prospect of success for the constituent assembly except upon the basis of the agreed procedure. Should the constitution come to be framed by a constituent assembly in which a large section of the Indian population had not been represented, His Majesty's Government could not, of course, contemplate—as the Congress have stated they would not contemplate—forcing such a constitution upon any unwilling parts of the country.[9]

If the constituent assembly was not worked under the Mission's Plan, partition would be the only alternative. The constitution it framed would not be imposed 'upon any unwilling parts of the country'. But Gandhi was unmoved. His direction to the Congressmen from Assam was clear, for he was untroubled by doubts when he met them on 15 December, 'I do not need a single minute to come to a decision, for on this I have a mind'. The Federal Court 'is a packed Court'. It will uphold London's interpretation. So, 'as soon as the time comes for the Constituent Assembly to go into sections you will say "Gentlemen, Assam retires"…. Else I will say Assam had only manikins and no men. It is an impertinent suggestion that Bengal should dominate Assam in any way'.[10]

Gandhi knew, of course, that his stand rendered partition inevitable; he was unfazed. His note on the constituent assembly, dated 17 December 1946, indicates that he was mentally prepared for partition. The constituent assembly should frame a constitution 'for all the Provinces, States and units that may be represented' in it. His 'Instructions to Congress Working Committee' dated 28/30 December 1946, envisaged partition and named the seceders from Pakistan—Assam, and the NWFP, 'the Sikhs in the Punjab and may be Baluchistan'. This will give 'Quaid-i-Azam Jinnah a universally acceptable and inoffensive formula for his Pakistan'.[11]

The All-India Congress Committee met on 5–6 January 1947 and resolved that 'it cannot be a party to any such compulsion or imposition against the will of the people concerned'.[12]

Jinnah had committed himself to reconvene the League's Council 'if the Congress unequivocally accepted the British Government's interpretation of the Grouping clauses in the Cabinet Mission's constitutional proposals for India'.[13]

That was not to be. The Pakistan which Jinnah had rejected on 25 April 1946 now become inevitable. It was a prospect that shattered his vision of Pakistan—maximum autonomy for the Pakistan provinces in a loose Indian federation. In 1960, B. Shiva Rao published a report of a discussion between Jinnah and Sir B.N. Rau, constitutional adviser to the constituent assembly, on 18 September 1946, in the course of which he asked for a clarification of crucial points. Shiva Rao noted, 'from the questions that he raised, it is a fair inference that his mind had not been finally made up against the League's participation in the Constituent Assembly'—nearly two months after it had withdrawn its acceptance of the Mission's Plan.[14]

One of the questions Jinnah asked was, 'In view of the confusion that has arisen about the "grouping clause", would it not be possible to set out its meaning in clear and unmistakable terms'. Jinnah also asked, 'Is it open to the Union Constituent Assembly to modify in any way the group or provincial constitutions as settled by the sections?' and about the machinery to resolve disputes. B.N. Rau's answer was that the correct position has now been accepted by the Congress. They had met on 18 September 1946 when Jinnah asked for the clarification in writing. Rau's reply on 22 September 1946 was evasive. The Congress persisted in its 'interpretation' until the end. On the other hand Jinnah persisted, with equal determination, to secure a return to the Cabinet Mission's Plan according to its original and correct meaning. Documents published years later by the

British government revealed that even at that late hour in December 1946 Jinnah was willing to work the plan if only the Congress gave up its interpretation that was designed to wreck the plan, as indeed it did.

At a meeting on 4 December with the members of the Mission—Stafford Cripps, Pethick-Lawrence, and A.V. Alexander—Jinnah and Liaquat Ali Khan complained of the Congress attitude. At the end, Jinnah threw a broad hint. The Muslim League's Council 'might accept' the plan if, as Cripps proposed, 'the Congress now accepted the implications of our interpretation'. On 6 December Jinnah moved a step further, he proposed 'an ad hoc tribunal of three of some standing judicial body' to resolve the dispute. The Secretary of State, Pethick-Lawrence rightly concluded on 13 December, that the Muslim League demanded that 'the next move should come from Congress in the shape of an acceptance of our interpretation of the Statement of May 16th'.[15]

The Congress had no intention of doing so. A promising year ended in defeat and despair. The last chance of preserving India's unity appeared on 16 May 1946. By December 1946 it was destroyed by Gandhi and the Congress. The law of contributory negligence provides a fair test: Who had the last clear chance of averting the mishap?

Jinnah and the Muslim League were not the only victims of the Congress' arrogance of power. It is, however, both historically false and politically unprincipled to single out Nehru alone for criticism on this score. It had seized all from the top to the bottom. Even a veteran like M.R. Jayakar, no friend of the League, was given a taste of it.

The constituent assembly held its first meeting on 9 December 1946. The League boycotted its proceeding. Jinnah and Liaquat Ali Khan were still in London. The next day the Congress president, J.B. Kripalani, moved for the appointment of a committee on 'Rules and Procedure of the Assembly'. The Hindu Mahasabha leader, Shyama Prasad Mukherjee, seconded a proposal by a member from Bengal that its remit should be widened thus, 'including Sections and Committees'. Nehru asked Kripalani to accept the amendment, which he did. Therefore, Jayakar uttered a word of caution:

> I am now putting before this assembly, will not be regarded as too cautious, but I am bound to point out a few considerations which I want the House to note carefully. These considerations are against the express mention of the words 'Sections and Committee'. My view is no doubt actuated by a feeling of caution, which I think is desirable at the present stage. Remember the word 'Sections'. You are asked by express terms to legislate for them in advance of their future formation. Remember 'Sections' include 'B' and 'C' Sections. Remember further that in 'B' and 'C' Sections there is likely to be — almost certainly to be — a preponderance of a certain group of men who are not present here today and who may be present at the late stage when these Sections begin to function. That group of men are not present here today under a feeling of suspicion, if not hostility.
>
> Would you like to legislate for them in advance at this stage, or would you not let the matter remain where it is, namely, that as the word 'Assembly' prima facie would include 'Sections' no rules can be framed by Sections 'A', 'B' and 'C' which are in conflict with the rules of the Assembly? This would be the usual constitutional rule. Would you not rather let matters rest at this, or would you go further and rub the point in by making an express mention of Sections implying thereby that we here today, in the absence of that group, make it obligatory by express words that the rules framed by the Assembly shall apply to the Sections. Such rubbing in is absolutely unnecessary, because the rules of the Assembly would prima facie include rules of the Sections. Remember that this group of men is not present here today and is, besides, watching these proceedings with jealousy and suspicion to discover whether you are taking anything out of their hands and deciding it finally in advance of their arrival? If you do so may it not interfere with their future arrival herein a friendly and trustful atmosphere? I therefore

suggest that the words as they stand in the original Resolution of Acharya Kripalani, may be accepted instead of going further to make an express mention of Sections and Committees.[16]

Jayakar's fears were justified. Rules were made, in effect, to control the sections. On 13 December, Nehru moved the Objectives Resolution. On 16 December, Jayakar moved a motion for postponing the debate 'to enable' the representatives of the League and the Indian states to participate in debate. He began by paying warm tributes to Motilal Nehru and to his children Jawaharlal Nehru and Vijaya Lakshmi Pandit. He was rudely heckled. Patel angrily asked 'May I know, Sir, if the Right Honourable Gentleman is interpreting here the policy laid down by His Majesty's Government?' G.B. Pant took the cue and was equally rude.[17] Jayakar's plea irked him because he had embarrassed the Congress. It had no time for the League on the plan and he was urging them to abide by the plan.

The president suspended discussion on Nehru's resolution on 21 December 1946. It was adopted by the assembly on 25 January 1947. Interestingly on 21 December, the assembly met *in camera*.[18] Before long, Jayakar resigned his membership of the assembly. The Muslim League Working Committee's resolution passed in Karachi on 31 January 1947, quoted chapter and verse for the assembly's rules, besides the Congress' pronouncements, to declare that since the Mission's Plan had been flouted the assembly should be dissolved. It finds place in few compilations and is reproduced in full in Appendix.

On 20 February 1947, Prime Minister Clement Attlee made an historic statement in the House of Commons. Differences between the political parties on the working of the constituent assembly persisted. 'It is of the essence of the [Cabinet Mission's] Plan that the Assembly should be fully representative'. There was no prospect of that. The uncertainty had to be ended. Power will definitely be transferred into 'responsible hands by a date not later than June 1948'. If there was no agreement on the constituent assembly, the British government will have to consider to whom the power should be handed over, 'whether as a whole to some form of Central Government for British India or in some areas to the existing provincial Governments, or in such other way as may seem most reasonable and in the best interests of the Indian people'.[19] This was intended to resolve the impasse in the interim government also.

The Congress Working Committee met in New Delhi on 6–8 March 1947 and passed three major resolutions. One welcomed Attlee's declaration of a deadline for the transfer of power. Another demanded the partition of Punjab. The reason cited was 'a way out which involves the least amount of compulsion. This would necessitate a division of the Punjab into two provinces, so that the predominantly Muslim part may be separate from the predominantly non-Muslim part'. It was stated that this applied to Bengal as well.

The third resolution read thus:

> In view of new developments which are leading to a swift transfer of power in India, it has become incumbent on the people of India to prepare themselves jointly and cooperatively for this change, so that it may be effected peacefully and to the advantage of all. The Working Committee, therefore, invite the All-India Muslim League to nominate representations to meet representatives of the Congress in order to consider the situation that has arisen and to devise means to meet it.

Even as the demand for the partition of India inevitably involved partition of these two provinces, the Congress demand for the partition of Punjab and Bengal was a tacit acceptance of the partition of India. Jinnah had always demanded that for any negotiations to be fruitful, the principle of the partition must first be accepted. Why then did he not respond to the invitation? The question of why the Congress leaders did not approach him for talks directly and in private before going public on this move also arises. Jinnah had, of course, every reason for resentment and even distrust given the Congress' disingenuous ploy of 'interpretation' in which it persisted to the very last.

Statesmanship lies, however, in rising above the bitterness of the past. A Congress–League pact on the partition would have radically improved the atmosphere in the country. It would have averted the carnage that followed the partition, assured a fair deal to the minorities and quite conceivably resulted in an accord on the question of the princely states and on some institutional links between the two sovereign states to facilitate mutual cooperation. Perhaps the proposal was too late in the day. Regardless, the League showed not the slightest interest in it and ignored it. Publication of the correspondence between the general secretaries of the Congress and the League, Shankarrao Deo and Liaquat Ali Khan, respectively, was triggered off by a claim by 'a member of the Muslim League Committee' in a statement to the Associated Press of India's correspondent in Bombay. He said that he was surprised at Nehru's statement in New Delhi that, so far, there had been no response from the Muslim League to the Congress invitation. 'The Muslim League leader said that the Muslim League was as anxious and as eager as the Congress to arrive at a mutual settlement...The Muslim League also realize the urgent need for a final decision regarding the future of our country, and is as anxious as the Congress to settle its differences with the Congress'.

Denying that the Muslim League was a stumbling block in the way of a settlement, the League leader said, 'Attempts have been made in the past to settle the differences at high level, but, unfortunately, these led us nowhere, because, there was no basis for joint discussions'.

He added, 'The Muslim League, therefore, now wishes to know from the Congress Working Committee, clearly and emphatically, the basis for any negotiations between the two parties'.[20]

The Congress General Secretary, Shankarrao Deo, immediately released the correspondence to the press with a prefatory statement. *Dawn* of 17 April 1947 published them in full. Shankarrao recalled the League leader's statement and said:

> While it is good to know that the League is anxious for a settlement it is difficult to understand what prevents its High Command from taking immediate steps to consider the Congress invitation. In order that the public may know how matters stand. I am releasing to the Press the correspondence that has recently passed between the General Secretary of the Muslim League and myself about which Press seems to have some knowledge already.

Shankarrao Deo wrote to Liaquat Ali Khan on 9 March 1947:

> Dear friend, I have pleasure in sending you herewith copies of three resolutions passed by the Working Committee at Delhi yesterday. I would like to draw your particular attention to resolution no. 2. Wherein an invitation has been issued to the Muslim League to send their representatives to meet representatives of the Congress. I shall be grateful if you could let me have an early reply so that further steps might be taken in this matter. (Sd.) Shankarrrao Deo.

On 9 March Nehru himself wrote to Liaquat Ali Khan inviting him to 'meet to discuss these matters'.[21]

Liaquat Ali Khan replied to Shankarrao Deo on 13 March 1947:

> Dear Sir, This is to acknowledge the receipt of your letter dated the 9th of March which I shall place before the next meeting of the Working Committee of the All-India Muslim League for their consideration. Yours truly, (Sd.) Liaquat Ali Khan.

Shankarrao Deo, wrote once again to Liaquat Ali Khan, on 11 April 1947:

> Dear Friend, May I draw your attention to your letter dated 13th March 1947 and request you to let me know when the next meeting of the Working Committee of the All-India Muslim League is likely to be held. As it is necessary for us to know at an early date whether your organisation is willing to send their representatives of the Congress. I would be obliged if you expedite your decision in the matter. Yours sincerely, (Sd.) Shankarrao Deo.

Liaquat Ali Khan replied on 14 April 1947:

> Dear Sir, with reference to your letter of the 11th April, 1947, I am to inform you that no date for the next meeting of the Working Committee of All-India Muslim League has been fixed as yet. In view of the discussions which are now in progress between the Viceroy and the Indian leaders, it is not likely that a meeting of the Working Committee will be called until a definite stage in the stalks has been reached. Yours truly, (Sd.) Liaquat Ali Khan.

Obviously the Muslim League preferred to negotiate with the Congress through the new Viceroy Louis Mountbatten, who was appointed by Attlee after he dismissed Archibald Wavell in February. How sincere the Congress' proposal was is hard to judge. Its preference from 1942 onwards was to negotiate with the British and it had wrecked the Mission's Plan systematically and with crass lack of integrity. This had generated distrust. Still, given the stakes the League should have probed the offer.

Mountbatten lost no time in grappling with the problem, after realizing the inevitability of the partition of India. Nehru indicated to Mountbatten on 8 April his readiness to accept the partition of Punjab and Bengal. But Azad feared such a denouement. 'He ardently supported the Mission's Plan'. It 'could be made to work' but 'a truncated Pakistan would spell disaster for the Mussalmans'.[22] The Plan died and with it the last hope of preserving India's unity.

DEMISE OF THE CABINET MISSION'S PLAN

Mountbatten tried to revise the Cabinet Mission Plan but failed. Documents in Volume X of *The Transfer of Power*, record the efforts he made despite his fears that success would elude him. He took up the matter with Vallabhbhai Patel on 25 April and received from him a long letter reiterating the Congress' stand. The viceroy replied through his principal secretary, Eric Mieville:

> H.E. feels that HMG's statement of 6 December is perfectly clear about the legal position and that the speeches by Sir Stafford Cripps and Lord Pethick-Lawrence, which you quoted, related to the undoubted fact that without a reasonable measure of agreement you cannot frame a constitution, and that if any outrageous attempt was made to force an unacceptable constitution on a province the constitution-making machine would break down whatever the legal rights of the parties might be.

Patel persisted, 'The statement of 6 December is merely clarificatory of a portion of the Cabinet Mission's Plan'. It was open season for quibbling. Mountbatten's reply on 16 May put paid to it:

> Provinces would acquire the right to opt out of a group (if the section decided to set one up) only after the first elections held under the new constitution, which had been framed by the section. There was never any question of the constitution being referred in the first instance to existing assemblies for approval.

> There always was inherent in this plan the risk that a provincial constitution might be rigged by the majority in a section; in the case of Assam, there undoubtedly has been a fear on the part of the present Assam Ministry that a constitution devised for Assam by Section C would be such as would in effect put them out of office. The answer to this is that they must trust the majority in Section C not to abuse its powers, in the same way as that majority in section C would have to trust the Congress majority in the Union Assembly not to abuse its power in regard to the federal subjects, etc.

This matter is of course most important from the point of view of both the major parties; and if only the position could be fully accepted and appreciated, there would still be a chance that the Cabinet Mission Plan could be made effective.[23]

What Patel did not know, of course, was that Mountbatten had had all his arguments carefully examined by George Abell who had served the viceroy's secretariat since 1945 and was familiar with the record. Patel's claim was found to be a false one. 'I think Home Member knows the position perfectly well', he wrote on 27 April. 'It was clear from what he said that even now the Congress would not give any sort of unequivocal acceptance of the Cabinet Mission's Plan which would satisfy Mr Jinnah'.

Jinnah had anticipated this realistically and told Mountbatten that:

> the whole basis of the Cabinet Mission Plan were that it had to be worked in a spirit of co-operation and mutual trust. In May 1946 there had been some prospect that this atmosphere could be created. Now, nearly a year later, ... it was clear that in no circumstances did Congress intend to work the Plan either in accordance with the spirit or the letter.[24]

Finally Mountbatten reported to London on 1 May, 'Jinnah has some justification to fear that the Congress do not mean to stick to their acceptance'. Its disingenuous interpretations betrayed intent to mislead. Once the constituent assembly began its work the Congress would use it as it pleased, leaving the League high and dry and the British bemused and acquiescent.[25]

The minutes of the British cabinet's meeting on 7 February 1947 recorded:

> Ministers agreed that by their refusal to join the Constituent Assembly, the Muslim League had placed themselves in the wrong. On the other hand, it could not reasonably be said that Congress

were acting fully in accordance with the Cabinet Mission's Plan. Their resolution of 6th January was not an unequivocal acceptance of His Majesty's Government's point of view and several of the rules of procedure which the Constituent Assembly had adopted were an attempt to amend the Plan to their advantage in important particulars.[26]

But let alone the Muslim League the Congress had nothing to offer even to the so-called 'nationalist Muslims'. Tej Bahadur Sapru went to the core of the problem in a letter to a friend on 4 October 1941: 'I have never attached any importance to Jinnah's demand of Pakistan, but the real question is, *as it has always been*, what is it that we are going to offer to the Muslims?'[27]

V.P. Menon made the same point in his authoritative work, *Transfer of Power in India*:

Nationalist Muslims found themselves in a particularly difficult position. They felt that, unless the Congress could reassure the Muslims, it would not be possible to win their support in the coming elections. Towards the end of August 1945, Abul Kalam Azad approached Gandhiji with a plan for a communal settlement. It was useless, he said, to enter into the causes of the communal problem or to apportion blame for it. Muslim fears could only be removed by devising a scheme under which they would feel secure. Any attempt to form a unitary government at the Centre would fail. Partition was against the interests of the Muslims themselves. As an Indian Muslim, he regarded partition as a defeatist policy and could not accept it. He suggested to the Congress that the future constitution of India must be federal with fully autonomous units; that the central subjects must only be of an all-India nature and agreed upon by the constituent unit, and that the units must be given the right of secession. There must be joint electorates both at the Centre and in the provinces, with reservation of seats and such differential franchise as might be needed to make electorates reflect the strength of population of the communities. There must be parity of Hindus and Muslims in the central legislature and the central executive till such time as communal suspicion disappeared and parties were formed on economic and political lines. There should also be a convention by which the head of the Indian federation would, in the initial period, be Hindu and Muslim by turn. Hindu friends were exhorted to leave entirely to the Muslims the question of their status in the future constitution of India. If Muslims were satisfied that the decision was not being imposed on them by a non-Muslim agency, they would drop the idea of partition and realize that their interests would be best served by a federated and united India.[28]

Neither Azad nor *The Collected Works of Mahatma Gandhi* reproduce the correspondence between Gandhi and Azad. Intercepted by the British, it was printed in the *Transfer of Power*, Vol. VI, pp. 155–7 and p. 172.

Muslim Leaguers were not the only ones to feel aggrieved by some policies of Congress ministries in 1937–9. Maulana Hifzurrahman, president of the pro-Congress Jamiat-ul-Ulema-i-Hind, complained bitterly to Kripalani, who was the Congress' general secretary in 1937 on the ministries' education policy and section of textbooks.[29]

A Congress sympathizer, Maulana Muhsin Sajjad of Bihar, who was also a leading figure of the Non-cooperation Movement, wrote a documented complaint to the Congress Working Committee on 22 December 1939. He particularly censured the Congress leaders' softness towards the leaders of the Hindu Mahasabha, V.D. Savarkar and B.S. Moonjee.[30]

The most devastating critique, however, came from Nehru's close friend, M. Asaf Ali. His memoirs reveal how marginalized he and Azad were in the Congress councils. In December 1943, Azad reviewed with him and Syed Mahmud 'the Congress Muslim position'. 'Personally I [Asaf Ali] think it is time that merciless self-criticism was undertaken by nationalist Muslims and Hindu Congressmen. Indian Muslims as a bulk are dissatisfied with the policies of the Congress, howsoever well intentioned they may have been. A practical politician would take note of it and alter the course of his policies....'[31] In July 1944, Asaf Ali noted that 'certain persons [that is, Jinnah] and policies are like the red rag to him [Nehru] and the very mention of them sends him into an unreasonable outburst of passion, expressed more in his tense face...the impression of a proud and unreasoning victim of volcanic emotions'.

He asked what the solution to the communal issue was 'if not the one proposed by Jinnah? Could any political progress be made without solving this question?... He [Nehru] was frankly not hopeful of any deal with Jinnah, who he thought was not aware of the world forces and economic developments....'[32]

Even in prison, Patel made no secret of his contempt for Congress Muslims. 'Patel & Co. have time and again, spoken in a manner rather ironical, indicating that Mahmud, I and (less marked) Maulana don't come up to their mark', Asaf Ali wrote.[33]

On 6 January 1948, Patel questioned Azad's patriotism.[34] But the unkindest cut was Gandhi's stance. On 24 July 1947, he wrote to Nehru opposing Azad's membership of the first Cabinet of free India. 'Sardar is decidedly against his membership'. So, 'name another Muslim for the Cabinet'.[35]

That was Azad's lot; insulted by Jinnah as 'a show-boy' and distrusted by Patel for his espousal of Muslim interests from a nationalist viewpoint. The nationalist Muslim had no role to play. The Congress left the field to the League.

زاہدِ تنگ نظر نے مجھے کافر جانا
اور کافر یہ سمجھتا ہے کہ مسلمان ہوں میں

(*The narrow minded pious brand me an Infidel
And the Infidel thinks I am a Muslim*) – Iqbal.

Notes

1. Latif Ahmed Sherwani, *Pakistan Resolution to Pakistan 1940–1947*, National Publishing House, Karachi, 1969, p. 139.
2. The Indian Annual Register, 1946, Vol. II, pp. 167–8; Shah Mohammed, *The Indian Muslims: A Documentary Record 1900–1947*, Vol. II, Meenakshi Prakashan, Meerut, p. 229.
3. *Collected Works of Mahatma Gandhi*, Vol. 85, p. 6.
4. ToP, Vol. VIII, p. 321.
5. Leonard Mosley, *The Last Days of the British Raj*, Weidenfeld & Nicolson, London, 1961, pp. 39–41; vide also ToP, Vol. VIII, pp. 312–3.
6. Ghosh, p. 193.
7. *Collected Works of Mahatma Gandhi*, Vol. 86, p. 162.
8. ToP, Vol. IX, pp. 239–40.
9. Ibid., pp. 295–6.
10. *Collected Works of Mahatma Gandhi*, Vol. 86, pp. 227–30.
11. *Collected Works of Mahatma Gandhi*, Vol. 86, pp. 235 and 285.
12. Anil Chandra Banerjee (ed.), *The Making of the Indian Constitution 1939–1947*, Vol. I, Documents, A. Mukherjee & Co., Calcutta, 1948, pp. 380–2.
13. Ibid., p. 372.
14. B.N. Rau, *India's Constitution in the Making*, Ed. by B.S. Rao, Allied Publishers, Bombay, 1963, pp. lii–liii.
15. ToP, Vol. IX, pp. 290–2 and 344–5.
16. Constituent Assembly Debates, Vol. I, pp. 24–7.
17. Ibid., pp. 77–8.
18. Ibid., pp. 166 and 172.
19. House of Commons Debates, Vol. 433, cols 1395–8.
20. *The Times of India*, 16 April 1947.
21. SWJN, Vol. 1, pp. 68–9.
22. ToP, Vol. X, p. 215.
23. Durga Das (ed.), *Sardar Patel's Correspondence; 1945–50*, Vol. IV, Navajivan Publishing House, Ahmedabad, pp. 30–5.
24. ToP, Vol. X, pp. 149–50.
25. Ibid., Vol. X, p. 541.
26. Ibid., Vol. IX, p. 639.
27. Rima Hooja (ed.), *Crusader for Self-Rule: Tej Bahadur Sapru and the Indian National Movement*, Rawat Publications, Jaipur and New Delhi, 1999, p. 342.
28. V.P. Menon, *The Transfer of Power in India*, Orient Longman Ltd., India, 1957, p. 221.
29. K.M. Ashraf, Vol. 2, pp. 291–300, for the text of his letter.

30. Mushirul Hasan, *Towards Freedom: Documents on the Movement for Independence in India*, ICHR, Oxford University Press, New Delhi, 2008, pp. 234–46.
31. Ibid., p. 272.
32. Ibid., p. 283.
33. Ibid., p. 315.
34. A.G. Noorani (ed.), *The Muslims of India: A Documentary Record 1947–2000*, Oxford University Press, New Delhi, 2003, p. 65.
35. *Collected Works of Mahatma Gandhi*, Vol. 88, p. 408.

7

An Embittered Separation

Even a year before the partition, none of the leaders of the two parties anticipated either the frenzied rush of events or the course they took; least of all the end result, although it was foreseeable. Surely by 1946 the alternatives were evident—either partition of India and of Punjab and Bengal, or a loose federation. In 1946, communal riots were the norm, even in a city like Bombay. Partition of Punjab, particularly, entailed carnage as Sikandar Hayat Khan accurately predicted even as early as in October 1938 to Penderel Moon.[1]

It would be facile and altogether wrong to state that events *overtook* the leaders. They had shaped the events. Jinnah expected the Congress to settle on the basis of a loose Union. He knew that Pakistan necessarily entailed partition of its two major provinces, Punjab and Bengal. But had he accepted that publicly he would have lost support in these crucial provinces.

Even when that prospect stared him in the face he assured one and all, as late as on 11 May 1947, that he was 'deadly against the partition of Bengal and the Punjab and we shall fight every inch against it'.[2] He was being less than candid to his followers, for on 16 May he had already agreed to terms of reference of the Boundary Commission for Punjab Bengal and Assam—'on the basis of ascertaining the contiguous majority areas of Muslims and non-Muslims *down to girdawar circles*'. The italicized words were omitted in the terms of reference of the Radcliffe Commission. The unit was not specified—district, taluka etc.[3]

It was a fundamental flaw in the strategy which Jinnah had adopted which led to this result—confrontational advocacy of a demand, which in the form he had put forth, none could accept, with not a hint of compromise. The hauteur and the rhetoric fouled the atmosphere. He had not prepared a position to fall back on. Events moved far too fast for him. He was unprepared, especially for the consequences of the Two-Nation Theory or of an iron-walled partition. Confident of his tactical skills, Jinnah proved a poor strategist. Like Gandhi, he, too, had gambled. His success in creating a state evoked universal admiration. His courage, independence and determination struck awe. At the root of every significant success in history lies a calculating intransigence. Things go wrong when they are not perfectly blended.

On 24 February, Gandhi reacted to the British government's announcement to quit realistically. 'This may lead to Pakistan for those provinces or portions which may want it.... The Congress provinces...will get what they want'.

He gave a formula on April 4: Jinnah to be prime minister of India—backed by a Congress majority in the constituent assembly—and liable to a dismissal at any moment. An elaboration of 10 April hinted at partition as an alternative to the League entering the constituent assembly. The League was offered an assembly freed from the Cabinet Mission's restrictions—with Jinnah as prime minister as a sweetener—or a Pakistan minus the NWFP. When neither worked, he said on 6 May: 'The Congress should in no circumstances be party to partition. We should tell the British to quit unconditionally'.

He wrote to Mountbatten on 8 May, asking him to 'leave the government of the whole of India including the States, to one party'. On 3 June 1947, the Partition Plan was published, which both the parties accepted. The next day Gandhi said: 'I tried my best to bring the Congress round to accept the proposal of May

16. But now we must accept what is an accomplished fact'—this was not true, of course, as he well knew. He had led the Congress and it followed him.

The line was clear and consistent: power must be transferred to a Congress government at the centre, which will *then* deal with the Muslim League. As Ambedkar pointed out, this was the core of the Rajaji formula which Gandhi offered to Jinnah in 1944. This was also the demand in 1947, after the compromise in the Mission's Plan had been torpedoed.

Seervai's comment on this iconic figure is fair. 'It is sad to think that Gandhi's rejection of the Cabinet Mission's proposal for an Interim Government, and of the Cabinet Mission Plan, should have had the unfortunate consequence of destroying the unity of a free India for which he had fought so valiantly and so long'.[4]

Gandhi had seemingly braced himself for partition in Rajaji's formula in 1944 and in his own 'Instructions to Working Committee' on 28/30 December 1946 ('a universally acceptable and inoffensive formula for his [Jinnah's] Pakistan'). The frenetic march of events since baffled him as they did everyone. The Congress Working Committee's demand for partition of Punjab and Bengal on 8 March 1947 implied acceptance of partition of the country.

Confronted with the realities that brooked no evasion, he became desperate. He loathed partition of the country he loved but never accepted any compromise with Jinnah which could have averted it. Jinnah did not loathe partition but dreaded it in the only form in which it could be granted. He would have jumped at any sensible compromise, in a manner had made his own, under a smokescreen of assertive rhetoric. He had accepted a Union of India on 25 April, even before the Simla Conference began, and persisted by dropping hints to the British ministers whom he met with in London until December 1946. If only the Congress would drop its crippling conditions, he was prepared to work the Cabinet Mission's Plan. He knew the risks. The Pakistan movement would lose steam. Party discipline would weaken. But the advantages of a compromise to all interests would emerge in bold relief as the processes of conciliation went underway. A constitution can only be drafted in this spirit, with the principal parties sharing power in the interim government while the constituent assembly did its job.

This, alas, was the farthest from the minds of Gandhi, Nehru, Patel, and their followers. But while Nehru and Patel preferred the partition of India to a union, which involved power sharing, Gandhi hated partition; only, he had no practicable compromise formula to offer. The one he floated in April 1947 verged on the absurd. It is necessary to peruse his documents to realize how impractical his effort was.

At the end of his interview with Mountbatten on 4 April, Gandhi dictated to the Chief of Staff, Lord Ismay an 'Outline of Draft Agreement'. It read thus:

> Mr Jinnah to be given the option of forming a Cabinet.
>
> The selection of the Cabinet is left entirely to Mr Jinnah. The members may be all Muslims, or all non-Muslims, or they may be representatives of all classes and creeds of the Indian people.
>
> If Mr Jinnah accepted this offer, the Congress would guarantee to co-operate freely and sincerely, so long as all the measures that Mr Jinnah's Cabinet bring forward are in the interest of the Indian people as a whole.
>
> The sole reference of what is or is not in the interest of India as a whole will be Lord Mountbatten, in his personal capacity.
>
> Mr Jinnah must stipulate, on behalf of the League or of any other parties represented in the Cabinet formed by him that, so far as he

or they are concerned, they will do their utmost to preserve peace throughout India.

There shall be no National Guards (of the League) or any other form of private army.

Within the framework hereof Mr Jinnah will be perfectly free to present for acceptance a scheme of Pakistan even before the transfer of power, provided however, that he is successful in his appeal to reason and not to the force of arms which he abjures for all time for this purpose. Thus, there will be no compulsion in this matter over a province or a part thereof.

In the Assembly the Congress has a decisive majority. But the Congress shall never use that majority against the League policy simply because of its identification with the League but will give its hearty support to every measure brought forward by the League Government, provided that it is in the interest of the whole of India. Whether it is in such interest or not shall be decided by Lord Mountbatten as man and not in his representative capacity.

If Mr Jinnah rejects this offer, the same offer to be made mutatis mutandis to Congress.

On 10 April, he discussed a related formula with the Congress Working Committee and gave it to Mountbatten the next day, writing on it in Hindi, 'Gandhi's draft'. It read:

1. So far as Pakistan is concerned and so far as the Congress is concerned nothing will be yielded to force. But everything just will be conceded readily if it appeals to reason. Since nothing is to be forcibly taken, it should be open to any province or part thereof to abstain from joining Pakistan and remain with the remaining provinces. Thus, so far as the Congress is aware today, the Frontier Province is with it (Congress) and the Eastern part of the Punjab where the Hindus and the Sikhs combined have a decisive majority will remain out of the Pakistan zone. Similarly in the East, Assam is clearly outside the zone of Pakistan and the Western part of Bengal including

Darjeeling, Dinajpur, Calcutta, Burdwan, Midnapore, Khulna, 24-Parganas, etc., where the Hindus are in a decisive majority will remain outside the Pakistan zone. And since the Congress is willing to concede to reason everything just, it is open to the Muslim League to appeal to the Hindus, by present just treatment, to reconsider their expressed view and not to divide Bengal.

2. It is well to mention in this connection that if the suggested agreement goes through, the Muslim League will participate fully in the Constituent Assembly in a spirit of co-operation. It might also be mentioned that it is the settled policy with the Congress that the system of separate electorates has done the greatest harm to the national cause and therefore the Congress will insist on joint electorates throughout with reservation of seats wherever it is considered necessary.
3. The present raid of Assam and the contemplated so-called civil disobedience within should stop altogether.
4. Muslim League intrigues said to be going on, with the Frontier tribes for creating disturbances in the Frontier Province and onward should also stop.
5. Frankly anti-Hindu legislation hurried through the Sind Legislature in utter disregard of Hindu feeling and opposition should be abandoned.
6. The attempt that is being nakedly pursued in the Muslim majority provinces to pack civil and police services with Muslims irrespective of merit and to the deliberate exclusion of Hindus must be given up forthwith.
7. Speeches inciting to hatred, including murder, arson and loot, should cease.
8. Newspapers like the *Dawn, Morning News, Star of India, Azad* and others, whether in English or in any of the Indian vernaculars, should change their policy of inculcating hatred against the Hindus.
9. Private armies under the guise of National Guards, secretly or openly armed, should cease.
10. Forcible conversion, rape, abduction, arson and loot culminating in murders of men, women and children by Muslims should stop.
11. What the Congress expects the Muslim League to do will readily be done in the fullest measure by the Congress.

12. What is stated here applies equally to the inhabitants of princes' India, Portuguese India, and French India.
13. The foregoing is the test of either's sincerity and that being granted publicly and in writing in the form of an agreement, the Congress would have no objection whatsoever to the Muslim League forming the whole of the Cabinet consisting of Muslims only or partly Muslims and partly non-Muslims.
14. Subject to the foregoing the Congress pledges itself to give full co-operation to the Muslim League Cabinet if it is formed and never to use the Congress majority against the League with the sole purpose of defeating the Muslims. On the contrary every measure will be considered on its merits and receive full co-operation from the Congress members whenever a particular measure is provably in the interests of the whole of India.[5]

Gandhi wrote to the viceroy on 11 April to say that except for Khan Abdul Ghaffar Khan, he had failed to carry his colleagues with him. He left for Patna the next day. Pyarelal glibly, if not devotedly, reproduces them and writes that Gandhi's had become a 'voice in the wilderness'. This reflects, vividly, South Asia's political culture of the personality cult; the Supreme Leader is never wrong. Tilak was the idol of the masses but never encouraged such a cult. Gandhi and Jinnah did. In India, debate erupted on who was the better successor, Nehru or Patel. In Pakistan, denigration of the level-headed Liaquat Ali Khan became a cottage industry.

In April, Mountbatten's talks with the leaders were in full swing and reached a breakthrough by May. Not surprisingly, because only one option was open—Plan B, partition of India and the provinces of Punjab and Bengal.

Gandhi's exertions need not have frightened Mountbatten since Gandhi had no sensible alternative to offer. But the viceroy was worried lest Gandhi threw a spanner in the works and wrecked the understandings that had been reached. Mountbatten gave full vent to his feelings against Gandhi in private communications

AN EMBITTERED SEPARATION 241

and did so in language that was characteristically intemperate and cheap.

In his personal report dated 5 June 1947, he wrote:

> Since Gandhi returned to Delhi on the 24th May, he has been carrying out an intense propaganda against the new plan (for partition), and although I have always been led to understand he was the man who got Congress to turn down the Cabinet Mission plan a year ago he was now trying to force the Cabinet Mission plan on the country. He may be a saint but he seems also to be a disciple of Trotsky.[6]

On 2 July 1947, the viceroy wrote to Prime Minister Attlee, 'My private opinion is that Gandhi is adopting his usual Trotsky attitude and might quite well like to see the present plan wrecked, so he is busy stiffening Congress attitude'.[7]

On 4 July, Mountbatten repeated his, by now favourite, expression in his personal report:

> The attitude of Gandhi continues to be quite unpredictable and as an example of what I have to contend with I attach as appendices 'A' and 'B' a copy of a letter I received from him dated 27th June, together with the reply I sent him on the next day. Needless to say everything he wrote in his letter was a complete misrepresentation, either deliberate or otherwise, of what I had said to him. He is an inveterate and dangerous Trotskyist.[8]

Never mind that this ignoramus hardly knew what Trotsky's ideology was. But to him 'Trotskyist' could only mean a destroyer, a wrecker.

Retrospect brings out the pattern of Gandhi and the Congress' repeated miscalculations after 1937. The first taste of power had produced delusions of absolute power and added to its arrogance towards all, even men like Jayakar. The Quit India Movement was predicated on the defeat of Britain and its allies in the war.

Pakistan was first dismissed as being economically unviable. It was conceded in the fond belief that Jinnah and his League would return to India in sackcloth and ashes when, perhaps, all sins would be forgiven.

Consequently, it never occurred to any one, even faintly, to publicly and extensively declare that in any event, the non-Muslim areas of Punjab and Bengal could never form part of Pakistan. The truth hit the people affected when all of a sudden, the inevitable happened. They had believed all along that their Quaid-i-Azam would not, as he was reputed, 'yield an inch of ground'. They did not know of the territorial concessions he had made in private since 1942, nor the fact that the stance he had adopted was forced on him by the Congress' refusal to deal with him as a partner in the enterprise. Deep within he had remained the conciliator of old. Only this time around, there was no Tilak with whom to forge a pact on national unity. An altogether different political ethos had possessed the land. Jinnah adopted the very weapons of mobilization which Congress had deployed for long. Both sides miscalculated with tragic consequences.

The record on the Congress' arrogant complacence is impressive. On 4 March 1947, shortly after Attlee's historic announcement of 20 February on the transfer of power to India by the end of June 1948, Patel confidently wrote to his old friend Kanji Dwarkadas, his assessment of the situation:

> Of course, the Labour Government have proved their bona fides to us and to the world but the Statement for the present, has resulted in our losing the Punjab. I am not, however, taking such a gloomy view about the Punjab as you do. Even if the League succeeds in forming the Ministry in the Punjab, it would only be for a period of a year and a quarter. Before next June, the Constitution must be ready and if the League insists on Pakistan, the only alternative is the division of the Punjab and Bengal. They cannot have Punjab as a whole or Bengal without civil war. I do not think that the British Government will agree to division. In the end, they will see the

wisdom of handing over the reins of Government to the strongest party. Even if they do not do so, they will not help the minority in securing or maintaining division, and a strong Centre with the whole of India, except Eastern Bengal and a part of the Punjab, Sind and Baluchistan, enjoying full autonomy under that Centre, will be so powerful that the remaining portions will eventually come in.[9]

He had assumed that (a) the British would not agree to the partition; (b) they would eventually hand over 'the reins of Government' to the Congress; (c) the NWFP would not become a part of Pakistan; and most importantly (d) 'the remaining portions', which comprise Pakistan, 'will eventually come in'. There was no warrant for any of these assumptions.

Mountbatten shrewdly understood the Congress' calculations. When he met Prime Minister Attlee, Cripps and a few others in London on 19 May to explain the partition proposal, he revealed that Jinnah's refusal to meet the Congress leaders in discussion rendered his task difficult. This explains why Nehru and Shankarrao Deo's letters to Liaquat, proposing direct talks, drew a blank. Jinnah adamantly maintained his refusal until an accord was reached on the 3 June Plan and then, too, for formal talks with the viceroy in the chair. History, assuredly, would have taken a different turn if he had risen to the occasion and held direct talks with Nehru and Patel since the principle of partition had been accepted in March.

Mountbatten proceeded to mention that with the threat of violence in the air, the Congress leaders 'were now inclined to feel that it would be to their advantage to be relieved of responsibility for the Provinces that would form Pakistan, while at the same time they were confident that those Provinces would ultimately have to seek re-union with the remainder of India.'[10]

The two sides separated in rancour and bitterness. Its depth can be gauged from Patel's remarks on 8 August. Jinnah flew to Karachi from Delhi on 7 August. Mosley records:

He left Delhi after delivering a conciliatory message in which he appealed to both Hindus and Muslims to bury the past and wished India success and prosperity. He got a bucket of water in his face in return from Sardar Patel who said in Delhi the following day: 'The poison has been removed from the body of India. We are now one and indivisible. You cannot divide the sea or the waters of the river. As for the Muslims, they have their roots, their sacred places and their centres here. I do not know what they can possibly do in Pakistan. It will not be long before they return to us'.[11]

Even after the partition, Nehru assured the Kashmiri leader, Sheikh Mohammed Abdullah, on 10 October 1947, 'As for Pakistan, it is in an infinitely worse position and I doubt very much if it can survive at all. Financially it will be completely bankrupt. It has no trained personnel, and the burdens it carries are such that it can hardly survive'.[12]

On the other side, as mentioned earlier, all the assumptions Jinnah had so fondly entertained were proved wrong, to no small extent because of his own hauteur: (a) there was no hope in sight for friendly relationship between the two new States whose leaders squabbled endlessly, even after both had accepted the Mountbatten Plan for partition; (b) the minorities in West Pakistan were leaving their hearths and homes. The carnage and massive transfers of population imperilled the minorities in both states; (c) an iron wall grew up in 1948 which rendered visits to each other's country, transfer of funds and holding of property in each other's country impossible, a divide which persists still; and (d) the two countries became locked in strife which shows no sign of ending. In the result, the partition did not 'solve the communal question' as Jinnah had hoped; it 'bisected it', to use the expression coined by the distinguished journalist Frank Moraes, an ardent admirer of Jinnah till the end ('the most completely honest politician I ever knew'). The presence of Hindus in West Pakistan was fundamental to Jinnah's concept of a modern secular state as also free travel between the two countries. That was not to be.

AN EMBITTERED SEPARATION   245

Jinnah told the meeting of leaders with the viceroy on 3 June that, 'it would be his intention in Pakistan to observe no communal differences. All those who lived there, regardless of creed, would be fully-fledged citizens'.

When the Council of the All-India Muslim League met on 9 June at the Imperial Hotel in Queensway (now Janpath), New Delhi, the proceedings were held *in camera*. But 'a source of the Intelligence Bureau' provided Patel, the Home Member, with a report of the proceedings—documents in *The Transfer of Power* volumes show that the Intelligence Bureau had thoroughly penetrated, both, the Congress and the League. Patel forwarded the report to Mountbatten. The plan was accepted by 460 votes to 8, which included Maulana Hasrat Mohani.

But not before Jinnah was questioned by members from UP, Bombay, Orissa, and Bengal about the fate of the Muslim minority in India. The report said, 'In reply to these questions, Mr Jinnah said that he could disclose nothing beyond his personal opinion that the safeguarding of the rights of Muslims minorities would depend upon the future relations between Hindustan and Pakistan'.[13]

It was a pathetic admission which the president made in 'his personal opinion'. In 1916, Jinnah was accused by Muslim leaders of Punjab, of sacrificing their rights for the protection of the rights for the Muslim minorities. Events cruelly brought about a transformation. He was now the champion of the rights of the Pakistan provinces. He had no solution to the problems his policies had created for the Muslim minority in India. They had to bear the brunt.

This was, of course, predictable and had been predicted by all outside the circles of the League. The predicament was not unique. At a seminar in Princeton, in December 1968, the Black leader, Roy Innis, advocated 'a social contract between the two main factions', the blacks and the whites. The blacks were not in a majority in a single state in the United States. Espousing 'black nationalism', he rejected 'integration'. He demanded, therefore, a union of 25 million blacks in communities in which they held sway; a 'nations like structure which is unique' with its own political institutions.

Carl Kaysen, who was an adviser to President John F. Kennedy, brought Roy Innis down to earth with these remarks.

> What you say may be a feasible goal, provided you and your colleagues have the magic, the organizational power, the drive, the leadership to organize and successfully exploit the misery in which most black Americans live. But what I think you're not taking into account is that the white society you would make your new social contract with, should you succeed, would not be today's moderately, mildly watered-down liberal white society. It would be a much more mobilized and repressive white society, in which the power equation between, in your language, 'you and us' would be more sharply drawn. Would you get a good bargain?[14]

Jinnah provided the leadership, 'the magic, the organizational power, the drive' of a kind that amazed admirers and critics alike. But the mobilization of Muslims, on the plank of a Two-Nation Theory and a separatist agenda, produced the Hindu backlash, which Nehru predicted in 1945, to the Communist Party's ideologue, Dr K.M. Ashraf.

From 1920 onwards, one thing led to another. K.M. Munshi called Gandhi's rise to eminence in Indian politics an 'avalanche' which swept all, except a few. Jinnah was the foremost among them and accurately predicted that Gandhi's movement 'would inevitably result in widespread violence'. But, Jinnah did not anticipate the consequences of his movement and its impact on the Muslim and Hindu masses.

Over two centuries earlier, the wise Edward Burke had warned 'the temper of the people amongst whom he presides ought to be the first study of a statesman. And the knowledge of this temper is by no means impossible for him to attain, if he has not an interest in being ignorant of what it is his duty to learn'.[15] None of the iconic figures Gandhi, Jinnah, and Nehru had a sure grasp of the temper of the people who loved them. They understood only in part. In this, Tilak was unique. He belonged to the masses.

None of the first three could have felt comfortable in the moral, legal, or political culture of the countries they had created. Muslims who left India to escape the massacres were not allowed to retain their homes. Vazira Fazila-Yacoobali Zamindar's stupendous research, establishes some of the grimmer and neglected happenings.[16]

The exodus of refugees brought in its train problems of relief and resettlement; the permit system, followed by passports and visas, and the ruinous laws on evacuee property. Her accounts of the Muslim exodus from Delhi and the Hindu exodus from Karachi reveal a lot. Delhi's Deputy Commissioner, M.S. Randhawa, earned deserved notoriety for his communal behaviour. The Chief Commissioner, Sahibzada Khurshid Ahmad, was undermined.

The author was surprised to discover, as many readers will be now, that in 1948, within months after partition:

> the tide turned and large numbers of north Indian Muslim refugees began to return to their homes in India. This return had enormous significance, for the first restrictions on movement in the region came in the form of an emergency permit system instituted by the Indian government to stem this tide and led to the introduction of citizenship provision ahead of the Constitution itself.

Differences arose between Nehru and the group comprising Patel, Rajendra Prasad, and very many others.

Randhawa documented on 1 June 1948:

> There are rumours that some trouble will take place in the last week of June...the return of Muslims in large numbers from Pakistan and the occupation of houses which have been lying vacant seems to be the major cause of these rumours. The refugees were living in the hope that they will be able to get these houses, but with the return of Muslims, these hopes are vanishing. Consequently they want to create panic among Muslims, by spreading rumours that some trouble will take place. Creation of so-called Muslim zones which are nothing but miniature Pakistan is also resented.

Khurshid Ahmed pencilled on the margin: 'I hope when D.C. says they are nothing but miniature Pakistan he is not explaining his own views but the views held by unbalanced refugees'. He held his tongue firmly in cheek, evidently.

In a note to the cabinet ministers on 12 September 1947, Nehru wrote:

> The disturbances in West and East Punjab have led to vast migrations across the border and an exchange of population is going on. This might be said to have been spontaneous, or under the stress of circumstances. Although exchange of population was occasionally mentioned during the past few months as a possible consequence of Pakistan, few people took it seriously and most of us criticized it as totally impracticable. Even after the disturbances began in the Punjab, we did not definitely encourage such an exchange, though we made arrangements for the removal of evacuees in danger of their lives. These arrangements developed till they became, in effect, arrangements for an exchange of population on a large scale....
>
> The Delhi disturbances have raised a novel aspect of this problem and we have now to consider it not merely in relation to the Punjab or the Frontier, etc., but in its all-India context. We have indeed to

think out carefully the exact policy we should pursue in future on this vital point so that the steps we may take in the present may not come in the way of our general policy.... We cannot be slaves of circumstances, as we have been to some extent during the past few weeks, being driven hither and thither by forces utterly beyond our control. We cannot ignore public opinion, of course, especially when there is strong feeling behind it. At the same time it would be dangerous for us to encourage any policies which might be based on emotional upheaval which exist today. That upheaval will die down to a large extent and then we shall have to face the consequences of any wrong policy that we might adopt. We have to think in terms of the future of India, what kind of India we envisages and hope to build, what its relations are going to be with Pakistan as well as the rest of the world. It is perhaps not necessary or desirable to come to final and concrete decisions immediately. Any attempt to do so might lead us into wrong decisions, because of the prevailing sentiment.

The disturbances in Delhi have brought the wider issue before us in all its grimness. The secession of certain parts of India and the formation of Pakistan has left India very predominantly non-Muslim, though it has still a considerable Muslim population. We have guaranteed in the constitution we are making the fullest rights to all minorities. That is common ground. It is clearly, however, that the part that Muslims have played in India has been very greatly reduced by the establishment of Pakistan. Such part as they can play can only be a cooperative part, and not one by compulsion which the great majority will never tolerate. There has been this element of compulsion in the past or threats, and this has led to the present unhappy situation and anger between the various communities.

Are we to aim at or to encourage trends which will lead to the progressive elimination of the Muslim population from India, or are we to consolidate, make secure and absorb as full citizens the Muslims who remain in India. That, again, involves our conception of India; is it going to be, as it has been in a large measure, a kind of composite state where there is complete cultural freedom for various groups, but at the same time a strong political unity, or do we wish to make it, as certain elements appear to desire, definitely a Hindu or a non-Muslim state?[17]

His anguish could not have been mitigated by recollection of the warnings he had consistently and prophetically delivered.

Jinnah and Nehru were two secularists who pursued policies and initiated trends over which they lost control and were overcome by forces neither respected. For none but none, had understood the temper of the people. Civil disobedience led to violence and disregard for the law. Nehru's denial of the minority's problems created a deadlock. Jinnah's Two-Nation Theory encouraged communalists and sectarian forces that have no interest in his 11 August 1947 speech.

Notes

1. Penderel Moon, *Divide and Quit*, Chatto & Windus, London, 1961, p. 20.
2. Mehrunisa Ali (ed.), *Jinnah on World Affairs: Select Documents*, Pakistan Study Centre, University of Karachi, 2007, p. 378.
3. ToP, Vol. X, p. 846.
4. H.M. Seervai, *Partition of India: Legend and Reality*, Oxford University Press, Karachi, 2005, p. 182.
5. Nayar, Vol. II, pp. 128–9 in facsimile; *Collected Works of Mahatma Gandhi*, Vol. 87, pp. 199–200 and 246–7 for texts of both documents.
6. ToP, Vol. XI, p. 160.
7. Ibid., p. 826.
8. Ibid., p. 896.
9. G. M. Nandurkar (ed.), *Sardar's Letters Mostly Unknown*, Vol. II, Sardar Vallabhbhai Patel Smarak Bhavan; Ahmedabad, p. 209.
10. ToP, Vol. X, p. 896.
11. Leonard Mosley, *The Last Days of the British Raj*, Weidenfeld & Nicolson, London, 1961, p. 248.
12. SWJN, Vol. 4, p. 269.
13. ToP, Vol. XI, p. 245.
14. Francois Duchene (ed.), *The Endless Crisis: America in the Seventies*, (Seminar Proceedings), Simon & Schuster, p. 103.
15. E.J. Payne, *Burke—Selected Works, Thoughts on the Present Discontents*, Clarendon Press, Oxford, 1904, p. 3.
16. Vazira Fazila-Yacoobali Zamindar, *The Long Partition and the Making of Modern South Asia*, Oxford University Press, Karachi, 2008.
17. S. Gopal and Uma Iyenger (eds.), *The Essential Writings of Jawaharlal Nehru*, Vol. I, Oxford University Press, New Delhi, pp. 164–5.

8

The United Bengal Episode

In April 1947, there was an excellent opportunity to lower the temperature and thus lessen the trauma of the partition. The premier of Bengal, Huseyn Shaheed Suhrawardy, was shaken by the implications for his province of Attlee's announcement on 20 February, to transfer power, if necessary, to a divided India. He wrote a letter to [the last British] governor of Bengal, Sir Frederick Burrows on 24 February, with a copy to Jinnah on 26 February, proposing an independent Bengal.[1]

Suhrawardy fired his opening salvo as early as on 13 March 1947, 'Whatever may be the form of the future constitution. I certainly visualize that the province of Bengal will attain an independent status'. He hinted at the immediate formation of an all-party government to replace the league Ministry which he headed.

A detailed exposition of the concept was made by Suhrawardy at a press conference in New Delhi on 27 April and by the secretary of the Bengal Provincial Muslim League, Abul Hashim, at Calcutta, on 29 April. Both, the viceroy and the governor, promoted it ardently till the last. Burrows tried to convince a sceptical Kiran Shankar Roy, leader of the opposition in the assembly, of its worth on 22 March.[2]

Suhrawardy spoke of 'an independent, undivided and sovereign Bengal, in a divided India, as a separate Dominion'.[3] 26 April 1947 was a day of crucial importance. Mountbatten met Suhrawardy as well as Jinnah that day. Suhrawardy told him that, 'he could get Mr Jinnah to agree that it need not join Pakistan if it was prepared to remain united'. He pleaded with the viceroy not to have a decision on partition until November, but secured only a brief respite since a decision had to be made 'within one month'.[4]

When Mountbatten met Jinnah later in the day he asked him 'straight out what his views were about keeping Bengal United at the price of its remaining out of Pakistan. He said, without any hesitation "I should be delighted, what is the use of Bengal without Calcutta. They had much better remain united and independent: I am sure they would be on friendly terms with us".'[5]

The fact that this represented a considered decision becomes apparent from the fact that Liaquat Ali Khan told Eric Mieville, principal secretary to the viceroy, at a dinner two days later that, 'he was in no way worried about Bengal as he was convinced in his own mind that the province would never divide. He thought that it would remain a separate state, joining neither Hindustan nor Pakistan'.[6] The loyalist Nazimuddin also endorsed the demand in press statements on 22 April and 9 May. Mountbatten won over Roy completely on 3 May, on the assurance of joint electorates.

He, however, received a letter of 2 May from Shyama Prasad Mookerjee pressing for Bengal's partition regardless of whether India remained one or not.[7] Mookerjee wrote in the same vein to Vallabhbhai Patel on 11 May, warning him about Sarat Bose's parleys with Suhrawardy. 'Even if a loose centre as contemplated under the Cabinet Mission Scheme is established, we shall have no safety in Bengal'. He was knocking at a door wide open. As well as assuring him, Patel wrote to other Bengali leaders, besides reproaching Sarat Bose himself, on 22 May. He told K.C. Neogy (13 May) that, 'the only way to save the Hindus of Bengal is to insist on partition of Bengal and to listen to nothing else', Binoy Kumar Roy was assured the next day in these terms, 'Bengal has got to be partitioned, if the non-Muslim population is to survive'.⁸

Nehru was also strongly opposed to the idea. He wrote to S.P. Mookerjee on 14 May that he was against 'a sovereign Bengal unconnected with the Union'.⁹ Nehru told Norman Cliff of *News Chronicle* on 27 May that 'he would agree to Bengal remaining united only if it remains in the Union'.¹⁰

Mountbatten reported to Burrows a talk he had had with Suhrawardy on 16 May, 'I warned him that Nehru was not in favour of an independent Bengal unless closely linked to Hindustan, as he felt that a partition now would anyhow bring East Bengal into Hindustan in a few years'.¹¹ In a discussion with Eric Mieville on 27 May, Nehru 'reacted strongly and said there was no chance of the Hindus there agreeing to put themselves under permanent Muslim domination which was what the proposed agreement really amounted to. He did not however, rule out the possibility of Bengal joining up with Hindustan'.¹² Nehru urged partition of Punjab and Bengal even if the Mission's Plan was accepted and India remained united.¹³

The only person who could have retrieved the situation for Sarat Bose and Suhrawardy was Gandhi. Bose met him at Sodepur Ashram on 10 May along with Abul Hashim. Hashim built his case for a united Bengal on the 'common language, common culture, and common history that united the Hindus and Muslims of Bengal alike' neither of whom wished to be ruled by 'Pakistanis who loved a thousand miles away'.

Gandhi put a couple of searching questions. What if Pakistan offered a 'voluntary federation' based on a common religion? Alternatively, if culture be the bond, Bengal's culture is derived 'from the priceless heirloom of all India'. What had he, then, to say of a 'voluntary association' between Bengal and the rest of

India? If that is so, and 'Bengal wishes to enter into voluntary association with the rest of India, what would you say about that?'

Having rejected, implicitly, association with Pakistan, Hashim could hardly endorse Gandhi's suggestion of a union with India. His silence drew from Gandhi the comment, 'You have not really made up your mind about Pakistan. Please think about it once more, and then we shall discuss the new proposal'.[14]

Suhrawardy tried his skills in persuasion with Gandhi on 11 and 12 May and was told 'a new Bengal could not be born in utter disregard of the past'. On 13 May Mookerjee pleaded his cause. Gandhi proposed that a decision by a majority of members of each community alone could suffice to establish a united Bengal or bring about its partition. This was a fair test.

Time was fast running out for Suhrawardy. He told Mountbatten on 14 May that, 'they had made good progress and on the whole he was hopeful of the result'. The viceroy had already obtained a copy of the document Bose and Roy had handed to Suhrawardy, which spoke of a 'Socialist' Republic of Bengal. Its text is not reproduced in any of the works. It was released to the press in Calcutta on 18 May by Fazlur Rehman and is reproduced here from the *Morning Herald*, a daily which was published for a brief period in Bombay. It read thus:

> (1) Bengal to be a sovereign Socialist Republic of Bengal will decide its relations with the rest of India. (2) The Bengal Legislature, after the constitution is framed and put into force, should be elected on the basis of adult franchise and joint electorate etc. (3) On para 1 and 2 being accepted by both parties and on Bengal being declared by His Majesty's Government as an independent state, the present Ministry will be dissolved and an Interim Government will be formed consisting of equal numbers of Muslims and Hindus (including the scheduled caste Hindus) but excluding the Chief Minister who will be a Muslim. The Home Minister shall be a

Hindu. (4) The Interim Government will give Hindus, including scheduled castes, and Muslims equal share in the service. (5) The British Government shall transfer power to Interim Government on or before June 1948. (6) An ad hoc constitution-making body consisting of 30 persons, 16 Muslims and 14 Hindus, will be set up by the Muslim League and the Congress respectively to frame a constitution.

Mountbatten warned that, 'it would debar their entry into the British Commonwealth'. The only other state that called itself socialist was the USSR. They could style themselves as a 'Free State' or simply Bengal. Burrows informed him that Bose was agreeable to the name 'Free State of Bengal'.[15] This explains the change in the text that was signed by Sarat Bose and Abul Hashim on 20 May at Bose's house, in the presence of Suhrawardy, his cabinet colleagues, Mohammed Ali Bogra, Fazlur Rehman, and Kiran Shankar Roy.

Bose forwarded it to Gandhi as 'a tentative agreement' under a covering letter dated 23 May. The agreement read thus:

1. Bengal will be a Free State. The Free State of Bengal will decide its relations with the rest of India.
2. The constitution of the Free State of Bengal will provide for election to the Bengal Legislature on the basis of joint electorate and adult franchise, with reservation of seats proportionate to the population amongst Hindus and Muslims. The seats as between Hindus and Scheduled Caste Hindus will be distributed amongst them in proportion to their respective population or in such manner as may be agreed among them. The constituencies will be multiple constituencies and the votes will be distributive and not cumulative. A candidate who gets the majority of the votes of his own community cast during the elections and 25 per cent of the votes of the other communities so cast will be declared elected. If no candidate satisfied these conditions, that candidate who gets the largest number of votes of his own community will be elected.
3. On the announcement by His Majesty's Government that the proposal of the Free State of Bengal has been accepted and that

Bengal will not be partitioned, the present Bengal Ministry will be dissolved and a new Interim Ministry brought into being consisting of an equal number of Muslims and Hindus (including Scheduled Caste Hindus) but excluding the Chief Minister. In this ministry, the Chief Minister will be a Muslim and the Home Minister a Hindu.

4. Pending the final emergence of a Legislature and a Ministry under the new constitution the Hindus (including Scheduled Caste Hindus) and the Muslims will have an equal share in the services including military and police. The services will be manned by Bengalees.

5. A Constituent Assembly composed of 30 persons, 16 Muslims, and 14 Hindus will be elected by the Muslim and non-Muslim members of the legislature respectively, excluding the Europeans.

20th May, 1947.
Sd/- Sarat Chandra Bose
Sd/- Abul Hashim[16]

Gandhi replied as follows:

Patna 25/5/47

My dear Sarat,

I have your note. There is nothing in the draft stipulating that nothing will be done by mere majority. Every act of Government must carry with it the co-operation of at least two-thirds of the Hindu members in the Executive and the Legislature. There should be an admission that Bengal has common culture and common mother tongue—Bengali. Make sure that the Central Muslim League approved of the proposal notwithstanding reports to the contrary. If your presence is necessary in Delhi I shall telephone or telegraph. I propose to discuss the draft with the Working Committee.

Yours
Bapu[17]

Sisir Bose records:

> Some changes were made in the terms relating to the future constitution of Bengal as a result of further talks that father had with certain League and Congress leaders.
>
> The authors of the terms continued their discussions with a view to improving them and these talks mostly centred round the provisions relating to (1) the Bengal Free State's relations with the rest of India and (2) elections to the Legislature. Those two paragraphs were redrafted as follows:
>
> Amended Paragraph 1: Bengal will be a Free State. The Free State of Bengal will decide its relations with the rest of India. The question of joining any Union will be decided by the Legislature of the Free State of Bengal by a two-thirds majority. Amended Paragraph 2: The Constitution of the Free State of Bengal will provide for election to the Bengal Legislature on the basis of joint electorate and adult franchise, with reservation of seats proportionate to the population amongst Hindus and Muslims.
>
> The seats as between Hindus and Scheduled Castes Hindus will be distributed amongst them in proportion to their respective population or in such manner as may be agreed among them. The constituencies will be multiple constituencies and the votes will be distributive and not cumulative.
>
> A candidate who gets the largest number of votes of his community cast during the elections and at least 25 per cent of the votes of the other communities so cast will be declared elected. If no candidate satisfies the above conditions then that candidate who gets the next largest number of votes of his own community cast during the elections and at least 25 per cent of the votes of the other communities so cast will be declared elected. If no candidate satisfies the above conditions then that candidate who gets the next largest number of votes of his own community cast during the elections and at least 25 per cent of the votes of the other communities so cast will be declared elected. If no candidate satisfies the conditions laid down in the previous sentence, then that

candidate who gets the largest number of votes out of the total votes polled will be elected.[18]

Father told the Associated Press of India in New Delhi on 31 May 1947 that he had discussed with Mahatma Gandhi the Bengal situation and particularly his plan for the formation of a Free State of Bengal as an alternative to its partition into two provinces. He expressed the belief that if the Congress High Command accepted his plan, then it would be easier to persuade the League High Command to agree to Mr Suhrawardy's scheme of United Bengal which was virtually the same as his own plan.

Father added, 'I have faith in my proposal and shall stick to it to the last. I shall meet other Congress leaders and explore all possibilities of preventing the partition of Bengal. I do not say that Bengal should remain outside the Union. What I say is that only a Free Bengal can decide her relations with the rest of India'.

While in London, Mountbatten received the Cabinet Committee's authorization 'to re-cast Statement so far as Bengal is concerned in the light of circumstances prevailing on June 2nd'.[19] Broadcast 'A' was to be used 'if it appears probable that Bengal will be partitioned'. Broadcast 'B', 'if it appears probable that Bengal will remain unified'. The only difference between 'A' and 'B' was an additional para which read, 'Bengal was one of the provinces for whom partition was demanded, but the newly formed Coalition Government of Bengal have asked for their case to be reconsidered, and this is reviewed in the statement which is shortly to be read out'.[20] It was that close as late as on 31 May 1947.

He met Suhrawardy immediately on his return to Delhi on 30 May. But he appreciated that it depended on accord between the leaders at the centre. Despite their broadcasts on 3 June, in which they accepted the Partition Plan, neither Sarat Bose nor Suhrawardy gave up hope. Bose wrote to Jinnah on 9 June seeking his support.

By now Gandhi felt that it was best to scotch the moves decisively. He wrote to Sarat Bose on 8 June:

> I have gone through your draft. I have now discussed the scheme thoroughly with Pandit Nehru and the Sardar. Both of them are dead against the proposal and they are of opinion that it is merely a trick for dividing Hindus and Scheduled Caste leaders.
>
> With them it is not merely a suspicion but almost a conviction. They feel also that money is being lavishly expended in order to secure Scheduled Caste votes. If such is the case you should give up the struggle at least at present. For the unity purchased by corrupt practices would be worse than a frank partition, it being a recognition of the established division of hearts and the unfortunate experiences of the Hindus. I see also that there is no prospect of transfer of power outside the two parts of India.

Unless he secured written assurance of 'the local Muslim League supported by the Centre', he should give up the struggle for Bengal's unity 'and cease to disturb the atmosphere that has been created for the partition of Bengal.[21] Both, Bose and Suhrawardy denied the charges of corruption.[22]

Sarat Bose's claim to Gandhi that a referendum of the Hindus of Bengal would have registered a vote against partition, was of doubtful validity. But his son Sugata Bose makes the perfect comment on the vote in the Bengal assembly pursuant to the Mountbatten Plan of 3 June:

> The charade of ascertaining 'the will of the people' carried out on 20 June 1947 has left the historian with a small advantage. It has put on record that the legislators of that part of Bengal which went to Pakistan overwhelmingly, rejected by 106 votes to 35, the offer of their partitioned inheritance. The decisive votes to partition Bengal were cast by 58 West Bengal legislators against 21 opposed.[23]

He recalled that:

Although it won far fewer votes than the Congress, the Muslim League emerged with an absolute majority in the 1946 elections by making a sweep of 115 of the 123 Muslim seats. The Congress took almost all the general seats and a majority of the scheduled caste seats, but ended up with a total of only sixty-two. Despite his majority, the League leader Suhrawardy's first instinct was to form a coalition ministry with the Congress. This did not suit the high commands of either party.

He traced the Congress' consistent refusal to share power since 1937.

On the related aspect of Muslim domination or union with Pakistan, which could have been excluded by treaty as was done in the case of Austria in 1955, Harun-or-Rashid points out:

> It was not fair to link the question of Bengal's independence with the possibility of domination by any party like the League. Numerically, Hindus and Muslims of Bengal were almost equal. In a joint electoral system based on universal franchise, as offered under the tentative agreement (also known as the Suhrawardy–Bose–Roy formula), a single communal party rule was seemingly an impossibility. Further, once granted independence, there was hardly any chance of Bengal joining (West) Pakistan.

It was a wilful refusal by the Congress to share power with the League which led to, both, the collapse of the Mission's Plan and defeat of the moves for a United Bengal as the third independent state on the subcontinent. The safeguards which Gandhi demanded for the Hindus of Bengal, in his letter to Sarat Bose on 25 May, were never offered to Muslims in the union either by him, or by the Congress. Indeed, the Muslim League never demanded that 'every act of Government' must be supported by two-thirds of the Muslims 'in the Executive and the Legislature'. This makes governance impossible. Gandhi's terms were impossible.

# NOTES

1. Harun-or-Rashid (ed.), *Inside Bengal Politics 1936–1947: Unpublished Correspondence of Political Leaders*, University Press Ltd., Dhaka, 2003, pp. 72–5. Vide also Harun-or-Rashid, *The Fore-shadowing of Bangladesh*, Asiatic Society of Bangladesh, Dhaka, 1987, Ch. 7, 'The Move for a United Independent Bengal', pp. 273–340.
2. ToP, Vol. X, p. 6.
3. *The Statesman,* 28 April 1947.
4. Ibid., pp. 448–9.
5. Ibid., p. 452.
6. Ibid., p. 452.
7. Ibid., p. 555.
8. Durga Das (ed.), *Sardar Patel's Correspondence: 1945–50*, Vol. IV, Navajivan Publishing House, Ahmedabad, pp. 34, 39 and 43.
9. SWJN, Vol. 2, p. 148.
10. ToP, Vol. X, p. 560.
11. Ibid., p. 850.
12. Ibid., p. 1013.
13. SWJN, Vol. 2, p. 68.
14. Nirmal Kumar Bose, *My Days with Gandhi*, Nishana, Calcutta, 1953, pp. 227–34.
15. ToP, Vol. X, p. 849 and 904 respectively.
16. Sisir Kumar Bose, *Remembering My Father*, Netaji Research Bureau, Calcutta, 1988, pp. 152–3.
17. Ibid., p. 153.
18. Ibid.
19. ToP, Vol. X, p. 971.
20. ToP, Vol. X, p. 1.
21. Nayar, Vol. II, pp. 187–8.
22. Ibid., p. 189–90.
23. Sugata Bose, 'A Doubtful Inheritance: The Partition of Bengal in 1947', in D.A. Low (ed.) *The Political Inheritance*, Pakistan, Delhi, 1982, pp. 130–43.

9

Assessing Jinnah

Only after India was divided, did the leaders come to terms with the grim realities. Jinnah espoused the secular ideal in his famous speech to Pakistan's constituent assembly on 11 August 1947; Nehru, who had rejected the concept of religious minorities in a plural society, fought manfully for secularism and for the Muslims' place in India till his dying day. Gandhi bravely fought communal violence. He was livid when idols were placed inside mosques. He said on 30 November 1947: 'It is the duty of those who have installed the idols to remove them from there.... By thus installing idols in the mosques, they are desecrating the mosques and also insulting the idols'.[1] When he went on a fast to demand protection of Muslims' lives he displeased Sardar Patel and enraged the Hindu fanatics. He *knew* he was courting death. Gandhi consciously chose the path and died a martyr's death.

It fell to Maulana Azad's lot to be vindicated. He spent the rest of his life in suppressed sadness. Years later, Chaudhry Khaliquzzaman ruminated over the post-partition scenario in a *tour d'horizon* with M.B. Naqvi, a senior journalist, and Zuhair Siddiqi. Naqvi's report in *Pakistan Economist* of 15 April 1979, makes sad reading as it recorded the thoughts of a politician who had claimed to be foremost in his advocacy of partition, in his memoir *Pathway to Pakistan* (1962). He was now a much sadder man. He stated:

> The manner in which he made alterations on a single theme for forty minutes was remarkable: 'It was all a mistake'. He was not talking

merely of the 1947 settlement of the old Hindu—Muslim problem of historical India. His scope was larger, it covered the whole orientation of Muslim politics during the British period of Indian history.... He said never be pessimistic about Urdu's future or gloomy over its present predicament; and he included in it the whole subcontinent. He called Urdu a *Chinnal Chhokri* who will eventually carve out for itself a place in the hearts of its most inveterate enemies and tormentors....

But on the more substantive issue of history Khaliquzzaman's judgement, despite its somewhat oracular nature, was emphatic: The 1947 settlement (of historical India) broke-down in 1971 and there is no use pretending nothing has happened. His main argument to prove this comprised just pointing out, the state of the Muslim community, or what used to be proudly called the Muslim India, now divided in three separate communities with hardly anyone daring to have any common link among themselves. His position is, in historical terms, stern indeed. First, apart from the fact that it did not actually solve the issue it set out to, viz. the Hindu–Muslim problem of historical India—and which has largely contributed to its failure—it has simply not worked. Something new is, therefore called for.... There was clear implication, as a corollary of the foregoing, that the over-simple 1947 arrangement has today lost its relevance in its original form. But by this he did not mean a simple rejection or some kind of a return—intellectual or political—to Akhand Bharat. That, he had felt sure, was an idle dream, never to be realized: That ignores almost every factor of history. But what he underlined was: Some new and close thinking was called for. He felt grieved that none of it was taking place in Pakistan; he did not know about India or Bangladesh.

Thirdly, here he did not only speak with some animation but some sorrow, 'look at the condition of the three isolated Muslim communities. They dare not communicate with one another.' And look at their political weight in the area: Pakistanis today are not one-third as important as the pre-independence Muslim India was. Are the Indian Muslim a third of their forebears in political weight? The Muslims of Bangladesh—well, you know, they do not count as much as even Pakistan.

But Azad had seen it all before and at the time of the partition. On 15 April 1946, Maulana Azad issued a statement about Pakistan, analyzing its implications:

> I have come to the conclusion that it is harmful not only for India as a whole but for Muslims in particular. And in fact it creates more problems than it solves.... The scheme of Pakistan is a symbol of defeatism.... It is a confession that Indian Muslims cannot hold their own in India as a whole and would be content to withdraw to a corner specially reserved for them.... Over 90 millions in number they are in quantity and quality a sufficiently important element in Indian life to influence decisively all questions of administration and policy. Nature has further helped them by concentrating them in certain areas.... I am prepared to overlook all other aspects of the problem and judge it from the point of view of Muslim interests alone. I shall go still further and say that if it can be shown that the scheme of Pakistan can in any way benefit Muslims I would be prepared to accept it myself and also to work for its acceptance by others. But the truth is that even if I examine the scheme from the point of view of the communal interests of the Muslims themselves. I am forced to the conclusion that it can in no way benefit them or allay their legitimate fears.
>
> Let us consider dispassionately the consequences which will follow if we give effect to the Pakistan scheme. India will be divided into two states, one with a majority of Muslims and the other of Hindus. In the Hindustan State there will remain 3½ crores of Muslims scattered in small minorities all over the land. With 17 per cent in UP, 12 per cent in Bihar and 9 per cent in Madras, they will be weaker than they are today in the Hindu majority provinces. They have had their homelands in these regions for almost a thousand years and built up well-known centres of Muslims culture and civilization there.
>
> They will awaken overnight and discover that they have become aliens and foreigners. Backward industrially, educationally, and economically they will be left to the mercies of what would then become an unadulterated Hindu raj.

On the other hand, their position within the Pakistan State will be vulnerable and weak. Nowhere in Pakistan will their majority be comparable to the Hindu majority in the Hindustan State.

In fact, their majority will be so slight that it will be offset by the economical, educational, and political lead enjoyed by non-Muslims in these areas. Even if this were not so and Pakistan were overwhelmingly Muslim in population, it still could hardly solve the problem of Muslims in Hindustan.

Two States confronting one another offer no solution to the problem of one another's minorities, but only lead to retribution and reprisals by introducing a system of mutual hostages. The scheme of Pakistan therefore solves no problem for the Muslims. It cannot safeguard their rights where they are in a minority nor as citizens of Pakistan secure them a position in Indian or world affairs which they would enjoy as citizens of a major State like the Indian Union.

It may be argued that if Pakistan is so much against the interest of the Muslims themselves, why should such a large section of Muslims be swept away by its lure? The answer is to be found in the attitude of certain communal extremists among the Hindus. When the Muslim League began to speak of Pakistan, they read into the scheme a sinister Pan-Islamic conspiracy and began to oppose it out of fear that it foreshadowed a combination of Indian Muslims with trans-Indian Muslim States. The opposition acted as an incentive to the adherents of the League.

He proposed a grant of full autonomy to the provinces. The Congress, however, had other ideas.

Azad told a group of Muslims from UP who were about to leave for Pakistan:

> You are going away from your motherland. Have you reflected on its consequences? Your fleeing from here will weaken the Muslims of India and a day might well come when the present people of Pakistan will rise to assert their individual identities. Bengalis, Punjabis, Sindhis, Baloch, and Pathan will claim separate

nationalities. Will not your status in Pakistan then become as precarious and helpless as that of uninvited guests?[2]

It would, however, be wrong to suggest that his own record was free from blemish or error. His qualities outweighed them.

Sir Chimanlal Setalvad delivered a fair verdict:

> It is futile to attempt to hide the naked truth by saying that force of circumstances has compelled the Congress to accept the partition of India and they had to submit to the inevitable. The circumstances were of their own creation, and what had once been warded off was made inevitable by their own deeds. The cherished boon of a united India had fallen into their lap, but they by their own want of political wisdom threw it out and made it beyond their reach....
>
> What has happened is indeed a great personal triumph for Mr Jinnah. Within seven years after the Lahore Pakistan resolution of 1940, he has succeeded in defeating a great political organisation of sixty years' standing with the backing of the large majority of the Indian people. But has he succeeded in doing good to the Muslims themselves and to his country? ...this division of India has laid the foundations of interminable quarries and chaos which will bring untold suffering to generations yet unborn.[3]

Jinnah was not exactly a picture of joy when Pakistan was established. Events had overwhelmed him and his miscalculations, rash as they were, diverted to a course he could not have imagined. His style foiled his policies.

The memoirs of A.R. Siddiqi, a Dehlavi who settled in Karachi after the partition, record the shock and trauma that Muslims felt in the historic city, as the implications of Pakistan emerged from the realm of slogan to the world of reality. If scholars and their students felt disoriented, one can imagine the pain of the ordinary Muslim.

A.R. Siddiqi writes:

> Our history teacher, the Dean of the Faculty of Arts, Dr Ishtiaq Hussain Qureshi, was quite a political activist, unflinchingly committed to the Pakistan movement, although he saw the emergence of Pakistan neither as a parting of the ways nor exactly as a partition of the country—it would be more of a 'political redefinition' of an Indian than anything else. The making of Pakistan was, to his mind, the best way for the two largest communities of the subcontinent, the Hindus and the Muslims, to live in peace and harmony and according to their own rights.[4]

> On which side of the divide would Delhi be, though? We believed that in all fairness it ought to become the joint capital of both countries, for it was utterly inconceivable to have a Pakistan without Delhi and its Delhiwallas....[5]

There was gloom in the office of *Dawn*, the Muslim League's organ, at Daryaganj in Old Delhi, when the Partition Plan of 3 June 1947 was announced. The League's Council accepted it at a meeting held in the Imperial Hotel at Janpath (then Queensway) in New Delhi.

> ...the mere thought of leaving the city for good was like a stab in my heart. At the India Coffee House, New Delhi, our daily haunt, I had heated arguments with a group of Hindu friends. Modest and quite on the defensive before the Partition Plan, they were becoming increasingly assertive, even aggressive. They would taunt me, saying, 'So your Mr Jinnah had to eat his words and accept his moth-eaten and truncated Pakistan? Why?' 'You just wait and see.... Nobody can beat Mr Jinnah on the political chessboard,' I would snap back...[6]

Little did he know that at the very moment in May 1947, when Jinnah publicly said he would not accept the partition of Punjab and Bengal, he was negotiating the terms of reference of the Boundary Commission in these provinces.

Siddiqi describes the culture of Old Delhi, the travails of the Mohajirs and their culture shock when they settled in Pakistan.

> The hope of projecting 100 million Indian Muslims as one nation under the magic spell of the Pakistan Movement was shattered on first contact with the harsh realities of provincialism. The emergence of the state of Pakistan saw the melting away of incipient nationalism, or nationhood, among Indian Muslims, and what had been a supreme achievement in reality was only a partial success.[7]

Siddiqi adds:

> Through many centuries of co-existence and interaction with the Hindus, the Muslims of the Ganga-Yamuna belt had evolved a cultural, linguistic, and dietary mix which was an exotic patchwork of Hindu–Muslim India. Over the years, the matrix assumed an all-India complexion *vis-à-vis* the essentially local-provincial cultures and languages.[8]

It is this composite culture that suffered the most, Urdu particularly. No one anticipated the imposition of travel barriers between India and Pakistan amidst the carnage.

What Raja Ram Narain Mauzun wrote of Sirajuddaulah's brave, but unsuccessful fight at the Battle of Plassey in 1787, is true of the misfortune that befell the subcontinent in 1857 after the Great Mutiny and even more so of the tragedy of 1947.

غزالاں تم تو واقف ہو، کہو مجنوں کے مرنے کی
دیوانہ مر گیا آخر کو ویرانے پہ کیا گزری

(*Oh Gazelles! You certainly know.*
Tell us of the death of Majnoon.
The frenzied lover died at last, but what befell the wilderness).

In any fair verdict, neither Jinnah's qualities, nor his failings and errors must be underestimated. If the Mission's Plan was an achievement, could he not have unbent to assure Assam that it would not be coerced and saved the plan? A Congress–League Pact in 1946 would have been in the spirit of the Lucknow Pact of 1916 between Jinnah and Tilak.

Some day, the verdict of history on Jinnah will be written definitively. When it is written, that verdict will be in the terms Gibbon used for Belisarius, 'His imperfections flowed from the contagion of the times; his virtues were his own, the free gift of nature or reflection. He raised himself without a master or a rival and so inadequate were the arms committed to his hand, that his sole advantage was derived from the pride and presumption of his adversaries'.[9]

His life and political career must be viewed as a whole. He faltered, but never stooped. In that selfless, steadfast concern for basic issues of public policy, even if it spelt isolation and wilderness more than once in his career, Jinnah set an example equalled by few.

In that rare mix of qualities of character, political insight, tactical skill, and tenacity of purpose, with failings like lack of imagination and incapacity to rise above the bitterness accumulated over the years, Jinnah sets examples of the highest order yet delivers warning of the havoc which an outstandingly able and dedicated leader can inflict on his people by his hubris.

Jinnah's vision of Pakistan was shattered with the partition of Punjab and Bengal, and the massive killings. For a secular Pakistan, the presence of a large, powerful, and articulate minority was indispensable. This exodus also affected Muslims in India adversely and with lasting consequences. In India the values of democracy and rule of law, which he cherished all his life, are respected. The fact remains that though he broke the mould of constitutional discourse and played with fire, the final responsibility for partition was not his. In the decisive phase in 1946, he thrice discarded partition in favour of a united India—on 25 April in a talk with Stafford Cripps, on 12 May in his own proposals in writing to the Cabinet Mission, and, finally, on 6 June when he got the Council of the Muslim League to accept the Cabinet Mission's Plan of 16 May 1946.

But a united India implied a sharing of power, which the Congress abhorred. Worse still, it had no role for Jinnah as a partner in a united India. He had 'no real place in the country' Nehru maintained repeatedly. The assertion was made first in a diary entry on 25 December 1943 ('keep Jinnah faraway'). It was made openly to the mediators, the Cabinet Mission, on 10 June 1946: Jinnah had 'no real place in the country'.

Jinnah was an expellee, not an exile. His dreams lie buried in India as well as in Pakistan. He might well have cried in the words the gifted poet Sahir Ludhianvi used in 1943 when he was honoured by the Ludhiana Government College, which had expelled him for communist activities:

تو آج بھی ہے میرے لیے جنتِ خیال
ہیں تجھ میں دفن میری جوانی کے چار سال

لیکن ہم ان فضاؤں کے پالے ہوئے تو ہیں
گر یاں نہیں تو یاں سے نکالے ہوئے تو ہیں

(*You are for me still the heaven of my dreams*
On your grounds lie buried four years of my youth.
But I have been brought up very much in its atmosphere
If I do not belong to it, I was at least expelled from this place).

NOTES

1. *Collected Works of Mahatma Gandhi*, Vol. 90, p. 144.
2. *Watan* (Delhi), March 1948, reproduced in *Kamalistan* (Delhi), Special Issue on Maulana Azad, March 1986.
3. *The Times of India*, 15 June 1947; see Appendix for the text.
4. Brigadier A.R. Siddiqi, *Partition and the Making of the Mohajir Mindset: A Narrative*, Oxford University Press, 2008, p. 17. It is a very evocative memoir.
5. Ibid., p. 20.
6. Ibid., p. 21.
7. Ibid., p. xviii.
8. Ibid., p. 108.
9. Edward Gibbon, *The Decline and Fall of the Roman Empire*, Vol. II, The Modern Library, New York, 1932, p. 240.

Appendices

Appendix 1

Jinnah's Defence of Tilak: The Court Proceedings

The Magisterial Proceedings

On Saturday, the 22nd July 1916 in the Court of Mr G.W. Hatch, I.C.S., District Magistrate of Poona, Mr James Adolphus Guider, Deputy Inspector-General of Police, C.I.D., lodged the following information against Mr B.G. Tilak under Section 108 Criminal Procedure Code.

The Information
(Exhibit No. 1)
In the Court of District Magistrate, Poona
JAMES ADOLPHUS GUIDER,
Deputy Inspector-General of Police, C.I.D.
Versus.
BAL GANGADHAR TILAK, B.A., LL.B., residing at Poona

Information under Section 108, C.P.C.

I, the above said James Adolphus Guider, do hereby lay the following information:

1. That the said Bal Gangadhar Tilak having previous convictions on charges of sedition, is orally disseminating as stated below, seditious matter, i.e., matter the publication of which is punishable under section 124A I.P.C.
2. That he delivered speeches on Home Rule,
   (a) At Belgaum on the evening of 1st May 1916 on the termination of the meeting held in connection with the Historical Research Association,
   (b) At Ahmednagar on the evening of 31st May 1916 in the open space behind the Kapad Bazar in reply to an address presented to him by the merchants of the Kapad Bazar,
   (c) At Ahmednagar again on 1st June 1916 in the Old Kapad Bazar, at an open-air mass meeting, all of which he brought, or attempted to bring, into hatred or contempt, or excited, or attempted to excite, disaffection towards His Majesty, or the Government established by law in British India.
3. That it is feared that he will continue to do the same.
4. Copies of speeches referred to in para 2 above are attached herewith as Appendix A, B & C.
5. Witness will be kept in attendance on the date of hearing.

(Sd.) S.C. Davar,   (Sd.) J.A. Guider
Public Prosecutor,
Poona: 22nd July 1916.

The Magistrate after reading the information asked Mr Guider to make an affidavit whereupon Mr Guider submitted it.

Mr Guider's Affidavit
(Exhibit No. 2)

James Adolphus Guider says on solemn affirmation.

The information presented by me today in the matter of Bal Gangadhar Tilak is correct to the best of my belief. It is based partly on information received from my subordinates, partly on records of my office, and on other sources.

I ask that a substantial security of say Rs 50,000 be demanded. He is a man of means, he owns the *Kesari* Press and the Gaikwad Wada. He is a man of considerable influence, and with wealthy friends. At the present moment his friends are collecting a sum of one lakh of rupees for presentation to him tomorrow, as a birthday gift. I ask that security should be taken for one year. I put in the 3 speeches and their translations on which I reply.

(Sd.) J.A. Guider,
before me
(Sd.) G.W. Hatch,
District Magistrate, Poona.

The Magistrate then issued the Preliminary Order and the summons which are given below:

Magistrate's Preliminary Order

Whereas I, G.W. Hatch, District Magistrate, Poona, have received information that Bal Gangadhar Tilak who resides at Poona within the limits of my jurisdiction disseminates seditious matter, in witness of which reports of speeches delivered by him at Belgaum on 1st May 1916, and at Ahmednagar on 31st May and 1st June 1916, on the subject of Home Rule have been produced before me:

I hereby require the said Bal Gangadhar Tilak to show cause why he should not be ordered to execute a bond for a sum of Rs 20,000 with two sureties each in a sum of Rs 10,000 for his good behaviour for a period of one year (section 108, 112 Criminal Procedure Code). Poona, 22-7-1916.

(Sd.) G.W. Hatch,
District Magistrate, Poona

* * *

APPENDIX 1

The Summons
Summons on Information of a Probable Breach of the Peace
(Section 114 of C.P.C.)

To,
    Bal Gangadhar Tilak,
    Narayan Peth, Poona City.

Whereas it has been made to appear to me by a credible information that you disseminate seditious matter, you are hereby required to attend in person at the office of the District Magistrate, Poona, on the 28th day of July 1916 at 12 noon to show cause why you should not be required to enter into a bond for Rs 20,000 and also to give security by the bond of two sureties each in the sum of Rs 10,000 that you will keep the peace for the term of one year.

Given under my hand and the seal of the Court this 22nd day of July 1916.

                                        (Sd.) G.W. Hatch,
                                    District Magistrate, Poona

The notice and the summons were served on Mr Tilak by Mr Boyd, the District Superintendent of Police, Poona, at Mr Tilak's residence in the Narayan Peth at about 10:30 A.M. on 23rd July 1916—which happened to be Mr Tilak's 61st birthday—when he was sitting amongst his numerous friends who had been there to offer their congratulations to him.

On 25th July 1916 Mr S.K. Damle, B.A., LL.B. pleader presented an application on behalf of Mr Tilak for postponement and for the copies of the information, affidavit and the translations of speeches of Mr Tilak, which formed the subject matter of the complaint. His request was granted and the case was postponed till 2nd August and copies were ordered to be supplied to him.

On 2nd August 1916 Khan Bahadur S.C. Davar appeared for Government and Mr S.K. Damle for Mr Tilak. After hearing the pleaders the case was again postponed till 7th August 1916 at 12 noon.

* * *

First Day's Proceedings
Monday, 7th August 1916.
(Before Mr G.W. Hatch Esq. I.C.S., District Magistrate, Poona)

In pursuance of the notice served on him Mr Bal Gangadhar Tilak appeared in person in the Court of the District Magistrate Poona at 12 noon precisely.

Mr B.D. Binning, Bar-at-Law assisted by M.N.M. Patwardhan Bar-at-Law and instructed by Khan Bahadur S.C. Davar, Government Pleader appeared for the crown. Mr Tilak was defended by the Hon'ble Mr Mahomed Ali Jinnah, Bar-at-Law, Mr D.S. Erulkar, Bar-at-Law assisted by Messrs R.P. Karandikar, High Court Pleader, S.R. Bakhle, B.A., LL.B. High Court Pleader, H.L. Patil, S.K. Damle, B.A., LL.B., N.C. Kelkar, B.A., LL.B. and S.G. Lele, District Pleaders.

At the outset Mr Binning proposed to call evidence to prove the speeches which were the subject matter of the charge.

Mr Jinnah suggested that the proper course would be to treat the case as a warrant case and that the prosecution should state what their case was before calling evidence.

Mr Binning said he had no objection to making a brief statement. He did not propose then to read the speeches and make comments. But he said the allegations were to the following effect:
1. That the British Government keeps India in a continual state of bondage or slavery.
2. That the British Government do not do their duty by India; that they administer it for the benefit of England or Great Britain.
3. That the British Government are not a real Government because they consider themselves insulted when told of things that have not been done and for the doing of which a desire is not now apparent.
4. That the British Government is full of self-conceit and thinks anything it does is perfect.
5. That the main object of the British Government and its officials is to fill their 'aching bellies'.
6. That intervening Collectors, Commissioners and other people are not wanted.
7. That all British rule except a mere nominal sovereignty is to be removed at an early moment.
8. That all British have in the course of 50 years failed to educate India so that it is fit to rule itself.
9. That they, the British, are unfit to rule and must go.
10. That the priests of the deity i.e. the British Government—the officials—must be removed because this priest or that priest does not do good to the people.
11. That responsible officials in India keep back from the King Emperor the full facts, hence justice is not done.

12. That the only reason the Viceroy and other officials in India get high pay is because India has to pay for them.
13. That the Bureaucracy's first idea is to see that their pay is secured.
14. That the present is a fit time of agitation for the getting of Home Rule.
15. That Government consider this agitation bad because they will be losers by it.
16. That all through the speeches a strong distinction is made between the administration in India and the Sovereign's wishes.
17. That under the Company's regime a letter used to come to the Governor General as follows: 'So much profit must be made this year: realize it and send it to us'; this was the administration; the people's good was not considered; this was not a good sort of administration; that Parliament under Queen Victoria did not approve of this system, but that now once more the administration of the country is in accordance with the Company's system.
18. That nobody in India told the Government and its servants to come here; that they are not wanted.
19. That the Government is not generous and wise and will not listen to what you have to say and redress your grievances.
20. That its sight is so affected as not to see the figures in its own reports.
21. That this Government is no Government at all because it evades its responsibilities.
22. That the chief question is whether a certain nation—India to wit is to be treated like beasts.
23. That if people stand in the road of this Home Rule movement they must be pushed out of the way by giving them a push.

Such remarks made to such audience by a person in the position of the respondent are certain to cause disaffection to the Government of this country. They are made under the guise but without the substance of a real agitation to obtain Home Rule for India which is a cloak for the malice for the maker.

Mr Binning then began to examine the Prosecution witnesses. Mr Trimbak Bhikaji Datre, Sub-Inspector, C.I.D. was the first witness called.

Trimbak Bhikaji Datre
Examination in Chief

Questioned by Mr Binning he said:

I was deputed to attend the 18th Provincial Conference at Belgaum in May last.

On the first May at 6 p.m. I attended a lecture delivered by Mr Tilak in the tent of the Conference. I attended the Conference and the meeting under the orders of Mr Guider. I took down the speeches in Marathi short-hand. My special work now is to take down speeches in Marathi short-hand. I have done this work for the last six years. I made short-hand notes of Mr Tilak's speech at Belgaum. (short-hand notes put in Ex. A.)

Mr Jinnah—They can only go in as corroborative evidence. They cannot go in as a speech delivered by Mr Tilak, but they can go in—only to show that short-hand notes of the speeches were taken.

The Magistrate made a note of Mr Jinnah's objection.

Q.—Did you put your short-hand notes into Marathi transcript? A—Yes, I turned it into long-hand with Mr Somnath Shanker Deshpande who was present at the lecture.

Q.—Is this a correct transcription from your short-hand notes? A.—Yes. It correctly represents what I heard Mr Tilak say. [Transcript put in as Ex. B.] At the time I took the short-hand notes, I was about four or five paces from Mr Tilak. There was a large crowd at Belgaum-lecture delivered Tilak. People of all kinds were there.

On the 31st May 1916 I attended a lecture delivered by Mr Tilak at Ahmednagar in an open space at the back of the cloth market at 7 p.m. All classes of people were there. I made short-hand notes of that lecture and I produce them. (Put in Ex. C.) I was about four or five paces from Mr Tilak when he made his speech.

Witness here put in his transcript of the speech, and said it was a correct transcript. [Ex. D.]

Q.—Did you further attend a lecture, delivered by Mr Tilak at Ahmednagar on the 1st June 1915? A.—Yes, I made short-hand notes of what Mr Tilak said.

[Put in Ex. E. and his transcript as Ex. F.]

Mr Jinnah reserved his cross examination.

Mr Anant Krishna Thakur, B.A., was the next witness Questioned by Mr Binning he said:

Anant Krishna Thakur
Examination in Chief

I am a B.A. of the Bombay University. I am employed in the Oriental Translator's Office for over ten years. I read the Marathi documents shown to me. I did not actually translate the documents but compared them with the English translated versions I hold in my hand. The translations are correct.

Mr Jinnah.—I should like to have the actual Translator here. I don't mind the documents going in, but I should like to know how the original Translator came to adopt certain terms. I object to the translations going in without the person who made the translations being called.

Mr Binning—I do not propose to call the original Translator. This witness's evidence is sufficient for my purpose.

Mr Jinnah's objection was noted and translations put in as Ex. G.H.I.

Mr Jinnah reserved cross examination. Mr Binning then tendered record of Mr Tilak's previous convictions.

Mr Jinnah objected to the 'previous convictions' being admitted at that stage of the proceedings. He was startled to find Mr Binning tendering the 'previous convictions.' He contended that to put them at that stage would certainly tend to prejudice the Magistrate's mind. This was a special case under Section 108 C.P.C.

The Magistrate said that what he had in his mind was I.L.R. 11 Bom. (Mr Khare's case).

Mr Binning quoted 32 I.L.R.P. 13 in support of his contention that the 'previous convictions' were admissible.

Mr Jinnah: To allow previous convictions to join at this stage is to rely upon the judgment of other persons.

The Magistrate said his order was that Mr Tilak's 'previous convictions' be admitted.

The record stated that on the first occasion Mr Tilak was sentenced to eighteen months imprisonment and on the second to three years' imprisonment on each of the two charges and to pay a fine of Rs 1,000.

Mr Jinnah said the fine had been remitted by the Government.

Mr Binning said he had no objection to the fine being dropped.

Mr Binning here closed his case.

Mr Jinnah's requests

Mr Jinnah said: Both in fairness to the Court and to the respondent Mr Binning ought to say what were the passages in the three speeches which came within Section 124A. Without that the Court could not say that it was satisfied that a *prima facie* case had been made out and called upon him to enter upon his defence. Again, without that it was not possible for the defence to meet the charge. The information did not show on what passages the prosecution relied.

The Magistrate observed that according to the information they relied on the whole speech.

Mr Jinnah submitted it was not shown which passage were seditious.

Mr Binning said he was not going to rely solely on individual passages, but he would rely upon the whole speech.

The Magistrate said he thought the prosecution were justified in saying that they would not be tied down to such and such sentence. Mr Binning had given indications of his case and enumerated the points on which he intended to ask the Court to confirm the rule.

Mr Jinnah said that that was not sufficient. His contention was that Mr Binning should point out passages in support of each of the allegations he had put forward. Taking for instance the first point that Mr Tilak had said that the British Government in India kept India in a continuous bondage, he submitted that Mr Binning should at least give the worst possible part of the speech to support that proposition. In the absence of that, supposing he were to say that there was not a single passage in the speech to support that point, how would the Court decide it?

Mr Binning then pointed out the passages on which he relied and added that apart from those passages he would rely on the general effect of the speech.

At this stage Mr Jinnah applied for a postponement to enable the defence to inspect the Marathi short-hand notes of the first witness.

Mr Binning did not object, and the case was adjourned till Tuesday, at 12:30 p.m.

The Magistrate ordered that opportunity should be given to the defence to examine the short-hand note-books in the presence of the representative of the prosecutions and also of an official of the Court.

* * *

APPENDIX 1

The Second Day's Proceedings
Tuesday, 8th August 1916

Sub-Inspector Trimbak Bhikaji Datre of C.I.D. was called by Mr Jinnah for cross examination. He deposed as follows:

These are the short-hand notes of the first lecture Ex. A. I can take down 110 to 120 words per minute in short-hand. Ordinary speakers can speak 110 words to a minute. Tilak speaks 70, 80 or 90 words to a minute. I took down everything he said; there might be some omissions owing to pencil requiring repairs. I don't remember whether my pencil had to be sharpened during Tilak's speech. There was one Deshpande also taking notes; he is a Police Sub-Inspector. He is a short-hand writer. There was no other. The short-hand notes produced (A.C.E.) are all in my hand-writing. Everything in Ex. A concerning Tilak's speech, was taken down at the time of the meeting. Deshpande also took short-hand notes. We prepared the transcript together. The transcript was prepared from both short-hand notes. There may be some words in his notes that are not in mine. How can there be a mistake when I take short-hand notes? No sentence was omitted; some words may have been omitted. On page 101 of my note-book I have omitted 'kahitikanee' as it was repeated frequently but I have made a mark to show that these words occurred at the place. There is no possibility of my mistaking 'Raj' and 'rajya' when used by the speaker. I don't think it is possible to confuse 'Rajya-vyavastha' and 'raj-vyavastha' I personally make no difference in the short-hand signs for 'raj' and 'Rajya'. Deshpande makes a difference between 'raj' and 'Rajya'. I am in the C.I.D. My pay is Rs 70 p.m. For the last five or six years I have been deputed to take notes of speeches. This transcription was completed in some 8 or 9 days. I put it before Mr Healy. Some portion of the transcript is in my hand-writing, some in Deshpande's.

Re-examined by Mr Binning.

I have no other work except making short-hand notes, and transcripts. On the whole this keeps me busy throughout the year; sometimes more and sometimes less. Pages 41 to 46 of the first speech are in my hand-writing.

Mr Jinnah then called Mr Anant Krishna Thakur, B.A. for cross examination.

Q.—'The sovereign's policy is in accordance with the Trading Company's policy.' Does not Sovereign's policy mean the State policy? A.: It does not mean the State policy, but the Sovereign's personal policy.

The Magistrate said, perhaps Mr Tilak used the word (Rajyadhoran) and the reporter took it down Rajdhaoran. Mr Jinnah said that was exactly his point.

On page 65 of my transcript I have: 'We have to go out by giving him a push.' The verb in this sentence is in the future-present tense.

Q.—Now is not this the correct translation?—'we may have to go by giving him a push.' A.—No.

Q.—Will you explain to the Court what you mean in Marathi by 'future present tense' A.—present intention of future thing.

Q.—'Future thing' in this sentence means 'intention'—does it not? A.—The 'present intention is first to give a push and then go out.'

Q.—Does not the translation really mean 'may have?' A.—There would be no sense of possibility in that.

Q.—Do you understand what this sentence we are discussing means? A.—Yes.

What is the meaning of the word Sirkar? A.—Government. Any other meaning would depend upon the context.

Q.—Is there a Marathi word for bureaucracy? A.—The word in Marathi would mean, as in current use, official class. I do not know if there is another expression in Marathi which conveys the meaning of the word bureaucracy.

Q.—Now you see that the word Sirkar is a comprehensive term in Marathi. Does it not apply to various other things, such as a Judicial Court? A.—By itself it would not be wrong to call a Judicial Court, Sirkar.

Q.—Would the word Sirkar be applicable to the Collector? A.—It would be applicable if used in connection with Collector's office. The term is used in connection with a Government Magistracy or Civil authority.

Q.—Look at your transcript, page 25. How do you translate the word 'ghamend?' Do you rely upon any dictionary for that? A.—No, because I know the meaning.

Q.—I have Candy's dictionary with me. I put it to you, would it not mean 'over-confidence?' A.—It is nearly so, reading it with the context. Q.—The word 'Dhoort' means 'rogue.' A.—The meaning is given in Dr Bhandarkar's first or second book of Sanskrit. But I did not look it up in a dictionary for the purpose of comparing it with the transcript.

Mr Jinnah to the Court:

My. Point is that the word 'rogue' is not a correct translation. It really means 'cunning.'

To witness—I suppose the common expression in Marathi means 'You are a very shrewd man.' A.—Yes.

Q.—'Gulamgiri' does not necessarily mean slavery? Being referred to Candy's dictionary the witness said Gulamgiri did not necessarily mean slavery. It may mean servility.

Q.—It may mean obsequiousness. A.—I don't know the word 'obsequiousness.' I don't claim to be an English scholar.

Q.—Who translated this transcript first? A.—Mr Oka, my superior in the Oriental Translator' Office, and I compared it and passed it. Mr Oka is in Bombay now. I saw him in Bombay about fortnight ago, and 4 or 5 days ago in Poona.

Q.—'Rajwyawasta' means the administration of the State; does it not?

Mr Binning: Before my learned friend goes any further, I will admit the correctness of his translations, whether the translation is correct or not.

Mr Jinnah (laughing). But I don't admit the other is right. Continuing he said: The translations accepted by Mr Binning should be noted down by the Court without leaving any ambiguity. And if the Court is prepared to admit them, then and then only I would proceed. Mr Binning thinks that he is at home, but I am in a court of law. I must proceed according to law.

Q.—Is the phrase used in Mr Tilak's speech used in the same sense as the well-known proverb in Marathi 'The loss is the master's but the storekeeper is worrying about it?' A.—I understood it to mean that the owner bears the expense but the granary-keeper does not like it. Apte's Marathi proverbs gave the meaning as 'the owner may sanction expenditure for certain things but his clerk hesitates.'

Q.—What do you mean by this passage of the translation, 'if the state of the administration remains as it does at present, England cannot give any rights among European Nations?' A.—There is no sense whatever in the passage.

Mr Jinnah to witness: Now I want you to go carefully through the three speeches and tell me wherever the word 'Gulamgiri' occurs what it means, and after that I am finished with your cross-examination. Look at your transcript at the end of page 34 and read it. [Witness read it in Marathi] and then said the translation was 'like a beast.'

Q.—Is there not a better way of translating this? Supposing I would suggest the word 'cattle'. A.—The expression really means lower beasts like dogs or pigs or any of the lower animals. The only correct translation is 'are like beasts, without taking into consideration their desires, and their aspirations.' The words 'Gura Sarakha' mean 'like cattle'.

Q.—What is the difference between the terms Guru and Pashu? A.— 'Guru' we call cows, and 'Pashu' all other beasts. The terms are not equivalent to each other. Guru won't include 'Pashu.' Man is certainly not included in the term 'Pashu.' I have heard the phrase before about going to sleep when the thief came.

Q.—Do you know that after the war broke out Mr Tilak made a declaration as to his policy and attitude towards Government? A.—I do not know that. It did not come into the Oriental Translator's Office.

With this was finished the cross-examination of Mr Thakur subject to the general answer the translation of the word 'Gulamgiri' in the three speeches.

SUB-INSPECTOR DATRE, CROSS EXAMINED

Q.—How many words a minute do you take down in Marathi short-hand? A.—110-120 words. Ordinarily a speaker in Marathi could speak 110 words a minute. Mr Tilak spoke at the rate of 70-80 or 90 words a minute.

Mr Binning then called witness Mr Somnath Shankar Deshpande, Sub-Inspector C.I.D. He deposed as follows:

I am a Sub-Inspector. I attended the lecture of Mr Tilak at Belgaum on 1st of May last, with sub-Inspector Datre and made short-hand notes of what Mr Tilak said. I correctly took down what I heard. I produce it. (Ex. K. & L. They were allowed to be put in on the footing as Ex. A. & C.) I was at a distance of 4-5 paces from Mr Tilak. I took one or two pencils with me on this occasion. (Shown transcript). This is the transcript Datre and I made. I did it correctly from my short-hand notes.

* * *

Third Day's Proceedings
Wednesday, 9th August 1916

Mr A. K. Thakur cross examined by Mr Jinnah:

I have looked through the speeches and I find 'Gulamgiri' translated as 'slavery' wherever the word occurs. I know Apte's Sanskrit Dictionary, it is well known. 'Pashu' is a Sanskrit word. 'Pashu' may mean cattle,—it would include cattle.

Re-examined by Mr Binning:

Dr Bhandarkar's 2nd book of Sanskrit is a well-known book and used in schools. Professor Ranade's 20th century English-Marathi dictionary is also a well-known work. The transcript page 2 of the 3rd speech shows 'Gulamgiri and dasya'; 'dasya' is correctly translated as 'bondage.'

Cross examined (by permission) by Mr Jinnah.

'Dasya' does not mean servitude. It does not mean 'service'. Servitude is not the common meaning of 'dasya'; as the dictionary gives it may mean 'servitude' and 'service'.

Sub-Inspector Somnath Deshpande, cross examined by Mr Jinnah, said for the last two years he had been a short-hand-writer and his pay was Rs 70. He sometimes omitted certain words. A whole sentence could never be lost. Sometimes a sentence might be taken down wrongly; sometimes there might be omissions and wrongly-taken-down sentences in his notes. Mr Tilak spoke about seventy to ninety words per minute.

At times there were applause and cheers in the speech. But he had every sentence which Mr Tilak uttered. Cheers and applause did not interfere with him so far as his hearing was concerned, as the lecturer stopped at that time. His experience was as soon as applause stopped the speaker began. He might have attended about hundred meetings. During those he had never missed a single sentence in spite of cheering and applause. At certain places there was a difference between his short-hand notes and those of Datre. The transcription was prepared after putting both their heads together. In his notes in certain places he had made remarks 'cannot make out.' There was a difference between 'raja' & 'rajya'. A listener could not make a mistake in listening to these words.

APPENDIX 1

Witness was asked to write both the words on a piece of paper and Mr Jinnah put it in and said he wanted to know the other by putting this in, his right of reply would be lost. He wanted the Magistrate's ruling.

Mr Binning said he was not going to dispute the defence's right of replying. Mr Jinnah need not scheme for it.

Mr Jinnah said Mr Binning seemed to think he was in his home. He was in Court and he wanted the Court's ruling.

The Magistrate said he would not object to Mr Jinnah's right of reply.

Continuing witness said he transcribed the notes in two or three days.

The Court then asked Mr Bal Gangadhar Tilak a few questions. He made a statement in reply which is given below.

Statement of the accused (taken in English).

Bal Gangadhar Tilak, 60 Brahmin, Literary writer, Poona City.

Question: Did you at Belgaum on 1 May and at Nagar on 31 May and 1 June deliver lectures or speeches, the subject of which in your own words—was 'swarajya'?

Answer: Yes on 'Swarajya' or 'Home Rule.' The notice about the lecture stated both words.

Question: Have you read the copies of the Marathi transcript taken by your pleaders?

Answer: Yes.

Question: Are they correctly reports of what you said.

Answer: Not verbatim.

Question: Are they substantially correct?

Answer: On the whole, in general, they may be correct; but I find in certain places there are omissions and imperfections.

Question: What was your object in delivering these lectures.

Answer: To defend and explain Home Rule and point out the best way of obtaining it; and to exhort people to become members of the Home Rule League.

Question: Can you explain Home Rule in a few words?

Answer: It is given in the lectures.

Question: Government have proceeded against you on two previous occasions for disseminating sedition?

Answer: Yes.

Question: You were convicted on both occasions?

Answer: Yes.

Question: Do you wish to make any other statement?

Answer: No; I leave it to my counsel.

(Sd.) B.G. TILAK.

Mr Jinnah said he was not going to call any evidence.

Mr Binning's Address

Mr Binning then addressed the Court. He said his position was extraordinary as he did not know what was the defence. As far as one could gather the defence was that certain of the words had been wrongly translated in the numerous passages in the speeches put in. But even if the corresponding meaning was put there, that would not alter the meaning of the speeches. Mr Binning's imperfect knowledge of Marathi placed him at a disadvantage. The word 'Dasya' was tried to be shown as not meaning 'slavery' but by that Mr Tilak wanted to show that India was in perpetual servitude. 'Bondage' must have been the meaning of the word. 'Dasya' and 'Gulamgiri' taken in conjunction with the context. The accused was always entitled to be given the benefit of the best meaning of the word. 'Dasya' meant 'Service'. Ranade's latest dictionary gave 'Dasya' as the meaning of 'Service' and against the word 'bondage' itself there was the same word in the same dictionary. In Candy's dictionary, on which the defence had relied, 'Dasya' was given as meaning 'servitude, service and servantship'. Apte's dictionary gave the meaning as 'servitude, bondage and slavery'. It was remarkable that an experienced and accomplished orator like Mr Tilak should have used a word which was so little used. Perpetual servitude was not better than slavery. 'Gulamgiri' was 'slavery' as it was the meaning given in Ranade's Dictionary. Again 'Dasya' was given for 'slavery' in Ranade's Dictionary. Coming to the word 'dhurta' the defence said it meant 'cunning person' but a cunning person was not an honourable person. Dr Bhandarkar had given 'rogue' as the meaning of that word. The word 'ghamenda' was translated as 'overweening confidence' but there was no difference between this meaning and the one given by the prosecution. He was not going to say whether Home Rule was or was not a perfectly legitimate aspiration and subject for discussion. Whoever by words spoken attempted to bring into hatred or contempt or attempted to excite disaffection towards His Majesty or Government established by law, should be punished. That was section 124A. His case was Mr Tilak was disseminating matter which was punishable under that section and that he should find security that he would not do so for one year.

Previous Convictions

Continuing Mr Binning said, the Magistrate must consider the fact that Mr Tilak has been twice convicted under Section 124A. In spite of the fact that he had been sentenced to eighteen months,—part, of which he was let off on certain conditions,—he was disseminating sedition.

Mr Jinnah said Mr Binning was saying that the term was remitted upon certain conditions, but surely that was not in the judgment. What business had Mr Binning to say that Mr, Tilak had not kept the promises?

Mr Binning admitted after some time that he (himself) was not entitled to say that. Continuing, he said Mr Tilak was convicted a second time to six years but not deterred by that he still made speeches. They had there to deal with a man whom no amount of warning and correction would correct. He would do it again. Something must be done to stop these speeches, otherwise he would probably do worse. Counsel then went into the following cases:

22 Bom. P. 112; 8 B.L.R.P. 457; 10 B.L.R. 866; 20 All. P. 55; 32 Mad. P. 27; 34 Cal. 991.

Counsel Continued:

When a man wrote or spoke words which caused his hearers to dislike the Government, to look with contempt upon the Government, or to hate the Government, then that man committed an offence under Section 124A. Any one was entitled to say about a particular Collector or Commissioner that he had done wrong. Mr Tilak had brought the officers of the Government into contempt. The words of the Section were, if you incited hatred or contempt or disaffection you came under the Act.

The Speeches Dealt With

Coming to the speeches Mr Binning said he did not know how it was that Home Rule was put down alongside Swarajya in the notices as a subject of the lectures. He had read the speeches with the greatest care and attention and it seemed to him that they did not advocate any definite scheme for Swarajya or Home Rule. They contained some amusing and some dull stories which were excellent from the literary point of view, but there was no definition given on Home Rule or Swarajya. Take, for instance, the speech at Belgaum. In this Mr Tilak made no definite or substantial statement about Home Rule or Swarajya. Counsel said the case he had to submit on behalf of the Government was that under the guise of advocating a Home Rule scheme, which did not exist, the respondent had made remarks in his speeches imputing, in the words of Sir Charles Farran, dishonest and immoral motives to the Government established in this country and that too after he: had been twice punished. Mr Binning then proceeded to read the first speech of Mr Tilak which was delivered at Belgaum and commented upon the passages to which the prosecution took exception. This speech, counsel said, was made to a very large audience consisting of all classes of people. The speaker commenced by asking what was Swarajya and though the question was asked more than once he did not attempt to define it. In the forefront of his speech he put forward the proposition that when they began to discuss Home Rule in India they immediately put themselves in a position to which the Government were opposed.

Mr Binning then referred to the passages in the speech which related to British officials, and in which it was alleged, they were charged with being conceited and with looking at their own interests only, and observed that they were clearly calculated to make those who heard the speech to dislike the Government. As far as he knew he had no more rights in this country than Mr Tilak had and was not entitled to do more than what Mr Tilak was entitled to do.

Mr Jinnah said it was an entirely incorrect statement to make. Mr Binning possessed more rights than Mr Tilak or the person he spoke of. Counsel must confine himself to the documents and must not make any incorrect statement. Mr Binning: The argument was that India was fit to govern itself, that the Government knew this perfectly well, that it would not give India power to govern itself and that it wrongly represented to the invisible Government at Home that India was not fit to govern itself. Counsel said if he were an Indian and were to listen to a speech like that, he would certainly feel a dislike for Government. Counsel asked, 'could anyone make a nastier accusation against his Government in any country?' It should be remarked that this utterance was received with cries of cheers and shame, cheers for the oratory and shame for the supposed disgraceful conduct of the Government. Then came the following passage 'Does the Emperor lose anything whether the administration is carried on by a Civil Servant or by our Brelvi Saheb? The rule, still remains. The Emperor still remains. The difference would be that the white servant who was with him would be replaced by a black servant. From whom then does this opposition come? This opposition comes from those people who are in power. It does not come from the Emperor.' Counsel said when such reflections were made they always caused annoyance to Europeans.

But the last paragraph, counsel said, was pregnant with remarks which must cause disaffection against the Government. It stated 'When there was the East India Company's rule in this country all matters were carried on a commercial principle. The whole attention was directed towards the question how might the Company's shareholders obtain a considerable profit. A letter used to come to the Governor-General here to this effect. "So much profit must be paid to us this year. Realise it and send it to us." This was the administration.' The speech proceeded 'The Sovereign's policy is in accordance with the trading company's policy. The administration of the kingdom is in accordance with the company's policy and in the meantime the proclamation has no effect.'

What Lord Hardinge Said

After referring to some more passages in the paragraph, counsel said a wrong idea seemed to prevail that Lord Hardinge, the late Viceroy, was in favour of giving Home Rule to India and a reference had been made in support of this to a speech made by him. Counsel said he would later on refer to it but in the meanwhile he would only say that what Lord Hardinge actually said was that there could be no objection to the Indians cherishing such an ideal and to their aspiring to get it at some distant time, but he said to seek to get it now was absolutely out of place. Counsel further took exception to the following remarks. 'But we do not want the State Secretary, who has been created as a son-in-law' He submitted that this was a deliberate statement suggesting that the appointment of the man who was at the head of affairs in connection with India was a job. Coming to the second speech, Mr Binning said it was more abusive than the first. He quoted a passage in which, after referring to the English Government as alien, Mr Tilak said, 'What is the result of Alienness? The difference between aliens and others is that the alien's point of view is alien, their thoughts are alien and their general conduct is such, that their minds are not inclined to particularly benefit those people to whom they are aliens. Alienness has to do with interests. Alienness is certainly not concerned with white and black skin. Alienness is not concerned with religion, etc The Government is alien. He is to be considered alien, who looks only to his own benefit, to the benefit of his own race, and to the benefit of his original country. If anybody has charged the Government with being alien he has done so in the above sense'. Counsel submitted that here the speaker suggested that the Government of this country were aliens, that they did not do their duty and that they only looked to the benefit of the English race. That was calculated to excite disaffection against the Government. Counsel next referred to a passage in which the speaker said that the intervening Collectors, Commissioners and other people were not wanted, and added: 'We are not inferior to them in point of bravery and education. We possess ability. Such being the case; why should we not get the rights? Why should the Emperor make a distinction between his black and white subjects? Who has given such advice to the Emperor'? Counsel said the suggestion here was that the Emperor would not make such a distinction if the officials referred to, among whom were included Viceroys, etc. did not keep back the true facts from him. Coming to another passage in which comparison was made between the salaries of the Viceroy and the Prime Minister counsel said it was here suggested that the Prime Minister got only Rs 5,000 a month, because English people would not pay him more. That was all nonsense. A Prime Minister was generally a person, who had already made a large fortune, and the question of money was no consideration to him. Again, the Prime Minister had not to entertain Indian and European Members of the Legislative Councils, etc.

Mr Jinnah said it was not a fact. The Viceroy and the Governor were paid additional allowances for entertaining people.

At this stage Mr Binning asked the Court to adjourn the proceedings.

* * *

Fourth day's Proceedings
Thursday, the 10th instant

The hearing of the case was resumed at 12 noon on Thursday.

'A Touch of the Old Tilak'

Mr Binning continuing said that Mr Tilak said the bureaucracy objected to the people saying the Government of India had not made the Indians fit to rule themselves. This was received with cheers and was likely to cause disaffection. If, on the other hand, Indians were fit to rule themselves, the Government were not telling this to people at Home in order not to give them Home Rule. 'In the present crisis if they were resolute they could turn the bureaucracy out. If they wished to remain slaves none would say "don't". What was the use of advising them who wished to remain in slavery? There was only one medicine and it was power'. Take it, said Mr Tilak, that was a touch of the old Mr Tilak. Again, suggestions were made that Indian and English subjects were not treated alike, there was distinction. Where there was wisdom there was power. That was an entirely new idea. The Ahmednagar audience was asked to believe that the Government had stopped their industries, which for the last fifty years were really prospering. That was a disgraceful statement to make. According to Mr Tilak, Indians who accepted Government offices were not manly. They had only the natures of animals, as animals did not possess the better qualities of man. There is no scope for men of education and manliness in India, said Mr Tilak. If they got 'Swarajya' instead of being treated like animals they would be treated like men. That was the most offensive remark calculated to create disaffection. When they got Home Rule they could do anything. Counsel hoped the millennium would then arrive. Again he said, 'Give us Home Rule first and we will settle with the Mahomedans afterwards,' but they must settle it first and Home Rule would come afterwards. They must take into consideration Mr Tilak's past when he said 'I don't tell you to do any unlawful thing. They must not be afraid of blustering and bawling.'

C.I.D. a Part of the Constitution

It was a most offensive remark against the C.I.D. who were a part of the British constitution in India. 'Did Mr Tilak really say,' asked counsel, 'that there was more peace in the time of the Peshwas than under the British Government?' That was not correct.

Mr Jinnah: How do you know it was not?

Mr Binning: I have both English and Indian histories.

Mr Jinnah said Elphinstone said that, and it was in his history.

Continuing, Mr Binning said they were not there because Mr Tilak advocated Home Rule; but because he had advocated it in a particular way and would continue doing so. The complaint against Mr Tilak was not that he advocated Home Rule, but he did it in an unpardonable way.

Manner Not Theme Culpable

After referring to some more passages, Mr Binning said that he had to say it again they were not there that day, because Mr Tilak had advocated any particular scheme of Home Rule; but they were there because of the way in which he had advocated it. As he said before, the complaint against Mr Tilak was that in advocating Home Rule, he said things which were quite unpardonable. There was nothing like a tangible scheme of Home Rule suggested in those speeches. Counsel said he had nothing to say about the merits of the Home Rule question. That was a matter entirely, outside this case. It was natural that the inhabitant of a country should desire and strive for powers to govern their country themselves. Personally it seemed to him that it was a perfectly good ideal to have before one without attempting to bring the Government into contempt and hatred. But unfortunately, that was not the attitude of Mr Tilak. If they looked at Mr Tilak's speeches they would find that their real object was not to put forward a coherent scheme of Swarajya, but it was to abuse the Government. First of all he said that the Government did not work for the people's good, that they would not listen to their grievances, and that they stopped their mouths and intellects.

Secondly, he said that the British official was full of overweening conceit and greed, and his first care was to see to his own pay and interests.

Thirdly, Mr Tilak charged the officials with deliberately misleading what was called 'the invisible government' namely the Sovereign, and the English people as to the condition of the people of India, who were fit to govern themselves by representing that they were not so fit.

Fourthly, he said that the Government themselves were unfit to govern India.

Fifthly and lastly, the general and main theme of the speeches was that the Government were carrying on the same policy as the East India Company which was to squeeze the people and make as large a profit as possible.

In short Mr Tilak charged the officials with greed, conceit, dishonesty and incompetence. Counsel observed that it was immaterial whether all those charges against the Government were true or not. He was not concerned with that. Even if they were true, as had been pointed out in the several cases, the mentioning of them was calculated to bring the Government into hatred and contempt.

Mr Jinnah said he agreed that the truth in such a case would be no justification.

Mr Binning said he would adopt that. Continuing, Mr Binning said that was the position with regard to those speeches, but before he stopped he should like to point out that if one applied to the representatives of the British

Government in India the words which Mr Tilak had applied to them, one was endeavouring to excite feelings of disaffection against the Government within the meaning of Section 124A.

He should also like to refer to one or two small points. Mr Jinnah had made a complaint that the man who originally made the translations was not called. Obviously there was nothing in it. So long as a responsible person said that he had compared the translations, what mattered who made them, as the man who made the translations originally was a man who in the opinion of the prosecution would not be a good witness to be submitted to the skilful cross-examination of Mr Jinnah. What was the good of calling him when they had perfectly competent man who was not likely to be confused in cross-examination?

Another point to which he wished to refer was the fact that though Mr Tilak had an ample opportunity himself of stating to the Court what his explanation about the speeches was, he had chosen to leave that to his counsel.

Mr Jinnah—He did it under instructions.

Mr Binning—But I feel bound to say for myself that his own explanation would appeal much more powerfully than that of his professional advisers.

Mr Jinnah's Address

Mr Jinnah then addressed the Court on behalf of Mr Tilak. He said he was rather in an embarrassing position because Mr Binning had told the Magistrate that the service to which he belonged was being attacked in the speeches. He hopes the Court would pay no attention to that and would rise above it and do his duty as a judge. It was a delicate matter because the judge belonged to the Service which was being attacked and he hoped he would give him the fullest liberty which the traditions of the bar had always allowed them. The first question was that they had not got Mr Tilak's speeches as speeches written by him.

Speeches Murdered

The speeches were taken down by short-hand writers, who were deputed by the C.I.D., with whom Mr Tilak was not a *persona grata*, evidently with the object of catching him for prosecution if possible. These two men took down the notes. His submission was that these witnesses were not frank or fair or honest because they would not have given the evidence they had, if they had been fair. They had told the Court it was impossible to make mistakes. But no judge would believe that. They not only made mistakes but murdered the speeches. They had, however admitted that certain sentences and words might have been taken down wrongly or omitted and it is very important to remember that, and it is a matter of common knowledge that short-hand writers spoil the speeches though unwittingly.

Then coming to the second process of transcribing, there was the further difficulty of comparing whether the transcript was accurate. They had transcribed what was thought to be Mr Tilak's speeches. Then they had the third process of translation. The man who had translated it was not brought before the Court because he was man of such a temperament, intelligence and nature that a cross-examination would confuse him. They had therefore a man who could not be confused by a cross-examination. The Court had seen in the course of the examination that certain words which had not been used had been used by the translator to make the speeches offensive.

Of course, Mr Tilak said that generally the substance of the speeches was correct, but there were omissions and imperfections in certain places. These were the circumstances in connection with the speeches which he asked the Court to bear in mind when taking them into consideration.

INTERPRETATION OF SECTION 124A

The first question that arose was this: whether the speeches came under Section 124A. The law had been laid down that the Court had to approach the statement in writing not in the light that Mr Binning had pointed out by looking at one sentence here and one passage there, but by looking at the whole speech. Lord Fitzgerald had laid down the law in 1868 in Sullivan's case, and that had been the law ever since which was adopted in the 'Bangabasi' case and in the Tilak trial by Justice Strachey who said that it would not be fair to judge of the intention by isolated passages or casual expression without reference to the context.

Continuing Mr Jinnah said that his proposition was that these speeches came under the second Explanation. They were comments expressing disapprobation of the measures of the Government with a view to bring about a change by lawful means. Without exciting hatred or contempt or disaffection. The only way to do so was by looking at the whole speeches.

PREVIOUS CONVICTIONS

He had urged at the time the record of convictions was tendered, that it should not be allowed. Section 108 was a preventive section. Therefore, if a man has committed similar acts before it would be a piece of evidence persuading the Court that he must be bound over. These convictions, however, could not carry much weight as the first conviction was in 1898 and the second about eight years ago. The Magistrate must not think, that because he was convicted, Mr Tilak was a bad man and whatever he said was under a disguise and it was terribly seditious. Mr Binning had asked the Court not to believe Mr Tilak because he had been convicted. Mr Jinnah hoped it would not take any notice of this. The first thing the Court had to bear in mind was this: Mr Binning had read the speeches as if they were some independent discourses or lectures. He had forgotten the purpose and the object and the occasion of these speeches altogether. The Court would find from the speeches themselves that Mr Tilak and those who agreed with him had decided to start a Home Rule League and a Home Rule League was established at Belgaum on that occasion. Mr Tilak had told the Court in his own words that the lectures were intended to advocate this propaganda of Home Rule, which was being attacked from certain quarters, both official and Indian. The lecture, therefore, was really intended to be an answer to the objections which were urged by those who were opposed to the Home Rule League and his object was to define the scope and to remove the misunderstanding so far as his school of thought was concerned. He wanted to demolish the arguments which bad been advocated against the Home Rule League. Mr Binning argued that Mr Tilak was a wicked fellow and wherever there was any passage not favourable to the prosecution, he put it down as a cloak, as a disguise, but whenever any strong comment appeared he labelled it as sedition.

Mr Binning had frankly and fairly said that he was not objecting to the Home Rule League propaganda being legitimately discussed, but he objected to the manner and method which Mr Tilak had adopted in advocating the movement. In other words, Mr Binning said that the advocacy of the Home Rule League and its propaganda was a mere cloak, and that Mr Tilak really wanted to libel the Government established by law to his heart's content. Mr Binning had further said that he did not wonder at it, considering that Mr Tilak had been twice convicted at the instance of the Government. Counsel said a grosser misrepresentation of these lectures could not possibly be imagined.

No other interpretation than a frank advocacy of Home Role can be put upon the speeches and Mr Tilak can never be supposed to be actuated by malice or with a desire to libel the Government. The Court could not do him greater injustice if Mr Binning's argument was accepted.

The Level of the Audience

His submission was that Mr Tilak went to Ahmednagar and Belgaum to establish Home Rule League and he wanted the people to join them and also pay subscriptions to carry on the work of the League. He had an audience of all classes and Mr Tilak took a great deal of pains to go to their level to make them understand the position. Of course Mr Binning had said it was all nonsense but they must consider the class of audience whom Mr Tilak had to address. In the first lecture he told them what the Government was. Mr Tilak was addressing an audience which was largely composed of ignorant people. He wanted to make them understand and he went into the most elementary principles. Why, in the name of Heavens, attribute dishonest motives to Mr Tilak and insist that he stood before an audience of 5,000 people and said what he did not believe and that the audience which heard these sentiments believed that he was not speaking the truth? Why imagine that hatred or contempt must be more in the mind of the audience, because he sketched the idea of Home Rule in a crude manner to a particular audience and the audience cheered him because they approved of what he had said, that Home Rule should be secured through the British and must be fostered by British Rule, etc. Was that sedition? Swarajya had been defined by Mr Tilak in a very clear manner. He put it briefly by saying that the management of their affairs should be in their own hands and that was the demand for Swarajya. Swarajya was the full authority for the management of their affairs and not that the British Government should go away and that the Germans should come here. Then he said the present position in India was this that they had a Civil Service—bureaucracy. Mr Tilak used the word Sarkar for the Civil Service. He found it very hard to make the audience understand the word Civil Service. The audience understood well that by the Government he did not mean the Government established by law. The whole of the burden of Mr Tilak's song was this: He said that the Civil Service had got a monopoly of power and that that system was not beneficial,—it was neither beneficial to the people of this country, nor to the English people,—and he said there must be a change. Therefore, really, this attack was an attack on this system, not on Government.

C.I.D. Government

Mr Jinnah asked what was the Government established by law? Suppose you attacked the Civil Service or the C.I.D. Mr Binning had said that the C.I.D. was the Government established by law. If the C.I.D. was Government by law established then he would say good-bye to all Government established by law in the country. Counsel's proposition was that the Civil Service was not the Government established by law, under Section 24A. Take the army system, was it sedition to attack it? Suppose he attacked the police or the forest service, was that sedition? When Mr Tilak said, 'You cannot cut grass or kill a tiger, he said there was the Civil Service whose permission they had to get to do everything. Mr Tilak meant: 'We want some better arrangement than this.' Mr Tilak did not attribute dishonesty or immortality to the Collectors. He said that there were certain grievances, which could be remedied and there were certain grievances which were without foundation, which if Indians had the management would still be there. There was the typical instance of the 'Opposition' who attacked the Government for not doing certain things which they did not do when they came into power. They had started the Home Rule movement to bring about a change in the present system of administration which they wanted to carry out by reasonable and practical methods which Mr Tilak had laid down at the end of the speech. Mr Tilak found fault with the present system of administration and said what 'Swarajya' meant. Then he said the change should be brought about partially, gradually and then fully. Mr Tilak said that the monopoly which the Civil Service were enjoying at the present time so far as the actual administration of the country was concerned, should not be continued and laid down a plan for so doing. Mr Tilak said the amendment was to be brought about through Parliament, they should not ask it from others. He said a petition was to be made to the English people and the English Parliament. They had to do everything legal for that purpose. He said they had grievances some of which were real and some of which were not, because they had not administration in their hands. The administration was managed by the Civil Service and they had the monopoly. The people were helpless, they could not do any small thing unless they obtained the permission of the Collector. This system must, therefore, be changed. Mr Tilak asked were they not going to put their heads together to bring about the change? It was admitted that the people of India were the most backward in the world and he said the British Government did not object to their having Home Rule; but there were the officials, not only European, but Indian. He urged to be determined to show their resoluteness to become members of this League and subscribe money and not to be frightened by the C.I.D. Mr Tilak said 'Be manly' and took pity for their condition. Mr Binning had said the moment a man said that they were backward and must rise, that meant that the bureaucracy kept them down like this. Nowhere had Mr Tilak said that the bureaucracy was keeping them down like animals. He did not charge the British people, on the contrary, if any of these facts were well known to the people, at Home, things would be improved. Counsel said he was not going to dispute for a moment that words here and there were strong. Some people might like them, but Mr Tilak never intended any offence or insult. When a person was on his legs before 4,000 or 5,000 people lecturing, there was likely to be a certain amount of excitement. Counsel had ascertained from Mr Tilak that he certainly did not mean to be offensive to certain individuals or officials. Mr Jinnah then went on to deal with the speeches and quoted the story of the three *Dhurtas* as was repeated by Sir Ramkrishne Bhandarkar in the Imperial Legislative Council which was not meant to be offensive. He could not imagine that the same Dr Bhandarkar, who had translated the Sanskrit word 'Dhurta' as rogue in his second book would have meant to say, in the Imperial Council that his opponents like the late Mr Gokhale and others were *rogues*. Mr Jinnah explained that what Mr Tilak meant was that the Home Rule League was the sheep which was carried over head by Mr Tilak and his friends and what he meant was that let others say anything *re* the Home Rule League, people need not be confused by the opponents. And the story was more applicable to his own countrymen i.e. the moderates. Where is the sting, the insult, the offence, then?

The Magistrate: The word *rogues* is quite immaterial to this story.

Mr Jinnah: Quite so; that is the point. Mr Tilak demolishes the arguments of unfitness, of driving away the English people, and of the fear of the C.I.D. There is nothing wrong in this. What he meant was 'Don't be simpletons.'

Now coming to the Commercial Policy of Company's Government, Mr Jinnah said that the Company's rule was bad and rotten. It is good that it has gone. Mr Jinnah after explaining the working of the Company Government said that of the Statute of 1858 was based on the model of administration of the Company's Government. But the proclamation which defined the policy of the Government remained a dead letter.

Criticism of a System

Mr Binning had said it was absurd to give a time limit for Home Rule, but the American Government had done that in the case of the Philippines. As to the argument of Mr Binning about the Secretary of State being called a son-in-law, Counsel submitted that it was urged by publicists in India and in England that the post of the Secretary of State as well as his Council should be abolished, because the post is occupied by a man who can not have the portfolio elsewhere yet such man possesses tremendous powers in his hands, and, as said by Lord Morley once, even the Governor-General is his agent. There is therefore no sedition in Mr Tilak's remarks on this point.

Counsel said where there was will there was way. Englishmen were aliens in this country, said counsel, and Mr Asquith and Lord Cromer had said that this was not the country of the domicile of Englishman. There was nothing offensive in that and counsel quoted Mr Asquith's speech in support. When Mr Asquith and Lord Cromer say the same thing it was alright, but if Mr Tilak says the same then it is sedition. As regards that part of the speech wherein Mr Binning was in doubt as to what Mr Tilak meant by saying 'We shall have to go by giving him a push' Mr Jinnah submitted that there must be something missing in it because as it stood it means nothing. The proper version is that Mr Tilak advocated the door of Parliament while learned aliens ask him to go to the other viz. the door of bureaucracy. But Mr Tilak did not want to go by that door as there they were likely to meet with an obstruction. This contingency Mr Tilak wanted to avoid, and he therefore advised his audience not to go by this other door. There was nothing improper in this. Coming to the point 'who told you to come here' in the speech, Counsel said that there are some civilians who grumble and complain that the climate is extremely hot and trying etc. and Mr Tilak sarcastically replies them 'who asked you to come here.' It is a mere taunt and not sedition.

Mr Asquith had said the Government of the country was in the hands of learned aliens and Mr Tilak had said nothing else. Mr Tilak wanted a thorough overhauling of administration and the Home Rule League was there for that purpose. It was a fact that Europeans were exiles in this land and were suffering from heat, etc, and Mr Tilak used it sarcastically. But how could there be sedition in that? Regarding invisible Government, counsel said the Secretary of State was invisible. The Government as was carried out from Downing street was invisible. That part of Government which was in Europe was invisible.

Counsel said his first proposition was this, if the criticism was the criticism of a certain set of administrators as stated by Mr Justice Strachey, it did not come under Section 124A. It was the criticism of a system and nothing else; and even according to Justice Strachey's dictum a severe, nay, even a perverse criticism thereof would be protected by the explanation which exempts from the operation of the section any disapprobation of a measure of Government caused for the purpose of getting that measure reformed, modified or repealed by lawful means. The change advocated was to be brought about by changing the existing law through Parliament. The Act of 1858 was nothing but a measure and was covered by the explanation of Section 124A. That because one Act had come into force, it did not prevent them from expressing disapprobation with a view to repealing or modifying it. In order to remove or repeal certain Acts they had to criticize the present policy and show the defects and flaws. Was not Mr Tilak entitled to say that the substitute he proposed was Home Rule which was a better system both in the interest of the Government and the people? Otherwise none would escape Section 124A.

As to the objection of Mr Binning regarding that part of the speech wherein Mr Tilak said 'we have lost out trade.' Counsel said that to any one who was acquainted with history it is a patent fact that India has lost her trade. Mr Tilak has not said that it is due to the scheming of the bureaucracy, still, Counsel submitted, it remains a fact. Those who knew the history of excise duty would be convinced that their hands were tied down altogether.

Aching Belly

Coming to that part of the speech *viz*. 'Remove the middle-men's aching belly', counsel said the translation 'aching belly' was a mere murder of the Marathi proverb. Mr Binning had said Mr Tilak wanted to bring the Government into contempt, but Mr Tilak had said nothing against the Government. Mr Tilak said the Government was all-right but they had certain officials who could not bear that certain rights should be given to the people and counsel submitted that that did not bring the Government into contempt although it was a severe criticism of Collectors and Commissioners.

Referring to the point of '*Badwas of Pandharpur*' and the 'Pujaris', Counsel said that Mr Tilak wanted to do away with the monopoly of these Civilians. It is not a venom against the white Civilians but against the system. He did not spare his own countrymen wherever they have got the monopoly. He said that an Indian Civilian is sometimes a worse bureaucrat than his brother. Continuing Mr Jinnah said that it is unfair and unjust to first report a man wrongly, then get it wrongly translated in the C.I.D. shop, and finally obtain a sanction and to base a prosecution thereon against Mr Tilak against whom there is already a strong prejudice. It is unjust to pick a word here, an expression there and say that it is sedition. Mr Tilak's speeches had been taken down by C.I.D. reporters who have no love for him and had been wrongly translated and counsel hoped that in the light of his explanation the Court would think of them favourably. Mr Tilak's only objection was that the present management was a monopoly and it must be finished. He did not incite to violence. There was nothing wrong in a man telling his countrymen to be men rather than remain in a fallen state. In concluding his remarks on the second speech Mr Jinnah submitted: Not only Mr Tilak but some members of the Civil Service have advocated such reforms (here the counsel referred the Court to the books written by Mr Houghton and Mr Fielding Hull on the subject of Home Rule). Mr Tilak wants to convey that the executive should be responsible to the people. He does not want the officers to be his servants. He wanted the officials to be responsible to the people as in other countries. Referring to the points of 'bondage' and 'slavery' and 'Parrot story', counsel submitted that there was not charge against the Government that they have kept the people in slavery but the condition of things brought about by this faulty system has resulted in a degeneration of the people of this country. Mr Tilak wanted to rouse his countrymen from their lethargy and there was no sedition in it. Merely having sufficient to eat is not the *summum bonum* of life. Sir Walter Lawrence formerly Private Secretary to the Viceroy, advocated a new form of Government and Mr Tilak has endorsed the same in his speech. What Mr Tilak wanted to impress upon his audience was that they should not remain fourteenth to the allusion about beasts, counsel said no imputation was there made against the Government that it was treating the people as beasts.

In conclusion Mr Jinnah submitted that no case had been made out by the prosecution for asking the Court to bind over Mr Tilak.

The court reserved judgment till Saturday.

Decision

On Saturday 12th instant the proceedings began at 12:35 P.M.

Mr Hatch.—Mr Tilak, you must enter into a bond of Rs 20,000 and give two sureties of Rs 10,000 each. I have given my reasons in my judgment of which a copy will be shortly given to you. You should consider yourself a fortunate man in that Government have not proceeded against you under the substantive Section 124A. Section 108 Cr. P.C. is a preventive Section and this should serve you and your friends as a warning.

Then Mr Tilak signed a bond of Rs 20,000 and tendered Mr Trimbak Hari Avte and Mr Ganpat Vithoba Morval as his sureties and they were accepted by the Magistrate.

APPENDIX 1

RULE AGAINST MR TILAK

Dist. Magistrate's Decision

The following is the full text of the decision of Mr G.W. Hatch Esq. I.C.S., District Magistrate, Poona, in the matter of the rule issued against Mr Tilak:

On the information laid by Mr J.A. Guider, Deputy Inspector-General of Police, C.I.D., Poona, this Court on 22 July 1916 issued a notice under Section 108, 112 Criminal Procedure Code, calling upon Bal Gangadhar Tilak to show cause why he should not be ordered to execute a bond for a sum of Rs 20,000, with two sureties each in a sum of Rs 10,000, for his good behaviour for a period of one year.

The information laid was to the effect that B.G. Tilak having previous convictions for sedition was orally disseminating seditious matter, that is matter, the publication of which is punishable under Section 124A I.P.C., and in witness thereof the reports prepared by short-hand writers in Marathi, of speeches delivered by Mr Tilak on 1st May 1916, 31st May 1916 and 1st June 1916, together with English translation of the same, were put in by Mr Guider.

A summons was issued to Mr Tilak returnable on 28th of July 1916; subsequently on the application of the defence a postponement was granted till 2nd August and again on the application of both parties till 7th August.

The evidence in support of this information has been heard. It consists of the statements of the two short-hand reporters and of an official from the Oriental Translator's office. The former testify that the Marathi transcripts of their short-hand (viz. Exhibits B, D and F) contain a correct account of what they heard Tilak say. The latter certifies that the English translations put in (viz. Exhibits C, H and I) are correct translations of Exhibits B, D and F.

The prosecution also put in a certificate under Section 511, clause (b) of the Criminal Procedure Code regarding Tilak's previous convictions for sedition. Counsel for Tilak objected to this record of previous convictions going in but his objection was over-ruled. Mr Jinnah (for Tilak) remarked that the five of Rs 1,000 under Section 153-A had been remitted by Government, and Mr Binning (for Government) admitted that this was so.

Tilak in reply to the Court admitted that the reports of his speeches were on the whole and generally speaking correct, although there were omissions and imperfections. His object, he said, was to defend and explain Home Rule, and point out the best way of obtaining it; also to exhort people to become members of the Home Rule League. Asked whether he could explain in a few words what he meant by Home Rule, he replied 'It is given in the speeches.'

The defence called no witnesses. Counsel for the defence has not seriously impugned the correctness of the translation of the speeches; but he objects to the translation of a few words, to which I will now refer.

In the first speech (Exhibit G) on page 3 it is suggested that the word 'the' in line 4 is superfluous: also that the word 'entity' in the middle of the page should be 'form;' on page 5 instead of 'conceit,' the defence suggest 'over-confidence'; on page 6, they object to 'rogue' as a translation of 'dhurt,' on page 7 for 'accumulated' they would read 'collected'; on page 8 for 'obstruction' they read 'hindrance,' on page 9 for 'Sovereign's Policy' 'State Policy.' This is the complete list of emendations in speech I and the only one of the least importance to the meaning in the opinion of this Court is the last. Here the Marathi transcript shows 'rajadhoran' 'sovereign's policy'. Had it shown rajyadhoran, the correct translation would have been 'State Policy'. One of the short-hand writers made no distinction between his short-hand version of raj and rajya, the other did. In any case it seems to the Court a reasonable possibility that the speaker may have been misheard. The general trend of the argument in speeches seems to fit in better with 'state policy' in place of 'sovereign's policy,' in the passage at the foot of page 9. I would, therefore, allow the defence the benefit of the doubt in this case and read 'State policy'.

In speech II (Exhibit H) two emendations are suggested on page 2. The first, 'administration of the state' instead of 'ruling power', is accepted by counsel for the prosecution; the second is an improved translation of a some what difficult passage regarding the meaning of the word 'aliens.' The improved translation will be found in the deposition of witness No. 2. It does not affect the argument.

In speech III (Exhibit I) the words 'slavery' and 'bondage' occurring at the foot of page 1 were challenged by the defence. The Marathi words are 'gulamgiri' and 'dasya' Witness No. 2 an experienced translator, asserts that these words are correctly translated, the defence asserts that the former should be translated as 'servitude,' for 'dasya' also they suggested the same word to the witness.

On page 3 the word 'beast' for 'pashu' is objected to, 'animal' or 'cattle' is suggested in its place.

Throughout the speeches wherever 'gulamgiri' appears, it has been translated 'slavery'—the defence prefers 'servitude.'

The above is a complete list of the points-so far as the Court has been able to note them-in which the defence impugn the translation. There are as might be expected, a few passages in which elisions appear to have occurred, making the meaning doubtful. On the whole, this Court finds no difficulty in coming to the conclusion that the English versions Exhibits G, H and I, are accurate translations of the Marathi transcripts (B, D and F); and it sees no reason to question the statement of the short-hand writers, men of experience in their profession, that the transcripts represent a true and complete account of what they heard Mr Tilak say.

Mr Binning for the prosecution relies upon the whole of the speeches. He indicated certain passages on which he chiefly relies-they are marked in red by the Court on Exhibits C, H and I. He states plainly that he does not call into question the propriety of the discussion of Home Rule. His instructions are to express no views on that subject. What he asked the Court to condemn, on the ground that they are seditious within the meaning of Section 124A of the Indian Penal Code, are the remarks made by Tilak in various parts of the speeches in which he imputes dishonest and corrupt motives to Government.

Analyzing briefly the speech delivered on 1 May, we find first of all an attempt to divide the Government existing in India at the present time into two portions, the 'invisible English Government', and the 'visible Government,' by whose hands the invisible Government is getting works done'. Mr Tilak says he does not desire to change the former, But that the latter should 'pass into other hands' and, as he explains later, by that he means 'into our own hands', the hands of the people of this country.

He goes on to tell his audience that it is not sedition to ask for the removal of a single official, be he a sepoy or a Governor. He then plainly indicates his opinion that the present administration is not being carried on well. He gives a list of alleged grievances—abolition of Kulkarni watans, forest 'zulum', spread of liquor drinking, absence of proper education, abolition of trial by jury at Belgaum, no college in Karnatic. Why, he asks, do these things exist? There is only one answer. 'If you had been the officials in their place, or if their authority had been responsible to the public opinion, these things would not have happened'. He goes on to tell his audience they are helpless; they can do nothing without a petition to the Collector. 'We want some better arrangement than this.' The present officials, not being selected by the people, think they know best—it is their conceit or over-confidence. Other bureaucrats say 'act according to our wishes we say, act according to our wishes, so that all grievances will be removed.'

Later on he refers to the visible Government in this country as the 'deities' between the people and the 'invisible king or Government.' 'God does not get angry; these deities get angry without reason,' he gives the instance of the panch trying to keep the administration of his own affairs out of the hands of their wards. They say he is half-mad, that he has bad habits; eventually they go before the court and get him adjudged mad. 'Some things like these have now begun to happen here.'

Then follows the story of the three rogues. Mr Jinnah for the defence sought to give this story a cachet of respectability by quoting it as delivered by Sir R. Bhandarkar in the course of a speech in Council, when he likened his opponents in the matter of the University Bill—including such a reputable person as the Hon'ble Mr Gokhale—to the three rogues of this story. But a story may be told in more than one way, and may carry more than one moral. Mr Tilak's object appears to have been to invite his audience to see a likeness between those Indians who do not advocate Home Rule and the rogues of the story; and to warn them to beware of the guiles of those persons who would deprive them of their rightful property i.e. Swarajya.

He next discusses the question of fitness. He indulges in some remarks which are admittedly offensive (i.e. Mr Jinnah for the defence admits them to be so) regarding the inexperienced youth from England, who, he suggests, lords it over the Mamlatdars of 60 years of age.

He concludes this discussion by the words 'How long will you teach us?.... Is there any end to this? Or must we just like this, work under you like slaves till the end?' He adds: 'These officers have control over the people's education and it is their duty to improve them; this duty remains on one side, they make attempts on the other side. They say that whatever attempts they make, it is impossible for these people to become fit for this work. I think that to place such excuses before the invisible Government is in a manner an occupation of securing one's own interest.'

After referring to the smooth working of the administration in the Native State of Mysore he remarks: 'They only object in saying that the Indians are not fit to carry on the administration is that they are always to be kept in slavery, that they are to be made to do work by labouring like slaves, and that the ways whereby their intellect and their ability may be developed are to be stopped'—sentiments greeted by his audience with cheers and cries of shame.

In the next paragraph (page 9) he refers to the money-making or trading policy of the East India Company; an administration in which the people's good was not considered. In 1858 the sovereign took the administration into his own hands; but the establishment of employees remained the same. The Director of the Company went, and the State Secretary came in his place; it is the latter and not the governor-general, who decides how much money is to be spent in India and what taxes are to be imposed. 'This is but a commercial policy' says Mr Tilak. 'Though the administration went into the hands of the Queen's Government, and although they issued a great proclamation, the 'sovereign's policy (or 'the state policy' in the alternative version) is not on the basis of the proclamation. The sovereign's policy is in accordance with the trading Company's policy, the administration of the kingdom is in accordance with the Company's policy. And in the meantime the proclamation has no effect (Laughter, cheers).'

A little later he says that the bureaucracy, the State Secretary and the Governor-General have been cajoling the people of India by promising them additional powers and places. Then follows an objectionable reference to the Educational Department, in which, though most of the subordinate servants are Indians, a Saheb is kept at the head 'to restrain their mouths and scope of their intellect.'

A little later the State Secretary is told that he is not wanted and is likened to the 'son-in-law', the suggestion apparently being that his appointment is the result of a job. A few lines lower down occurs this sentence: 'I say again, if the nation is to get happiness, if the thousands of complaints, that have arisen to-day, are to be removed, then first of all change this system of administration,'

APPENDIX 1

The audience are told that if they get Swarajya, all their difficulties will disappear. If additional expenditure is to be met it will be met voluntarily and will not oppress their minds. Then follows a somewhat important sentence. 'Learned aliens may tell us, when we are passing through this door, that we should not pass through this door but through that; but if any one comes and stands there and (begins to) tell us not to go through it, then we have to (or alternatively rendered 'shall have to') go out by giving him a push. The very same is the case with Swarajya. This is the obstruction of the bureaucracy.'

Mr Jinnah suggests that 'this door' is the door of Parliament, also that there is something missing in the sentence.

Tilak then passes on to a reference to the extravagance of paying a Collector Rs 2,500. If they say they want this big pay on account of the hardships of the climate etc. he replies by asking 'who told them to come here? We did not ask them.'

A few lines further down he tells his audience that he proposes to go on placing the subject (before the people) at every place in order to forward the Home Rule movement.

So ends speech No. 1, delivered on 1st May 1916 at the 18th Provincial Conference at Belgaum before a large audience, composed of 'people of all sorts' (witness No. 1).

What have the defence to say about this speech? Mr Jinnah tells this Court that *the criticism in speech No. 1 is the criticism of a certain set of administrators* and refers to Mr Justice Strachey's remarks in 22 Bombay at page 135 to the effect that the Government established in British India means 'British rule and its representatives as such the existing political system as distinguished from any particular set of administrators.'

The Court has no hesitation in rejecting this suggestion the quotations given above provide complete grounds for its refutation.

Mr Jinnah's next line of defence is that the Act of 1858 (i.e. the act under which the Government of India is constituted; since repealed and consolidated by an Act of 1915,) is nothing but a measure which may lawfully be disapprobated with a view to its repeal or modification. Mr Tilak in order to get it altered must show how the system set up by that Act is bad and defective. He proposes to get it altered in a law-ful manner, by going to Parliament; he must be allowed to criticize the system and expose its abuses or he will have no chance of getting it altered.

The simple answer to this is that his criticisms must be such that they do not fall within the scope of Section 124A of the Indian Penal Code. That Section has been explained and commented on in numerous reported cases. It is agreed that Tilak's first trial reported in 22 Bombay is the most complete exposition of the law. On page 137 Mr Justice Strachey distinguishes between disaffection and disapprobation. In 8 Bombay Law Reporter, page 438, is found a definition of Government established by law in India; it amplifies Mr Justice Strachey's definition on page 135 of 22 Bombay. I do not propose to discuss the law at length; it is now well understood. Disaffection in the words of Mr Justice Strachey means 'absence of affection or enmity....' 'A man may criticize or comment on any measure or act of Government. ....may express the strongest condemnation of such measures, and he may do so severely and even unreasonably, perversely and unfairly.... But if he goes beyond that and whether in the course of comments on measures he, holds up the Government itself to hatred or contempt...as for instance by attributing to it every sort of evil and misfortune suffered by the people, or dwelling adversely on its foreign origin or character or imputing to it base motives, or accusing it of hostility to indifference to the welfare of the people, then he is guilty under the Section.' The quotations made above from the Belgaum speech include samples of three out of the four things which a man may not do.

Accordingly this Court has no hesitation in deciding that B.G. Tilak in his speech delivered at Belgaum on 1 May 1916 did speak words calculated to bring into hatred or contempt the government established by law in British India, and did attempt to excite disaffection towards that Government, and that thereby he disseminated matter punishable under section 124A of the Indian Penal Code.

Of the two speeches subsequently delivered at Ahmednagar, it is not necessary to speak at great length. They contain seditious passages undoubtedly; a few only will be quoted here, though others can be found. In the speech of 31 May (Exhibit H) on page 2, he describes the Government as alien, and defines alien as follows: 'He is to be considered alien who does not do this duty (i.e. those things whereby the nation may become eminent and be benefited), but looks; only to his own benefit, to the benefit of his own race, and to the benefit of his original country.' He says the people have been complaining of their grievances for the past 20 or 25 years, but 'the Government (he repeats the phrase) is alien. It does not know.... However much you may clamour, however much you may agitate, whatever the number of grounds you may show, its sight is so affected as not to see the figures drawn from its own reports and set before it.' A little further on 'Government has a sort of religious duty to perform; a sort of responsibility rests on its shoulders. I say that when a Government evades this responsibility, it is no Government at all.' He then compares the officials of the Government in India to the middlemen, or keepers of granaries, who according to the Indian proverbial expression, are worried (literally 'whose bellies ache') when the master spends his money freely. He gives the proverb a sting by telling his audience that the intervening middlemen's aching bellies should be removed-lending colour to a suggestion, which is not apparent in the proverb in its usual form, that the middlemen are greedy and self-interested and on that account obtrude themselves between the master and the people.

In a later passage he invites attention to the fact that he desires to retain the rule of the English Government and does not desire a German Government in its place. Mr Jinnah asks the Court to note this passage, as an evidence of Tilak's good faith and loyalty.

In another passage Tilak complains that while money cannot be found for education, it can be found for increasing the pay of the bureaucracy. Later he says: 'Their first lookout is to see how their pay will be secure.'

Again he declares the present Government unfit to rule because in 50 years they have not educated the Indians up to a point when they can rule themselves. He describes their 'deceit' and 'shuffling' in the matter of pronouncing the Indian unfit. He tells his audience that they must have the courage to laugh in the saheb's face instead of in their homes. He finally exhorts them thus; 'if you wish to remain slaves, do so. No one says, do not. What is the use of giving advice to him hundreds of times who likes slavery? He who is willing to remain in slavery may do so freely. But this is not the condition of citizens.' Mr Jinnah says: Mr Tilak's only object is to wake people up out of their lethargy. Doubtless. But when in order to do so, he tells them they are 'slaves' or are 'in servitude'—if that translation is preferred—not once, but ten or a dozen times in the course of the three speeches—then he must not complain if he is charged with attempting to excite disaffection towards the Government responsible, as he alleges, for keeping them in this unfortunate plight.

In the 3rd speech (Exhibit I) delivered on the following day, there are two passages which I will quote. The first develops the slavery theme: it runs thus: 'Our industries must be improved. But why it was stopped? Who stopped it? If we begin to look out for the cause of this (it will appear that) we did not stop this industrial reform, we did not stop this economic reform. In that nation in which there is a way and there is liberty to use and show one's ability, good qualities flourish. But when there is utter slavery and bondage, what qualities will be developed? Nothing will happen except with the pleasure of the master.' Mr Jinnah says again he is trying to wake up his audience; to the ordinary man he appears to be trying to alienate the affection of his listeners, to cause that absence of affection or enmity towards the Government which constitutes disaffection and disloyalty. A little later Tilak drives his point home still more by telling the people that unless they get the administration change, 'every man in India will become more and more effeminate. The duty we have to do is that. Such are the institutions of slavery.'

The second important passage is concerned with his statement of what constitutes the national question. The chief question is whether a certain nation is to be treated like beasts or considering the people in the nation to be men, their sentiment, their desire for liberty is to bend in some direction and they are to be brought and placed in the rank 'of civilized nations.' The defence suggest that 'beast' is too strong a word. After referring to the available dictionaries and studying the context, the Court concludes that an English writer or orator would certainly have used the words 'brute beasts' in this connection and that the word 'pashu' in Tilak's mouth meant that and nothing else. There are other offensive passages in this speech calculated to alienate

APPENDIX 1

the affection of his audience from the rulers, but it is unnecessary to quote from it further.

Looking at these speeches as whole, fairly, freely, and without giving undue weight to isolated passages, what impression do they convey to us, and what impression must we believe they conveyed to the audience to which they were addressed? The impression I gather from them is that Tilak wishes to disaffect his audience towards the Government, in order that they may 'wake up' (to adopt Mr Jinnah's words) to their present unhappy condition, join Home Rule League and help him in his agitation for a change in the administration of the country. He is addressing an ignorant audience, —Counsel for the defence insisted upon this point—and he knows that he cannot interest them in his argument unless he can illustrate it forcibly; so he tells them that they are slaves, that their grievances remain unredressed, that the Government only considers its own interests which are alien to theirs, and intends to keep them in slavery on the untrue excuse that they are not fit to rule themselves.

Mr Jinnah's contention that it is not the Government that Tilak is attacking but only the Civil Service, will be discarded at once by any one who reads the speeches through. The speaker refers frequently to the Bureaucracy using the English word; but the context and trend of his argument throughout shows that he is referring to the whole system of Government and the whole body of officials in India from the Governor-General down to the Police sepoy.

Tilak has been twice convicted under Section 124A; the first time in 1897, the second in 1908.

He finished his term of imprisonment for the second offence only two years ago. He has proclaimed his intention in the Belgaum speech of talking again upon this subject. Accordingly I am satisfied that in order to maintain his good behaviour it is necessary that he should execute a bond with two sureties as set out in my order of 22 July last. I direct that he do enter into a bond in a sum of Rs 20,000, with two sureties each in a sum of Rs 10,000 to be of good behaviour for a period of one year (Section 108 Criminal Procedure Code.)

(12.8.1916.)   (Sd.) G.W. Hatch,
District Magistrate, Poona.

On the 23rd of August Mr Tilak files the following revisional application in the High Court of Judicature at Bombay against the order of the District Magistrate of Poona.

APPENDIX 1

IN HIS MAJESTY'S HIGH COURT OF JUDICATURE AT BOMBAY

CRIMINAL REVISION APPLICATION
No. 232 of 1916

BAL GANGADHAR TILAK Residing at Poona
V/s.
KING EMPEROR

The humble petition of Bal Gangadhar Tilak Residing at Poona

(Before the Hon. Justice Beaman
AND
Hon. Justice Sir John Heaton).

RESPECTFULLY SHOWETH:-

That the petitioner was called upon by Mr Hatch, District Magistrate, Poona, to furnish security for good behaviour under Section 108 Cri. P. Code and was by his order dated 12 August 1916 required to enter into a bond in a sum of Rupees 20,000 with two sureties each in a sum of Rs 10,000 to be of good behaviour for a period of one year.

Being aggrieved by this order Your Lordships' petitioner bags to approach this Honourable Court with a prayer that Your Lordships will be pleased to send for the Record and papers of the case and set aside the order on the following among their grounds:

1. That the Lower Court misunderstood Sec. 124A. The Indian P. Code and failed to duly notice its second explanation.

2. The learned Magistrate omitted to follow the provisions of section 117 of the Cri. P.C. in the conduct of the case after the appearance before him of the petitioner to show cause as required by his notice in that he failed to examine the informant in petitioner's presence.

3. That the Lower Court committed an error in law in admitting at the stage it did, evidence of petitioner's previous convictions recorded more then 6 years ago and in using the same for the purpose of construing the speeches of Petitioner.

4. That the learned Magistrate was wrong in law in accepting as proved the particular words and passages for which petitioner is bound over, without legal and legally sufficient evidence.

5. That the learned Magistrate allowed his judgment to be influenced by notes of the shorthand writers regarding 'cheers' &c. without legal proof of the same.

6. That the three speeches as presented to the Court by the prosecution are not the verbatim reports of petitioner's speeches and cannot legally be made the bases of an order under Sec. 108 Cri. P.C.

7. That petitioner is not legally liable to be proceeded against under Section 108 Cri. P. Code.

8. That the Lower Court misconstrued the speeches and their scope though it was specially explained by the petitioner in his speeches.

9. That the main object of petitioner in the speeches being to bring about a change in the system of administration by an amendment in the Government of India Act which is only a measure within a meaning of explanation II of Section 124 Cri. P. Code, the speeches fall under the 2nd explanation to Section 124 A.I.P.C.

10. That the speeches (not even one or any part of them) are not offensive within the meaning of Section 124A Indian Penal Code.

11. That in supporting 'Home Rule for India' petitioner never intended to use nor has used any expressions offensive within the meaning of S. 124A but is stating his case for Home Rule Regarding which (Home Rule) itself the prosecution has got nothing to say and which Home Rule or Swarajya has been held to be a legitimate object by Indian Law Report 34 Calcutta 991 so that members of a public meeting may be exhorted to work for its attainment.

12. The Lower Court has misunderstood the expression 'Government established by law in British India, appearing in Section 124A and it erred in assuming it to stand for 'Government' as defined in Section 17 of the P. Code.

13. The finding that the speeches or the passages quoted in the judgment are likely to create disaffection is not supported either by proper and natural construction of the speeches as a whole, or by any direct evidence on the point.

14. That the evidence of the shorthand reporters standing by itself is insufficient in law to support the final order passed and the notes not being 'evidence' nor the translations there is no legal evidence in the case to sustain the order.

15. The 'Notes' are admittedly inaccurate and incomplete in places, they are not legally admissible as any evidence. The man originally translated has not been examined in proof of the translation and the evidence of Mr Thakore is not good evidence.

16. That the passages relied on by the Lower Court in Support of its decision are read by the Court irrespective of their context in which they appear.

17. That in translation Marathi passages lose their real tenor and acquire a different spirit and form this the Lower Court has failed to note.

18. That the significance of Marathi proverbs and parables is not properly brought out in the translations and therefore the translations are really not a proper test to understand the passages and illustrations in Marathi.

19. That the amount of security is excessive. And that for this act of kindness Your Lordship's petitioner shall as in duty bound ever pray.

Bombay
23rd August 1916

Sd. S.R. Bakhle,
Pleader for the Applicant

Mr S.R. Bakhle, B.A., LL.B., High Court Pleader, appeared on 30th of August 1916 on behalf of Mr Tilak before the Hon. Mr Justice Beaman and the Hon. Justice Sir John Heaton and argued in favour of admitting the application.

Mr Bakhle, in the course of his argument, said that the object of the speeches was to criticize the machinery and not the Government established by law, and the question, whether they were seditious or not, ought to have been considered by taking into consideration the speeches as a whole. The translations were admittedly inaccurate.

Mr Justice Beaman: All that becomes a pure question of fact. The Magistrate believes it to be so and it is a question of fact whether they were or were not to that character.

Mr Justice Beaman urged that he also complained of several irregularities. In the first place the complaint on whose information the summons was issued ought to have been examined under Section 117 of the Code, in order to inquire into the truth of the information upon which the action had been taken.

Mr Justice Beaman: There was an inquiry was there not and certain witnesses were examined?

Mr Bakhle: But Mr Guider was the informant and he was not examined.

Mr Justice Beaman: What would be the use of examining Mr Guider? What could you have learnt from him except that three speeches were made? The section does not state that the informant should be examined.

Mr Bakhle: The next irregularity is that the learned Magistrate had these speeches before him. They were tried to be proved by the short-hand notes. They are not evidence at all. They were put in merely to refresh the memory of the witnesses.

Mr Justice Beaman: What's wrong with that? Nobody says that they are evidence as such of the speeches. They are merely used to refresh the memory of the witnesses. There is no irregularity in that.

Mr Bakhle: The third irregularity was that these speeches were translated in Bombay by one person. He is not examined, but they are put in through another person and he is asked whether the translation is a correct translation.

Mr Justice Beaman: What is the sense in that argument? Here is a Marathi document which is translated and it is shown to a person who knows Marathi very well and he says that the translation is accurate.

Mr Bakhle: The other irregularity consisted in taking evidence of previous convictions of Mr Tilak before the inquiry was over instead of at the end of the inquiry.

Mr Justice Beaman: There is no question of any enhancement of punishment. Besides as you already stated the amount of the bond required to be executed was already stated in the notice to Mr Tilak as required by the Code.

Mr Tilak is well known to all and some of the incidents of his life are known to most of us. That is the injustice you complain of?

Mr Justice Heaton: There is not a shadow of any injustice or unfairness done or shown to your client. You may have a cause for complaint on merits.

Mr Bakhle then read the judgment of the lower court and commented that the speeches read as a whole merely put before the audience a scheme for the administration of the Government. Mr Tilak wanted only a change in the administration. He distinguished between the supreme Government and the machinery used by that Government. He had no quarrel with the British Government. The change he sought was only by an amendment of the Government of India Act.

Their Lordships granted a rule in the matter.

IN THE HIGH COURT OF JUDICATURE AT BOMBAY

CRIMINAL REVISION APPLICATION
NO. 232 of 1916

BAL GANGADHAR TILAK APPLICANT
vs.
KING EMPEROR RESPONDENT

(Before the Hon, Justice Sir Stanley Batchelor
AND
Hon. Mr Justice Shaha)
Wednesday, 8th November 1916

The Hon. Mr Mohammad Ali Jinnah with Messrs Joseph Baptista and Erulkar, Barristers-at-law, instructed by Messrs. Bakhle, Modak and Karandikar High Court Pleaders appeared for the applicant while the Hon. Mr Jardine Messrs. Strangman and N.M. Patwardhan barristers-at-law instructed by Mr S.S. Patkar, Government pleader and Khan Bahadur S.C. Davar appeared for the crown.

The Hon. Mr Jinnah addressed the Court as follows:

Your Lordships please, in this case, my lords, the Magistrate... an order under Sec. 108 of the Cr P.C. The order runs in this way. (Reads the order as follows: 'direct that he does enter into bond in a sum of Rs 20,000 with two sureties each in a sum of Rs 10,000 to be of good behaviour for a period of one year Sec. 108, Cr. P.C.,') Now if your Lordships will turn to Sec 119, Cr. P.C., the charge we have got to meet is this. (Reads Sec. 108 as follows: *Security for good behaviour from persons disseminating seditious matter'* — whenever a Chief Presidency or District Magistrate, or a Presidency Magistrates or a Magistrate of the First class specially empowered by the Local Government in this behalf, has information that there is within the limits of his jurisdiction any who, within or without such limits, either orally or in writing, disseminates or attempts to disseminate or any wise abets the dissemination of—

(a) Any seditious matter, that is to… the publication of which is punishable… 124A of the I.P.C. or

(b) Any matter the publication of which is punishable under Sec. 152 A of the I.P.C. or

(c) Any matter concerning a Judge which amounts to criminal intimidation or defamation under the I.P.C.,

such Magistrate may (In manner hereinafter) require such person to show cause why he should not be ordered to execute a bond, with or without securities, for his good behaviour for such period, not exceeding 1 year, as the Magistrate thinks fit to fix.) Therefore, the first thing that the Court has got to find out is whether in this case the Appellant, by speeches, disseminates or attempts to disseminate any seditious matter. To put it shortly, whether he comes within the meaning of Sec. 124A. In this case orally speeches were delivered. Therefore, my lords, the first question that your lordships have got to consider is whether there is sedition in the words uttered in the 3 speeches which he delivered at these 3 meetings. Now, the first question that your lordships will have to consider is what does Sec. 124A say (reads the section.) Whoever by words, either spoken or written, or by signs, or by visible representation, or otherwise, brings or attempts to bring into hatred or contempt, or excites or attempts to excite disaffection towards, Her Majesty or the Government established by Law in British India shall be punished with transportation for life or any shorter term, to which fine may be added, or with imprisonment which may extend to three years, to which fine may be added, or without fine. 'The appellant is not charged with having done, what is said in this section towards His Majesty. From his finding, your lordships will see, the Magistrate holds that the 'appellant' did speak words calculated to bring into hatred or contempt the Government established by law in British India.' Therefore, the first question, which I have to submit to your lordships, is this; 'What is the Government established by law in British India?' I submit that the Magistrate has taken entirely a wrong view of our criticism which is directed towards the Government, which, the Magistrate says, is the Government established by law in British India. The first question which your lordships will have to consider is 'what is the Government that is by law established in British India?' Now, I shall point out to your lordships that really the Government by law established in British India is not, at all, attacked in any way in these speeches, I am going to point out to your lordships no less than 47 passages, which go to show that in these 3 speeches there is not a single word against the Government established by law in British India. On the contrary, in these 47 passages Mr Tilak has made it quite clear that the British rule or the British Government is beneficial. Now, Sec. 16 of the I.P.C. defines what is the 'Government of India.' Sec. 16 says 'The words "Government of India" denote the Governor-general of India in Council or, during the absence of the

Governor-general of India from his Council, the President in Council or the Governor-general of India alone, as regards the powers which may be lawfully exercised by them or him respectively.' Now, as regards the words 'Government,' as distinguished from the 'Government of India,' Sec. 17 says this; 'The word "Government" denotes the person or persons authorized by law to administer executive Government in any part of British India.'

Bachelor J.: The question is whether in Section 124A 'Government' is Government of India.

Mr Jinnah: In Sec.17 the term is 'Government,' which is defined there.

Bachelor J.: Section 124A says 'or the Government established by law in British India.'

Mr Jinnah: If you take the definition of the term 'Government,' as given in Sec. 17, then in Sec., 124A the words 'Established by law in British India,' after the word 'Government,' are superfluous. There is no meaning in them. Therefore, I say that by the term 'Government' what is meant is Government not in a concrete form but Government in an abstract form, that is to say 'Constitutionally established Government.' If you attack that Government in a manner which is likely to cause disaffection, then it falls within Sec. 124A. If you take, my lords, first of all, 'Government,' as defined in Sec. 17, then any police sepoy would come under that section. Any executive person or persons, authorized by law to administer the executive Government in any part of British India, would come under that section. Any Collector would come under it. Any individual authorized to administer executive powers would come under it, but I submit, Section 17 has nothing whatever to do with 'the Government established by law in British India.' Then, Section 16 gives you another definition of the term 'Government,' but, I don't say, that definition is a definition of the phrase, 'The Government established by law in British India,' therefore, Secs. 16 and 17 do not apply at all. That is my submission. Therefore, the only authoritative pronouncement on this phrase, 'Government established by law in British India,' as far as I am able to see, is given by Mr Justice Batty in 8 B.L.R. 438. (Reads the page from about the middle downwards). Your lordships will see that, according to Mr Justice Batty, it is an abstract conception which is called 'Government.' (Reads the page further).

Batchelor J.: That is quite so, no doubt. I only want to test your argument about Secs. 16 and 17 as regards the words 'Government established by law in British India.' In Sec. 17 what is contemplated by the term 'Government' is a collective conception. This is my idea that 'Government does not mean an individual or individual officials;' Government is an abstract conception.

Mr Jinnah: Then, your lordships will see what he says later on. (Reads further from the judgment of Mr Justice Batty.). According to Mr Justice Batty, 'Government does not mean that it is transitory, occasional and temporary, but that it is vital and permanent. My submission, therefore, my lords, is this that the speeches that Mr. Tilak made are nothing but a criticism of a certain system of administration and not of the whole administration. Remember this also that he is only dealing with a certain portion of the whole system of administration, such as, the Military Service, the Forest Service and so forth. Mr Tilak deals with one part of the whole system of administration, which is the Civil Service and which, in India, constitutes the Bureaucracy. The whole of the criticism, the whole of the comment, is directed towards that part of the whole system of Government. The comment is directed towards a particular phase of the system of administration, a particularly specified phase of that system, namely, the Bureaucracy having the monopoly of all the powers and being not responsible to the people.

Batchelor J.: Then you don't say that the whole of the Civil Service should be abolished, but that it should be brought under control?

Mr Jinnah: Brought under control of the people and made responsible to the people.

Batchelor J.: Yes, you don't say that this Service should be done away with. You want Officers, you want men to carry on the administration. What you really criticize is that under the present constitution of the Government of India the Bureaucracy are not under the control of the people and are not responsible to the people, and that they should be brought under the control of the people and made responsible to the people and should not be done away with entirely?

Mr Jinnah: Yes. Now, if your lordships turn to the Explanations to Section 124A, you will find that the Magistrate was wrong in giving the meaning that he has given to the word 'disaffection,' as defined by Mr Justice Strachey.

Batchelor J.: Yes. You have the expression 'disaffection' defined. (Reads the definition of 'disaffection.')

Mr Jinnah: It must be something active. Something more than a passive feeling. Your lordships will find that in Explanation 2 to Section 124A. (Reads it). My submission, my lords, is this that you should read the speeches of Mr Tilak as a whole. I don't think it will be disputed: it is laid down over and over again, that you cannot look at a passage here and a passage there, but that you have to read the whole speech, and reading these 3 speeches as a whole, my submission, my lords, is this that they are nothing but a comment or an expression of disapprobation of the measures of Government with a view to obtain their alteration by lawful means. In this case the next point I have to establish is the point of intention. Your lordships will remember that in every criminal case, and I should say the more so in a case of this character the intention of the writer or speaker is absolutely essential. It is of the utmost importance. You must, first of all, be satisfied that the writer or speaker has intended to cause disaffection, and how are you going to be satisfied? The intention must be gathered from the writings to speeches themselves. If you look at these speeches, the 'onus' really is on the prosecution to prove the intention. With regard to this question of intention, I can also point out to your lordships no less than 47 passages, which I have picked out from the speeches and which go conclusively to show that there is no doubt, my lords, that there is not the slightest doubt than Mr Tilak never intended to cause disaffection towards Government established by law in British India. There is one more thing that I ought to say before I come to these passages. You will remember, my lords, how there speeches are before you now. When the speeches were delivered, the shorthand writers, the C.I.D. shorthand writers, were there and they took down the notes in shorthand. Of course, strictly speaking, those notes can be utilized for refreshing the memory and nothing else. The substance of the speeches generally is correct. Mr Tilak himself admits that. Your lordships will agree with me to this extent that in a speech taken down by a shorthand writer a wrong phrase here or a wrong phrase there or a wrong word here or a wrong word there makes a lot of difference in a particular passage, and, therefore, I ask your lordships to take these speeches as a whole. I ask your lordships to read speeches and examine them. There is no doubt with regard to the translation except that of some words.

Batchelor J.: This is what you mean to say: that the speeches must be read as a whole to find out what the speaker means.

Mr Jinnah: Yes. There was a great deal of discussion with regard to the translation of certain words. The translation of those words was challenged.

Batchelor J.: This is what you say: we have to remember that we should take the passages as a whole and not look to the translation of any particular words. We both have read the 3 speeches. You may argue on that footing. We don't want to shorten your argument.

Mr Jinnah: Then I won't read the speeches. I ought to draw your lordships attention to the Government of India Act of 1915. With regard to that my submission is this that you will find there what is meant by the 'Government established by law in British India.' (Reads a section of the Act.) First of all, you have His Majesty the King-Emperor. There is no complaint about that (Reads Sections 1 and 2 of the Act.) Your lordships will see that the 'Government of India by law established in British India' is really, first of all, the King-himself and the Parliament also, because the Parliament, that is the British Parliament, has got certain powers. Then, what is done is this; certain powers are delegated to the Secretary of State for India only for a certain purpose. (Reads Section 2 of the Act.) Then, you have the Governor-General in Council. Then, I will ask your lordships to turn to Section 33 of the Act. (Reads it.) Here, the important words are 'Vested to maintain the law.' Therefore, as I am telling you, my lords, strictly speaking, if you take, first of all, Justice Batty's judgment, you get this that the 'Government established in British India by law' is really the King-Emperor and Parliament, which gives certain powers to the Secretary of State for India and only certain powers of superintendence, direction and control, are given to the Governor-General in Council. Therefore, you cannot possibly go beyond the very words 'The Governor-General in Council'; that is the Government. Then you have various Services for instance, the Military Service, the Forest Service and the Civil Service. I say it is open to any citizen to say that a particular Service should be removed in a particular way. I submit any individual is entitled to criticise any Service even unreasonably, then he does not cause disaffection against the Government established by law in British India. Then, my lords, with regard to the question of intention, I may also point out to your lordships a passage in the 'Laws of England' by Lord Salisbury, Vol. 9, p. 445. A Seditious intention is an intention—(1) to bring into hatred or contempt, or to excite disaffection against, the King or the Government and Constitution of the United Kingdom, or either House of Parliament, or the administration of Justice (n); or (2) to excite the King's subjects to attempt, otherwise than by lawful means, the alteration of any matter in Church or State by law established; or (3) to incite any person to commit any crime in disturbance of the peace; or (4) to raise discontent or disaffection amongst his Majesty's subjects' or (5) to promote feelings of ill-will and hostility between different classes of such subjects.

But an intention is not seditious if the object is to show that the King has been misled or mistaken in his measures, or to point out errors or defects in the Government or Constitution with a view to their reformation, or to excite the subjects to attempt by lawful means the alteration of any matter in Church or State by law established, or to point out, in order to their removal, matters which are producing, or having a tendency to produce, feelings of hatred and ill-will between classes of the King's subjects.

In this as in other offences the person is deemed to intend the consequence which would naturally follow from his conduct at the time, and in the circumstances, in which the words were used.

He, first of all, deals with what is sedition. There is not much difference between the law of sedition in England and here. This is what he says. (Reads P. 463 already mentioned.) Here the important words are 'the State by law established.' That is certainly an abstract conception of the term 'Government.' Therefore, my lords, the prosecution have got really to satisfy your lordships that Mr Tilak intention is what they say it is. The Magistrate says in his judgment—I will point out the passage to your lordships when I come to deal with the judgment—that, no doubt, Mr Tilak was criticizing the measures of Government, but that to that extent, he was only using the argument as a mere cloak. I say, the prosecution have got to satisfy your lordships what Mr Tilak's intention was. It is no use saying his argument is a mere cloak really to cause disaffection and to bring hatred or dislike, in the minds of his hearers, for the government by law established in British India. I will tell your lordships what the intention of Mr Tilak was when he delivered these speeches. First of all, your lordships will remember this that the Home Rule League is established at Belgaum. That is admitted. There is no doubt about it, and, of course, in the Lower Court, Mr Binning said he would not express any opinion about this movement at all, and, therefore, I take it that the Home Rule League is not an unconstitutional organisation and that there is nothing against it. Now, what happens? Mr Tilak goes to Belgaum, and in Belgaum what does he do? He makes a speech, and the object of his making the speech was to convince his audience that the Home Rule League was a good thing. He began to tell his audience clearly that he wanted to convince them as to 'what we are asking for? What is the thing that we ought to have?' And Mr Tilak wanted to convince the audience in this way in order that the audience might become members of the League, and, of course, it is always desirable to have members and to get subscription for membership, that is the object with which Mr Tilak was giving these lectures. Therefore, I say, Mr Tilak had no particular object in having the intention at this juncture to disseminate sedition. His object was a definite object, namely, to try to convince people that the Home Rule League organisation was a good thing. Now, your lordships, we will take the first speech. What he does in this speech is to divide the Government into an 'Invisible Government' and a 'Visible Government'. Then he says 'The question of 'Swaraja' is not about the Emperor, not about this invisible Government....' So far as the Emperor is concerned, Mr Tilak has nothing to say against him. He distinctly says that fanatical nations never rise and that there must be a Government. Now, I ask your lordships the simple question: 'Can you imagine a lecturer, starting with the praise of the British Rule, can ever possibly create prejudice against the British Rule in this country and yet put before his audience these ideas of advancement 'through their sympathy, through their anxious care, through their high sentiments?' He says these things about the British Government and then he says 'this is how we have to secure our own good.' This is really what he says to effect his purpose. Does a man, starting with these words, really want to cause disaffection? Remember what he further says: 'it is an undoubted fact that we must secure our good under their protection.' My lords, can that be disputed by anybody? For the people of this country must try and secure their own good with the aid of the English nation. Then he says 'One Government will remain invisible Government, and the visible Government changes every moment.... We do not wish to change the invisible Government—English Government.' Here he gives his abstract conception of what he wants to remain and what he wants to be changed. Next he says the 'Swaraja' agitation, now existing in India, is for the change of the Ministry.... We want to remain under the shelter of the English rule.' My lords, the audience must be really the most perverted to be disaffected against the British Rule when a speaker, remember, my lords, throughout his speech, does not say a single word against the British Government. Here are the passages which I have picked out from the speech which are pregnant with the admissions that I have read to your Lordships. If the man wanted to cause disaffection he would have done so in the very introduction of his speech, and he would have gone on hammering and setting out the object which he had at heart. But that is not the case here. Here you find, my lords, at various stages of the speech sentiments are brought out and attempts made to make it clear as to what his object was, namely, to object to the present system of administration. He says: 'We do not want this system,.... I am sure that by the grace of God your next generation will not fail to obtain the fruit of this work, though it may not be obtained in your life time.' My lords, this is Mr Tilak's first speech. Now, there are 24 passages in this speech; I have numbered them, my lords; they are not at the beginning or at the end; they are spread out throughout the speech, at various points, where he wants to make it clear what he really wants, namely, a change in the system of administration and nothing else. Now, let us turn to the objections realised to this first speech. If your lordships will turn to the speech, you will find that some of the objections made by the prosecution were really under some misconception of what the speaker really meant. Turn to page 22 to see their objection. I think, my lords, I don't see how I can avoid reading the speech; I must read it that is the only way of dealing with it.

Batchelor J.: Read all the 3 speeches. I don't wish you to shorten your argument. If you want to read these passages, do so; we are entirely in your hands.

Mr Jinnah: My lords, if you turn to page 22, line 37, there Mr Tilak says what 'Swaraja' is. He asks 'What is 'Swaraja'?' And he makes his meaning clear from line 50. He says. Those who are ruling over you do not belong to your religion,.... It is carried on through those who are now servants, (viz.), the State Secretary, Viceroy, Governor, below him the Collector, the Patil, and, lastly, the police sepoy. 'Now, my lords, if you say you object to any particular official or a particular member of Government or the Secretary of States, is that sedition? Is that wrong? Is there anything wrong? All that he says is that.' If you want really to do anything, at all, you have to go to the Collector, you have no power yourself; you cannot manage your own affairs. We want a better arrangement than that. We want to have our little finger in the management of our own affairs. Then a great point was made of the passage. 'I am so much educated, I get so much pay, I possess so much ability — why should I do any thing which would be harmful to others?' The only answer is: 'Because you have such conceit. There is one way, there is no rule about it. He whose belly is pinched has experience about it.' Now, my lords, that word 'conceit' ought to be 'overconfident.'

Batchelor J.: We have nothing to do with what the word means. It may mean conceit or overconfidence.

Shah J.: What is the original for 'conceit?' I cannot make it out.

Mr Jinnah: 'Ghamend.'

Batchelor J.: Speaking entirely for myself, it does not matter whether the word means 'conceit' or 'overconfidence.'

Mr Jinnah: 'Conceit' is more offensive.

Batchelor J.: It may be offensive, it is no concern of ours.

Mr Jinnah: No. This is one of the passages to which the prosecution object, I don't know, my lords, what is wrong in it. Another thing which they complain of is the passage: 'he whose belly is pinched has experience about it.' I think, my lords, obviously this is not properly taken down. What Mr Tilak means to say is that when anything is asked from the officials, they are so overconfident that they do not listen to us. Therefore, he says that he whose belly is pinched has experience.

Batchelor J.: You see, we say in English 'it is the wearer of the shoe that knows where the shoes pinches.'

Mr Jinnah: Quite so, that is it. Some of the officials are overconfident about their own management, which they are perfectly honestly doing their best to keep properly, but, they cannot realize what defects the people of the country see in the management.

Your lordships then comes is the story of the three rogues referred to by Mr Tilak. Of this story the prosecution complain strongly. This story of three rogues is, my lords, not intended to apply to the English people. It is really intended to apply to those, who are really the opponents of the Home Rule League organisation, and if you read that passage in the speech very carefully, you will see that what Mr Tilak is driving at is this. He says 'I say the Home Rule League is a good thing. I want you also to agree with me.' His object is to persuade people to join the League, to become its members and not to become simpletons like the gentleman in the story of the three rogues, occurring in the Panchatantra, because says he 'People will come and tell you all sorts of stories against the Home Rule League organisation.' This is, my lords, the story of the 3 rogues, which is given in this speech: 'A villager had come taking a sheep on his head. One rogue said to him 'there is a she-goat on your head.' The second said 'there is a dog on your head.' The third one said quite a third thing. He threw away the sheep. The rogues took it away. Our condition is like that.'

Batchelor J.: This story is a sort of a story reported in one of the Law Reports?

Mr Jinnah: This story has been told in the Legislative Council.

Batchelor J.: This story is symbolic? This man is carrying something?

Mr Jinnah: It was real sheep.

Batchelor J.: Yes, and one of them said it was a dog, and the other man said it was something else. The man, who carried the sheep on his head, was a such a simpleton that he was confused and he threw the sheep away from his head.

Batchelor J.: The man met three men one after another?

Batchelor J.: Yes, After they had told him in 3 different ways that it was not the sheep that he was carrying on his head, he threw it away. Mr Tilak says to the audience 'Don't be such simpletons.' Mr Tilak does not use the term rogues in respect of any particular race or a particular class of people or a particular community. The term is used against the opponents of the Home Rule League organisation. Remember, my lords, this story was used by Dr Bhandarkar in the Legislative Council.

Batchelor J.: There is such a story told of a man called Montgomery in one of the plays of Shakespeare. (The story was briefly related here.) What I think is the meaning of this story is this: 'If you think this is a good thing, you must not give up that good thing, simply because a succession of persons comes to you—first the one, then the second, and after him the third—and says 'this is this, that or the other.'

Mr Jinnah: Yes, that is right. Now, instead of carrying the sheep on his shoulders, Mr Tilak wants to carry the Home Rule League organisation. (Laughter.) He says to the audience 'Here is my League, it is a good thing, I don't care what a succession of people may tell you one after another against it.'

Shah J.: Is not the gravamen of the offence there that he likens those who take a different view to his own to the 3 rogues in the story?

Mr Jinnah: That is not sufficient. I don't know what the prosecution really say about this. The story applies to every body who is an opponent of the Home Rule League organisation.

Mr Jardine: So far as one can make it out the 'three rogues' represent the people who protest against the Home Rule League organisation, and they are so called because they do it knowing it to be a good thing.

Mr Jinnah: First of all, my lords, my submission is this that this story is used absolutely innocently. It does not mean that what others say is dishonest. Your lordships will find that even Dr Bhandarkar, in the Legislative Council, has used this very story against those certain honourable colleagues who said the University Bill was not a good thing. Dr Bhandarkar told this whole story in the Legislative Council and said 'I don't like to be such a simpleton as the man in that story and I will not drop this thing, because there are certain colleagues who say it is not a good thing.' Do your lordships think Dr Bhandarkar was there guilty of even discourtesy?

Batchelor J.: We have got nothing to do whether it is discourteous or not.

Mr Jardine: The appellant calls the people cheat who don't want this thing by repeating the story of the three rogues.

Mr Jinnah: I don't wish to take up your lordships' time if your lordships have understood it in that way. I don't want really to trouble your lordships. Reading the whole of that passage, it may be discourteous.

Batchelor J.: We are sitting here as Judges to see whether a criminal offence is committed or not. We have nothing to do with discourtesy or courtesy.

Mr Jinnah: Then, I won't trouble your lordships with the passage.

Mr Jinnah: 'Your Lordships remember, Mr Tilak is here trying to meet the argument of unfitness, and he says this 'why is it we are not fit?' And he says that the Hon'ble Sir S.P. Sinha and other members of the Executive Council did not say they were not fit when they were offered their posts. Further, Mr Tilak refers to the condition of service of the Assistant Collector of the age 21 and the Mamlatdar of the age of 60 who has to become the subordinate of the young Assistant Collector, what Mr Tilak says is this that under the present system of administration what happens is this that you get young men to come out, at the age of 21, as Assistant Collectors, and they are given large powers, larger than the other officers like Mamlatdars, who are men who have so much more experience. That is the only argument that Mr Tilak is using in this passage and, I ask, my Lords, 'why should this illustration be construed, in the name of goodness, into sedition against Government?' Mr Tilak points out the experience of one officer compared with the experience of other, and tells you how the system is working.

Batchelor J.: Subject to what the Advocate-General may say, we don't think there is anything in that.

Mr Jinnah: The Lower Court said on this point that this passage was a sort of an insinuation that the Bureaucracy thought that they are the repositories of experience. That is not so. What Mr Tilak says is this: 'At the present, time, science has made progress, knowledge has increased and experience has accumulated in one place; therefore, we are to-day more fit to be given the management of our affairs, than we were before, because now we have got experience, we have got knowledge.' My Lords, this is Mr Tilak's contention. If a man criticizes a particular system of administration, if he wants to make out a case that the system is a bad one or a defective one or one that is not conducive to the good of the people, if a man finds fault with such a system, how else is he to describe it? And, then, Mr Tilak says 'Better say "it is not to be given."' What he means to say is this 'say straight way "we won't give it."' Then, he further says 'what I say is, "don't apply the words *Not fit* to us."' This, my Lords, is Mr Tilak's last argument. He, no doubt, argues here with anger when he says 'Better say "it is not to be given." What I say is "don't apply the words *not fit* to us. Don't say we are not fit."' Then he says 'but how long will you teach us—for one generation, two generations, or three generations? Is there any end to this, or must we, just like this, work under you like slaves till the end? Set some limit.' My Lords, Mr Tilak says all this because he wants to strengthen his argument that 'we fare fit.' This, my Lords, is the passage which was complained of. Then you turn to the next page half down the 29th page.

Batchelor J.: In the middle on page 29 Mr Tilak says 'Hence, the only object in saying that the Indians are not fit to carry on the administration is that they are always to be kept in slavery, that they are to be made to do work by labouring like slaves, and that the ways, whereby their intellect and their ability may be developed, are to be stopped.' This is a passage which seems to us dead against you.

Mr Jinnah: In this passage, my Lords, Mr Tilak is dealing with the argument of unfitness. He argues that it is not correct that 'we are not fit.' He says at the top of his page 'What is going on in the Khalsa territory?' Then he takes the example of the Mysore State. He says that that State is only almost next door to Belgaum, and there you, find that the whole administration is managed by the Indian people, and therefore, asks Mr Tilak 'why are we not fit when the next door neighbours are?' He says 'The king of Mysore is a Hindu, the Minister is a Hindu, the subjects are Hindus, the Lower officers are Hindus.

They carry on the administration of such a large kingdom of Mysore, but it is said that the people of the two districts (British) beyond Mysore cannot carry it on in that manner. There are six districts in the Mysore territory, hence it is like saying that six are fit and eight are not fit.' Thus, my Lords, is another argument on the point of fitness. Then further on he says 'leave these districts to us, and see how we administer them.' He further says 'keep yourself aloof for ten years and see whether it can be done or not. If it cannot be done take us under tour control after ten years. You are free to do so.' My Lords, he says 'leave the districts to us for ten years, and if you find that we cannot administer them properly, then take them away from us straight off. Take them straight away from us after ten years if we have made a mess.' My Lords, Mr Tilak is here arguing with the objectors, who say that Indians are not fit to carry on the administration, and he asks if Indians are always to be kept in slavery. My Lords, the term 'Slavery' is here used as political slavery, that is to say, that in the present conditions of the political rule people are to get no rights. It is not 'slavery' in the sense that we understand it as meaning 'Gulamgiri.' You know, my Lords, that when a man gets very angry he says 'I am not your "Gulam"', please.

Batchelor J.: When a man is angry he says 'Am tumara Gulam nai hai.'

Mr Jinnah: When a man gets angry and says 'I am not your Gulam,' he means to say 'I am not to follow your behests.'

Batchelor J.: When you are angry with me and say 'I am not your Slave,' you mean—

Mr Jinnah: What Mr Tilak says is this 'hence the only object in saying that the Indians are not fit to carry on the administration is that they are always to be kept in slavery, that they are to be made to do work by labouring like slaves, and that the ways, whereby their intellect and their ability may be developed, are to be stopped.' What, my Lords, Mr Tilak's argument is, is this 'if I am fit, you go on using all sorts of arguments and illustrations and so on, and so on, and to say I am unfit.'

Shah J.: You mean to say it is an expression of impatience with the other side?

Batchelor J.: I remember reading many years ago the Aesop's Fables in Marathi, where I have read word for 'moral,' which is 'Tatparya': that word means rather the result than the motive.

Mr Jinnah: The exact equivalent would be 'upshot.'

Mr Jardine: It does not mean 'Upshot.' It comes nearer to 'The object.'

Mr Jinnah: Your Lordships will remember this passage is not directed towards the Government. It is really directed towards the objectors. Mr Tilak does not say, my Lords, for a moment, that it is, the Government that objects. You will see my Lords, that he makes that clear that the objection does not come from Government. He makes that clear. He includes among the objectors both Indians as well as Englishmen. He does not confine his remarks to one class. Then, he goes on to say 'What do we ask for? Do we say "Drive away the English Government?"' Further he says, 'From whom then does this opposition come? This opposition comes from those who are in power,' that is, he means, the people who are carrying on the Government—the members of the Civil service. He says, 'It does not come from the Emperor.'

'This argument is brought forward by men whose interest lies in deceiving you. Do not care about it at all.' This argument, says Mr Tilak, is brought forward by some whose interests are opposed to public interests, and who are those people? Those are the people, he says, who are in power and who happen to have the monopoly of power at the present moment, and this, says Mr Tilak, he wants to be changed. It is not attack, I admit, my Lords, on Government as Government established by Law in British India.

Batchelor J.: The passage is used in the sense that it attacks those whose interests are opposed to the country's interests.

Mr Jinnah: Then, I don't think I need trouble your Lordships with the rest of that page, because there is no complaint about it. At page 30 they complain about the whole of that first paragraph. There, again, my Lords, what Mr Tilak is doing is to give a historical quotation as to what the Government was before the Queen assumed the reign of the territories in India.

What Mr Tilak says is this, that 'the Proclamation has remained ineffective, and you have the roots or the foundations of the system, which existed at the time of the Company's rules, still existing.' He says 'these roots and foundations still exist, and, therefore, it is not good.' That is the whole of his argument throughout the speech, if you read that speech, my Lords, you will see that what he says is that you had the Company's rule which was based on purely commercial principles in India. Then he says that in the place of the Company's Board of Directors you have got the Secretary of State. That is perfectly correct, if you look to the Act of 1858. Formerly, all the powers, which are now vested in the Secretary of State, were vested in the Company's Director. I want to draw your Lordships' attention to what Mr Tilak says in this page. He says 'The Sovereign—The Parliament took the administration into their hands, but the establishment of employees, which then existed, has remained just as before.' That is perfectly correct. 'Therefore,' says Mr Tilak, 'the roots or foundations of the old system were continued, so that, the establishment of employees, which then existed has remained just as before.' His object is to say that the roots or foundations of the old system have continued since 1858. Then we come to page 31. Mr Tilak says 'To put the matter very briefly, Mr Dadabhai Nawroji, who is one of those living persons who saw this arrangement and pointed out its defects, began this work.'

Batchelor J.: What is objected here?

Mr Jinnah: The whole of this passage is objected to.

Mr Jardine: I rely on the preceeding page and the top of this page and lower down of this page also.

Mr Jinnah: Mr Tilak says further 'Then arose these Legislative Councils.... We shall publish them in the 'Bombay Government Gazette.' 'This is the only difference. Nothing is got from this.' My Lords, here, Mr Tilak is dealing with the question of the Legislative Councils having power to make speeches only. He says they can only make speeches which, instead of being published in news-papers would be published in the 'Bombay Government Gazette.'

Batchelor J.: What is objectionable here?

Mr Jinnah: I don't know what they really object to. This was the passage objected to. In this passage Mr Tilak further says 'The hope of getting is held out.... Thus, this Bureaucracy has been cajoling us.'

Batchelor J.: Was this passage objected to in the Lower Court?

Mr Binning: Would your Lordships allow me to explain what happened in the Lower Court?

Batchelor J.: No.

Mr Jinnah: I don't know whether they object to the words 'Thus this Bureaucracy has been cajoling us?' By these words Mr Tilak means that 'The Bureaucracy are putting us off.'

Mr Jardine: I object to the passage in the middle, where Mr Tilak says 'The hope of getting is held out. There is a *shlok* (stanza) in the *Mahabharat,* which says 'Hope should be made dependent upon time,' and a few lines later on.

Mr Jinnah: What does this passage come to? It comes to this that 'Some arguments are advanced in one respect or another. We are told "You are not fit." Our demands are put off.' My Lords, does it cause disaffection towards Government to say 'We make these demands; right or wrong, we make these demands, these are our demands, which are being put off. They are being put off on some excuse or another.' Is this argument, my Lords, likely to cause disaffection? Is this whole paragraph such as would entitle the Court to say to a man 'You are guilty under section 124A?' What is wrong in saying that 'our demands are being put off by the Secretary of State for India?' It may be that the demands may be right or the demands may be wrong, but is it wrong to say that 'our demands are put off?' I don't think there is any complaint about the remaining passages on this page. Then, your Lordships, we come to page 32; this is what is really complained of, namely, 'We do not want the State Secretary, who has been created as a son-in-law.' Your Lordships, while reading this speech, should remember that what Mr Tilak means is this that the Secretary of State as an individual, is like the son-in-law, which is an Indian phrase and means that the man has got no right *'de jure'* but *'de facto.'* He is in your house simply because he has been married to your daughter. He is in reality a boss in your house, simply because he has been married to your daughter. This is an Indian idea, meaning a man who has got no legal rights, but who still somehow or other, makes himself master of the situation. My Lords, when, in this passage, Mr Tilak says 'For the last five or fifty years the State Secretary and the Governors-General have been cajoling us in this manner—have kept us afloat,' what he means is this that you have got the State Secretary or the Governor-General who cannot do anything. They are nothing but agents and responsible to no one, in face, though, in theory, to Parliament.

APPENDIX 1

If Mr Tilak says in this passage that this state of things is intolerable, what is wrong? Is it sedition to say that the Secretary of State for India's position, under the present conditions, is intolerable? 'Learned aliens may tell us when we are passing like this through this door, that we should not pass through this door but through that; but, if anyone comes and stands there and (begins to) tell us not to go through it, then we have to go out by giving him a push. The very same is the case with 'Swaraja.' 'This is the obstruction of the Bureaucracy. We do not want such obstruction.' My Lords, I tell you what Mr Tilak's idea is. His idea is this. Mr Tilak says 'Now. This is our position. This is what we want. We want to have "Swarajya," and, for that purpose, we want this Home Rule organisation.' My Lords, here, Mr Tilak makes it clear as to what his position is as regards the Home Rule League organisation. He says he has a reform to be brought about by going to Parliament. He says 'We want to go through this door—the door of Parliament; we want to follow this road. We don't follow another road.' Then he says 'The very same is the case with "Swaraja." This is the obstruction of the Bureaucracy. We do not want such obstruction.' What he means to say is that 'there are two methods by which Indian reform can be secured, and one of them is to go over the head of the Bureaucracy, to go to Parliament. Either go over the head of the Bureaucracy, or go through the Bureaucracy. I am going to follow this read of Home Rule League organization, I want it to go to Parliament. I don't want the road of the Bureaucracy.' I think, there is something missing, my lords. His idea is this, that the 'Bureaucracy tells us "don't do this; don't do that; you go through this road;" I want to go through the other road,' that is what he means when he says 'Learned aliens may tell us, when we are passing like this through this door, that we should not pass through this door but through that; I prefer to go through the other door, namely, to go over the head of the Bureaucracy to Parliament,' further, Mr Tilak says 'the demand for "Swaraja" is such that it has nothing to do with sedition, it has nothing to do also with the invisible government. This domestic arrangement should be managed by you yourselves, and, by doing so, what will happen is that, in the first place, your minds will remain in peace.' Then, my lords, there is a complaint made about what Mr Tilak says at p. 32: 'But now the principal question is "Who told them to come here from there? We did not call them."' That is really the very old, old argument used when a man says that he has come from cold climate to the hot climate and has got his health spoiled.

There, my lords, he is making out a case for Home Rule. Now, my lords, read that speech as a whole, and see what the result is—whether the result is such as must lead any member of the audience, who has got any intelligence, at all,—with regard to those that have got no intelligence, it does not matter—take the case of intelligent persons and see whether the result would be such as to lead them to entertain feelings of disaffection towards British Government. Undoubtedly, throughout the speech there is a condemnation—a direct condemnation of the system which prevails, at present in the whole administration of this country, which is only a part of the Government, and Mr Tilak says that that system should be changed, because that system is bad, and, for that purpose, further says, 'We want to go to Parliament, we want to petition the British nation, we want to petition the British Parliament to have that Act changed.' I ask, my lords, what is wrong in that? Why is that sedition? You may find an expression here and there very strong or very discourteous, but it is not seditious. And when you are making out a case for the notice of the audience, when you are criticizing a particular measure, my lords, you cannot help advancing arguments, which must be telling arguments. You cannot help advancing facts and evidence in support of the case which you are making very strong. I quite agree with your Lordships. Your lordships have nothing to do with how strong the argument may be, how discourteous it may be, or even if it is offensive, so long as Mr Tilak has not done what is prohibited by Sec. 124A. If you read the whole of the speech, you will see that it does not cause disaffection towards the Government established by law in British India. Then, my lords, we come to the next speech. The first passage is this: 'The question is always asked.... This is an honour to them, but should we not tell it to do those things which it does not do?' I only want to point out to your lordships that Mr Tilak had no intention to cause disaffection: it is a very essential ingredient to find out whether the man intended to cause disaffection or not, and that can be gathered from his speech. You have this passage clearly to indicate what the state of his mind was, what the intention of the man was, what his 'mens rea' was. You have to find the intention from the language, and if you look at the language in this passage, you will find that it does not show you that his intention is to create disaffection towards the Government established by law in British India. The whole of the second speech shows that he does not come within the section of sedition. And what is sedition really? Sedition is nothing but slander. Sedition is slander of Government. This speech clearly shows that when Mr Tilak delivered this speech, he had no intention to cause disaffection in the minds of his hearers towards Government. He distinctly says in the speech.—'Do not think that I am speaking only about the whites, we do not want this system.'....

Batchelor J.: There is passage at page 35 which seems to us to be against you. It is about the middle of the page: 'Such has become the condition, that such things, as would be beneficial to the country cannot be carried out.'

Mr Jinnah: My lords, he says 'the business of commission agency has remained, but what has happened in it is that the profit which this country derived from it, is lost to us and goes to the English. The thing is that the men and the business are the same as before, but owing to a change in the ruling power, we cannot do some things. Such has become the condition that such things as would be beneficial to the country cannot be carried out.' I think this sentence is not properly translated. He further says 'At first, we thought that since the English Government was (as) a matter of fact, alien, there was no sedition in calling them so.... If anybody has charged this Government with being alien, he has done so in the above sense.' Now, my lords, what does he mean by this passage? He is trying to define 'alien' according to his own ideas, and his idea is that a man is an alien not because he does not belong to the same religion or race or caste or creed or colour as himself, but a person who does not wish good to India. That, I submit, my lords, is the whole summing up of Mr Tilak argument.

Batchelor J.: The speaker says that a man is not alien merely because he differs in religion or colour or religion or caste; he calls a man alien whose interests are opposed to or counter against the interests of the people of this country. He means 'Government is alien' in that sense.

Mr Jinnah: I submit he does not say that. You see, the whole of his point is this that in India the administration is not carried on to the benefit of the people, he says that the way in which the administration is carried on is not to the benefit of the people, at the present moment, and he does not say that a man is an alien, because he belongs to a different religion or caste or race or colour or anything of that kind. He also says that here is a certain system which is managed by a certain class of men who have got vested interests and, therefore, are not really doing good to India. He has not said this of the real Government, of the British Government, for that you have got to read the whole speech.

Batchelor J.: He does not say of the King, but he says of the Government, he means 'Government is alien.'

Mr Jinnah: He does not mean the Government established by law in British India. He is referring to certain number of persons, who are managing the administration of the country.

Batchelor J.: I suppose what was held against you by the Court below was the words 'The king looks to his own benefit, to the benefit of his own race, and to the benefit of his original country.' What have you to say to that?

Mr Jinnah: What Mr. Tilak says is that that king is to be considered alien, who does not do his duty and that the king who does his duty is not an alien. If a man does not do his duty and if he is such a man as would come within this description then no doubt, he is an alien. He is an alien who, no matter what his religion, what his caste, or what his creed, who does not do his duty. Therefore, the king, who does his duty is not an alien, no matter what his race, or colour or religion or creed. Only he is to be considered an alien, who does not do his duty. That is perfectly true; for a person, who does not do his duty, in a sense goes against the interests of India, and so, says Mr Tilak, is an alien.

Batchelor J.: Look at the bottom of page 35, (Reads 'Government is alien.') This Government is not for our interest but for its own interests and, in that sense, is a foreign Government.' That is the obvious sense of what appears at the bottom of page 35?

Mr Jinnah: I say, my Lords, that is, no doubt, a criticism of the Bureaucratic system of administration. He says he has a complaint against that system of administration.

Batchelor J.: Against which system of administration?

Mr Jinnah: Against the Bureaucratic system of administration. If you read the whole of this passage, I say, you will see that Mr Tilak is attacking this system of administration. He says 'this particular system of administration is in the hands of a certain number of people.' My Lords, I don't want to shelve the answer. What I understand the meaning of this passage is this. That Mr Tilak very clearly says.—'This particular class of administrators have got vested interests. Their own interests are opposed to the interest of the people,' and, therefore, he says.—'You place this complaint of yours, this grievance before Parliament, and ask for the alteration of the system, because, the administrators are not under the control of the people, are not responsible to the people, and have got to look to their own interests, which interests are antagonistic to the interests of the people.'

Batchelor J.: The whole question is whether it is not the case that this article creates disaffection in the minds of the hearers. That is the point. If it does, it comes under the section.

Mr Jinnah: My Lords, first of all, let us consider this. What Mr Tilak tells his audience is this. 'The British Government is the best Government for us. The British Rule has been most beneficial to us. We have really to make progress under the protecting hand of the British Rule, but we have got this iron wall, namely, this particular system, which is a part of the government in this country. This system of administration of the country is in the hands of a certain set of people who, in my opinion, cannot possibly do justice to our demands; it is a form or a sort of an interested system of Government, which has got its own interests to look to and which, therefore, cannot possibly do justice to our demands and cannot treat us conscientiously. Therefore, we say that this system ought to be changed.' Is that sedition, my, Lords? Is that sedition, is that really causing disaffection towards the government established in British India by Law? What is the idea of sedition, my Lords?' Your Lordships know the root idea of sedition, which is that certain results must follow your writing or speeches. That was the root idea of sedition, that is to say, what a speaker or writer says or writes must bring about certain results,— revolution or a state of things not compatible with the existence of lawful authority.

Batchelor J.: The question is whether it may bring about a feeling of enmity towards Government or a feeling of dislike towards Government. The question is whether he is trying to bring about enmity towards Government. I want you to answer this question. What would be the effect of this attack on Government in the presence of a Maratha audience of intelligence—would it be to excite a feeling of enmity against Government, what is your answer to that question?

Mr Jinnah: If it was an intelligent audience, they would have understood what the object of Mr Tilak was in making these remarks. They would certainly have entertained no feeling of enmity towards Government. This intelligent audience would have said 'Let us put our heads together and see whether we can change this system of administration, that is a stumbling block in our way.' I say, no intelligent audience would have been disaffected by this speech.

Mr Jinnah: My lords, the word 'Sarkar' is translated as 'Government.' But, I submit, if you read the speech from beginning to end, you will see what the point is of Mr Tilak.

Shah J.: The original ward is 'Sarkar.'

Mr Jinnah: My lords, I have heard the Mamlatdar being called the 'Sarkar' I have been puzzled a great deal by this translation of the word 'Sarkar' by the word 'Government.' 'Sarkar' does not mean 'Government,' it is an elastic word, and there is no other word in Marathi to express the idea of 'Sarkar,' that is the 'Bureaucracy.' 'Sarkar' here means the 'Bureaucracy.' The audience could never understand by 'Sarkar' anything like the 'Government.' The word is taken from Sanskrit. Even the witness himself has admitted that the word 'Sarkar' is used for the 'Administration.'

Batchelor J.: I do not question it for a moment.

Mr Jinnah: Therefore, may I ask the Court to judge what the meaning of this passage is by reading the whole speech? Read the whole of this page. The word 'Sarkar' there is translated as 'Government,' but it does not mean the 'Government established by law in British India,' it undoubtedly means 'Administration.' It means nothing else. There is no other meaning. That is all that I have to submit to your Lordships on that point. Further he says 'We want the rule of the English, which is over us, but we do not want these intervening middleman,' 'keepers of granaries,' as he calls them. There, again, my Lords, is an attack on the Bureaucracy; it is the Civil Service that is attacked by the term 'intervening middlemen.' Calling these Civil Servants 'intervening middlemen,' that is, 'the keepers of granaries,' he says further 'the grain belongs to the master. The provision belongs to the master.' Then he says 'Remove the intervening middlemen's aching belly and confer these powers upon people, so that they may duly look to their domestic affairs.' My lords, a great deal was made of the term 'aching belly' in the Lower Court. I don't know what they are going to say here. Here, my lords, the shorthand writers, who took this portion down, did not take down the original Marathi speech correctly.

Mr Jardine: I am not going to rely on the question of 'aching belly.'

Mr Jinnah: That is all right. This, again, my Lords, is an attack on the Bureaucracy; it is the Civil Service that is attacked. I do urge this on your lordships, my lords, that when you find that the word 'Sarkar' is translated by the Translator as 'Government,' it really does not mean the 'Government' in the sense in which it is contemplated by section 124A. Your Lordships may understand that by the word 'Sarkar' it is really the Civil Service for the

Bureaucracy that is intended by the speaker. Then, your lordships will find among these speeches, again, a very strong sentiment of loyalty expressed, which is not compatible with the man's intention to cause sedition or disaffection. Your Lordships will see that what Mr Tilak complains is that the present Bureaucracy consider things from their own point of view—very differently from what would be the case, if the 'authority were to be given into our hands.' My Lords, Mr Tilak makes his position very clear as to his object. There are these speeches. I submit, my lords, that any intelligent man, who heard these speeches, would certainly not be disaffected towards the Government established by law in British India, within the meaning of Section 124A. The, we come to the third speech.

(At this stage the Court adjourned for lunch.)

When the Court re-assembled after lunch, the Hon'ble Mr Jinnah resumed his address as follows:

My Lords, I don't know whether I have made myself quite clear with regard to your Lordships' point about 'The Government is alien.' The first thing, my lords, that I want to speak to your lordships is this. Mr Tilak tries his best in this very passage, to get rid of the prejudice, which may be there on account of race, colour or religion and so on. He says there may be any man—he may be a Christian or he may belong to a different race, or he may be a white man; that does not make him an alien. He tries to imply this, that so long as those who are in charge of the administration have their interests in conflict with ours in some matters, no doubt, to that extent, they are aliens. Therefore, I say, that Mr Tilak, when he said that 'The Government is alien,' had no intention really to cause disaffection. There is no reason to suppose on this account, that he wanted to cause disaffection or to excite contempt or hatred for the British Government. Supposing he wanted to do that, he could have easily said 'look at these people, they do not belong to our race, at all; they are aliens; they are Christians; and so on and so forth. My Lords, the impression that he created upon the minds of the audience was that it does not make a man alien because he is of a different religion or a different caste or a different race, and so on. He says his theory of an alien is that he is an alien, connected with the administration of this country, whose interests conflict with the interests of the country. And, then, my Lords, he gives an illustration and takes, for instance, the case of the 'Swadeshi' industries being taxed. He takes the case of Excise Duty, and so on. Therefore, when he says 'their interests conflict with ours,' he admits that in that respect they are aliens. But, my Lords, my complete answer to your question is this that the word 'Government,' in the sentence 'Government is alien'; is used by the translator for the original Marathi word 'Sarkar,' which does not mean, if you read the context of this speech, 'the Government by law established in India.' On the contrary, it is absolutely clear—if you read the whole speech, it is quite clear that 'Government' there means nothing but administration of the Bureaucrats, who are managing the Government, and he is really attacking the Bureaucracy—a certain set of officers, who are managing the administration. 'Government' there, my Lords, means nothing more than 'Bureaucracy.' Then, my Lords, coming to the third speech, your Lordships will find, again, that Mr Tilak makes his intention quite clear—he never intended to cause disaffection. Take the third speech, where he says by '"Swaraja" it is not meant that the English should be driven away.'

And (if the matter) be considered from such a standpoint, then there is no other way (to accomplish this) than (the acquisition of) 'Swaraja', than 'the possession of authority.' If you look at the passage, your Lordships will see that Mr Tilak says 'If the Native Collectors remain and, in the end, the English Collectors come, we want them. There is no objection to say. "Remove such and such a man (and) make such and such an arrangement in such and such a place."' My Lords, there was a great deal of discussion about the word 'Beasts' in the passage which I have read, namely, 'The chief question is whether a certain nation is to be treated like beasts.' Our suggestion is not that they are treated like cattle, but all that Mr Tilak really wishes to say is 'Why should our people not have the same liberty, and why should they not have the ordinary desires and sentiments like other nations, and why should they not make progress?' My Lords, it is a common expression; it means this; it means nothing else. Then, my Lords, Mr Tilak gives the story of a parrot, and that was objected to. I really don't know, my Lords, what is wrong about that story. Mr Tilak says 'The Collector of Nagar looks to sanitation'.... This is not our original natural, sentiment—the natural human sentiment. As that is not the parrot's natural sentiment, just so this is not the natural sentiment of our nation.

Mr Jardine: I don't complain of the parrot's story, my Lords.

Mr Jinnah: Then I shall leave the story alone............There is no question which is not dependent upon 'Swarajya.' There is nothing else, my Lords, that I can think of in this speech, unless your Lordships will desire me to explain something. There is nothing else that had been objected to in the Lower Court. I don't know what objections will be made here. Now, my Lords, I say that taking these speeches as a whole, they are criticisms of the system—of only a part of the whole administration. What has really happened is that Mr Tilak has told his audience that the Home Rule League organization is a good movement, that they should become members of the League, and that they should bring about a change in the system of administration; and how that has to be done Mr Tilak makes quite clear. He says that that has to be done by placing the matter before the British public and the British Parliament and by getting this statute amended in Parliament. Now, if your Lordships will look to the judgment of the learned Magistrate, your Lordships will find that this is his finding at page 90; 'Looking at these speeches, as a whole, fairly, freely, and without giving undue weight to isolated passages, what impression do they convey to us, and what impression must we believe they conveyed to the audience to which they were addressed? The impression I gather from them is that Mr Tilak wishes to disaffect his audience towards the Government, in order that they may "Wake up" (to adopt Mr Jinnah's words) to their present unhappy condition, join his Home Rule League, and help him in his agitation for a change in the administration of the country. He is addressing an ignorant audience—counsel for the defence insisted upon this point.' My Lords, I don't know why the learned Magistrate says the audience was ignorant. May be that the audience was not highly intelligent, but to say that the audience was ignorant, there is no justification for it. However, the judgment proceeds: 'And he (Mr Tilak) knows that he cannot interest them in his argument unless he can illustrate it forcibly; so, he tells them that they are slaves, that their grievances remain unredressed, that the Government only considers its own interests, which are alien to theirs, and intends to keep them in slavery on the untrue excuse that they are not fit to rule themselves.'

Batchelor J.: Was the audience of Maratha agriculturists?

Mr Jinnah: We have got evidence, my lords, that they were of all classes of people—merchants and various classes of people. Your lordships will not, please understand me to say that I want to convey that the audience was intellectual. I do not say that. But, I think, it is quite wrong to say that they were ignorant. Mr Tilak knew that he was addressing an audience with reference to a political question; so he knew that the audience could follow him; otherwise, he would have wasted his breath. (Laughter.) Very well. Then the Magistrate further says this in his judgment: 'Mr Jinnah's contention, that it is not the Government that Mr Tilak is attacking, but only the Civil Service, will be discarded at once, by anyone who reads the speeches through. The speaker refers frequently to the Bureaucracy—using the English word—but the context and trend of his argument throughout shows that he is referring to the whole system of Government and the whole body of officials in India—from the Governor General down to the police sepoy.' Now, my lords, it is for your lordships to decide whether you are not satisfied that the real attack was on the Civil Service and that Mr Tilak is simply seeking to have a change in the system of administration in the country. I say that all these three speeches clearly show that here is a criticism and an attack upon the system of administration of the Civil Service. That is all that I have to submit, my lords.

The Advocate-General's Reply

The Hon. Mr M.R. Jardine, the Advocate-General, replied as follows on behalf of the Crown:

My Lords, with regard to the expression 'Government established by law in British India,' my submission is that there is possibly a great deal of hair splitting upon what the expression substantially means. There is no substantial doubt as to what it means. My learned friend, without citing any authority for his proposition, suggested that it means the Sovereignty, the Crown, the House of Parliament, and nothing more. In the absence of any authority for that very narrow construction of that phrase, I do not propose to deal further with it. But, I would point out to your lordships that it seems to me that the suggestion of my learned friend merely brings the Government of this country within a measurable distance of being helpless against the attacks by people in this country. The meaning of the term 'Government' is 'administration that is carried on by those persons who are authorized by law to do so,' If that was not correct, then, I say, the Government of the country would be impossible. I need not labour, my lords, in laying stress upon the result that would be derived if my learned friend's suggestion, as regards the meaning of the expression 'Government established by law in British India,' were accepted, because that expression has been dealt with in the judgment of Justice Strachey in this Court. That judgment, or rather, the summing up in that case, was referred to the Full Bench in that particular case, and it was also laid before the Privy Council, and was there ably argued by persons of great eminence in the English Bar. It is hardly likely that those arguments would have escaped the notice of this Court.

Shah J.: Does not the Full Bench, in that case, think that the point of the meaning of the 'Government by law established in British India' was a very minor point in the case?

Mr Jardine: Yes then, my learned friend suggests that the Indian Penal Code protects everybody except the Government, who are responsible for the administration of the country.

Batchelor J.: It is not here only the question of fact; here, you have the abstract thing 'Government.' If you wish to attack the Government, it would be through one of its agencies, as, for instance, the Forest Department or the unfortunate Civil Service Department, to which I belong, or various other Departments. If you attack one of these agencies, you attack Government, and the purpose will be served I think that is what it comes to.

Mr Jardine: That is really what Mr Justice Strachey says, and the Privy Council has repeated as much. After Justice Strachey's judgment, that expression, which occurred in the original section remains, but the section itself is amended. That must be regarded as a substantially correct law. Then, my lords, with regard to the effect of the speeches in this case.

Shah J.: Do you say that all members of a particular service would be members of Government within the meaning of the section, or that the 'Government by law established in British India' would simply mean 'Government,' as defined in the Government of India Act, and that it may be possible to bring Government into contempt or hatred or disaffection in a variety of ways by attacking members of some Service by which the Government is carried on? Can 'Government' include the Services within the meaning of the section? Is that your view? I want to know what your view is.

Mr Jardine: It is quite sufficient for my purpose to say that 'Government' includes those persons who are vested with the Executive Government in any particular Presidency, and they are, of course, responsible for the way the administration is carried on, although the administration may be carried on by Junior officials. You cannot separate the administration from most of these employees.

Shah J.: Take, for instance, a concrete case. Suppose there is a criticism against the members of the Civil Service or the Forest Department; would you say that is against Government by law established in British India? Would you say the Government is criticised there?

Mr Jardine: I should certainly say, my lords, that because the Civil Service forms a very large part of the administration, they are a substantial agency of the administration; the administration consists largely of Civilians. What I submit, my lords, is this that the members of the Civil Service are persons who have power to carry on the work, and you cannot distinguish those persons from their juniors; they are the accredited agents, and they have to be protected; otherwise, it seems to me that Government can never be protected at all. I am now coming to the speeches, my lords. My submission, with regard to them, is this. They are an attack on everything except His Majesty and the House of Parliament. It is perfectly true that in various passages the King-Emperor is excluded from criticism. I don't know how it strikes the Court with regard to this exclusion of His Majesty; it seems to me that the exclusion is merely because he is treated as an invisible Government—as inoperative Government. However that may be, here Mr Tilak is not charged with attacking the King. The whole of his charge is against the operative system of Government. The whole of his attack is against the operative system of Government, from which the King and the Parliament are excluded. It is quite obvious, if he had done anything else—if he had attacked the King or the Parliament, he would have been in a very different position. What Mr Tilak is charged with is not for that which he has not done, but for what he has done. The King and Parliament are excluded from his criticism, but they are contrasted with the Government in this country. A great stress has been laid upon various passages in these speeches to show that Mr Tilak does not seek separation. Here, again, he is not charged with the desire of separation, whether he has that desire or not; though I would point out that his references to separation are marked in their expression by the fact that he is generally contrasting the Bureaucracy of England with the Bureaucracy of Germany. There seems to be not too much advantage to be derived from his remark 'We don't want to apply to Germany or France.' My submission is that I think it a fair criticism of his speeches to say that he refers to the invisible Government in one place, and to the visible Government in another place, and directly he refers to the visible Government, he refers to it in a sense as if that Government has fallen under his ban.

APPENDIX 1

The Advocate-General then referred to certain passages where Government was called alien and argued that Mr Tilak distinguished Government from bureaucracy when it suited him.

Mr Jardine: I submit, My Lords, my learned friend has not really grappled or had not attempted to grapple with the real charges that were made against his client. He has not read the Magistrate's judgment to your Lordships, presumably, he has not read it himself. At page 78—rather towards the end— you have what the Magistrate says: 'Mr Binning for the prosecution relies upon the whole of the speeches. He indicates certain passages on which he chiefly relies—they are marked red by the Court on Exhibits G.H. and I. He states plainly that he does not call into question the propriety of the discussion of Home Rule. His instructions are to express no views on that subject. What he asked the Court to condemn, on the ground that it is seditious within the meaning of section 124A of the Indian Penal Code, are the remarks made by Mr Tilak in various parts of the speeches, in which he imputes dishonest and corrupt motives to Government.' On that part of the case, my lords, my learned friend has not seriously dwelt. The charges made by the speaker were that the Government was 'alien' and hence hostile to the interests of the people. Mr Tilak had also charged Government with holding out hopes without any intention of fulfilling them, and that the Government of this country was, as in the Company's time, purely a money-making business. There were frequent references to the slavish condition of people. My Lords, at page 25—in the middle of the page, your Lordships will find a number of measures are referred to, and then it is suggested that those measures are due to the fact that the 'Government is not in our own hands.' I don't object to the criticism, but I do object to the suggestion that the Government of the country is carried on by a Bureaucracy who possessed all the powers of the Government.

Batchelor J.: The speaker complains of specific Government measures and says that they are due because the power is in the hands of a certain class instead of in the hands of the people of India.

Mr Jardine: I don't object to that, but I say if you read the whole of the speech, you will find that it is suggested to the audience that the Government of India is responsible for certain measures and that it does not do what the people like. That is exactly what it comes to. Then look at page 28, where there is a passage referring to the Mamlatdar of ripe experience being lorded over by a young Civilian.

Batchelor J.: Is it not a fair criticism?

Mr Jardine: It may be, my Lords! But taking it with the rest of the speech, I submit, you will find that the speaker is trying to work upon the feelings of the audience, not so much against the system of administration, but in order to induce the people to join the Home Rule League because, the speaker said, they should think that 'this Government is unjust and deliberately trying to oppress the people.' My learned friend said that throughout these speeches you find credit being given to the Civil Service or the Bureaucracy. I don't wish to read the speeches in order to save time, my Lords, and I think this might be conceded that the Bureaucracy is given some credit, but, so far as I know, I can refer to no passage in which Mr Tilak has given credit to the Bureaucracy for any desire for the welfare of the country.

Batchelor J.: Look at page 36, about ten lines from the bottom.

Mr Jardine: Certain good things are said of the Bureaucracy. My point is this that although Mr Tilak admits, from time to time, that the Bureaucracy has done good to the country, he has never given them credit, so far as I can see, for disinterested motives for any desire to do good to the country, which they are governing.

Batchelor J.: I think that there are several passages where he does that.

Mr Jardine: My point is this. I cannot say he does not concede that the Government is efficient.

Batchelor J.: Quite so.

Mr Jardine: What I do wish to draw the Court's attention to is this. My point is about motive. I submit there is no passage in these speeches where a recognition is made that there may be a desire on the part of the Bureaucracy to do their best for this country except for the indirect advantage of the country from which they come. I should not have troubled your Lordships with these observations had not my learned friend drawn your Lordships' attention to the fact that Mr Tilak was describing some good things about the Bureaucracy. He admits they are industrious and educated, but, throughout, he ascribes their good actions to interested motives.... Now, my lords, if your Lordships want me to argue that imputation of hostility or indifference to the people on the part of the Government would come within Sec. 124A.

Batchelor J.: There is no doubt about the law. I don't know how the Magistrate came to mean 'disaffection' as absence of affection.

Mr Binning: I was there and, as far as I remember, I read the whole of the section.

Batchelor J.: 'Disaffection' is not 'absence of affection.'

Mr Binning: No, my lords.

Batchelor J.: This is a clear mistake of the Magistrate.

Mr Jardine: I think so.

Batchelor J.: In 32 Bombay, page 134 you have this laid down: Disaffection is not absence of affection.

Mr Jinnah: We have got the definition of 'disaffection' distinctly now, my lords.

Mr Jardine: I submit, my lords, that the language used in these speeches would raise a feeling of enmity; I cannot imagine how it would strike your lordships. I say it would not produce any other result.

Batchelor J.: When a man is criticizing, he is 'pro tanto' exciting a feeling, but he is entitled to criticize?

Mr Jardine: Undoubtedly.

APPENDIX 1

Batchelor J.: Very well. If a man is entitled to criticize to that extent he is entitled to excite feelings of disapprobation—you admit that?

Mr Jardine: Undoubtedly. The question here is my lords, not whether the effect of these speeches is to raise in the minds of his hearers a feeling of disapprobation; here the question is of raising a feeling of downright hostility towards Government.

Batchelor J.: Does he go so far as that?

Mr Jardine: I submit that is the result of these speeches, my lords. If you attribute wrong motives, you produce disapprobation. But if you attribute directly dishonest motives, then you are getting a totally different result; the result would be to excite great deal more than disapprobation. Disapprobation of measures is one thing; but when you begin to impute motives, when you suggest dishonest motives, then, I say, you are evidently getting into matters which would excite enmity; not mere disapprobation.

Batchelor J.: Supposing you are delivering a speech and I happen to be present. Assume I am a typical Maratha. When that speech is over, what do you think would be the effect of that speech on my mind? Is it not possible that it would have the effect of producing in my mind the feeling that the Government, in the opinion of any reasonable man, has not done for the Empire all that it should have done?

Mr Jardine: My lords, here Mr Tilak tells people that Government is taking too much tax. It is an attack on the system and not on the measure of the Government.

Shah J.: If there is a speech and not a written article, and if the speaker deals with his subject, is he not entitled to a certain amount of indulgence so far as the actual effect of his action is concerned, the speech being not like a written article?

Mr Jardine: He is entitled to such indulgence, but he has got to keep within the limits of the law. There is no reason why he should not keep himself within the section, so far as the subject matter is the measures; otherwise, it seems to me—

Shah J.: There is no question about it; he must keep himself within the limits of the law. Supposing he transgresses the bounds of law, would there be no difference observed between his speech and a written matter?

Batchelor J.: Would there be no allowance made in his case?

Mr Jardine: I don't know why he should be differently treated if he said for instance that certain things should be done in cold blood? In this case Mr Tilak is telling his hearers that Government is deliberately deceiving people and deliberately doing things for their own country's advantage. There is nothing before your lordships to show that the speaker did not mean exactly what he said. My only submission is that feeling of disapprobation and feeling of enmity stand on totally different planes of criticism. When you impute motives of dishonesty, you raise in the minds of the hearers—I say a large number of them—I don't say everybody—a feeling of actual hostility towards Government.

Now, my learned friends' argument was that it was necessary to show intention on the part of the speaker to create disaffection. My contention is that there was intention to create a feeling that would be likely to excite feeling of disaffection. My further submission is that, for the purpose of Section 108 the question of intention on the part of the speaker is entirely immaterial. In a criminal case there must be intention. My submission is that when you are dealing with Section 108, it is not necessary that there should be intention at all.

Shah J.: Clause A of Section 124A says that seditious matter is a matter which is punishable under Section 124A.

Mr Jardine: There it is the matter that is punishable and not the person.

Batchelor J.: How is matter punishable? (Laughter.)

Mr Jardine: It is not, my lords. That is the wording of the sections. The matter is described in Section 124A.

Shah J.: What is the difference between Clauses A and B of Section 124A?

Batchelor J.: Intention is to be derived from actual words?

Mr Jardine: My submission, my lords, is this that here the question is that there would likely be that effect; therefore the question of intention does not arise.

Batchelor J.: Man's intent is to be gathered from the effect, the natural effect which his words may produce?

Mr Jardine: Yes, and not from his language merely. Intention cannot be deduced from language; then it would be said it did not come within the section.

Batchelor J.: Just so.

Mr Jardine: A man may say something in the heat of oratory; it is not a case in which he should be punished. Here, if Mr Tilak was carried away by his own eloquence and said something which he did not mean, it would not be the case for punishment. It would obviously not be a case for putting in force a section of this sort; that case would fall under another section. (Reads 43 Calcutta, 544.) In this case it is distinctly laid down that when you are dealing with certain circumstances, you may find there may be no intention; yet, the matter of this sort should not be disputed.

Batchelor J.: Very well.

Mr Jardine: Therefore, my lords, my submission is that the learned Magistrate's order is perfectly correct, and there is no provision in the law which entitles the appellant to a revision of this order.

The Hon. Mr Jinnah, for Mr Tilak, said as follows in reply to the Hon. Advocate-General:

I should like to point out to your lordships something which, perhaps, has escaped my learned friend, Mr Jardine. Your lordships will find the passage at page 70. It is in the judgment of the Magistrate. [Reads the passage].

I submit, my lords, that Mr Tilak is addressing an audience of 2,000 people and, naturally, when he is delivering the speech, there are cheers and confusion and laughter in the meeting. For this result one cannot say that Mr Tilak has done something for which he is responsible. I simply say there is a great difference between the man standing to deliver a speech and the man who is deliberately sitting down to write an article. Then he is cool and collected. I submit, my lords, here is an attack on the Bureaucracy really, and I say it was not intended to cause disaffection against Government. The criticism may by very severe but it was within the section, and if you cannot convict a man under Section 153 and if you cannot convict a man under Section 124A, then my lords, my submission is that you cannot call upon him to give security. You call him to give security provided he has committed an offence. It is open to Government to bind a man over if in a particular case they don't think it worth while to prosecute him and obtain his conviction. But in order to deal with a man under Section 108, the Court must be satisfied that an offence has been committed. Take the case of a lunatic, my lords. Suppose he goes and makes a speech as a lunatic and he does use language which clearly falls under Section 124A. Then, he being a lunatic, he has not committed the offence. In this case, my lords, I have said I have picked 47 passages from these three speeches. They show that to an ordinary mind they do not convey the idea of causing disaffection. These 47 passages rebut the presumption of the intention which my learned friend, Mr Jardine, wishes to bring home to my client.

Batchelor J.: You rely on the forty-seven passages as showing the general purport of the speeches which would not produce that effect?

Mr Jinnah: Yes. I would refer your lordships to what Lord Halisbury says on the question of intention. (Reads from Lord Halisbury's Laws of England.) In the present case, my lords these forty-seven passages show the intention of the speaker, the intention which permeates these three speeches.

Batchelor J.: We shall deliver judgment tomorrow morning.

(Adjourned till Thursday, 9-11-16, 11:30 a.m.)

Justice Batchelor's Judgment

The Hon. Justice Sir Stanley L. Batchelor in delivering his judgment said:

This is an application by Mr B.G. Tilak praying this Court to revise the Order made by the District Magistrate of Poona under Sec. 108 and the following sections of the C.P.C.

The Order complained of directs that applicant do enter into a bond in a sum of Rs 20,000 with two sureties each in a sum of Rs 10,000 to be of good behaviour for a period of one year. The ground of the Order was that in the learned District Magistrate's opinion the applicant disseminated seditious matter in the three speeches which are now upon the record.

These speeches were admittedly made by Mr Tilak. They were made in the Marathi language, but their translations before us are, it is admitted, substantially correct, and in my view nothing turns upon certain small niceties of expression in which, the defence suggest that the official translation contains slightly harsher words than the Marathi warrants. Thus the only question, is whether in the three speeches the applicant is proved to have excited or to have attempted to excite disaffection towards the Government established by law in British India within the meaning of Section 124A of the Indian Penal Code. In my opinion the application does not give rise to any real question of law. But I must notice a mistake of law into which the learned Magistrate has inadvertently fallen.

Following Mr Justice Strachey's original pronouncement to the Jury in *Queen Empress* vs. *Bal Gangadhar Tilak* (I.I.R. 22 Bombay, p. 112), he has held that 'disaffection' is the equivalent merely of 'absence of affection.' I cannot say whether this expression did or did not influence the learned Magistrate's decision, but it is plain that it may have done so. It is, I think, equally plain that this construction of the word 'disaffection' is opposed to all ordinary English usage in words compounded with the particle 'dis.' Dislike for instance, is not a mere absence of liking, nor is disgust for a thing a mere absence of taste for it. This, indeed, was recognized by the Full Bench which amended Mr Justice Strachey's definition. See the Report I.L.R. 22 Bombay at p. 151. The present explanation, No. 1, appended to Section 124A, now sets the point at rest. With these definitions before us I say that there is not, in my opinion, any real doubt about the law governing the case. Next, there were on behalf of the defence two preliminary arguments on which a word must be said. It will only be a word, because in my judgment the points taken are wholly devoid of substance or merit.

First, then it was said that there could be no excitement or disaffection in these speeches, inasmuch as the speaker openly and sincerely professed his loyalty to his Majesty the King—Emperor and the British Parliament. To that I have only to say that as I read Section 124A, it is clear that to a charge of exciting disaffection towards the Government established by law in British India, a profession, however sincere, of loyalty to His Majesty and the British Parliament, is no answer whatever.

Secondly, it was contended that the speeches could not in law offend against Section 124A, because the speaker's attack was made not on the Government *nomination* but on the Civil Service only. That, I think, is not quite so in fact. But assuming it to be so, it affords no answer to the charge, for the Government established by law acts through a human agency, and, admittedly the Civil Service is its principal agency for the administration of the country in times of peace. Therefore, where, as here, you criticize the Civil Service *en bloc*, the question whether you excite disaffection against Government or not seems to me a pure question of fact. You do so if the natural effect of your words, infusing hatred of the Civil Service, is also to infuse hatred or contempt of the established Government whose accredited agent the Civil Service is. You avoid doing so if preferring appropriate language of moderation, you use words which do not naturally excite such hatred of Government. It is, I think, a mere question of fact.

Passing now to the speeches themselves, they must be read as a whole. A fair construction must be put upon them straining nothing either for the Crown or for the applicant, and paying more attention to the whole general effect than to any isolated words or passages. The question is, whether upon such fair construction these speeches offend under Section 124A or not.

Now, first, as to the general aim of the speaker, it is, I think, reasonably clear that in contending for what he describes as 'Swarajya,' his object is to obtain for Indians an increased and a gradually increasing share of political authority and to subject the administration of the country to the control of the people or the peoples of India. I am of opinion that the advocacy of such an object is not *per se* an infringement of the law, nor has the learned Advocate-General contended otherwise.

I wish to be understood as confining these last observations to the case which we have before us and to the object which, as I have explained, these speeches seem to me to pursue. I desire to guard myself from being supposed to say that the advocacy of 'Swarajya' is in all cases permissible. That is a point upon which it is not necessary now to pronounce an opinion, and upon which I refrain from pronouncing an opinion. For, as I understand it, the word 'Swarajya,' may have a dozen different meanings in the mouths of as many speakers. The remarks, which I have made are applicable only to the object aimed at in these speeches, as I have already defined that object.

We must now turn to the actual language employed by the applicant noting especially the methods which the speaker advocates for ensuring the political changes which he seeks. First it is a matter for observation that he formally and expressly repudiates all intention of sedition. That of course is by no means conclusive. But it is a fact to be considered along with other facts. For I am bound to say that a candid reading of the whole speeches does not convince me that the repudiation of disloyalty is feigned or artificial. Now the intention to create disaffection must, of course, be proved, and following the usual rule that a man must be taken to intend the natural and probable consequences of his own acts, we must seek for the speaker's intention in the language which he has used.

In the course of the argument comments were made, and properly made, on the form of many expressions to be found in the addresses, this form being in many cases offensive or insulting in the personal sense. These matters, however, though they may convict the speaker of bad taste, or bad temper, do not seem to me to go very far towards convicting him of a violation of the criminal law. Now, it not being contended that the main object of the speaker's advocacy is in itself forbidden we must see whether there is anything in the language used or the methods urged which fairly brings the applicant within the penal section. The answer must of course depend on the effect likely to be produced by the speeches on the minds of the hearers. Would that effect naturally and probably be to excite disaffection as defined in the section or to excite only such measure of disapprobation as is not forbidden by the law? The arguments which we have heard to assist us in answering this question are no doubt helpful. But it must be borne in mind that all such arguments necessarily concentrate upon certain selected passages, whereas the Court's aim is to decide upon the general effect of the speeches as a whole. Probably, the fairest way to ascertain that effect is to read the three speeches from beginning to end quietly and attentively, remembering the arguments, and remembering the politically ignorant audience whom Mr Tilak was addressing. I have so read these speeches not once, but several times, and the impression left on my mind is that on the whole, despite certain passages which are rightly objected to by the prosecution, the general effect would not naturally and probably be to cause disaffection, that is, hostility or enmity or contempt, but rather to create a feeling of disapprobation of the Government, for that it delays the transference of political power to the hands of those whom the speaker designates as 'the people.' For this conclusion I can only appeal to the general purport of all the three speeches as a whole. They cover 34 pages of print and of course I cannot set them out *in extenso* in this judgment. I must, therefore, perforce refer to particular passages of particular consequence. But I wish it to be understood that my decision is based not on particular passages, but upon the general effect.

I proceed now to cite a few passages is order to show what in the speaker's own language is the meaning of that *Swarajya* which he was advocating to his audience. He tells them:

'But however good may be the arrangement made by other people, still it is not the case that he who wants to have the power to make this arrangement always approves of it. This is the principle of "Swarajya." If you got the powers to select your Collector, it cannot be said with certainty that he would do any more work than the present Collector. Perhaps he may not do. He may even do it badly. I admit this.... To put it briefly, the demand that the management of our affairs should be in our hands is the demand for "Swarajya." ...If you carry on such an effort now for 5 or 25 years, you will never fail to obtain its fruit.'

This passage is important as showing that the speaker does not expect that the political change which he advocates is to come suddenly or by a stroke of the pen. In other passages he uses the following language:

'Confer those powers upon the people, so that, they may duly look to their domestic affairs. We ask for "Swarajya" of this kind. This "Swarajya" does not mean that the English Government should be removed, the Emperor's rule should be removed and the rule of some one of our Native States should be established in its place.... But we must do those things which relate to business, trade, religion and society. Unless the power of doing those things comes partially into our hands in the end, it must come fully,—unless it comes fully into our hands, it is impossible for us to see a time of plenty, the dawn of good fortune, advantage or prosperity. Water cannot be drunk with others' mouths. We ourselves have to drink it.... The first duty is, take a portion of this authority into your possession, it does not matter if you take a little portion of it.... A new king is not wanted. But give into our possession a portion of the powers by losing which our condition is being reduced to that of orphans.'

The above passages show the nature of the demand made. With this demand as a political theme I have of course no concern whatever, and I decline to say a word upon the subject. My concern is to say only that as a Judge I find nothing in it that offends against the law.

Passing now to an enquiry as to the methods advocated for securing the result proposed, I set out the following excerpts as indicating the speaker's general views: 'It is an undisputed fact that we should secure our own good under the rule of the English people themselves, under the supervision of the English nation, with the help of the English nation, through their sympathy, through their anxious care, and through those high sentiments which they possess.... In this manner, good management is to be asked for in this administration. Amendment is to be brought about in the present law; it is to be brought about through Parliament. We will not ask for it from others. We have not to get this demand complied with by petitioning France. The Allies may be there, we have not to petition them. The petition is to be made to the English people, to the English Parliament.... Owing to the war which is now going on in Europe, it has begun to be thought that unless all the many parts of the British Empire unite together, that Empire would not attain as much strength as it should. It has so happened now that a consciousness has been awakened in them that they stand in need of aid from other countries called Colonies, belonging to them—Australia, Canada and New Zealand,—which are inhabited by Sahebs. If you take advantage of this awakened consciousness, you too have this opportunity of acquiring some rights. No one tells you to obtain these rights by the use of the sword. But today the nation's mind has undergone a change. India can give some help to England. If India be happy England too will acquire a sort of glory, a sort of strength and a sort of greatness. This consciousness has been awakened in England.... On the day on which you will be ready to do this particularly in these days after the war is over—the administration shall have to be changed in some respects at least.... I don't say to any of you that you should do unlawful things in order to acquire these rights. There is a lawful way.'

In all these passages which I have cited as fairly typical of the speeches as fairly exemplifying the speaker's general drift, not only is there nothing illegal, but there is a distinct pleading that the political changes advocated should be obtained by lawful and constitutional means.

I need not lengthen this judgment by reference to the large mass of arguments used. It is enough to say that in my opinion the bulk of these arguments are free from legal objection and I notice as among such arguments that the contentions that Indian Administrators govern Native States without complaint; that in British India British officials are paid too highly, and Indians, though they are free to discuss, have no effective control over finance or policy; that the present officials being in fact alien by race, though able and industrious men, do not readily understand the needs of the people. Now all this may be politically wise or politically foolish. With that I say, again I have no concern. But it is in my judgment, fair political criticism not obnoxious to Section 124A. Yet it is arguments such as these which form the bulk of these three addresses, and the applicant is entitled to be judged rather by his general tenor and purport than by any selected passages. It must also, in fairness to the applicant, be stated that these speeches are not all mere condemnation. In one passage of the speech of the 31 May 1916, he says, speaking of the Government and of the material improvements which the Government has made in the country, 'I do not say that these things have not been done, done well and have been done better by the British Government than they would have been done by the former Governments; this is an honour to them. But should we not tell it to do those things which it does not do.'

If matters rested here, the applicant's defence would, in my opinion, be very strong. Unfortunately matters do not rest here, and there are two or three passages which, undoubtedly, as they stand, are to my mind impossible of justification. Nor has Mr Tilak's learned counsel made any substantial or successful attempt to justify them. If these passages stood alone or if I could bring myself to think that they fairly reflected the speaker's general meaning, I should feel bound to confirm the Magistrate's Order. I don't intend to give those offensive passages any further publicity by repeating them in this judgment. I shall sufficiently identify them by saying that one passage occurring in the first speech, refers to keeping Indians in a position of slavery or servitude, and another passage in the second speech describes the Government as an 'alien Government looking mainly to its own interests.' In my mind the only real difficulty in this case has been to decide whether these passages alone can properly be used as affording a sufficient ground for the learned Magistrate's Order. Upon the best consideration that I can give to this difficult question, and having regard to the whole tenor of the speeches, I think that the answer should be in the applicant's favour. I think so, not because these passages in themselves can be justified, but because their obvious objectionableness is somewhat mitigated by the contexts of the arguments in which they occur, and because I don't regard them as fairly characterizing the general effect of the speeches as a whole. There is no reason to think that, in these long speeches delivered orally, these particular passages, which occupy no specially prominent place in the addresses, would specially impress themselves on the minds of the audience so as to override the general effect. That general effect is not, I think, shown to exceed the limits of fair criticism as defined in Explanations 2 and 3 of Section 124A. On these grounds, I am of opinion, that the rule should be made absolute, the order under revision being set aside. The bonds, if they are executed, must be cancelled and discharged.

Justice Shah's Judgment

Justice Shah in delivering a concurring judgment said:

This is an application for revising an order made by the District Magistrate of Poona. The order is made in proceedings taken under Section 108 Criminal Procedure Code against the petitioner, and directs him to enter into a bond in a sum of Rs 20,000, with two sureties, each in a sum of Rs 10,000, to be of good behaviour for a period of one year.

The information under Section 108 Criminal Procedure Code, against the petitioner was that he had orally disseminated seditious matter, that is, matter the publication of which was punishable under Section 124A of the Indian Penal Code, by making three speeches on the subject of 'Swarajya' or Home Rule, one at Belgaum on the 1st May, and the other two at Ahmednager, on the 31st May and 1 June last.

The learned District Magistrate has come to the conclusion that these speeches contain matter the publication of which is punishable under Section 124A, I.P.C., and the order in question is based on this conclusion.

The principal question to be decided on this application is whether the matter complained of is such that its publication is punishable under Section 124A, I.P.C.

At the outset it may be mentioned that no objection is taken to the main theme of the lecture viz 'Swarajya' or Home Rule for India on behalf of the Crown, nor is it suggested that the word 'Swarajya' is used in any offensive sense in those speeches. The learned Advocate-General has contended before us, as it was contended before the Lower Court, that the matter disseminated by the petitioner is seditious on account of the remarks made in various parts of his speeches imputing dishonest and corrupt motives to Government by law established in British India.

It has been argued that the Lower Court is wrong in holding that 'disaffection' within the meaning of Section 124A means 'absence of affection.' The learned District Magistrate purports to quote the words of Mr Justice Strachey. But it seems to me that in view of the observations of the Full Bench consisting of Farran C.J., Candy and Strachey J.J. in the case of *Queen Empress vs. Bal Gangadhar Tilak*, (I.L.R. 22 Bom. at p. 151) and of the judgments in *Queen Empress vs. Ramchandra Narayan* and another (I.L.R. 22 Bom 152) it is clear that 'disaffection' does not mean 'absence of affection.' The section as it stood when these cases were decided was repealed in 1898, and the present Section 124A was substituted for it. The first explanation to the section seems to indicate that 'disaffection' cannot mean 'absence of affection' within the meaning of the section. I agree on this point with the observations of Mr Justice Batty in the case of *Emperor vs. Bhaskar* (8 Bom. L.R. p. 437). The learned

Advocate-General does not contend otherwise; and the point is not of any practical importance in the case.

There has been some argument as to the meaning of the expression 'Government established by law in British India' and the observations of Mr Justice Strachey in Tilak's case and Mr Justice Batty in Bhasker's case on this point have been referred to.

For the purposes of this case, it seems to me to be sufficient to state that the expression would mean the various Governments constituted by the statutes relating to the Government of India now consolidated into the Government of India Act of 1915 (V and VI George V Ch. 61), and would denote the person or persons authorized by law to administer executive Government in any part of British India. The Hon. Mr Jinnah has argued that all the criticism directed against the Indian Civil Service, generally described as 'bureaucracy' in the speeches, cannot, under any circumstances, be treated as criticism against the 'Government by law established in British India.' I am unable to accept this argument. It may be that the various services under the control of the Government by law established in British India do not form part of the Government within the meaning of the section; and it may be that the criticism directed against any of the services in not necessarily criticism of the 'Government by law established in British India.' But the feelings which it is the object of Section 124A to prohibit, may be excited towards the Government in a variety of ways; and it seems to me that it is possible to excite such feelings towards the Government by an unfair condemnation of any of its services. Whether in a particular case the condemnation of any service is sufficient to excite any feelings of hatred or contempt or disaffection towards the 'Government by law established in British India,' must depend upon the nature of the criticism, the position of the service in the administration and all the other circumstances of that case. It would be a question of fact to be determined in each case with reference to its circumstances. But as a matter of law it cannot be said that the condemnation of a particular service under the 'Government by law established in British India' can never be sufficient to excite any of the feelings prohibited by Section 124A towards such Government.

I now come to the question as to whether the publication of the matter contained in these speeches is punishable under Section 124A. It is quite clear that the speaker must not bring or attempt to bring into hatred or contempt, or excite or attempt to excite disaffection towards His Majesty or the 'Government established by law in British India;' and it is also clear that even in the case of comments falling under Explanation 2 or 3 of the Section, this essential condition must be observed. In the present case Mr Jinnah has laid great emphasis on the fact that throughout the speeches the speaker has expressed his loyalty to His Majesty. But this cannot avail him. He is not charged with exciting disaffection towards His Majesty. The Crown case is that he has attempted to bring into hatred or contempt or to excite disaffection towards the

APPENDIX 1

Government established by law in British India; and it is no answer to this charge to say that he has expressed his loyalty to His Majesty.

The speeches in question were delivered in Marathi and are very long. It is necessary to determine the intention of the speaker in delivering these speeches. The intention must be gathered primarily from the language used; and if on reading the speeches, the reasonable and natural and probable effect of the speeches on the minds of those to whom they were addressed, appears to be that feelings of hatred, contempt or disaffection would be excited towards the Government, the petitioner's case must fail.

The question, therefore, is one of determining reasonable, natural and probable effect of the speeches taken as a whole on the minds of those to whom they were addressed. I have read these speeches for myself. They have been fully discussed on both sides, and various passages have been referred to. I do not consider it necessary to deal with these passages in detail. The speeches must be read as a whole 'in a fair, free and liberal spirit.' In dealing with them one 'should not pause upon an objectionable sentence here or a strong word there.' They should be dealt with 'in a spirit of freedom' and not viewed 'with an eye of narrow criticism.' The case should be viewed 'in a free, bold, manly and generous spirit' towards the petitioner (see R.V. Burns 16 Cox at p. 362.) In the present case it is clear from the various passages in the speeches that the avowed object of the petitioner was to create a public opinion in favour of Home Rule for India, and to induce the hearers to join the Home Rule League. It is also clear from the speeches that he did not advocate for the achievement of his object any means other than strictly constitutional means. Under these circumstances it is clear that in determining the general effect of the speeches care should be taken not to attach undue importance to the objectionable passages. Undoubtedly there are some objectionable passages in these speeches. Particularly the references to the condition of slavery and to the alien character of the rule are unfair and improper. It seems to me, however, that the petitioner is entitled to the benefit of the argument that the general effect of the speeches taken as a whole should be considered, as that would be the impression left on the minds of the hearers. It is possible that different minds might estimate this effect differently. Under the circumstances, I have done my best to consider the passages in the speeches in favour of the petitioner on the one hand and in favour of the Crown case on the other; and to estimate their effect. I am unable to say that the natural and probable effect of the speeches taken as a whole on the minds of those to whom they were addressed, would be to bring into hatred or contempt, or to excite disaffection, towards the 'Government established by law in British India.' I am not, therefore, prepared to hold that the matter disseminated by the petitioner is seditious within the meaning of Section 108, Cl. (a) Criminal Procedure Code. I do not ignore the fact that there are some passages, which, if they stood by themselves, might justify the inference against the accused. But their effect in the course of long speeches orally delivered is a different matter.

The learned Advocate-General has attempted to save the order by urging that even if the publication of the matter be not punishable under Section 124A on account of the criminal intent of the petitioner not being established, the Court could still make an order under Section 108 Criminal Procedure Code and that this is a fit case for making the order contemplated by the section. He has relied upon the case of *Sitalprasad vs. Emperor* (I.L.R. 43 Cal. 591). But it seems to me that it is essential under Section 108, Cl. (a) that the matter disseminated must be shown to be seditious. The words of the section are clear and must be given effect to. I do not think that this view renders Section 108 of the Criminal Procedure Code unnecessary. It seems to me that the section affords an additional remedy to the Crown which may be more appropriate in certain cases than an actual prosecution on a charge under Section 124A. I am unable to follow Sitalprasad's case in view of the clear words of the section.

I, therefore, concur in the order proposed by my learned brother.

After the judgments were delivered Mr Jinnah told their Lordships that Mr Tilak had already executed the bonds; so unless their Lordships directed their cancellation they would stand and therefore he asked the Court to order their cancellation.

The Court therefore ordered that the said bonds be cancelled.

Appendix 2

Jinnah's Battles for Press Freedom

Quaid-i-Azam Mohammed Ali Jinnah belonged to a generation of leaders the like of whom we are unlikely to see again. They do not make such men any more. Their politics were as elevated as their character. They were cultured men of the world but had ideals to which they were committed. They knew the power of the word, spoken and written, founded journals and fought for press freedom in those heady days of the struggle for independence from British rule.

Gandhi founded *Young India* and *Harijan* to which he contributed regularly. Nehru founded the *National Herald* which was run to the ground by those he trusted. Even in his eighties Rajaji, the great dissenter who got the Madras Congress Legislature Party to pass a resolution in April 1942 accepting Pakistan for the sake of national unity, founded a lively weekly *Swarajya* to which he contributed a column regularly. Jinnah founded *Dawn* which flourishes still. His articles were few and far between. One is particularly famous, the one in *Time and Tide* of London on 9 January 1940 two months before the Lahore resolution. Decades earlier, he was an active Chairman of the Board of Directors of the *Bombay Chronicle* whose editor Benjamin Guy Horniman called the British owned *The Times of India* the 'Old woman of Bori Bunder.' As a lawyer Jinnah fought two particularly notable cases concerning press freedom. One concerned his friend Bal Gangadhar Tilak, the other the *Chronicle* itself.

It is however in his speeches in the Central Legislative Assembly and on public platform that he expressed comprehensively and clearly his view on freedom of the press. For nearly three decades he seized every opportunity that came his way to expound his outlook. Interesting and, indeed, instructive as it is to read a speech by itself, one gets a fuller picture of what Walter Lippmann called his 'public philosophy' if one considers them as a whole. They form a rich heritage, a great corpus of enlightened pronouncements. This writer is indebted to compilations by Syed Sharifuddin Pirzada, Riaz Ahmed and an excellent but neglected volume on 'Jinnah as a Parliamentarian' by I.A. Rehman, Mohammed Jafar, and Ghani Jafar.

As far back as on 20 December 1913 Jinnah called upon the Indian Congress and the All-India Muslim League, which he had joined that year the 'most representative organisations in the country' as he called them to consider jointly issues of common concern like the Press Act. He was presiding over a meeting of the Anjuman-i-Islam in Bombay.

In order to protest against the use of the Press Act against several newspapers, the Council of Bombay Presidency Association met on 8 June 1916 and appointed a Committee 'to draft a memorial for the purpose and submit it to the Council within a fortnight'. Predictably, Jinnah was nominated a member of that committee.

In 1916 Jinnah was invited to preside over the Bombay Provincial Conference a step which Gandhi lauded in these words:

> It has chosen as President a person who holds a respected position in the eyes of both parties. It is decided accordingly that it would be in the fitness of things to elect as President a learned Muslim gentleman. This is not for the first time that Ahmedabad has shown such wisdom. It has done so on many previous occasions. Our President, Mr Jinnah, is an eminent lawyer; he is not only a member of the Legislature but also the President of the biggest Islamic Association in India. He has placed us under a great obligation by accepting the presidentship of this small conference. All of you must have rejoiced at it as much as I have done.

In his presidential address on 21 October 1916 Jinnah said:

> The Press Act was a most unwelcome measure from its very inception. It has been characterised as a serious menace to the freedom of the Press in India; but the harsh manner in which it is enforced has roused the strongest opposition and created great discontent. The safeguards provided by the Act have proved illusory and incapable of being enforced as declared by the High Court of Calcutta. It is high time that the Government appointed a committee of official and non-official members to consider its working since 1910 and recommend what course should be adopted to allay the just public resentment and discontent with regard to this measure.

A crowded public meeting of the citizens of Bombay was held on 30 July 1917 under the auspices of the Presidency Association over which Jinnah presided. In view of Jawaharlal Nehru's cheap remark to Mountbatten at their first meeting in Delhi in 1947 that success came late to Jinnah, it bears mention that present on the dais was a galaxy of eminence—Tilak, Motilal Nehru, Sarojini Naidu, Bhulabhai Desai, Omar Sobhani, M.R. Jayakar and others. It was to protest against the internment of Annie Besant and a couple of other leaders in Madras. Jinnah said:

> It seems obvious that, if we accept the policy of the Government, all constitutional and lawful agitation will in effect be stopped, that the freedom of speech and the press and the right of public meeting under the British flag is henceforth to be regulated by the arbitrary judgment and decision of a Provincial Governor or Government, that the Executive are to decide what is lawful and constitutional propaganda without reference to the Courts of Justice of His Majesty the King-Emperor.

In September 1918 G.S. Khaparde moved a resolution in the Imperial Legislative Council which read: 'This Council recommends to the Governor-General in Council that a committee consisting of an equal number of officials and non-official Indians be appointed to inquire into and report on (a) the effect produced on the Press in India by the legislation relating to it, and by the

APPENDIX 2   353

Defence of India (Consolidation) Rules, 1915; and (b) the moral and material conditions of the Press in India.' Jinnah's frank speech deserves to be quoted in extenso:

> Sir, when the Press Act was passed in 1910, I happened to be a Member of this council. At that time the position, sir, was this—I think the Hon'ble the Home Member will bear me out—that we had got already sufficient provisions in our ordinary codes and our ordinary laws, to deal adequately with most of the offences which he described in his speech, but that could only be done by means of judicial proceedings.
>
> It was then suggested in 1910 that we had so many instances of papers which I will characterise as erring papers, papers which spread sedition and disaffection, and were the cause more or less of political crimes, that those papers could not well and adequately be dealt with by the weapons which already existed in the armoury of the law. Therefore, the Government came before this council and put forward this case, that the council must give power to the Executive to deal with such offences, because it was urged that the consequences of adopting judicial proceedings were sometimes worse in their result, although it could secure a conviction against the culprit. Sir, if you will refer to the proceedings of 1910, you will find that almost every non-official Member, feeling as he did that the Press Act was striking a blow at the liberty of the Press which we all prize, still came to the conclusion that, having regard to the circumstances, he could not refuse them.
>
> Sir, this Act has the defect of all measures which do not come under the purview of judicial supervision; because it is measure which has got to be administered by the Executives. This measure has remained on the Statute book for seven years, and I venture to say that, notwithstanding the extreme instances the Hon'ble the Home Member was pleased to cite, there are cases where this Act has been maladminstered and has been oppressively worked. It is no use citing instances of an extreme character. We know all that, and we regret it. It was because of these extreme cases that the Government were in a position to come before this Council and ask for these extraordinary powers which you have got at present. We regret them and we unwillingly gave you that power. But the question today is this—How has that power been exercised, and how is this Act to be administered. I have no hesitation in saying that the Act has been administered in a most arbitrary manner; and you cannot prevent it, you cannot avoid it because you must remember that we are all human; and when such arbitrary powers are given to Heads of Department and to Executive Officers, it must be remembered that they are human, they have got likes and dislikes, and they have their prejudices. And remember this, that there is no appeal, it is final. Seven years have passed since this Act became law, and we feel that it is time that a proper inquiry was held; and if you hold the inquiry, I say, protect the innocent, protect those journalists who are doing their duty and who are serving both the public and the Government by criticizing the Government freely, independently, honestly— which is an education for any Government.'

This was typical of him. He was balanced, ready to consider an opposing viewpoint and willing to admit a mistake. He knew that the British bribed sections of the press and asked in the assembly on 24 February 1924 what subsidy the Government of India paid to Reuters and the Associated Press of

India. The answer was none. They were paid for 'copies supplied' as newspapers did.

On 5 March 1921 the Press Association of India held a public meeting on Press Day at the Excelsior Theatre in Bombay which flourishes still. As ever Jinnah presided. He admitted to his mistake as the *Bombay Chronicle's* report brings out. He called for the repeal of the Press Act, 1910 evidently regretting his support to it in 1910:

> Fortunately or unfortunately the speaker happened to be a member of the Imperial Legislative Council that passed that Act. The late Mr Gokhale and several other prominent representatives of theirs in the Council, at the time, were told that things were taking place in India which it was impossible for the Government to control. The Press in the country was being conducted in such a way that it was impossible to apply to it the ordinary laws of the land. When Government seriously and in all ordinances placed certain matters before the representatives of the people, such as they were at the time, it showed on the part of those representatives a desire to help the administration of this country and they were induced, because of the exceptional circumstances which were placed before them to give their assent to that legislation. That was in 1910. Many of those members, he would assure them, were most unwilling and many of them were hesitant to allow a statute of that character to be placed on the statute book of any government. But arguments and reasons were placed for the moment which induced most of them to say: 'Very well we shall give you this power and let us see how it is going to be used.

That was in the year 1910. The Act had been enforced and the Act had been administered and he wanted them to follow him when he said in what spirit of reasonableness the leaders of the country gave this power into the hands of the executive. And since 1910 they had watched the working of the Act and the administration of the Act and they had found, and he was voicing the opinion of the educated all over the country, that one thing had come out clearly from this Act—that the Act had done no good to anybody. It had repressed and stunted their natural growth. It had not allowed the Press of this country to be independent, fearless and responsible. He was sure that it was clearly shown by now that instead of helping the very object, the Act had been a perfect failure. The only thing the Act had been able to achieve was this. That it had placed certain powers in the hands of the executive officers who had gratified their idiosyncrasies and oppressed the Press.'

He recalled Khaparde's motion and government's refusal to order an inquiry.

> That Act was nothing else than a source of irritation and a source of resentment to the Press of this country. Government might forfeit the security, but they were not going to prevent in the year 1921 the people from exercising their fullest liberty of speech and of writing. That was a grave reflection upon any Government that prevented its people from honestly, independently and fearlessly expressing their opinion and views. He went further and said that public opinion in India was getting healthier and sounder. He was seeing the fruits of it in front of him that repressive

Act they were going to carry on the administration of this country now, they were much mistaken. The liberty of the press was the most valuable thing and if that liberty was touched in any way it undermined the authority of the Government more than it undermined the authority of the people. The Press Act must be repealed. Indians did not want a modification of it.

By now the *Bombay Chronicle* was engulfed in one crisis after another. It had been founded by Pherozeshah Mehta in 1912. Differences arose after his death in November 1915. Horniman its first editor walked out without prior notice along with a majority of the staff after denouncing in the paper the pro-British attitude of the directors. The shareholders and the owners of the Indian newspapers upheld his stand and elected a new board of directors with Jinnah as its chairman. He succeeded in restoring harmony between the editorial and management wings of the paper. Jinnah resigned because he differed with its editorial support to the non-cooperation movement despite the editor's assurances of neutrality but he continued as director. He was succeeded as chairman by M.R. Jayakar whose memoirs *The Story of My Life* (Vol. I) records the whole story including Jinnah's correspondence with the authorities.

On 26 April 1919, Horniman was suddenly arrested and deported to England. It was over an inaccurate report by a correspondent. Simultaneously censorship was imposed on the paper. Jinnah protested strongly at this. To save the paper the directors deposited the maximum security under the Press Act. In 1919 Jayakar became chairman of the board. It instructed the editor Syed Abdullah Brelvi on 18 June 1919 not to 'identify' the paper with the non-cooperation movement. Pre-censorship was lifted that day but Brelvi flouted the instructions.

Judging by a press statement by one of the directors, Jamnadas Dwarkadas, on 16 April 1921, Jinnah's resignation as chairman was accepted by the board much later. He had appeared for the paper with M.K. Azad at the Esplanade Police Court on 18 December 1917 when Horniman was asked to deposit a security of Rs 2,000. The order was upheld by the court. In 1916 he had succeeded in the High Court in setting aside an order for a bond for good behaviour against Tilak on the ground of seditious speeches.

On 10 February 1924 in the Central Assembly Jinnah vehemently attacked the government for deporting Horniman and set the record straight.

> The Honourable the Home Member really reminded me, as if he was pleading before a third class magistrate. What happened was that a special correspondent of the *Bombay Chronicle* sent a report and what is more, Sir, even the Government notification admitted that the appearance of the bullets did lend colour to this conclusion that they were soft nose bullets, and that information was sent by a correspondent of the *Bombay Chronicle*. Mr Horniman was not responsible for it but that very correspondent on further examination of those bullets sent a further report. That report, I am prepared to prove anywhere you like, was not allowed to go out of Delhi and was detained. In the meantime Mr Horniman was deported under the Defence of India Act on a charge not of distributing his paper amongst the troops but

on a charge of having written two articles. The security was forfeited and censorship was imposed upon the paper and thereupon the *Bombay Chronicle* had to suspend its publication. It was after Mr Horniman was deported and when the Secretary of State for India was heckled—I do not know who was responsible—but it was then that this case was made out against Mr Horniman and Mr Montagu had to put forward that case. So far, Sir, with regard to the soft-nosed bullets, and I will add one thing more. This telegram which was sent by the *Bombay Chronicle* correspondent was detained and in the meantime the paper was suspended by us ourselves for the simple reason that the editor was deported, security was forfeited and censorship was imposed upon the paper. Therefore, the Board of Directors had in the meantime to suspend the paper. After five or six days the correspondent wrote to us a letter saying: 'I sent you this telegram contradicting my first report on further examination of the character of these bullets and how is it has not appeared in your paper? Sir, the very first day when the *Chronicle* re-appeared after its suspension this explanation was published in that paper; and, as I said before, even the Government notification-an challenge to the Home Member to look it up—admitted that the appearance of the bullets was that of soft-nosed bullets. Is that the case on which you deport a man?

His approach to two issues which unduly exercise some people today, obscenity and criticism of religion was liberal. He assumed that others would be as liberal. For instance he said on 20 February 1925 on Dewan Chaman Lall's Obscene Publications Bill.

Sir, if there is truly a work of art or literature or science, which is truly a work of art or literature or science, and if it is published or sold with a bona fide object, I ask Mr Chaman Lall—and I appeal less to his imagination, less to his enthusiasm, and more to his common sense and reason—to say is there any Magistrate, unless he is absolutely devoid of honesty, who would condemn it? It is not a question of law. Mr Chaman Lall waxes eloquence. I ask him, can he cite to me a single case where any Magistrate, whom he treated with such contempt as third class Magistrates and fourth class Magistrate's convicted the accused in such a case.

He trusted the judiciary and always opposed expansion of executive power. In 1926 the Penal Code was amended to enlarge the ambit of sedition in S.153-A by adding the words 'any matter calculated or likely to promote feelings of enmity or hatred' between different communities. On 25 August 1926 Jinnah opposed this amendment.

Are we going to put this measure on the Statute-book permanently? I think my Honourable friend, the Home Member will admit that this is a power which is an extraordinary power, an unusual power, and there are other interests which have got to be taken into consideration. And that is the liberty and freedom of the Press. And printing and publishing our opinions. That is a matter which ought not by ignored. Now, are you going to put this Bill permanently on the statute-book? Well, Sir, I have given thought to it and I appeal to this House not to allow the Government, however much they may be scared by the crisis which faces us, to take away from this House the power of enacting it into a Statute permanently. Therefore, I should say that this Statute should be enforced for a limited period. But, apart from that the second point is that the definition which is adopted here, is, I submit, much too wide. And it is clear departure from the terms of section 99-A. The object the Home Member has is to deal with the matter which would come under section 153-A. Instead of confining himself to that definition of section 153-A, the words which we are asked now to accept are as follows: after the words 'seditious matter' the words 'or any matter calculated or likely to promote feelings of enmity or hatred between different classes of His Majesty's subjects shall be inserted'.

Well, now, these words, let me tell you, are very wide and it will be impossible, I fancy, for the High Court to deal with any application for revision and come to a different conclusion from the decision of the Local Government if you have these words. You will at once negative the right which is given under the Criminal Procedure Code to go to High Courts, it will become useless. Therefore, these are the two matters about which I am very anxious, namely that we must carefully define the matter which it is intended to confiscate or forfeit and the Statute should be enforced for a limited period.'

Religious bigotry has gripped this unfortunate subcontinent, in India, Pakistan and Bangladesh. This is what the founder of Pakistan said in the assembly on 5 September 1927.

We in this House wish to make it clear that in future no wanton vilification or attack on any religion shall be permitted then let us proceed with this Bill. Let us enact a measure which will give us security against these scurrilous writers of the character now described. I thoroughly, endorse the principle, that while this measure should aim at those undesirable persons who indulge in wanton vilification or attack upon the religion of any particular class or upon the founders and prophets of a religion, we must also secure this very important and fundamental principle that those who are engaged in historical works, those who are engaged in the ascertainment of truth and those who are engaged in bona fide and honest criticisms of a religion shall be protected.

Assertive of the privileges of the House he was also assertive of the right of free speech outside the House, namely freedom to publish the speech in the House and claim privilege. He said on 6 September 1935:

The principle is this; freedom of speech; this is the answer for you to consider, that the freedom of speech gives me a right to publish it, and that I am not punishable. That is the question we have to decide, that the executive, wherever they are, have to observe this rule that once I have the privilege of freedom of speech, it gives me as a consequential privilege, the privilege of publishing it.

But by far his finest exposition on freedom of speech and, thus of the press, was made on 19 March 1930 while denouncing an order prohibiting Vallabhbhai Patel from speaking for one month at public meetings. It was a stellar performance and deserves quotation at length not least because, contrary to the falsehood by M.C. Setalvad in his memoirs *My Life*, Jinnah's research in law was thorough. He said he disagreed with the Non-Cooperation Movement but defended the participants' right to freedom of speech.

Sir, there is this movement in the country. The Government of India do not like it, I do not like it; your reasons may be different from my reasons; but we agree. I do not like it; and you do not like it. Now the question that I want to put you is this. Are you going to deal with this movement with the responsibility of the Government of India, or are you going to leave this movement to be dealt with by petty Magistrates in such manner as they may consider proper? According to the statement of the Honourable the Home Member, Sardar Vallbhbhai had made several speeches before. Were those speeches against the law? Did he transgress the limits of law or did he not? I have no information. If he was going to make a speech or speeches of the kind which he had already made in regard to which he had already transgressed the limits of law, and if he had already committed offences or infringed the law, then, Sir, your proper course, the proper course on the part of the authorities in that district should have been Sardar Vallabhbhai Patel ought to have been prosecuted long ago for an offence, but an order should not be passed which goes to the root of the principle of liberty of speech. Sir, the precedent that the Government of India are creating, this is what I am afraid of, and that is where the danger lies—the precedent they are creating is a dangerous precedent, and I want this House to understand that this is a very important issue. What is the real issue before the House? Sir, I will read in the language, which is certainly much better than I can command, a small passage to the House, and I think any one who is a student of history and of political movements in other countries will appreciate this passage and will see the point that I am trying to impress upon the Government. 'Liberty of opinion of course is open to abuse...'

Sir Hugh Cocke: What is that book please? Mr M.A. Jinnah: it is called 'American Government and Politics' by Beard, 4th Edition, Library Edition. It is not mine. It is the Library Edition of the House. Therefore, I think my Honourable friend Sir Hugh Cocke is now thoroughly satisfied. Liberty of opinion, lf course, is open to abuse; it is constantly abused; but far more open to abuse is the right to suppress opinion and far more often, in the long history of humanity, has it been abused. Still all matters of sentiment may be put on one side. It is hard, cold proposition; by what process are we most likely to secure orderly and intelligent government, by the process of censorship or that of freedom? On this question a comparison of English and Russian history is illuminating.

Do you want to follow the Russian history or the English History?

Sir, I shall continue to read the passage now: 'again and again those who have attempted to stop the progress of opinion by the gallows and prison have merely hastened their own destruction by violence.' I maintain most emphatically that there was no emergency. Vallabhbhai Patel had made no speech or speeches which came within the purview of the Penal Code.

With the launch of the movement for the establishment of Pakistan, the Quaid-i-Azam concentrated on dissemination of the League's policy 'to reach the masses'. His heart was set on founding an English daily in Delhi. The story of the birth of *Dawn* needs no recounting here. It began as a weekly on 19 October 1941 with Ahmed Hasan as editor and Z.A. Suleri and Aziz Beg on the editorial team. Pothan Joseph joined *Dawn* on 1 October 1942. The first issue of the daily came out on 12 October. He had worked in Calcutta on M.A.H. Ispahani's *Star of India*. In the beginning of 1945 he left *Dawn* to become principal press officer to the Government of India. Poonam Abraham acted as editor. Altaf Hussain left government service to join *Dawn* as its editor on 1 October 1945. Jinnah's correspondence with Ispahani records problems they faced in dealing with Pothan Joseph. In April 1945 Jinnah asked Ispahani to inquire of Arthur Moore, former editor of *The Statesman* whether he would accept editorship of *Dawn*.

In 1992 a biography of Pothan Joseph was published by T.J.S. George which records not only Jinnah's commitment to freedom of the press but also to editorial independence. It reproduces an article Joseph had written on Jinnah.

> He could never stand spend thrift mentality though he was capable of tolerating a certain degree of newspaper bohemianism.... Jinnah as the paramount chief of Dawn never vexed me with instructions as to editorial policy; never, not even in the most complicated situation when I showed signs of swaying on the rails. I discerned his mind by a sort of common understanding, and in my regular conversations with him of an evening, he would in a quiet disinterested and detached manner give his views on the bearings of some current development. There was no trace of pressure or censure, and he was anxious to test his views by inviting criticism in the seclusion of his drawing room, though never, so to speak, within the hearing of the gallery.... Once he sensed that you had the hang of the case, conversation was virtually over and the editor was free to follow his own technique of exposition.
>
> The notion of his having been a common bully in argument is fantastic, for the man was a great listener and he was very patient in reply unless perverse opposition roused in him the browbeating spirit. He was really a man with a heart, but determined never to be duped or see friends let down. He didn't care a hang about being represented as Mir Jaffer or as Judas Iscariot. No one could buy him, nor would he allow himself to be betrayed by a kiss. As an employer, Jinnah was exacting but he had the gift of stimulating in those who served him a sense of pride and also confidence that they could rely on him for a square deal.... Jinnah was a class by himself.

Appendix 3

The Lucknow Pact, 1916

Scheme of Reforms passed at the 31st session of the Indian National Congress held at Lucknow on 29 December 1916, and adopted by the All-Indian Moslem League at its meeting on 31 December 1916.

L.—PROVINCIAL LEGISLATIVE COUNCILS

1. Provincial Legislative Councils shall consist of four-fifths elected and of one-fifth nominated members.
2. Their strength shall be not less than one hundred and twenty-five members in the Major Provinces, and from five to seventy-five members in the Minor Provinces.
3. The members of Councils should be elected directly by the people on as broad a franchise as possible.
4. Adequate provision should be made for the representation of important minorities by election, and that the Mohammedans should be represented through special electorates on the Provincial Legislative Council.

Punjab	One half	of the elected Indian members
United Provinces	30 per cent	of the elected Indian members
Bengal	40 per cent	of the elected Indian members
Behar	25 per cent	of the elected Indian members
Central Provinces	15 per cent	of the elected Indian members
Madras	15 per cent	of the elected Indian members
Bombay	One-third	of the elected Indian members

Provided further that Mahomedans shall not participate in any of the other elections to the Legislative Councils.

Provided further that no Bill, nor any clause thereof, nor a resolution introduced by a non-official member affecting one or the other community, which question is to be determined by the members of that community in the Legislative Council concerned, shall be proceeded with, if three-fourths of the members of that community in the particular Council, Imperial or Provincial, oppose the bill or any clause thereof or the resolution.

5. The head of the Provincial Government should not be the President of the Legislative Council, but the Council should have the right of electing its President.
6. The right of asking supplementary questions should not be restricted to the member putting the original question but should be allowed to be exercised by any other member.

7. (a) Except customs, post, telegraph, mint, salt, opinion railways, army and navy, and tributes from Indian States, all other sources of revenue should be provincial. (b) There should be no divided heads of revenue. The Government of India should be provided with fixed contributions from the Provincial governments, such fixed contributions being liable to revision when extraordinary and unforeseen contingencies render such revision necessary. (c) The Provincial Council should have full authority to deal with all matters affecting the internal administration of the Province, inculcating the power to raise loans, to impose and alter taxation and to vote on the Budget. All items of expenditure and all proposals concerning ways and means for raising the necessary revenue should be embodied in Bills and submitted to the Provincial Council for adoption. (d) Resolutions on all matters within the purview of the Provincial Government should be allowed for discussion in accordance with rules made in that behalf by the Council itself. (e) A resolution passed by the Legislative Council shall be binding on the Executive Government, unless vetoed by the Governor in Council, provided however that if the resolution is again passed by the Council after an interval of not less than one year, it must be given effect to. (f) A motion for adjournment may be brought forward for the discussion of a definite matter of urgent public importance if supported by not less than one-eighth of the members present.
8. Any special meeting of the Council may be summoned on a requisition by not less than one-eighth of the members.
9. A Bill, other than a Money Bill, may be introduced in Council in accordance with the rules made in that behalf by the Council itself, and the consent of the Government should not be required therefore.
10. All Bills passed by Provincial legislatures shall have to receive the assent of the Governor before they become law, but may be vetoed by the Governor-General.
11. The terms of office of the member shall be five years.

Source: Christine E. Dobbin, *Basic Documents in the Development and Modern India and Pakistan, 1835–1947*, London, New York, Van Nostrand Reinhold Company, 1970, pp. 72–4.

Appendix 4

Jinnah's Fourteen Points, 1929

The League after anxious and careful consideration most earnestly and emphatically lays down that no scheme for the future constitution of the government of India will be acceptable to Mussulmans of India until and unless the following basic principles are given effect to and provisions are embodied therein to safeguard their rights and interests.

(1) The form of the future Constitution should be federal with the residuary powers vested in the Provinces.
(2) A uniform measure of autonomy shall be granted to all Provinces.
(3) All Legislatures in the country and other elected bodies shall be constituted on the definite principle of adequate and effective representation of Minorities in every Province without reducing the majority in any Province to a minority or even equality.
(4) In the Central Legislature, Mussulman representation shall not be less than one third.
(5) Representation of communal groups shall continue to be by means of separate electorates as at present: provided it shall be open to any community, at any time, to abandon its separate electorate in favour of joint electorate.
(6) Any territorial redistribution that might at any time be necessary shall not in any way affect the Muslim majority in the Punjab, Bengal, and the North-West Frontier Province.
(7) Full religious liberty, i.e. liberty of belief, worship and observance, propaganda, association and education, shall be guaranteed to all communities.
(8) No Bill or resolution or any part thereof shall be passed in any Legislature or any other elected body if three-fourths of the members of any community in the particular body oppose such a Bill, resolution or part thereof on the ground that it would be injurious to the interests of the community or in the alternative, such other measure is devised as may be found feasible and practicable to deal with such cases.
(9) Sindh should be separated from the Bombay Presidency.
(10) Reforms should be introduced in the North-West Frontier Province and Baluchistan on the same footing as in other Provinces.
(11) Provision should be made in the Constitution giving Muslims an adequate share, along with the other Indians, in all the Services of the State and in local self-governing bodies having due regard for the requirements of efficiency.
(12) The Constitution should embody adequate safeguards for the protection of Muslim culture and for the protection and promotion of Muslim

education, language, religion, personal laws and Muslim charitable instructions and for their due share in the grants-in-aid given by the State and by local self-governing bodies.
(13) No Cabinet, either Central or Provincial, should be formed without there being a proportion of at least one-third Muslim Ministers.
(14) No change shall be made in the Constitution by the Central Legislature except with the concurrence of the States constituting the Indian Federation.

Source: Christine E. Dobbin, *Basic Documents in the Development and Modern India and Pakistan, 1835–1947*, London, New York, Van Nostrand Reinhold Company, 1970, pp. 93–4.

Appendix 5

Jinnah–Rajendra Prasad Pact, 1934

I. It is hereby agreed that in Punjab

(1) The franchise qualifications of the three communities—Mussalmans, Hindus and Sikhs shall be so modified as to reflect the population of each community in the voting register.
(2) The Electorates shall be joint.
(3) (a) that so far as the Punjab Legislative Council is concerned, the distribution of the 175 seats into 10 special constituencies, and four seats for Europeans and Indian Christians, and 161 General seats including four seats for women given in His Majesty's Government's decision (amongst Hindus, Sikhas and Muslims) shall stand. (b) If women are to be given direct election in ordinary territorial constituencies, then the whole Province will be distributed amongst 161 single member constituencies, then the whole Province will be distributed amongst 161 single member constituencies otherwise among 157 single member constituencies, the distribution will be territorial on population basis; and there shall be no overlapping of constituencies. The constituencies allotted to each community will be such wherein its percentage of voters is largest.
(4) Each one of the above clauses is an essential part of the agreement.

II. It is requested that the franchise proposals in the white paper for the Punjab Legislative Council be revised and the decision given by His Majesty's Government on the communal question modified as in the agreement above.
The two questions stand or fall together

1. Franchise to be so framed and adjusted as to reflect the proportion of population of the various communities in the Electoral Rolls for the Provinces and the Centre and for that purpose differential franchise to be adopted wherever necessary.
2. There shall be no overlapping of electorates or constituencies.
3. That in the Punjab the Sikhs shall choose the number of constituencies for the seats allotted to them in the award, and thereafter the Hindus will have the choice to fix on such constituencies as they may desire for the number allotted to them, and the remaining constituencies shall be allotted to the Mussalmans as in the award excluding the seats allotted to the Europeans, Anglo Indians, Indian Christians and special constituencies.
4. In Bengal it is agreed between the Hindus and Mussalmans that if any seats are obtained from Europeans, they shall be divided between the Hindus and Mussalmans in proportion to their population in that

Province. Joint efforts to be made by the Hindus and Mussalmans to persuade the Europeans to release as many seats as they can possibly do from the quota allotted to them from the award. Subject to this the seats allotted to the Mussalamans under the award are to remain reserved for them, excluding the seats given to Europeans, Anglo Indians, Indian Christians and special Constituencies.

5. As regards the other Provinces the number of seats reserved for the Mussalmans to be as given in the award exclusive of special constituencies and those allotted to Europeans, Anglo Indians and Indian Christians.
6. Similarly seats allotted to Mussalmans for the Central Legislature by the award to remain reserved for them.
7. On that basis it is agreed that joint Electorate shall replace separate Electorates in all the Provinces and in the Centre.

Source: Marguerite Rose Dove, *Forfeited Future: The Conflict over Congress Ministries in British India 1933–1937*, Chanakya Publications, Delhi, 1987, pp-463-464

Appendix 6

The Lahore Resolution, 1940

While approving and endorsing the action taken by the Council and the Working Committee of the All-Indian Muslim League, as indicated in their resolutions dated the 27th of August, 17th and 18th of September and 22nd of October 1939, and 3rd of February 1940 on the constitutional issue, this Session of the All-Indian Muslim League emphatically reiterates that the scheme of Federation embodied the Government of India Act, 1935, is totally unsuited to, and unworkable in the peculiar conditions of this country and is altogether unacceptable to Muslim India.

It further records it emphatic view that while the declaration dated the 18th of October 1939, made by the Viceroy on behalf of His Majesty's Government is reassuring in so far as it declares that the policy and plan on which the Government of India Act, 1935, is based will be reconsidered in consultation with the various parties, interests and communities in India, Muslim India will not be satisfied unless the whole constitutional plan is reconsidered *de novo* and that no revised plan would be acceptable to the Muslims unless it is framed with their approval and consent.

Resolved that it is the considered view of this Session of the All-India Muslim League that no constitutional plan would be workable in this country or acceptable to the Muslims unless it is designed on the following basic principle, *viz*. that geographically contiguous units are demarcated into regions which should be so constituted, with such territorial readjustments as may be necessary, that the areas in which the Muslims are numerically in a majority as in the North-Western and Eastern zones of India should be grouped to constitute 'Independent States' in which the constituent units shall be autonomous and sovereign.

That adequate, effective and mandatory safeguards should be specially provided in the constitution for minorities in these units and in the regions for the protection of their religious, cultural, economic, political, administrative and other rights and interests in consultation with them and in other parts of India where the Mussalmans are in a minority adequate, effective and mandatory safeguards shall be specifically provided in the constitution for them and other minorities for the protection of their religious, cultural, economic, political, administrative and other rights and interests in consultation with them.

This Session further authorizes the Working Committee to frame a scheme of constitution in accordance with these basic principles, providing for the assumption finally by the respective regions of all powers such as defence, external affairs, communications, customs and such other matters as may be necessary.

Source: Resolutions of All-India Muslim League from December 1938 to March 1940, published by (Nawabzada) Liaquat Ali Khan, M.A. (Oxon), M.L.A. (US), Barrister-at-Law, Honorary Secretary, All-India Muslim League, Delhi, pp. 47–8.

Appendix 7

Stafford Cripps' Offer, 1942

The conclusions of the British War Cabinet as set out below are those which Sir Stafford Cripps has taken with him for discussion with the Indian Leaders and the question as to whether they will be implemented will depend upon the outcome of these discussions which are now taking place.

His Majesty's Government, having considered the anxieties expressed in this country and in India as to the fulfillment of the promises made in regard to the future of India, have decided to lay down in precise and clear terms the steps which they propose shall be taken for the earliest possible realization of self-government in India. The object is the creation of a new Indian Union which shall constitute a Dominion, associated with the United Kingdom and the other Dominions by a common allegiance to the Crown, but equal to them in every respect, in no way subordinate in any aspect of its domestic or external affairs.

His Majesty's Government therefore make the following declaration:-

(a) Immediately upon the cessation of hostilities, steps shall be taken to set up in India, in the manner described hereafter, an elected body charged with the task of framing a new Constitution for India.

(b) Provision shall be made, as set out below, for the participation of the Indian States in the constitution making body.

(c) His Majesty's Government undertake to accept and implement forthwith the Constitution so framed subject only to:-
(i) the right of any Province of British India that is not prepared to accept the new Constitution to retain its present constitutional position, provision being made for its subsequent accession if it so decides.

With such non-acceding provinces, should they so desire. His Majesty's Government will be prepared to agree upon a new Constitution, giving them the same full status as Indian Union, and arrived at by a procedure analogous to that here laid down.

(ii) the signing of a Treaty which shall be negotiated between His Majesty's Government and the constitution-making body. This Treaty will cover all necessary matters arising out of the complete transfer of responsibility from British to Indian hands; it will make provision, in accordance with the under takings given by His Majesty's Government, for the protection of racial and religious minorities; but will not impose any restriction on the power of the Indian Union to decide in the future its relationship to the other Member States of the British Commonwealth.

Whether or not an Indian State elects to adhere to the Constitution, it will be necessary to negotiate a revision of its Treaty arrangements, so far as this may be required in the new situation.

(d) the constitution-making body shall be composed as follows, unless the leaders of Indian opinion in the principal communities agree upon some other form before the end of hostilities:-

Immediately upon the result being known of the provincial elections which will be necessary at the end of hostilities, the entire membership of the Lower House of the Provincial Legislatures shall, as a single electoral college, proceed to the election of the constitution-making body by the system of proportional representation. This new body shall be in number about one tenth of the number of the electoral college. Indian States shall be invited to appoint representatives in the same proportion to their total population as in the case of the representatives of British India as a whole, and with the same powers as the British Indian members.

(e) During the critical period which now faces India and until the new Constitution can be framed His Majesty's Government must inevitably bear the responsibility for and retain control and direction of the defence of India as part of their world war effort, but the task of organizing to the full the military, moral and material resources of India must be the responsibility of the Government of India with the co-operation of the peoples of India. His Majesty's Government desire and invite the immediate and effective participation of the leaders of the principal sections of the Indian people in the counsels of their country, of the Commonwealth and of the United Nations. Thus they will be enabled to give their active and constructive help in the discharge of a task which is vital and essential for the future freedom of India.

Sources: Lord Privy Seals' Mission, Cmd. 6350 (1942), 4-5. Christine E. Dobbin, *Basic Documents in the Development and Modern India and Pakistan, 1835–1947*, London, New York, Van Nostrand Reinhold Company, 1970, pp 139

Appendix 8

The C.R. Formula, 1944

The basis of The Gandhi-Jinnah talks was the offer made by Mr Rajagopalachariar to Mr Jinnah in April 1944 which, according to the somewhat incredible* story told by Mr Rajagopalachariar, was discussed by him with Mr Gandhi in March 1943 when he (Mr Gandhi) was fasting in goal and to which Mr Gandhi had given his full approval. The following is the text of Mr Rajagopalachariar's formula popularly spoken of as the C. R. Formula:

(1) Subject to the terms set out below as regards the constitution for Free India, the Muslim League endorses the Indian demand for Independence and will co-operate with the Congress in the formation of a provisional interim government for the transitional period.

(2) After the termination of the war, a commission shall be appointed for demarcating contiguous districts in the north-west and east of India, wherein the Muslim population is in absolute majority. In the areas thus demarcated, a plebiscite of all the inhabitants held on the basis of adult suffrage or other practicable franchise shall ultimately decide the issue of separation from Hindustan. If the majority decide in favour of forming a sovereign State separate from Hindustan, such decision shall be given effect to, without prejudice to the right of districts on the border to choose to join either State.

(3) It will be open to all parties to advocate their points of view before the plebiscite is held.

(4) In the event of separation, mutual agreements shall be entered into for safeguarding defence, and commerce and communications and for other essential purposes.

(5) Any transfer of population shall only be on an absolutely voluntary basis.

(6) These terms shall be binding only in case of transfer by Britain of full power and responsibility for the governance of India.

Source: B.R. Ambedkar, *Pakistan or the Partition of India*, Thacker & Co. Ltd., Bombay, 1946, p. 408.

---

*The formula was discussed with Mr Gandhi in March 1943 but was not communicated to Mr Jinnah till April 1944.

Appendix 9

Jinnah's Offer of 12 May 1946

(Copies sent to Cabinet Mission and Congress.)

PRINCIPLES TO BE AGREED TO AS OUR OFFER

1. The six Muslim Provinces (Punjab, NWFP, Baluchistan, Sindh, Bengal and Assam) shall be grouped together as one group and will deal with all other subjects and matters except Foreign Affairs, Defence and Communications necessary for Defence, which may be dealt with by the Constitution-making bodies of the two groups of Provinces—Muslim Provinces (hereinafter named Pakistan Group) and Hindu Province—sitting together.
2. There shall be a separate Constitution-making body for the six Muslim Provinces named above, which will frame Constitutions for the Group and the Provinces in the Group and will determine the list of subjects that shall be provincial and Central of the (Pakistan Federation) with residuary sovereign powers vesting in the Provinces.
3. The method of election of the representatives to the Constitution-making body will be such as would secure proper representation to the various communities in proportion to their population in each Province of the Pakistan Group.
4. After the Constitutions of the Pakistan Federal Government and the Provinces are finally framed by the Constitution-making body it will be open to any Province of the Group to decide to opt out of its Group, provided the wishes of the people of that Province are ascertained by a referendum to opt out or not.
5. It must be open to discussion in the joint Constitution-making body as to whether the Union will have a Legislature or not. The method of providing the Union with finance should also be left for decision of the joint meeting of the two Constitution-making bodies, but in no event shall it be by means of taxation.
6. There should be parity of representation between the two Groups of Provinces in the Union Executive and the Legislature, if any.
7. No major point in the Union Constitution which affects the communal issue shall be deemed to be passed in the joint Constitution-making body, unless the majority of the members of the Constitution-making body, of the Hindu Provinces and the majority of the members of the Constitution-making body of the Pakistan Group, present and voting, are separately in its favour.

8. No decision, legislative, executive or administrative, shall be taken by the Union in regard to any matter of controversial nature, except by a majority of three-fourths.
9. In Group and Provincial Constitutions fundamental rights and safeguards concerning religion, culture and other matters affecting the different communities will be provided for.
10. The Constitution of the Union shall contain a provision whereby any Province can, by a majority vote of its Legislative Assembly, call for reconsideration of the terms of the Constitution, and will have the liberty to secede from the Union at any time after an initial period of ten years.

These are the principles of our offer for a peaceful and amicable settlement and this offer stands in its entirety and all matters mentioned herein are interdependent.

Source: *Papers Relating to the Cabinet Mission and India, 1946*, Government of India Press, 1946, pp. 20–3.

Appendix 10

The Congress' Offer of 12 May 1946

1. The Constituent Assembly to be formed as follows:-

    (i) Representatives shall be elected by each Provincial Assembly by Proportional representation (single transferable vote). The number so elected should be one-fifth of the number of members of the Assembly and they may be members of the Assembly or others.//
    (ii) Representatives from the States on the basis of their population in proportion to the representation from British India. How these representatives are to be chosen is to be considered later.

2. The Constituent Assembly shall draw up a constitution for the Federal Union. This shall consist of an All-India Federal Government and Legislature dealing with Foreign Affairs, Defence, Communications, Fundamental Rights, Currency, Customs and Planning as well as such other subjects as, on closer scrutiny may be found to be intimately allied to them. The Federal Union will have necessary powers to obtain for itself the finances it requires for these subjects and the power to raise revenues in its own right. The Union must also have power to take remedial action in cases of the constitution and in grave public emergencies.

3. All the remaining powers shall vest in the Provinces or Units.

4. Groups of Provinces may be formed and such groups may determine the Provincial subjects which they desire to take in common.

5. After the Constituent Assembly has decided the constitution for the All-India Federal Union as laid down in paragraph 2 above, the representatives of the Provinces may form groups to decide the Provincial constitutions for their group and if they wish, a group constitution.

6. No major point in the All-India Federal Constitution which affects the communal issue shall be deemed to be passed by the Constituent Assembly unless a majority of the members of the community or communities concerned present in Assembly and voting are separately in its favour. Provided that in case there is not agreement on any such issue, it will be referred to arbitration. In case of doubt as to whether any point is a major communal issue, the Speaker will decide or, if so desired, it may be referred to the Federal Court.

7. In the event of a dispute arising in the process of constitution-making the specific issue shall be referred to arbitration.

8. The constitution should provide machinery for its revision at any time subject to such checks as may be desired. If so desired, it may be

specifically stated that this whole constitution may be reconsidered after ten years.

Note by the Congress on the Principles to be Agreed Upon as Suggested on Behalf of the Muslim League, Dated 12 May 1946

The approach of the Muslim League is so different from that of the Congress in regard to these matters that it is a little difficult to deal with each point separately without reference to the rest. The picture as envisaged by the Congress is briefly given in a separate note. From consideration of this note and the Muslim League's proposals the difficulties and the possible agreement will become obvious.

The Muslim League's proposals are dealt with below briefly:-

(1) We suggest that the proper procedure is for one Constitution-making body or Constituent Assembly to meet for the whole of India and later for groups to be formed if so desired by the Provinces concerned. The matter should be left to the Provinces and if they wish to function as a group they are at liberty to do so and to frame their own constitution for the purpose.

In any event Assam has obviously no place in the group mentioned, and the North-West Frontier Province, as the elections show is not in favour of this proposal.

(2) We have agreed to residuary powers, apart from the central subject vesting in the Provinces. They can make such use of them as they like and, as has been stated above, function as a group. What the ultimate nature of such group may be cannot be determined at this stage and should be left to the representatives of the Provinces concerned.

(3) We have suggested that the most suitable method of election would be by single transferable vote. This would give proper representation to the various communities in proportion to their present representation in the legislatures. The population proportion is taken, we have no particular objection, but this would lead to difficulties in all the Provinces where there is weightage in favour of certain communities. The principal approved of would necessarily apply to all the Provinces.

(4) There is no necessity for opting out of a Province from its group as the previous consent of the Provinces is necessary for joining the group.

(5) We consider it essential that the Federal Union should have a Legislature. We consider it essential that the Union should have power to raise its own revenue.

(6 and 7). We are entirely opposed to parity of representation as between groups of Provinces in the Union executive or legislature. We think that the provision to the effect that no major communal issue in the Union constitution shall be deemed to be passed by the Constituent Assembly unless a majority of the members of the community or communities concerned present and voting in the Constituent Assembly are separately in its favour, is a sufficient and ample safeguard of all minorities. We have suggested something wider and including of communities than has been proposed else where. This may give rise to some difficulties in regard to small communities, but all such difficulties can be got over with reference to arbitration. We are prepared to consider the method of giving effect to this principle so as to make it more feasible.

Source: *Papers Relating to the Cabinet Mission and India, 1946*, Government of India Press, 1946, pp. 20–3.

Appendix 11

The Cabinet Mission's Plan of 16 May 1946

1. On the 15th March last just before the dispatch of the Cabinet Mission to India, Mr Attlee, the British Prime Minister, used these words:–

> 'My colleagues are going to India with the intention of using their utmost endeavors to help her to attain her freedom as speedily and fully as possible. What form of Government is to replace the present regime is for India to decide; but our desire is to help her to set up forth with the machinery for making that decision...
>
> 'I hope that the Indian people may elect to remain within the British Commonwealth. I am certain that she will find great advantages in doing so...
>
> 'But if she does so elect, it must be by her own free will. The British Commonwealth and Empire is not bound together by chains of external compulsion. It is a free association of free peoples. If, on the other hand, she elects for independence, in our view she has a right to do so. It will be for us to help to make the transition as smooth and easy as possible.'

2. Charged in these historic words, we—the Cabinet Ministers and the Viceroy—have done our utmost to assist the two main political parties to reach agreement upon the fundamental issue of the unity or division of India. After prolonged discussions in New Delhi we succeeded in bringing the Congress and the Muslim League together in conference at Simla. There was a full exchange of views and both parties were prepared to make considerable concessions in order to try to reach a settlement, but it ultimately proved impossible to close the remainder of the gap between the parties and so no agreement could be concluded. Since no agreement has been reached, we feel that it is our duty to put forward what we consider are the best arrangements possible to ensure a speedy setting up of the new constitution. This statement is made with the full approval of His Majesty's Government in the United Kingdom.

3. We have accordingly decided that immediate arrangements should be made whereby Indians may decide the future constitution of India, and an interim Government may be set up at once to carry on the administration of British India until such time as a new constitution can be brought into being. We have endeavored to be just to the smaller as well as to the larger sections of the people; and to recommend a solution which will lead to a practicable way of governing the India of the future and will give a sound basis for defence and a good opportunity for progress in the social, political and economic field.

4. It is not intended in this statement to review the voluminous evidence which has been submitted to the Mission; but it is right that we should state that it has shown an almost universal desire, outside the supporters of the Muslim League, for the unity of India.

5. This consideration did not, however, deter us from examining closely and impartially the possibility of a partition of India; since we were greatly impressed by the very genuine and acute anxiety of the Muslims lest they should find themselves subjected to a perpetual Hindu-majority rule. This feeling has become so strong and widespread amongst the Muslims that it cannot be allayed by mere paper safeguards. If there is to be internal peace in India it must be secured by measures which will assure to the Muslims a control in all matters vital to their culture, religion, and economic or other interests.

6. We therefore examined in the first instance the question of a separate and fully independent sovereign state of Pakistan as claimed by the Muslim League. Such a Pakistan would comprise two areas one in the North-West consisting of the provinces of the Punjab, Sindh, North-West Frontier, and British Baluchistan; the other in the North-East consisting of the provinces of Bengal and Assam. The League were prepared to consider adjustment of boundaries at a later state, but insisted that the principle of Pakistan should first be acknowledged. The argument for a separate state of Pakistan was based, first, upon the right of the Muslim majority to decide their method of government according to their wishes, and, secondly, upon the necessity to include substantial areas in which Muslims are in a minority, in order to make Pakistan administratively and economically workable.

The size of the non-Muslim minorities in a Pakistan comprising the whole of the six provinces enumerated above would be very considerable as the following figures* show:-

	Muslim	Non-Muslim
North-Western Area:		
Punjab	16,217,242	12,201,577
North-West Frontier Province	2,788,797	249,270
Sind	3,208,325	1,326,683
British Baluchistan	438,930	62,701
	22,653,294	13,840,231
	62.07 per cent	37.93 per cent
North-Eastern Area:		
Bengal	33,005,434	27,301,091
Assam	3,442,479	6,762,254
	36,447,913	34,063,345
	51.69 per cent	48.31 per cent

*All population figures in this statement are from the most recent census taken in 1941.

The Muslim minorities in the remainder of British India number some 20 million dispersed amongst a total population of 188 million.

These figures show that the setting up of a separate sovereign state of Pakistan on the lines claimed by the Muslim League would not solve the communal minority problem; nor can we see any justification for including within a sovereign Pakistan those districts of the Punjab and of Bengal and Assam in which the population is predominantly non-Muslim. Every argument that can be used in favour of Pakistan can equally, in our view, be used in favour of the exclusion of the non-Muslim areas from Pakistan. This point would particularly affect the position of the Sikhs.

7. We, therefore, considered whether a smaller sovereign Pakistan confined to the Muslim majority areas alone might be a possible basis of compromise. Such a Pakistan is regarded by the Muslim League as quite impracticable because it would entail the exclusion from Pakistan of (a) the whole of the Ambala and Jullundur divisions in the Punjab; (b) the whole of Assam except the district of Sylhet; and (c) a large part of Western Bengal, including Calcutta, in which city the percentage of the Muslim population is 23.6 per cent. We ourselves are also convinced that any solution which involves a radical partition of the Punjab and Bengal, as this would do, would be contrary to the wishes and interests of a very large proportion of the inhabitants of these provinces. Bengal and the Punjab each has its own common language and a long history and tradition. Moreover, any division of the Punjab would of necessity divide the Sikhs, leaving substantial bodies of Sikhs on both sides of the boundary. We have therefore been forced to the conclusion that neither a larger nor a smaller sovereign state of Pakistan would provide an acceptable solution for the communal problem.

8. Apart from the great force of the foregoing arguments there are weighty administrative, economic and military considerations. The whole of the transportation and postal and telegraph systems of India have been established on the basis of a united India. To disintegrate them would gravely injure both parts of India. The case for a united defence is even stronger. The Indian Armed Forces have been built up as a whole for the defence of India as a whole, and to break them in two would inflict a deadly blow on the long traditions and high degree of efficiency of the Indian Army and would entail the gravest dangers. The Indian Navy and Indian Air Force would become much less effective. The two sections of the suggested Pakistan contain the two most vulnerable frontiers in India and for successful defence in depth the area of Pakistan would be insufficient.

9. A further consideration of importance is the greater difficulty which the Indian States would find in associating themselves with a divided British India.

10. Finally, there is the geographical fact that the two halves of the proposed Pakistan state are separated by some seven hundred miles and the

communications between them both in war and peace would be dependent on the goodwill of Hindustan.

11. We are therefore unable to advise the British Government that the power which at present resides in British hands should be handed over to two entirely separate sovereign states.

12. This decision does not however, blind us to the very real Muslim apprehensions that their culture and political and social life might become submerged in a purely unitary India, in which the Hindus with their greatly superior numbers must be a dominating element. To meet this the Congress have put forward a scheme under which provinces would have full autonomy subject only to a minimum of central subjects, such as foreign affairs, defence and communications.

Under this scheme provinces, if they wished to take part in economic and administrative planning on a large scale, could cede to the centre optional subjects addition to the compulsory ones mentioned above.

13. Such a scheme would, in our view, present considerable constitutional advantages and anomalies. It would be very difficult to work a central executive and legislature in which some minister, who dealt with compulsory subjects, were responsible to the whole of India while other ministers, who dealt with optional subjects, would be responsible only to those provinces who had elected to act together in respect of such subjects. This difficulty would be accentuated in the central legislature, where it would be necessary to exclude certain members from speaking and voting when subjects with which their provinces were not concerned were under discussion, Apart from the difficulty of working such a scheme, we do not consider that it would be fair to deny to other provinces, which did not desire to take the constitutional subjects at the centre, the right to form themselves into a group for a similar purpose. This would indeed be no more than the exercise of their autonomous powers in a particular way.

14. Before putting forward our recommendations we turn to deal with the relationship of the Indian States to British India. It is quite clear that with the attainment of independence by British India, whether inside or outside the British commonwealth, the relationship which has hitherto existed between the Rules of the States and the British Crown will no longer be possible. Paramountcy can neither be retained by the British Crown nor transferred to the new government. This fact has been fully recognized by those whom we interviewed from the States. They have at the same time assured us that the States are ready and willing to co-operate in the—development of India. The precise form which their co-operation will take must be a matter for negotiation during the building up of the new constitutional structure and it by no means follows that it will be identical for all the States. We have not therefore dealt with the States in the same detail as the provinces of British India in the paragraphs which follow.

15. We now indicate the nature of a solution which in our view would be just to the essential claims of all parties and would at the same time be most likely to bring about a stable and practicable form of constitution for All-India.

We recommend that the constitution should take the following basic form:-

(1) There should be a Union of India, embracing both British India and the State which should deal with the following subjects: foreign affairs, defence, and communications, and should have the powers necessary to raise the finances required for the above subjects.

(2) The Union should have an executive and a legislature constituted from British India and States representatives. Any question raising a major communal issue in the legislature should require for its decision a majority of the representatives present and voting of each of the two major communities as well as a majority of all the members present and voting.

(3) All subjects other than the Union subjects and all residuary powers should vest in the provinces.

(4) The States will retain all subjects and powers other than those ceded to the Union.

(5) Provinces should be free to form groups with executives and legislatures, and each group could determine the provincial subjects to be taken in common.

(6) The constitutions of the Union and of the groups should contain a provision whereby any province could by a majority vote of its legislative assembly call for a reconsideration of the terms of the constitution after an initial period of ten years and at ten-yearly intervals thereafter.

16. It is not our object to lay out the details of a constitution on the above programme but to set in motion machinery whereby a constitution can be settled by Indians for Indians.

It has been necessary, however, for us to make this recommendation as to the broad basis of the future constitution because it became clear to us in the course of our negotiations that not until that had been done was there any hope of getting the two major communities to join in the setting up of the constitution-making machinery.

17. We now indicate the constitution-making machinery which we propose should be brought into being forthwith in order to enable a new constitution to be worked out.

18. In forming any assembly to decide a new constitutional structure the first problem is to obtain as broad-based and accurate a representation of the whole population as is possible. The most satisfactory method obviously would be by election based on adult franchise, but any attempt to introduce such a

step now would lead to a wholly unacceptable delay in the formulation of the new constitution. The only practicable course is to utilize the recently elected Provincial Legislative Assemblies as electing bodies. There are, however, two factors in their composition which make this difficult. First, the numerical strengths of Provincial Legislative Assemblies do not bear the same proportion to the total population in each province. Thus, Assam, with a population of 10 million has a Legislative Assembly of 108 members, while Bengal, with a population six times as large, has an Assembly of only 250. Secondly, owing to the weightage given to minorities by the Communal Award, the strengths of the several communities in each Provincial Legislative Assembly are not in proportion to their numbers in the province. Thus the number of seats reserved for Moslems in the Bengal Legislative Assembly is only 48 per cent of total although they form 55 per cent of the provincial population. After a most careful consideration of the various methods by which these points might be corrected. We have come to the conclusion that the fairest and most practicable plant would be...

(a) to allot to each province a total number of seats proportional to its population, roughly in the ratio of one to a million, as the nearest substitute for representation by adult suffrage.
(b) to divide this provincial allocation of seats between the main communities in each province in proportion to their population.
(c) to provide that the representatives allocated to each community in a province shall be elected by members of that community in its Legislative Assembly.

We think that for these purposes it is sufficient to recognize only three main communities in India, General, Moslem and Sikh, the 'General' Community including all persons who are not Moslems or Sikhs. As smaller minorities would upon a population basis have little or no representation, since they would lose the weightage which assures them seats in Provincial Legislatures, we have made the arrangements set out in paragraph 20 below to give them a full representation upon all matters of special interest to minorities.

19. (i) We therefore propose that there shall be elected by each Provincial Legislative Assembly the following numbers of representatives, each part of the Legislative Assembly (General, Moslem or Sikh) electing its own representatives by the method of proportional representation with single transferable vote:-

APPENDIX 11

Table of Representation

Section A

Province	General	Muslim	Total
Madras	45	4	49
Bombay	19	2	21
United Provinces	47	8	55
Bihar	31	5	36
Central Provinces	16	1	17
Orissa	9	0	9
Total	167	20	187

Section B

Province	General	Muslim	Sikh	Total
Punjab	8	16	4	28
North-West Frontier Province	0	3	0	3
Sind	1	3	0	4
Total	9	22	4	35

Section C

Province	General	Muslim	Total
Bengal	27	33	60
Assam	7	3	10
Total	34	36	70
Total for British India	292		
Maximum for Indian States	93		
Total	385		

Note: In order to represent the Chief Commissioners' Provinces there will be added to Section A the member representing Delhi in the Central Legislative Assembly, the member representing Ajmer-Merwara in the Central Legislative Assembly and a representative to be elected by the Coorg Legislative Council.

To Section B will be added a representative of British Baluchistan.

(ii) It is the intention that the States would be given in the final Constituent Assembly appropriate representation which would not, on the basis of the calculation of population adopted for British India, exceed 93; but the method of selection will have to be determined by consultation. The States would in the preliminary stage be represented by a negotiating committee.

(iii) Representatives thus chosen shall meet at New Delhi as soon as possible.

(iv) A preliminary meeting will be held at which the general order of business will be decided, a chairman and other officers elected and an Advisory Committee (see paragraph 20 below) on rights of citizens, minorities and tribal and excluded areas set up. Thereafter the provincial representatives will divided up into three sections shown under A, B and C in the Table of Representation in sub-paragraph (i) of this paragraph.

(v) These sections shall proceed to settle provincial constitutions for the provinces included in each section and shall also decide whether any group constitution shall be set up for those provinces and if so with what provincial subjects the group should deal. Provinces should have power to opt out of groups in accordance with the provisions of sub-clause (viii) below.

(vi) The representatives of the sections and the Indian States shall reassemble for the purpose of setting the Union constitution.

(vii) In the Union Constituent Assembly resolution varying the provisions of paragraph 15 above or raising any major communal issue shall require a majority of the representatives present and voting of each of the two major communities. The Chairman of the Assembly shall decide which, if any, resolution raise major communal issues and shall, if so requested by majority of the representatives of either of the major communities, consult the Federal Court before giving his decision.

(viii) As soon as the new constitutional arrangements have come into operation it shall be open to any province to elect to come out of any group in which it has been placed. Such a decision shall be taken by the legislature of the province after the first general election under the new constitution.

20. The Advisory Committee on the rights of citizens, minorities and tribal and excluded areas will contain due representation of the interests affected and their function will be to report to the Union Constituent Assembly upon the list of fundamental rights, clauses for protecting minorities, and a scheme for the administration, of tribal and excluded areas, and to advise whether these rights should be incorporated, in the provincial, the group or the Union constitutions.

21. His Excellency the Viceroy will forthwith request the provincial legislatures to proceed with the election of their representatives and the States to set up a negotiating committee.

It is hoped that the process of constitution-making can proceed as rapidly as the complexities of the task permit so that the interim period may be as short as possible.

22. It will be necessary to negotiate a treaty between the Union Constituent Assembly and the United Kingdom to provide for certain matters arising out of the transfer of power.

23. While the constitution-making proceeds the administration of India has to be carried on. We attach the greatest importance therefore to the setting up at once of an interim Government having the support of the major political parties. It is essential during the interim period that there should be the maximum of cooperation in carrying through the difficult tasks that face the Government of India. Besides the heavy tasks of day-to-day administration, there is the grave danger of famine to be countered, there are decisions to be taken in many matters of post-war development which will have a far-reaching effects on India's future and there are important international conferences in which India has to be represented. For all these purposes a government having popular support is necessary. The Viceroy has already started discussions to this end and hopes soon to form an interim Government in which all the portfolios, including that of War Member, will be held by Indian leaders having the full confidence of the people. The British Government recognizing the significance of the changes, will give the fullest measure of co-operation to the Government so formed in the accomplishment of its tasks of administration and in bringing about as rapid and smooth a transition as possible.

24. To the leaders and people of India, who now have the opportunity of complete independence, we would finally say this. We and our Government and countrymen hope that it would be possible for the Indian people themselves to agree upon the method of framing the new Constitution under which they will live. Despite the labours which we have shared with the Indian parties and the exercise of much patience and goodwill by all, this has not been possible. We, therefore, now lay before you proposals which, after listening, to all sides and after much earnest thought, we trust will enable you to attain your independence in the shortest time and with the least danger of internal disturbance and conflict. These proposals may not, of course, completely satisfy all parties, but you will recognize with us that, at this supreme moment in Indian history, statesmanship demands mutual accommodation and we ask you to consider the alternative to the acceptance of these proposals. After all the efforts which we and the Indian parties have made together for agreement, we must state that, in our view, there is small hope of a peaceful settlement by the agreement of the Indian parties alone. The alternative would, therefore, be a grave danger of violence, chaos and even civil war. The gravity and duration of such a disturbance cannot be foreseen, but it is certain that it would be a terrible disaster for many millions of men, women and children. This is a possibility which must be regarded with equal abhorrence by the Indian people, our own countrymen and the world as a whole. We therefore lay these proposals

before you in the profound hope that they will be accepted and operated by you in the spirit of accommodation and goodwill in which they are offered. We appeal to all who have the future good of India at heart to extend their vision beyond their own community or interest to the interests of the whole 400 millions of Indian people.

We hope that the new independent India may choose to be a member of the British Commonwealth. We hope in any event, that you will remain in close and friendly association with our people. But these are matters for your own free choice. Whatever that choice may be, we look forward with you to your ever-increasing prosperity among the greatest nations of the world and to a future even more glorious than your past.

Source: *Papers Relating to the Cabinet Mission and India, 1946*, Government of India Press, 1946, pp. 1–7.

Appendix 12

Statement Made by Mr M.A. Jinnah, President of the All-India Muslim League, 22 May 1946

I have now before me the statement of the British Cabinet Delegation and His Excellency the Viceroy dated 15th of May, 1946, issued at Delhi. Before I deal with it I should like to give a background of the discussions that took place at Simla from the 5th of May onwards till the Conference was declared concluded and its breakdown announced in the official Communiqué dated 12th May, 1946.

We met in the conference on the 5th of May to consider the formula embodied in the letter of the Secretary of State for India, dated 27th April, 1946, inviting the League representatives.

The formula was as follows:-

'A Union Government dealing with the following subjects: Foreign Affairs, Defence and Communications. There will be two groups of provinces, the one of the predominantly Hindu provinces and the other of the predominantly Muslim provinces, dealing with all other subjects which the provinces in the respective groups desire to be dealt with in common. The provincial governments will deal with all other subjects and will have all the residuary sovereign rights.'

The Muslim League position was that:

Firstly, the zones comprising Bengal and Assam in the North East and Punjab, N. W. F. P., Sind and Baluchistan in the North-West of India constituted Pakistan zones and should be constituted as a sovereign independent State; and that an unequivocal undertaking be given to implement the establishment of Pakistan without delay;

Secondly, that separate constitution-making bodies be set up by the peoples of Pakistan and Hindustan for the purpose of framing their respective constitutions;

Thirdly, that minorities in Pakistan and Hindustan be provided with safeguards on the lines of the Lahore Resolution;

Fourthly, that the acceptance of the League demand and its implementation without delay were a sine qua non for the League co-operation and participation in the formation of an interim Government at the Centre;

Fifthly, it gave a warning to the British Government against any attempt to impose a Federal constitution on a united India basis, or forcing any interim arrangement at the Centre contrary to the League demand; and that Muslim India would resist if any attempt to impose it were made. Besides, such an attempt would be the grossest breach of faith of the declaration of His Majesty's Government made in August, 1940, with the approval of the British Parliament and subsequent announcements by the Secretary of State for India and other responsible British statesmen from time to time, reaffirming the August Declaration.

'We have never contemplated that acceptance by the Muslim League and the Congress of our invitation would imply as a preliminary condition full approval by them of the terms set out in my letter. These terms are our proposed basis for a settlement and what we have asked the Muslim League Working Committee to do is to agree to send its representatives to meet ourselves and representatives of the Congress in order to discuss it.'

The Congress position in reply to the invitation was stated in their letter of 28th April that a strong Federal Government at the Centre with present provinces as federating units be established and they laid down that Foreign Affairs, Defence, Currency, Customs, Tariffs 'and such other subjects as may be found on closer scrutiny to be intimately allied to them' should vest in the Central Federal Government. They negatived the idea of grouping of provinces. However, they also agreed to participate in the Conference to discuss the formula of the Cabinet Delegation.

After days of discussion no appreciable progress was made and, finally, I was asked to give our minimum terms in writing. Consequently we embodied certain fundamental principles of our terms in writing as an offer to the Congress, in the earnest desire for a peaceful and amicable settlement and for the speedy attainment of freedom and independence of the peoples of India. It was communicated to the Congress on the 12th of May and a copy of it was sent to the Cabinet Delegation at the same time.

The following were the terms of the offer made by the Muslim League Delegation:

(1) The six Muslim provinces (Punjab, N. W. F. P., Baluchistan, Sind, Bengal and Assam) shall be grouped together as one group and will deal with all other subjects and matters except foreign Affairs, Defence and Communications necessary for Defence, which may be dealt with by the Constitution-making bodies of the two groups of provinces—Muslim province (hereinafter named Pakistan Group) and Hindu Provinces—sitting together.

(2) There shall be a separate Constitution-making body for the six Muslim provinces named above, which will frame Constitutions for the (Group and the provinces in the Group and will determine the list of subjects that shall be Provincial and Central (of the Pakistan Federation) with residuary sovereign powers vesting in the provinces.

(3) The method of election of the representatives to the Constitution-making body will be such as would secure proper representation to the various communities in proportion to their population in each province of the Pakistan Group.

(4) After the Constitution of the Pakistan Federal Government and the provinces are finally framed by the Constitution-making body, it will be open

to any province of the Group to decide to opt out of its Group, provided the wishes of the people of that province are ascertained by a referendum to opt out or not.

(5) It must be open to discussion in the joint Constitution-making body as to whether the Union will have a Legislature or not. The method of providing the Union with finance should also be left for decision of the joint meeting of the two Constitution-making bodies but in no event shall it be by means of taxation.

(6) There shall be parity of representation between the two Groups of provinces in the Union Executive and the Legislature, if any.

(7) No major point in the Union Constitution which affects the communal issue shall be deemed to be passed in the joint Constitution-making body, unless the majority of the members of the Constitution-making body of the Hindu provinces and the majority of the members of the Constitution-making body of the Pakistan Group, present and voting, are separately in its favour.

(8) No decision, legislative, executive or administrative, shall be taken by the Union in regard to any matter of controversial nature, except by a majority of three fourths.

(9) In Group and Provincial Constitutions fundamental rights and safeguards concerning religion, culture and other matters affecting the different communities will be provided for.

(10) The Constitution of the Union shall contain a provision whereby any province can, by a majority vote of its Legislative Assembly, call for reconsideration of the terms of the Constitution and will have the liberty to secede from the Union at any time after an initial period of ten years.

The crux of our offer, as it will appear from its text was, *inter alia*, that the six Muslim provinces should be grouped together as Pakistan Group and the remaining as Hindustan Group and on the basis of two Federations we were willing to consider the Union or Confederation strictly confined to three subjects only, i.e. Foreign Affairs, Defence and Communications necessary for Defence, which the two sovereign Federations would voluntarily delegate to the Confederation. All the remaining subjects and the residue were to remain vested in the two Federations and the provinces respectively. This was intended to provide for a transitional period as after an initial period of ten years we were free to secede from the Union. But, unfortunately, this most conciliatory and reasonable offer was in all its fundamentals not accepted by the Congress as will appear from their reply to our offer. On the contrary, their final suggestions were the same as regards the subjects to be vested with the Centre, as they had been before the Congress entered the Conference; and they made one more drastic suggestion for our acceptance that the Centre 'must also have power to take remedial action in cases of breakdown of the constitution and in grave public emergencies'. This was stated in their reply dated 12th May, 1946, which was communicated to us.

At this stage the Conference broke down and we were informed that the British Cabinet Delegation would issue their statement which is now before the public.

To begin with, the statement is cryptic with several lacunas and the operative part of it is comprised of a few short paragraphs to which I shall refer later.

I regret that the Mission should have negatived the Muslim demand for the establishment of a complete sovereign State of Pakistan, which we still hold is the only solution of the constitutional problem of India and which alone can secure stable governments and lead to the happiness and welfare, not only of the two major communities, but of all the peoples of this subcontinent. It is all the more regrettable that the Mission should have thought fit to advance commonplace and exploded arguments against Pakistan and resorted to special pleadings, couched in a deplorable language, which is calculated to hurt the feelings of Muslim India. It seems that this was done by the Mission simply to appease and placate the Congress, because when they come to face the realities, they themselves have made the following pronouncement embodied in the paragraph 5 of the statement which says:-

> 'This consideration did not, however, deter us from examining closely and impartially the possibility of a partition of India; since we were greatly impressed by the very genuine and acute anxiety of the Muslims lest they should find themselves subjected to a perpetual Hindu majority rule.
>
> 'This feeling has become so strong and widespread amongst the Muslims that it cannot be allayed by mere paper safeguards. If there is to be internal peace in India it must be secured by measures which will assure to the Muslims a control in all matters vital to their culture, religion and economic or other interests.'

And again in paragraph 12:

> 'This decision does not, however, blind us to the very real Muslim apprehensions that their culture and political and social life might become submerged in a purely unitary India, in which the Hindus with their greatly superior numbers must be a dominating element.'

And now what recommendations have they made to effectively secure the object in view and in the light of the very clear and emphatic conclusion they arrived at in paragraph 12 of the statement?

I shall now deal with some of the important points in the operative part of the statement:-

(1) They have divided Pakistan into two what they call Section B (for the North-Western Zone) and Section C (for the North-Eastern Zone).
(2) Instead of two constitution-making bodies only one Constitution-making body is devised with three sections A, B and C.

APPENDIX 12

(3) They lay down that:
'There should be a Union of India, embracing both British India and the States, which should deal with the following subjects: Foreign Affairs, Defence and Communications; and should have the powers necessary to raise the finances required for the above subjects.'

There is no indication at all that the Communications would be restricted to what is necessary for Defence nor is there any indication as to how this Union will be empowered to raise finances required for these three subjects, while our view was that finances should be raised only by contribution and not by taxation.

(4) It is lad down that:
'The Union should have an Executive and a Legislature constituted from British Indian and States representatives. Any question raising a major communal issue in the Legislature should require for its decision a majority of the representatives present and voting of each of the two major communities as well as a majority of all the members present and voting.'

While our view was:
(a) that there should be no Legislature for the Union, but the question should be left to Constituent Assembly to decide;
(b) that there should be parity of representation between Pakistan Group and the Hindustan Group in the Union Executive and Legislature, if any; and
(c) that no decision, legislative, executive or administrative, should be taken by the Union in regard to any matter of a controversial nature, except by a majority of three-fourths; all these three terms of our after have been omitted from the statement.
No doubt, there is one safeguard for the conduct of business in the Union Legislature that:-

'any question raising a major communal issue in the Legislature should require for its decision a majority of the representatives present and voting of each of the two major communities as well as majority of all members present and voting.' Even this is vague and ineffective. To begin with, who will decide and how as to what is a major communal issue and what is a minor communal issue and what is a purely, non-communal issue?

(5) Our proposal that Pakistan Group should have a right to secede from the Union after an initial period of ten years, although the Congress had no serious objection to it, has been omitted and now we are only limited to a reconsideration of terms of the Union Constitution after an initial period of ten years.

(6) Coming to the Constitution-making machinery, here again, a representative of British Baluchistan is included in section B, but how he will be elected, is not indicated.

(7) With regard to the Constitution-making body for the purpose of framing the proposed Union Constitution, it will have an overwhelming Hindu majority, as in a house of 292 for British India the Muslim strength will be 79, and, if the number allotted to India States, 93, is taken into account, it is quite obvious that the Muslim proportion will be further reduced as the bulk of the States representatives would be Hindus. This Assembly, so constituted, will elect the Chairman and other officers and, it seems, also the memebers of the Advisory Committee, referred to in paragraph 20 of the statement, by a majority and the same rule will apply also to other normal business. But, I note, that there is only one saving clause which runs as follow:-

'In the Union Constituent Assembly resolutions varying the provisions of paragraph 15 above or raising any major communal issue shall require a majority of representatives present and voting of each of the two major communities. The chairman of the Assembly shall decide, which (if any) of the resolutions raise major communal issues and shall, if so requested by a majority of the representatives of either of the major communities, consult the Federal Court before giving his decision.'

It follows, therefore, that it will be the Chairman alone who will decide. He will not be bound by the opinion of the Federal Court, nor need anybody know what that opinion was, as the Chairman is merely directed to consult the Federal Court.

(8) With regard to the provinces opting out of their Group, it is left to the new legislature of the province after the first general election under the new constitution to decide, instead of a referendum of the people as was suggested by us.

(9) As for paragraph 20 which runs as follows:-

'The Advisory Committee on the rights of citizens, minorities and tribal and excluded areas should contain full representation of the interests affected, and their function will be to report to the Union Constituent Assembly upon the list of Fundamental Rights, the clauses for the protection of minorities and a scheme for the administration of the tribal and excluded areas and to advise whether these rights should be incorporated in the provincial, Group, or Union constitution.'

This raises a very serious question indeed, for, if it is left to the Union Constituent Assembly to decide these matters by a majority vote, whether any of the recommendations of the Advisory Committee should be incorporated in the Union Constitution, then it will open a door to more subjects being vested in the Union Government. This will destroy the very basic principle that the Union is to be strictly confined to three subjects.

These are some of the main points which I have tried to put before the public after studying this important document. I do not wish to anticipate the decision of the Working Committee and Council of the All-India Muslim League, which are going to meet shortly at Delhi. They will finally take such decisions as they may think proper after a careful consideration of the pros and cons and a through and dispassionate examination of the statement of the British Cabinet Delegation and His Excellency the Viceroy.

Appendix 13

Resolution Passed by the Congress Working Committee on 24 May 1946

The Working Committee has given careful consideration to the Statement dated 16th May, 1946, issued by the Delegation of the British Cabinet and the Viceroy on behalf of the British Government, as well as the correspondence relating to it that has passed between the Congress President and the members of the Delegation. They have examined it with every desire to find a way for a peaceful and co-operative transfer of power and the establishment of a free and independent India. Such and India must necessarily have s strong central authority capable of representing the nation with power and dignity in the counsels of the world. In considering the Statement, the Working Committee have kept in view the picture of the future, in so far as this was available to them from the proposals made for the formation of a Provisional Government and the clarification given by members of the Delegation. This picture is still incomplete and vague. It is only on the basis of the full picture that they can judge and come to a decision as to how far this is in conformity with the objectives they aim at. These objectives are: independence for India, a strong though limited, central authority, full autonomy for the provinces, the establishment of a democratic structure in the centre and in the units, the guarantee of the fundamental rights of each individual so that he may have full and equal opportunities of growth, and further that each community should have opportunity to live the life of its choice within the larger framework.

The Committee regret to find a divergence between these objectives and the various proposals that have been made on behalf of the British Government, and, in particular, there is no vital change envisaged during the interim period when the Provisional Government will function, in spite of the assurance given in paragraph 23 of the Statement. If the independence of India is aimed at, then the functioning of the Provisional Government must approximate closely in fact, even though not in law, to that independence and all obstructions and hindrances to it should be removed. The continued presence of a foreign army of occupation is a negation of independence.

The Statement issued by the Cabinet Delegation and the Viceroy contains certain recommendations and suggests a procedure for the building up of a Constituent Assembly, which is sovereign in so far as the framing of the constitution is concerned. The Committee do not agree with some of these recommendations. In their view it will be open to the Constituent Assembly itself at any stage to make changes and variations, with the proviso that in regard to certain major communal matters a majority decision of both the major communities will be necessary.

The procedure for the election of the Constituent Assembly is based on representation in the ratio of one to a million, but the application of this principle appears to have been overlooked in the case of European members of Assemblies, particularly in Assam and Bengal. Therefore, the Committee expect that this oversight will be corrected.

The Constituent Assembly is meant to be a fully elected body, chosen by the elected members of the Provincial Legislatures. In Baluchistan there is no elected assembly or any other kind of chamber which might elect a representative for the Constituent Assembly. It would be improper for any kind of nominated individual to speak for the whole province of Baluchistan, which he really does not represent in any way.

In Coorg the Legislative Council contains some nominated members as well as Europeans elected from a special constituency of less than a hundred electors. Only the elected members from the general constituencies should participate in the election.

The Statement of the Cabinet Delegation affirms the basic principle of provincial autonomy and residuary powers vesting in the Provinces. It is further said that Provinces should be free to form groups. Subsequently, however, it is recommended that provincial representatives will divide up into sections which "shall proceed to settle the Provincial Constitutions for the Provinces in each section and shall also decide whether any Group Constitution shall be set up for those Provinces". There is a marked discrepancy in these two separate provisions, and it would appear that a measure of compulsion is introduced which clearly infringes the basic principle of provincial autonomy. In order to retain the recommendatory character of the Statement, and in order to make the clauses consistent with each other, the Committee read paragraph 15 to mean that, in the first instance, the respective provinces will make their choice whether or not to belong to the section in which they are placed. Thus the Constituent Assembly must be considered as a sovereign body with final authority for the purpose of drawing up a constitution and giving effect to it.

The provisions in the Statement in regard to the Indian States are vague and much has been left for future decision. The Working Committee would, however, like to make it clear that the Constituent Assembly cannot be formed of entirely disparate elements, and the manner of appointing State representatives for the Constituent Assembly must approximate, in so far as is possible, to the method adopted in the Provinces. The committee are gravely concerned to learn that even at this present moment some State governments are attempting to crush the spirit of their people with the help of armed forces. These recent developments in the States are of great significance in the present and for the future of India, as they indicate that there is no real change of policy on the part of some of the State governments and of those who exercise paramountcy.

A Provisional National Government must have a new basis and must be a precursor of the full independence that will emerge from the Constituent Assembly. It must function in recognition of that fact, though changes in law need not be made at this stage. The Governor-General may continue as the head of that Government during the interim period, but the Government should function as a cabinet responsible to the Central Legislature. The status, powers and composition of the Provisional Government should be fully defined in order to enable the Committee to come to a decision. Major communal issues shall be decided in the manner referred to above in order to remove any possible fear or suspicion from the minds of a minority.

The Working Committee consider that the connected problems involved in the establishment of a Provisional Government and a Constituent Assembly should be viewed together so that they may appear as parts of the same picture, and there may be co-ordination between the two, as well as an acceptance of the independence that is now recognised as India's right and due. It is only with the conviction that they are engaged in building up a free, great and independent India, that the Working Committee can approach this task and invite the co-operation of all the people of India. In the absence of a full picture, the Committee are unable to give a final opinion at this stage.

5. I am quite clear that the spirit in which the Government is worked will be of much greater importance than any formal document and guarantees. I have no doubt that, if you are prepared to trust me, we shall be able to co-operate in a manner which will give India a sense of freedom from external control and will prepare for complete freedom as soon as the new Constitution is made.

6. I sincerely hope that the Congress will accept these assurances and will have no further hesitation in joining to co-operate in the immense problems which confront us.

7. In the matter of time table you will be aware that the All-India Muslim League Council is meeting on June 5th, at which we understand decisive conclusions are to be reached. I suggest therefore that if you summon your Working Committee to reassemble in Delhi on Friday the 7th, it may be possible for final decisions to be made by all Parties on all outstanding questions early in the following week.

Appendix 14

Statement Issued by the Cabinet Mission in New Delhi, 25 May 1946

The Delegation have considered the statement of the President of the Muslim League dated 22nd May and the resolution dated 24th May of the Working committee of the Congress.

2. The position is that since the Indian leaders after prolonged discussion failed to arrive at an agreement the Delegation put forward their recommendations as the nearest approach to reconciling the views of the two man parties. The scheme stands as a whole and can only succeed if it is accepted and worked in a spirit of co-operation.
3. The Delegation wish also to refer briefly to a few points that have been raised in the statement and resolution.
4. The authority functions of the Constituent Assembly and the procedure which it is intended to allow are clear from the Cabinet Delegation's statement. Once the Constituent Assembly is formed and working on this basis there is no intention of interfering with its discretion or questioning its decisions. When the Constituent Assembly has completed its labours, His Majesty's Government will recommend to Parliament such action as may be necessary for the cession of sovereignty to the Indian people, subject only to two matters which are mentioned in the statement and which, we believe, are not controversial, namely: adequate provision for the protection of the minorities (paragraph 20 of the statement) and willingness to conclude a treaty with His Majesty's Government to cover matters arising out of the transfer of power (paragraph 22 of the statement).
5. It is a consequence of the system of election that a few Europeans can be elected to the Constituent Assembly. Whether the right so given will be exercised is a matter for them to decide.
6. The representative of Baluchistan will be elected in a joint meeting of the Shahi Jirga and the non-official members of the Quetta municipality.
7. In Coorg the whole Legislative Council will have the right to vote but the official members will receive instructions not to take part in the election.
8. The interpretation put by the Congress resolution on paragraph 15 of the statement, to the effect that the Provinces can in the first instance make the choice whether or not to belong to the Section in which they are placed, does not accord with the Delegation's intentions. The reasons for the grouping of the Provinces are well known and this is an essential feature of the scheme and can only be modified by agreement between the parties. The right to opt out of the groups after the constitution making has been completed will be exercised by the people themselves, since at

the first election under the new provincial Constitution this question of opting out will obviously be a major issue and all those entitled to vote under the new franchise will be able to take their share in a truly democratic decision.

9. The question of how the States representatives should be appointed to the Constituent Assembly is clearly one which must be discussed with the States. It is not a matter for decision by the Delegation.
10. It is agreed that the interim Government will have a new basis. That basis is that all portfolios including that of the War Member will be held by Indians and that the members will be selected in consultation with the Indian political parties. These are very significant changes in the Government of India and a long step towards independence. H. M. G. will recognise the effect of these changes, will attach the fullest weight to them and will give to the Indian Government the greatest possible freedom in the exercise of the day-to-day administration of India.
11. As the Congress statement recognises, the present Constitution must continue during the interim period and the interim Government cannot, therefore, be made legally responsible to the Central Legislature. There is, however, nothing to prevent the members of the Government, individually or by common consent, from resigning if they fail to pass an important measure through the Legislature or if a vote of non-confidence is passed against them.
12. There is, of course, no intention of retaining British troops in India against the wish of an independent India under the new Constitution; but during the interim period, which it is hoped will be short, the British Parliament has under the present Constitution the ultimate responsibility for the security of India and it is necessary, therefore, that British troops should remain.

Appendix 15

Letter from Viceroy to Mr Jinnah, 4 June 1946

PERSONAL AND CONFIDENTIAL

You asked me yesterday to give you an assurance about the action that would be taken if one party accepted the scheme in the Cabinet Delegation's statement of the 16th May, and the other refused.

2. I can give you on behalf of the Cabinet Delegation my personal assurance that we do not propose to make any discrimination in the treatment of either party; and that we shall go ahead with the plan laid down in the statement so far as circumstances permit if either party accepts; but we hope that both will accept.

3. I should be grateful if you would see that the existence of this assurance dose not become public. If it is necessary for you to tell your Working Committee that you have an assurance, I should be grateful if you would explain to them this condition.

Appendix 16

**Resolution Passed by the All-India Muslim League Council,
6 June 1946**

1. This meeting of the Council of the All-India Muslim League, after having carefully considered the Statement issued by the Cabinet Mission and the Viceroy on 16th May, 1946, and other relevant statements and documents officially issued in connection therewith, and after having examined the proposals set forth in the said statement in all their bearings and implications, places upon record the following views for the guidance of the Nation and direction to the Working Committee.

2. That the reference made, and the conclusions recorded, in paras. 6, 7, 8, 9, 10 and 11 of the Statement, concerning the Muslim demand for the establishment of a full Sovereign Pakistan as the only solution of the Indian Constitutional Problem are unwarranted, unjustified, and unconvincing, and should not therefore have found a place in a State document issued on behalf and with the authority of, the British Government. These paragraphs are couched in such language, and contain such mutilations of the established facts, that the Cabinet Mission have clearly been prompted to include them in their Statement solely with the object of appeasing the Hindus, in utter disregard of Muslim sentiments. Furthermore, the contents of the aforesaid paragraphs are in conflict and inconsistent with the admissions made by the Mission themselves in paras. 5 and 12 of their Statement, which are to the following effect: First, the Mission 'were greatly impressed by the very genuine and acute anxiety of the Muslims lest they should find themselves subjected to a perpetual Hindu majority rule.' Second, 'this feeling has become so strong and widespread amongst the Muslims that it cannot be allayed by mere paper safeguards.' Third, 'If there is to be internal peace in India it must be secured by measures which will assure to the Muslims a control in all matters vital to their culture, religion, economic or other interests.' Fourth, 'Very real Muslim apprehensions exist that their culture and political and social life might become submerged in a purely unitary India, in which the Hindus, with their greatly superior numbers, must be the dominating element.' In order that there may be no manner of doubt in any quarter, the Council of the All-India Muslim League reiterates that the attainment of the goal of a complete sovereign Pakistan still remains the unalterable objective of the Muslims in India for the achievement of which they will, if necessary, employ every means in their power, and consider no sacrifice or suffering too great.

3. That notwithstanding the affront offered to Muslim sentiments by the choice of injudicious words in the preamble to the Statement of the Cabinet Mission, the Muslim League, having regard to the grave issues

involved, and prompted by its earnest desire for a peaceful solution, if possible, of the Indian constitutional problem, and inasmuch as the basis and the foundation of Pakistan are inherent in the Mission's plan by virtue of the compulsory grouping of the six Muslim Provinces in Section B and C, is willing to co-operate with the constitution-making machinery proposed in the scheme outlined by the Mission, in the hope that it would ultimately result in the establishment of complete sovereign Pakistan, and in the consummation of the goal of independence for the major nations, Muslims and Hindus, and all the other people inhabiting the vast subcontinent.

It is for these reasons that the Muslim League is accepting the scheme, and will join the constitution-making body, and it will keep in view the opportunity and right of secession of Provinces or groups from the Union, which have been provided in the Mission's plan by implication. The ultimate attitude of the Muslim League will depend on the final outcome of the labours of the constitution-making body, and on the final shape of the constitutions which may emerge from the deliberations of the that body jointly and separately in its three sections. The Muslim League also reserves the right to modify and revise the policy and attitude set forth in this resolution at any time during the progress of the deliberations of the constitution-making body, or the Constituent Assembly, or thereafter if the course of events so require, bearing in mind the fundamental principles and ideals here before adumbrated, to which the Muslim League is irrevocably committed.

4. That with regard to the arrangement for the proposed Interim Government at the Centre, this Council authorizes its President to negotiate with the Viceroy and to take such decisions and actions as he deems fit and proper.

Appendix 17

Letter from Mr Jinnah to Viceroy, 8 June 1946

During the course of our discussions regarding the Interim Government at Simla and thereafter at Delhi on the 3rd of June after my arrival and before the meeting of the Muslim League Working Committee took place, you were good enough to give me the assurance that there will be only twelve portfolios, five on behalf of the League, five congress, one Sikh and one Christian or Anglo-Indian; and that, as regards the portfolios, the most important portfolios will be equally divided between the League and the Congress in the Distribution thereof, further details being left open for discussion.

With your previous permission I informed the Working Committee of this assurance and this was one of the most important considerations which weighed with them together with the statement of the Cabinet Mission. These two together formed one whole and, as such, the Council of the All-India Muslim League has given its final decision on the 6th June. I may further inform you that similarly I had to repeat the assurance to the Council before they finally gave their approval. As you know, the meeting of the All-India Muslim League Council was held in camera and, there again, the house showed great opposition to the scheme in the beginning. During the course of discussions at a very early stage large body of opposition was satisfied when I made the statement in answer to the very pressing question as to what our position will be with regard to the Interim Government. But for this assurance we would not have got the approval of the Council to the scheme. As requested by you I took as much care as possible to see that it did not become public.

Finally, you state in answer to question 5 that 'No decision of a major communal issue could be taken by the Interim Government if the majority of either of the main parties were opposed to it.' You further say that you had pointed this out to the Congress President and he had agreed that the Congress appreciated this point. In this connection I desire to point out that we had accepted this principle for the long-term arrangement in the Union Legislature and it could possibly be applied to the provisional Government if it was responsible to the Legislature and was composed of representatives on the population basis of major communities. It could not be applied to the Provisional Government formed on a different basis altogether. It was pointed out by us in my letter of the 13th June, 1946*, that it would make administration impossible and deadlocks a certainty. Even in the question as framed by Mr Jinnah it is stated 'In view of the substitution of 14 now proposed for the original 12,' no major communal issues should be decided if the majority of the Muslim Members are opposed to it. Thus this question arose after the substitution of 14 for 12, i.e., after your statement of 16th June. In this statement no mention is made of this rule. This very important change has been introduced, almost casually and certainly without our consent. This again gives the power of veto or obstruction to the Muslim League in the Provisional Government.

We have stated above our objections to your proposals of 16th June as well as to your answers to the questions framed by Mr Jinnah. These defects are grave and would render the working of the Provisional Government difficult and deadlocks a certainty. In the circumstances your proposals cannot fulfil the immediate requirements of the situation or further the cause we hold dear.

My Committee have, therefore, reluctantly come to the conclusion that they are unable to assist you in forming a Provisional Government as proposed in your statement of 16th June, 1946.

With regard to the proposals made in the statement of 16th May, 1946, relating to the formation and functioning of the constitution-making body, the Working Committee of the Congress passed a resolution on the 24th May, 1946, and conversations and correspondence have taken place between your Excellency and the Cabinet Mission on the one side and myself and some of my colleagues on the other. In these we have pointed out what in our opinion were the defects in the proposals. We also gave our interpretation of some of the provisions of the statement. While adhering to our views, we accept your proposals and are prepared to work them with a view to achieve our objective. We would add, however, that the successful working of the Constituent Assembly will largely depend on the formation of a satisfactory Provisional Government.

Appendix 18

Resolution of the Congress Working Committee, 25 June 1946

On May 24, the Working Committee passed a Resolution on the Statement dated May 16 issued by the British Cabinet Delegation and the Viceroy. In this Resolution, they pointed out some defects in the Statement and gave their own interpretation of certain parts of it.

Since then, the Committee has been continuously engaged in giving earnest consideration to the proposals made on behalf of the British Government in the statements of May 16 and June 16, and have considered the correspondence in regard to them between the Congress President and Members of the Cabinet Delegation and the Viceroy. The Committee has examined both these sets of prudence and the opening out of avenues leading to the rapid advance of the masses economically and socially, so that their material standards may be raised and poverty, malnutrition, famine and lack of the necessaries in life may be ended, and all the people of the country may have freedom and the opportunity to grow and develop according to their genius.

These proposals fall short of these objectives. Yet the Committee has considered them earnestly in all their aspects because of their desire to find some way for the peaceful settlement of India's problem and the ending of the conflict between India and England.

The kind of independence which Congress has aimed at is the establishment of a united democratic Indian Federation with a Central authority which would command respect from the nations of the world, maximum provincial autonomy, and equal rights for all men and women in the country. The limitation of the Central authority, as contained in the proposals as well as the system of grouping of Provinces, weakened the whole structure and was unfair to some provinces, such as the North-West Frontier Province, and Assam, and to some of the minorities, notably the Sikhs.

The Committee disapproved of this. They felt, however, taking the proposals as a whole, that there was sufficient scope for enlarging and strengthening the Central authority and for fully ensuring the right of a Province to act according to its choice in regard to grouping, and to give protection to such minorities as might otherwise be placed at a disadvantage. Certain other objections were also raised on their behalf, notably the possibility of non-nationals taking any part in the Constitution-making. It is clear that it would be a breach both of the letter and the spirit of the statement of May 16 if any non-Indian participated in voting or standing for election to the Constituent Assembly.

In the proposals for an Interim Government contained in the Statement of June 16, the defects related to matters of vital concern to the Congress. Some of these have been pointed out in a letter of June 25, from the Congress President to the Viceroy. The Provisional Government must have power and authority and responsibility and should function, in fact if not in law, as a de facto independent Government leading to the full independence to come. The Members of such a Government can only hold themselves responsible to the people and not to any external authority. In the formation of a Provisional or other Government, Congressmen can never give up the national character of Congress or accept an artificial and unjust parity, or agree to a veto of a communal group. The Committee are unable to accept the proposals for the formation of an Interim Government as contained in the Statement of June 16.

The Committee have, however, decided that the Congress should join the proposed Constituent Assembly with a view to framing the Constitution of a free, united and democratic India.

While the Committee have agreed to Congress participation in the Constituent Assembly, it is, in their opinion, essential that a representative and responsible provisional national Government be formed at the earliest possible date. The continuation of an authoritarian and unrepresentative Government can only add to the suffering of the famishing masses and increase discontent. It will also put in jeopardy the work of the Constituent Assembly, which can only function in a free environment.

The Working Committee recommends accordingly to the All-India Congress Committee and for the purpose of considering and ratifying this recommendation they convene an emergent meeting of the All-India Congress Committee in Bombay on July 6 and 7.

Appendix 19

All-India Congress Committee's Resolution of 6 January 1947

The A. I. C. C. having considered the events that have taken place in the country since the Meerut Session of the Congress in November last, the statement issued by the British Government on December 6, 1946, and the statement of the Working Committee of December 22, 1946, advises Congressmen as follows:

The A. I. C. C. endorses the statement of the Working Committee of December 22, 1946, and expresses its agreement with the views contained therein.

While the Congress has always been agreeable to making a reference to the Federal Court on the question of interpretation in dispute such a reference has become purposeless and undesirable owing to recent announcements made on behalf of the British Government. A reference could only be made on an agreed basis, the parties concerned agreeing to abide by the decision given.

The A. I. C. C. is firmly of opinion that the constitution for a free and independent India should be framed by the people of India on the basis of as wide an agreement as possible. There must be no interference whatsoever by any external authority, and no compulsion of any province or part of a province by another province. The A. I. C. C. realizes and appreciates the difficulties placed in the way of some provinces, notably Assam, the N. W. F. P. and Baluchistan and the Sikhs in the Punjab, by the British Cabinet's scheme of May 16, 1946, and more especially by the interpretation put upon it by the British Government in their statement of December 6, 1946. The Congress cannot be a party to any such compulsion or imposition against the will of the people concerned, a principle which the British Government have themselves recognized.

The A. I. C. C. is anxious that the Constituent Assembly should proceed with the work of framing a constitution for free India with the goodwill of all parties concerned and, with a view to removing the difficulties that have arisen owing to varying interpretations, agree to advise action in accordance with the interpretation of the British Government in regard to the procedure to be followed in the sections. It must be clearly understood, however, that this must not involve any compulsion of a province and that the rights of the Sikhs in the Punjab should not be jeopardized. In the event of any attempt at such compulsion, a province or part of a province has the right to take such action as may be deemed necessary in order to give effect to the wishes of the people concerned. The future course of action will depend upon the developments that take place and the A. I. C. C. therefore directs the Working Committee to advise upon it, whenever circumstances so require, keeping in view the basic principle of provincial autonomy.

Appendix 20

All-India Muslim League Council Resolutions adopted at Kaiser Bagh in Bombay on 29 July 1946

RESOLUTION I

On the 6th of June 1946, the Council of the All-India Muslim League accepted the Scheme embodied in the Statement of the Cabinet Delegation and the viceroy dated May 16, 1946 and explained by them in their statement dated May 25, 1946. The Scheme of the Cabinet Delegation fell far short of the demand of the Muslim nation for the immediate establishment of an independent and fully sovereign State of Pakistan, comprising the six Muslim provinces, but the Council accepted a Union Centre for 10 years strictly confined to three subjects, viz. Defence, Foreign Affairs and Communications as the Scheme laid down certain fundamentals and safeguards and provided for the grouping separately of the six Muslim Provinces in Sections B and C for the purpose of framing their Provincial and Group Constitutions unfettered by the Union in any way; and also with a view to end the Hindu-Muslim deadlock peacefully and accelerate the attainment of freedom of the peoples of India. In arriving at this decision, the Council was also greatly influenced by the statement of the President, which he made with the authority of the Viceroy that the Interim Government, which was an integral part of the Mission's Scheme, was going to be formed on the basis of a formula, viz. 5 Muslim League, 5 Congress, 1 Sikh and I Indian Christian or Anglo Indian, stipulating that the most important portfolios would be distributed equally between the two major parties, the Muslim League and the Congress. The Council authorized the President to take such decision and action with regard to further details of setting up the Interim Government as he deemed fit and proper. In that very Resolution the Council also reserved the right to modify and revise this policy, if the course of events so required.

The British Government committed a breach of faith with the Muslim League in that the Cabinet Delegation and the Viceroy went back on the original formula of 5:5:2 for the setting up of the Interim Government to placate the Congress.

Having gone back on the original formula, upon the faith of which the Muslim League Council had come to their decision on the 6th of June, the Viceroy suggested a new basis of 5:5:3 and, after carrying on considerable negotiations with the Congress and having failed to get the Congress to agree to it, intimated to the parties on the 15th of June that he and the Cabinet Delegation would issue their final statement with regard to the setting up of the Interim Government.

Accordingly, on the 16th of June the President of the Muslim League received a Statement embodying what was announced to be the final decision for setting up the Interim Government by the Viceroy, making it clear that if either of the two major parties refused to accept the statement of June 16, the Viceroy would proceed to form the Interim Government with the major party accepting it and such other representatives as were willing to join. This was explicitly laid down in Paragraph 8 of the Statement of June 16.

Even this final decision of the Cabinet Mission of the 16th June, with regard to the formation of the Interim Government, was rejected by the Congress, whereas the Muslim League definitely accepted it. Though this proposal was different from the original formula of 5:5:2, the Muslim League accepted it because the Viceroy had provided safeguards and given other satisfactory assurances which were contained in his letter dated the 20th June 1946, addressed to the President of the Muslim League.

The Viceroy, however, scrapped the proposal of the 16th June and postponed the formation of the Interim Government on the plea concocted by the 'legalistic talents' of the Cabinet Mission, putting a most fantastic and dishonest construction upon Paragraph 8 of the Statement, to the effect that as both the major parties, i.e. the Muslim League and the Congress had accepted the Statement of May 16, the question of the Interim Government could only be taken up in consultation with the representatives of both the parties *de novo*.

Even assuming that this construction was tenable, for which there is no warrant, the Congress, by their conditional acceptance with reservations and interpretations of their own as lad down in the letter of the President of the Congress, dated the 25th of June, and the Resolution of the Working Committee of the Congress passed at Delhi on the 26th of June, repudiating the very fundamentals of the scheme had, in fact, rejected the Statement of the 16th of May and there was therefore no justification, whatsoever, for abandoning the final proposals of the 16th of June.

As regards the proposal embodied in the statements of the 16th and 25th of May of the Cabinet Delegation and the Viceroy, the Muslim League alone of the two major parties has accepted it.

The Congress have not accepted it because their acceptance is conditional and subject to their own interpretation, which is contrary to the authoritative statements of the Delegation and Viceroy issued on the 16th and the 25th of May. The Congress have made it clear that they do not accept any of the terms or the fundamentals of the Scheme, but that they have agreed only to go into the fundamentals of the Scheme, but that they have agreed only to go into the Constituent Assembly and to nothing else; and that the Constituent Assembly is a sovereign body and can take such decisions as it may think proper in total disregard of the terms and the basis on which it was proposed to be set up. Subsequently this was made further clear and beyond any doubt in the speeches that were made at the meeting of the All-India Congress Committee in Bombay on the 6th of July by prominent members of the Congress, to a press conference on July 10 in Bombay, and then again, even after the debate in the Parliament, in a public speech by him at Delhi on the 22nd of July.

The result is that of the two major parties, the Muslim League alone has accepted the statements of May 16 and 25 according to the spirit and the letter of the proposals embodied therein and in spite of the attention of the Secretary of State for India having been drawn to this situation by the statement of the President of the Muslim League of July 13 from Hyderabad, Deccan, neither Sir Stafford Cripps in the House of Commons, nor Lord Pethick-Lawrence in the House of Lords, in the course of the recent debate, have provided or suggested any means or machinery to prevent the Constituent Assembly from taking decisions which would be *ultra vires* and not competent for the Assembly to take. The only reference that the Secretary of State made to this serious situation was a mere expression of pious hope when he stated that "that would not be fair to the other parties who go in."

Once the Constituent Assembly were summoned and met, there was no provision or power that could prevent any decision from being taken by the Congress with its overwhelming majority, which would not be competent for the Assembly to take or which would be *ultra vires* of it, and however repugnant it might be to the letter or the spirit of the Scheme. It would rest entirely with the majority to take such decisions as they may think proper or suit them; and the Congress have already secured by sheer numbers and overwhelming Hindu Caste majority, whereby they will be in a position to use the Assembly in the manner in which they have already declared, i.e. that they will wreck the basic form of the Grouping of the Provinces and extend the scope, powers and subjects, as laid down in Paragraph 15 and provided for in Paragraph 19 of the Statement of May 16.

The Cabinet Delegation and the Viceroy, collectively and individually, have stated on more than one occasion that the basic principles were laid down to enable the major parties to join the Constituent Assembly, and that the Scheme cannot succeed unless it is worked in a spirit of co-operation. The attitude of the Congress clearly shows that these conditions, precedent for the successful working of the Constitution-making Body, do not exist. This fact, taken together with the policy of the British Government of sacrificing the interests of the Muslim nation and some other weaker sections of the peoples of India, particularly the Scheduled Castes, to appease the Congress, and the way in which they have been going back on their oral and written solemn pledges and assurances given from time to time to the Muslims, leaves no doubt that in these circumstances the participation of the Muslims in the proposed Constitution-making machinery is fraught with danger; and the Council therefore, hereby withdraws its acceptance of the Cabinet Mission's proposals, which was communicated to the Secretary of State for India by the President of the Muslim League on the 6th of June, 1946.

Resolution II

Whereas the Council of the All-India Muslim League has resolved to reject the proposals embodied in the Statement of the Cabinet Delegation and the Viceroy dated the 16th of May, 1946, due to the intransigence of the Congress, on one hand, and the breach of faith with the Muslims by the British Government, on the other; and

whereas Muslim India has exhausted, without success, all efforts to find a peaceful solution of the Indian problem by compromise and constitutional means; and

whereas the Congress is bent upon setting up Caste-Hindu Raj in India with the connivance of the British; and

whereas recent events have shown that power politics and not justice and fair play are the deciding factors in Indian affairs; and

whereas it has become abundantly clear that the Muslims of India would not rest contented with anything less than the immediate establishment of an Independent and fully sovereign State of Pakistan, and would resist any attempt to impose any Constitution-making machinery or any Constitution, long-term or short-term, or the setting up of any Interim Government at the Centre without the approval and consent of the Muslim League;

the Council of the All-India Muslim League is convinced that now the time has come for the Muslim nation to resort to Direct Action to achieve Pakistan to assert their just rights, to vindicate their honour and to get rid of the present British slavery and the contemplated future Caste-Hindu domination.

This Council calls upon the Muslim nation to stand to a man behind their sole representative and authoritative organization, the All-India Muslim League, and to be ready for every sacrifice.

This Council directs the Working Committee to prepare forthwith a programme of Direct Action to carry out the policy enunciated above, and to organize the Muslims for the coming struggle to be launched as and when necessary.

As a protest against, and in token of their deep resentment of the attitude of the British, this Council calls upon the Musalmans to renounce forthwith the titles conferred upon them by the alien Government.

Appendix 21

The Muslim League Working Committee's Resolution of 31 January 1947

On January 31, 1947, at Karachi the Working Committee of the All-India Muslim League in a lengthy resolution not only refused to summon its council, which on July 29, 1946, withdrew the League's acceptance of the Cabinet Mission's Plan, but called upon the British Government to declare that the plan had failed, in view of the rejection by the Congress of the British Government's statement of December 6, 1946.

The following is the full text of the resolution which was adopted after 200 minutes' discussion:

The Working Committee of the All-India Muslim League have given careful consideration to the statement issued by His Majesty's Government on December 6, 1946. The resolution passed thereafter by the Congress Working Committee on December 22, 1946 and by the All-India Congress Committee on January 6, 1947, the speeches delivered by responsible leaders of the Congress at the AICC session referred to above, and the proceedings of the Constituent Assembly during its two sessions so far held; and record their views as follows:–

By their statement of December 6, His Majesty's Government admitted that the interpretation which the Muslim League had always put on Paragraphs 19 (V) and 19 (VIII) of the Cabinet Mission's statement of May 16 was the correct one and accorded with the intention of the Cabinet Mission and His Majesty's Government. By that statement it was also proved that the Congress, on the other hand, had 'put forward a different view' and therefore had not accepted what His Majesty's Government themselves described as 'this fundamental point', namely, that decision in the Sections, including questions relating to the setting of the constitutions of provinces included in each Group, should, in the absence of agreement to the contrary, be taken by a simple majority vote of the representatives in the Sections.

His Majesty's Government furthermore, added that 'this statement, as so interpreted must therefore be considered an essential part of the scheme of May 16 for enabling the Indian people to formulate a constitution which His Majesty's Government would be prepared to submit to Parliament'. Accordingly, in their statement of December 6, they urged the Congress to accept 'this reaffirmation of the intention of the Cabinet Mission', or, in the alternative, to refer the point to the Federal Court at a very early date.

In their statement of December 6 His Majesty's Government also affirmed that the Congress had agreed that other questions of interpretation of the statement of May 16 which might arise might be referred by either side to the

Federal Court, whose decisions should be accepted, and, on the assumption that the Congress had agreed to this procedure, His Majesty's Government asked the Muslim League also to agree to it in order to ensure that 'the procedure both in the Union Constituent Assembly and in the Sections, may accord with the Cabinet Mission's Plan.'

Thirdly, His Majesty's Government, in the last paragraph of their statement of December 6, reiterated the fact that 'there has never been any prospect of success for the Constituent Assembly except upon the basis of the agreed procedure,' and they repeated the assurance: 'should the constitution come to be framed by a Constituent Assembly in which a large section of the Indian population had not been represented, His Majesty's Government would not, of course, contemplate—as the Congress have stated they would not contemplate—forcing such a constitution upon any unwilling parts of the country.'

The meaning and the application of this assurance were further clarified by Sir Stafford Cripps in his speech in the House of Commons on December 12, 1946, when he said 'but the Government also had to envisage the possibility in the clause in the final paragraph of the statement.' This was perhaps a statement of the obvious—that if the Muslim League could not be persuaded to come into the Constituent Assembly, then parts of the country where they were in a majority could not be held to be bound by the results.

The situation created by the issue of this statement by His Majesty's Government was that the onus of taking the next step fell on the Congress and they were called upon:

1. To accept honestly and unequivocally the correct interpretation of Paragraphs 19 (V) and 19 (VIII) of the Cabinet Mission's statement of May 16, which interpretation had been already accepted by the Muslim League, or to refer the point to the Federal Court;
2. To reaffirm that they accepted the procedure for the settling of other questions of interpretation that might arise, so that the decision should accord with the basic and fundamental principles of the scheme of 16th May, 1946, namely, that either side could refer such questions to the Federal Court, whose decisions would be binding on all concerned; and
3. To postpone the session of the Constituent Assembly which had been called for December 9, 1946, pending settlement of the dispute over fundamental points of principle and procedure which had been brought to the fore by the statement of December 6 and the correct interpretation of which the Congress had not accepted, as was made clear in that statement, there being no prospect of success for the Constituent Assembly without such agreement, particularly on the part of the Congress.

The Working Committee of the All-India Muslim League regret to note that the Congress have reacted to the situation created by the statement of December

6 in a manner which shows that they are determined to adhere to their own views and interpretations of fundamental provisions in the Cabinet Mission's statement of May 16, which militate against clearly expressed intentions and interpretations of the authors of that statement as well as of His Majesty's Government as a whole and which destroy the very basis on which constitutional plan set forth in that statement had been drawn up.

By their resolution of December 22, the Congress Working Committee rejected the suggestion that the point in dispute should be referred to the Federal Court if the Congress did not accept 'this reaffirmation of the intention of the Cabinet Mission', and that Committee decided to convene a meeting of the All-India Congress Committee for the purpose of giving a decision on the issues raised by the statement of December 6. The Working Committee of the Congress, however, in their resolution indulged in an attack on the British Government for their renewed interpretation and clarification which had called the Congress bluff, and on the Muslim League for no other fault except that its stand had been at last vindicated.

The All-India Congress Committee by its resolution passed on January 6, purported 'to agree to advice action in accordance with the interpretation of the British Government in regard to the procedure to be followed in the section', about which there never was any doubt in the mind of any sane and honest person, but it immediately added the following qualifying clauses:

- It must be clearly understood, however, that this must not involve any compulsion on a province and that the rights of the Sikhs in the Punjab should not be jeopardized;
- In the event of any attempt at such compulsion, a province or part of a province has the right to take such action as may be deemed necessary in order to give effect to the wishes of the people concerned; and
- The future course of action will depend upon the development that takes place and the AICC, therefore, directs the Working Committee to advice upon it, whenever circumstances so require, keeping in view the basic principle of provincial autonomy.

These qualifying clauses, in the considered opinion of the Working Committee of the All-India Muslim League, confer the right of veto within the Section on 'a province', and what is more absurd, on 'a part of a province', as well as on the Sikhs in the Punjab, and therefore they completely nullify the advice or so-called 'acceptance' by the Congress of the December 6 statement, and this AICC resolution is no more than a dishonest trick and jugglery of words by which the Congress has again attempted to deceive the British Government, the Muslim League and public opinion in general.

The question or issue was a very simple one. What was required was a straight and honest answer and not these evasions, equivocations and camouflage from one of the two major contracting parties to the questions whether the Congress honestly and sincerely agreed to the proposals of the 16th of May as clarified by His Majesty's Government on the 6th December 1946, and whether they were prepared to honourably abide by them and carry out the letter and spirit of the proposals which were put before the two major parties by the British Government, who were merely acting as mediators, as, unfortunately the two major parties had failed to come to any agreement at Simla and the conference at Simla had broke down.

Of the second point in His Majesty's Government's statement of December 6, namely, the procedure whereby either side could refer other questions of interpretation to the Federal Court, the resolution of the AICC makes no mention but the mover of the resolution, Pandit Jawaharlal Nehru, on being questioned on the second day of the AICC's deliberations as to whether the Congress had agreed to this procedure, categorically answered in the negative and declared:

> Apart from this, in view of the recent development and the statement of December 6, which produces a new situation, I am not prepared to admit for an instant that we have agreed to any future procedure about references, whatever the future brings we shall have to consider it. I should like to make it perfectly clear that we are giving no assurances about any references in regard to any other matters to the Federal Court. ... We are not going to commit ourselves at the present moment to any reference to the Federal Court or any other authority. We shall decide—or the Constituent Assembly shall decide—as we think best in the circumstances.

With regard to the third point, namely, that if a constitution came to be framed by a Constituent Assembly in which a large section of the Indian population had not been represented, 'such a constitution would not be forced upon any unwilling parts of the country,' the AICC resolution, in Paragraph 3, completely distorts the meaning and application of this principle and makes this an excuse to instigate a section of the population of Assam, the North-West Frontier Province, the Sikhs and even Baluchistan to revolt against decisions that might be taken by the relevant Sections sitting as a whole and by a simple majority vote. In the opinion of the Working Committee of the All-India Muslim League the subsequent decision of the Assam Provincial Congress not to abide by the procedure laid down for Sections and its reiteration that 'the constitution for Assam shall be framed by her own representatives only is a direct result of this instigation and is a step taken by Assam Congressmen in collusion with the All-India leaders of the Congress.

The Constituent Assembly met on December 9 and subsequent dates and thereafter on January 20 and subsequent dates and has already taken decisions of vital character so far as it is known to the public; and as some of the sittings were held *in camera* it is very difficult to get correct information as to what other resolutions it has passed or what decisions it has already taken. It has passed a resolution known as the Independent Sovereign Republic Resolution laying down the objectives.

It is not only a proclamation of India as an Independent Sovereign Republic but it lays down fundamentals of the constitution. As was admitted by, Pandit Jawaharlal Nehru, the mover of the resolution, it is a very vital resolution. It lays down the essentials of the next constitution; several things which are mentioned there are fundamentals of the constitution. It speaks of a Republic or 'Union', functions and powers vested in the 'Union' or as are inherent or implied in the Union and resulting, therefrom, and talks of present boundaries, States and present authorities, the residuary powers, powers being derived from the people, minority rights and fundamental rights.

There are undoubtedly fundamentals of the constitution and they are beyond the limit of the powers and the terms of the scheme of the Cabinet Mission of May 16 and the resolution is therefore illegal, *ultra vires* and not competent for the Constituent Assembly to adopt.

Next, it has appointed several committees and has proceeded to elect an advisory committee, referred to in Paragraph 20 of the statement of the Cabinet Mission and the Viceroy on the rights of citizens, minorities, tribal and excluded areas. Further, it has appointed a steering committee and various other committees and as some of the decisions have been taken *in camera* it is very difficult to say what resolutions it has passed or decisions it has taken. It has also passed the rules of procedure and assumed control of Sections by means of these rules for which there is no warrant or justification particularly, Rule 63, which runs as follows:

1. The Assembly shall, before finally settling the Union constitution, give an opportunity to the several provinces and States, through their legislatures to formulate, within such time as it may fix, their views upon the resolutions of the Assembly outlining the main features of the constitution or, if the Assembly so decides, upon the preliminary draft of the constitution.
2. Before the constitution of any provinces is finally settled or the decision to set up a group constitution for the section in which the province is included is finally taken, an opportunity shall be given to the province concerned through its legislature to formulate, within such time as may be fixed for the purpose of its views (a) upon the resolution outlining the main features of the constitution or, if the majority of the representatives of the province in the Assembly so desire upon the preliminary draft of such constitution, and (b) upon the preliminary decision of the Section concerned as to whether a group constitution shall be set up for the provinces included in the Section and, if so, with what provincial subject the group should deal?

And lastly, it has appointed a committee to define the scope of the Union subjects, whereas the position was made quite clear, immediately after the statement of May 16 was issued, by the Secretary of State for India in his broadcast and by Sir Stafford Cripps at his press conference where he read out an explanatory statement. Both of them stated in the clearest possible terms, to the time and manner in which group constitutions were to be framed by the Sections concerned before the Union constitution was taken up.

The Secretary of State said: 'After a preliminary meeting in common, these representatives of the provinces will divide themselves up into three Sections. These Sections will decide upon provincial and group matters. Subsequently they will reunite to decide upon the Constitution for the Union.'

Sir Stafford Cripps at his press conference said: 'So the three Sections will formulate the provincial and Group Constitutions and when that is done they work together with the States' representatives to make the Union Constitution. That is the final phase' and the Union is strictly confined to three subjects.

It is clear from the above that the Constituent Assembly in which only the Congress Party is represented, has taken divisions on principles and procedure, some of which exceed the limitations imposed by the statement of May 16 on the Constituent Assembly's functions and powers at the preliminary stage and, which further impinge upon the powers and functions of the Sections. By taking these decisions in the Constituent Assembly and by appointing a packed committee consisting of individuals chosen by the Congress, the Congress has already converted that truncated assembly into a rump and something totally different from what the Cabinet Mission's statement has provided for.

In view of these facts and circumstances the Working Committee of the All-India Muslim League are definitely of the opinion that the Congress, by rejecting this final appeal of His Majesty's Government to accept the correct interpretation of the fundamental procedure of the Cabinet Mission's statement of May 16, and by having already, by the resolution and decisions taken in two sessions, converted the Constituent Assembly into a body of its own conception, has destroyed all fundamentals of the statement of May 16 and every possibility of a compromise on the basis of the Cabinet Mission's constitutional plan. The Working Committee, accordingly, call upon His Majesty's Government to declare that the constitutional plan formulated by the Cabinet Mission as announced on May 16, has failed, because the Congress, after all these months of efforts, have not accepted the statement of May 16, 1946, nor have the Sikhs, nor have the Scheduled Castes.

The proposals of May 16 could only be given effect to and carried out if the two major parties agreed to accept them. The Congress had not, and have not accepted and do not accept them, although the Muslim League had accepted by their resolution the statement of May 16 as far back as June 6, 1946. But in view of the fact that the Congress refused to accept the proposals *in toto* and unequivocally, the Muslim League had to withdraw its acceptance on July 19, 1946.

The Working Committee of the All-India Muslim League are therefore, emphatically of the opinion that the elections to, and thereafter the summoning of the Constituent Assembly, in spite of strong protests and most emphatic objections on the part of the Muslim League, was *ab initi* void, invalid and illegal as not only the major parties had not accepted the statement but even the Sikhs and the Scheduled Castes had also not done so: and that the constitution of the Constituent Assembly and its proceedings and decisions are *ultra vires* invalid and illegal and it should be forthwith dissolved.

In view of these facts and circumstances the Working Committee are clearly of the opinion that as the Congress, as a major contracting party, has not accepted the statement of May 16 as clarified by the statement of His Majesty's Government of December 6, no useful purpose will be served by summoning a meeting of the Council of the All-India Muslim League to reconsider its decision of July 29, 1946, whereby it had withdrawn the acceptance of the Cabinet Mission's plan of May 14. – A.P.I

The Times of India, February 1947

Appendix 22

The Partition Plan of 3 June 1947

STATEMENT MADE BY HIS MAJESTY'S GOVERNMENT, 3 JUNE 1947

INTRODUCTION

1. On 20th February, 1947, His Majesty's Government announced their intention of transferring power in British India to Indian hands by June 1948. His Majesty's Government had hoped that it would be possible for the major parties to co-operate in the working-out of the Cabinet Mission's Plan of 16th May, 1946, and evolve for India a constitution acceptable to all concerned. This hope has not been fulfilled.
2. The majority of the representatives of the Provinces of Madras, Bombay, the United Provinces, Bihar, Central Provinces and Berar, Assam, Orissa and the North-West Frontier Province, and the representatives of Delhi, Ajmer-Merwara and Coorg have already made progress in the task of evolving a new Constitution. On the other hand, the Muslim League Party, including in it a majority of the representatives of Bengal, the Punjab and Sind, as also the representative of British Baluchistan, has decided not to participate in the Constituent Assembly.
3. It has always been the desire of His Majesty's Government that power should be transferred in accordance with the wishes of the Indian people themselves. This task would have been greatly facilitated if there had been agreement among the Indian political parties. In the absence of such an agreement, the task of devising a method by which the wishes of the Indian people can be ascertained has devolved on His Majesty's Government. After full consultation with political leaders in India, His Majesty's Government have decided to adopt for this purpose the plan set out below. His Majesty's Government wish to make it clear that they have no intention of attempting to frame any ultimate Constitution for India; this is a matter for the Indians themselves. Nor is there anything in this plan to preclude negotiations between communities for an united India.

THE ISSUES TO BE DECIDED

4. It is not the intention of His Majesty's Government to interrupt the work of the existing Constituent Assembly. Now that provision is made for certain Provinces specified below, His Majesty's Government trust that, as a consequence of this announcement, the Muslim League representatives of those Provinces, a majority of whose representatives are already participating in it, will now take their due share in its labours. At the same time, it is clear that any Constitution framed by this Assembly cannot

apply to those parts of the country which are unwilling to accept it. His Majesty's Government are satisfied that the procedure outlined below embodies the best practical method of ascertaining the wishes of the people of such areas on the issue whether their Constitution is to be framed:

(a) in the existing Constituent Assembly; or
(b) in a new and separate Constituent Assembly consisting of the representatives of those areas which decide not to participate in the existing Constituent Assembly.

When this has been done, it will be possible to determine the authority or authorities to whom power should be transferred.

BENGAL AND THE PUNJAB

5. The Provincial Legislative Assemblies of Bengal and the Punjab (excluding the European members) will therefore each be asked to meet in two parts, one representing the Muslim majority districts and the other the rest of the Province. For the purpose of determining the population of districts, the 1941 census figures will be taken as authoritative. The Muslim majority districts in these two Provinces are set out in the Appendix to this Announcement.
6. The members of the two parts of each Legislative Assembly sitting separately will be empowered to vote whether or not the Province should be partitioned. If a simple majority of either part decides in favour of partition, division will take place and arrangements will be made accordingly.
7. Before the question as to the partition is decided, it is desirable that the representatives of each part should know in advance which Constituent Assembly the Province as a whole would join in the event of the two parts subsequently deciding to remain united. Therefore, if any member of either Legislative Assembly so demands, there shall be held a meeting of all members of the Legislative Assembly (other than Europeans) at which a decision will be taken on the issue as to which Constituent Assembly the Province as a whole would join if it were decided by the two parts to remain united.
8. In the event of partition being decided upon, each part of the Legislative Assembly will, on behalf of the areas they represent, decide which of the alternatives in paragraph 4 above to adopt.
9. For the immediate purpose of deciding on the issue of partition, the members of the Legislative Assemblies of Bengal and the Punjab will sit in two parts according to Muslim majority districts (as laid down in the Appendix) and non-Muslim majority districts. This is only a preliminary

step of a purely temporary nature as it is evident that for the purposes of final partition of these Provinces a detailed investigation of boundary questions will be needed; and, as soon as a decision involving partition has been taken for either Province, a Boundary Commission will be set up by the Governor- General, the membership and terms of reference of which will be settled in consultation with those concerned. It will be instructed to demarcate the boundaries of the two parts of the Punjab on the basis of ascertaining the contiguous majority areas of Muslims and non-Muslims. It will also be instructed to take into account other factors. Similar instructions will be given to the Bengal Boundary Commission. Until the report of a Boundary Commission has been put into effect, the provisional boundaries indicated in the Appendix will be used.

Sind

10. The Legislative Assembly of Sind (excluding the European members) will at a special meeting also take its own decision on the alternatives in paragraph 4 above.

NORTH-WEST FRONTIER PROVINCE

11. The position of the North-West Frontier Province is exceptional. Two of the three representatives of this Province are already participating in the existing Constituent Assembly. But it is clear, in view of its geographical situation, and other considerations, that, if the whole or any part of the Punjab decides not to join the existing Constituent Assembly, it will be necessary to give the North-West Frontier Province an opportunity to reconsider its position. Accordingly, in such art event, a referendum will be made to the electors of the present Legislative Assembly in the North-West Frontier Province to choose which of the alternatives mentioned in paragraph 4 above they wish to adopt. The referendum will be held under the aegis of the Governor-General and in consultation with the Provincial Government.

BRITISH BALUCHISTAN

12. British Baluchistan has elected a member but he has not taken his seat in the existing Constituent Assembly. In view of its geographical situation, this Province will also be given an opportunity to reconsider its position and to choose which of the alternatives in paragraph 4 above to adopt. His Excellency the Governor-General is examining how this can most appropriately be done.

APPENDIX 22

ASSAM

13. Though Assam is predominantly a non-Muslim Province, the district of Sylhet which is contiguous to Bengal is predominately Muslim. There has been a demand that, in the event of the partition of Bengal, Sylhet should be amalgamated with the Muslim part of Bengal. Accordingly, if it is decided that Bengal should be partitioned, a referendum will be held in Sylhet district, under the aegis of the Governor-General and in consultation with the Assam Provincial Government, to decide whether the district of Sylhet should continue to form part of the Assam Province or should be amalgamated with the new Province of Eastern Bengal, if that Province agrees. If the referendum results in favour of amalgamation with Eastern Bengal, a Boundary Commission with terms of reference similar to those for the Punjab and Bengal will be set up to demarcate the Muslim majority areas of Sylhet district and contiguous Muslim majority areas of adjoining districts, which will then be transferred to Eastern Bengal. The rest of the Assam Province will in any case continue to participate in the proceedings of the existing Constituent Assembly.

REPRESENTATION IN CONSTITUENT ASSEMBLIES

14. If it is decided that Bengal and the Punjab should be partitioned, it will be necessary to hold fresh elections to choose their representatives on the scale of one for every million of population according to the principle contained in the Cabinet Mission's Plan of 16th May, 1946. Similar elections will also have to be held for Sylhet in the event of its being decided that this district should form part of East Bengal. The number of representatives to which each area would be entitled is as follows:

Province	General	Muslims	Sikhs	Total
Sylhet District	1	2	Nil	3
West Bengal	15	4	Nil	19
East Bengal	12	29	Nil	41
West Punjab	3	12	2	17
East Punjab	6	4	2	12

15. In accordance with the mandates given to them, the representatives of the various areas will either join the existing Constituent Assembly or form the new Constituent Assembly.

ADMINISTRATIVE MATTERS

16. Negotiations will have to be initiated as soon as possible on administrative consequences of any partition that may have been decided upon:

   (a) Between the representatives of the respective successor authorities about all subjects now dealt with by the Central Government, including Defence, Finance and Communications.
   (b) Between different successor authorities and His Majesty's Government for treaties in regard to matters arising out of the transfer of power.
   (c) In the case of Provinces that may be partitioned as to administration of all provincial subjects such as the division of assets and liabilities, the police and other services, the High Courts, provincial institutions, &c.

THE TRIBES OF THE NORTH-WEST FRONTIER

17. Agreements with tribes of the North-West Frontier of India will have to be negotiated by the appropriate successor authority.

THE STATES

18. His Majesty's Government wish to make it clear that the decisions announced above relate only to British India and that their policy towards Indian States contained in the Cabinet Mission Memorandum of 12th May, 1946, remains unchanged.

NECESSITY FOR SPEED

19. In order that the successor authorities may have time to prepare themselves to take over power, it is important that all the above processes should be completed as quickly as possible. To avoid delay, the different Provinces or parts of Provinces will proceed independently as far as practicable within the conditions of this Plan, the existing Constituent Assembly and the new Constituent Assembly (if formed) will proceed to frame Constitutions for their respective territories: they will of course be free to frame their own rules.

IMMEDIATE TRANSFER OF POWER

20. The major political parties have repeatedly emphasised their desire that there should be the earliest possible transfer of power in India. With this desire His Majesty's Government are in full sympathy, and they are

willing to anticipate the date of June 1948, for the handing over of power by the setting up of an independent Indian Government or Governments at an even earlier date. Accordingly, as the most expeditious, and indeed the only practicable, way of meeting this desire His Majesty's Government propose to introduce legislation during the current session for the transfer of power this year on a Dominion status basis to one or two successor authorities according to the decisions taken as a result of this announcement. This will be without prejudice to the right of Indian Constituent Assemblies to decide in due course whether or not the part of India in respect of which they have authority will remain within the British Commonwealth.

FURTHER ANNOUNCEMENTS BY GOVERNOR-GENERAL

His Excellency the Governor-General will from time to time make such further announcements as may be necessary in regard to produce or any other matters for carrying out the above arrangements.

APPENDIX

The Muslim-majority districts of the Punjab and Bengal according to the 1941 census

1. **THE PUNJAB**
   Lahore Division — Gujranwala, Gurdaspur, Lahore, Sheikhupura, Sialkot.
   Rawalpindi Division — Attock, Gujrat, Jhelum, Mianwali, Rawalpindi, Shahpur.
   Multan Division — Dera Ghazi Khan, Jhang, Lyallpur, Montgomery, Multan, Muzaffargarh.
2. **BENGAL**
   Chittagong Division — Chittagong, Noakhali, Tippera.
   Dacca Division — Bakerganj, Dacca, Faridpur, Mymensingh.
   Presidency Division — Jessore, Murshidabad, Nadia.
   Rajshahi Division — Bogra, Dinajpur, Malda, Pabna, Rajshahi, Rangpur.

Appendix 23

India Divided: Who is to Blame for Partition?
By Sir Chimanlal Setalvad

The die is cast. India is to be partitioned into Hindustan and Pakistan with all the grave dangers inherent in such partition. If the agreement to partition had been the result of mutual goodwill and understanding between the major parties, one might have hoped for harmonious working and the establishment of mutual confidence, leading ultimately to complete understanding and the emergence of a united India. But in this case the British Government had to put before the parties the best solution they could think of and the force of circumstances has compelled the Congress and the Muslim League to accept it. The force of circumstances, as I will show later, was of their own creation.

The solution has been reluctantly accepted by the Congress and the Muslim League and both dislike it; the League has failed to get all that it wanted and the Congress had to accept what had been most repugnant to them, the division of India. The Muslim League will be casting sorrowful and covetous glances at the part of Bengal (including Calcutta) and Punjab that will be separated and thrown into Hindustan. If Assam goes into Hindustan it is likely this will add to the League's bitterness. Their feelings will be the same as those of France regarding the provinces of Alsace and Lorraine of which she was deprived as the result of the first Franco-German war. Hindustan will also harbour similar feelings with regard to the non-Muslim population within the portions of Bengal and Punjab that will go under the sway of Pakistan. There will be added bitterness by the always present disappointment at their being denied their cherished goal of one United India. The question of minorities, instead of being solved by partition will be intensified. On any supposed or real grievances of the minorities in Hindustan or Pakistan, conflict will arise. The two parts of India will maintain separate armed forces and if Pakistan is not efficiently equipped the whole country will suffer from some ambitious invader from the North. Similarly, if Hindustan with it extensive seaboard does not maintain an efficient naval force, the whole country will again suffer.

THE STATES

Then contemplate what is going to happen to the Indian States. The first repercussion of a divided India is the dissolution of the Chamber of Princes. Some big States are sure to refuse to join either Hindustan or Pakistan and will become independent sovereign States, maintaining their own armed forces. Of the rest some may join Pakistan and others may join Hindustan.

With patches of Pakistan in the East and the West, with the United Provinces and Bihar intervening, administrative difficulties will arise and the Muslim

League has already started their demand for a corridor extending over 1,200 miles to connect Eastern Bengal and West Punjab.

It is legitimate to enquire who is responsible for this debacle. In my view all the parties concerned, viz the Congress, the British Government and the Muslim League are all more or less responsible, although on the facts set forth, the Congress should get the first prize. Lord Mountbatten has said that the riots killed the Cabinet Mission's Scheme. This is not correct. The scheme had been killed by the wobbling and vacillating attitude of one party. The riots only firmly fixed the nails in the coffin and put it beyond resurrection.

MISSION'S PLAN

Without going into earlier events which gave birth to and strengthened they cry of Pakistan let us examine the course of events subsequent to May 16, 1946 on which date the Cabinet Mission plan was published. That plan, as everyone knows, provided a scheme for a united India with a Centre dealing with only a few important subjects like defence, communication and foreign relations and the power to raise money for these purposes, leaving the provinces completely autonomous with all residuary powers vested in them. The scheme also provided for the formation of an interim Government representative of the Congress, the Muslim League and other minorities. On June 6, the Muslim League accepted both the interim and the long-term schemes.

The Congress, on the other hand, instead of promptly accepting the whole scheme, raised a variety of questions about its interpretation and raised objections to clauses grouping the provinces in different sections. They thus repudiated one of the fundamentals of the scheme. They further contended that the Constituent Assembly was a sovereign body and could put its own interpretation upon the provisions of the scheme. A prominent Congress leader said that they had agreed to nothing except entry into the Constituent Assembly. On June 26, the Congress accepted the long-term plan but rejected the interim government scheme. June 29, the Muslim League Council withdrew its acceptance of both the interim and long-term schemes and directed its Working Committee to declare forthwith a programme of direct action.

From June 1946, onwards, the Congress carried on a campaign against grouping and sections, and August 10, while purporting to accept the scheme in its entirety, still repudiated the grouping system. It was not till December 22, after His Majesty's Government issued their statement of December 6, that the Congress accepted the Cabinet Mission's scheme in its entirety and with the interpretation put upon it by the Cabinet Mission itself. They closed the stable door long after the horse had run away. If the Congress had displayed statesmanship and obvious common sense by accepting the Cabinet Mission's scheme in its entirety and with the interpretation which they ultimately accepted immediately after the acceptance by the Muslim League on June 6, the Cabinet Mission Plan for a united India would have been set working. It was obvious that the Muslim League had with great difficulty persuaded itself to accept the Cabinet Mission scheme both interim and long-term, and it would have been wisdom on the part of other parties to complete the deal and not give any opportunity or excuse to the League to go back on acceptance. On the country, as pointed out above, the Congress leaders carried on propaganda in the country for months, and even on January 10, 1947, Mr Gandhi advised Assam to stay out of the grouping.

Britain's Part

The British Government must also share the blame for what has happened. As soon as the Muslim League accepted the scheme, Lord Wavell should have hustled the other party and persuaded them to accept the whole scheme. The British Government should have from the beginning firmly announced their interpretation of the disputed clauses as soon as the controversy arose, and not allowed wrangling about them for months. Further, when the Muslim League expressed their willingness to join the Interim Government, Lord Wavell should have clearly stipulated that their coming in the Interim Government must be dependent on their agreeing to enter the Constituent Assembly.

It is futile to attempt to hide the naked truth by saying that force of circumstances has compelled the Congress to accept the partition of India and they had to submit to the inevitable. The circumstances were of their own creation, and what had once been warded off was made inevitable by their own deeds. The cherished boon of a united India had fallen into the lap, but they by their own want of political wisdom threw it out and made it beyond their reach. Some Congress leaders have argued that they could not coerce unwilling parts of the country to join the Union. Between May 16 and June 29, 1946, there was no question of coercing anyone. The Muslim League had accepted both parts of the united India scheme of the Cabinet Mission, but the Congress missed the opportunity of closing the deal. Others say that the partition scheme is better than the Cabinet Mission scheme as in the latter there was a weak centre. This attempt at face-saving is futile. A common Central Government was a great thing to achieve. Although the Centre had only a few subjects, by experience and mutual consent its field could have been enlarged as was done in the case of the United States, Canada and Australia.

The Future

As regards the Muslim League what has happened will be regarded by them as a great triumph though, as already pointed out, such a triumph has come to them by the bungling tactics of the other parties. What has happened is indeed a great personal triumph for Mr Jinnah. Within seven years after the Lahore Pakistan resolution of 1940, he has succeeded in defeating a great political organization of sixty years standing with the backing of the large majority of the Indian people. But has he succeeded in doing good to the Muslims themselves and to his country? When the whole world is trying to integrate, it is no service to India to disintegrate the country, India divided and speaking with two voices cannot pull her proper weight in the councils of the nations. But above all, this division of India has laid the foundations of interminable quarrels and chaos which will bring untold suffering to generations yet unborn. This is what the League has accomplished. U Aung San was quite correct when he said the other day that the partition of India will endanger the peace not only of India but of Asia and the whole world.

The Times of India, 15 June 1947

Appendix 24

Jinnah's Speech to Pakistan's Constituent Assembly on 11 August 1947

Presidential address to the Constituent Assembly of Pakistan at Karachi

Mr President Ladies and Gentlemen!

I cordially thank you, with the utmost sincerity, for the honor you have conferred upon me—the greatest honour that is possible for this Sovereign Assembly to confer—by electing me as your first President. I also thank those leaders who have spoken in appreciation of my services and their personal references to me. I sincerely hope that with your support and your co-operation we shall make this Constituent Assembly an example to the world. The Constituent Assembly has got two main functions to perform. The first is the very onerous and responsible task of framing our future constitution of Pakistan and the second of functioning as a full and complete sovereign body as the Federal Legislature of Pakistan. We have to do the best we can in adopting a provisional constitution for the Federal Legislature of Pakistan. You know really that not only we ourselves are wondering but I think, the whole world is wondering at this unprecedented cyclonic revolution which has brought about the plan of creating and establishing two independent sovereign Dominions in this subcontinent. As it is, it has been unprecedented; there is no parallel in the history of the world. This mighty sub-continent with all kinds of inhabitants has been brought under a plan which is titanic, unknown, unparalleled. And what is very important with regard to it is that we have achieved it peacefully and by means of an evolution of the greatest possible character.

Dealing with our first function in this Assembly, I cannot make any well-considered pronouncement at this moment, but I shall say a few things as they occur to me. The first and the foremost thing that I would like to emphasize is this-remember that you are now a sovereign legislative body and you have got all the powers. It, therefore, places on you the gravest responsibility as to how you should take your decisions. The first observation that I would like to make is this: you will no doubt agree with me that the first duty of a government is to maintain law and order, so that the life, property and religious beliefs of its subjects are fully protected by the State.

The second thing that occurs to me is this: One of the biggest curses from which India is suffering- I do not say that other countries are free from it, but, I think, our condition is much worse-is bribery and corruption. That really is a poison. We must put that down with an iron hand and I hope that you will take adequate measures as soon as it is possible for this Assembly to do so.

Black-marketing is another curse. Well I know that black-marketers are frequently caught and punished. Judicial sentences are passed or sometimes fines only are imposed. Now you have to tackle this monster which today is a colossal crime against society, in our distressed conditions, when we constantly face shortage of food and other essential commodities of life. A citizen who does black-marketing commits, I think, a greater crime than the biggest and most grievous of crimes. These black-marketers are really knowing, intelligent and ordinarily responsible people, and when they indulge in black-marketing, I think they ought to be very severely punished, because they undermine the entire system of control and regulation of foodstuffs and essential commodities, and cause wholesale starvation and want even death.

The next thing the strikes me is this: Here again it is a legacy which has been passed on to us. Along with many other things, good and bad, has arrived this great evil-the evil of nepotism and jobbery. This evil must be crushed relentlessly. I want to make it quit clear that I shall never tolerate any kind of jobbery, nepotism or any influence directly or indirectly brought to bear upon me. Wherever I will find that such a practice is in vogue or is continuing any where, low or high. I shall certainly not countenance it.

I know there are people who do not quite agree with the division of India and the partition of the Punjab and Bengal. Much had been said against it. But now that it has been accepted, it is the duty of everyone of us to loyally abide by it and honorably act according to the agreement which is now final and binding on all. But you must remember, as I have said, that this mighty revolution that has taken place is unprecedented. One can quite understand the feeling that exists between the two communities wherever one community is in majority and the other is in minority. But the question is, whether it was possible or practicable to act otherwise than what has been done. A division had to take place. On both sides, in Hindustan and Pakistan, there are sections of people who may not agree with it, who may not like it, but in my judgment there was no other solution and I am sure future history will record its verdict in favour of it. And what is more it will be proved by actual experience as we go on that was the only solution of India's constitutional problem. Any idea of a united India could never have worked and in my judgment it would have led us to terrific disaster. May be that view is correct; may be it is not: that remains to be seen. All the same, in this division it was impossible to avoid the question of minorities being in one Dominion or the other. Now that was unavoidable. There is no other solution. Now what shall we do? Now if we want to make this great State of Pakistan happy and prosperous we should wholly and solely concentrate on the well-being of the people, and especially of the masses and the poor. If you will work in co-operation, forgetting the past, burying the hatchet, you are bound to succeed. If you change your past and work together in a spirit that everyone of you, no matter to what community he belongs, no matter what relations he had with you in the past, no matter what is his colour, caste or creed, is first, second and last a citizen of this State with equal rights, privileges and obligations, there will be no end to the progress you will make.

I cannot emphasize it too much. We should begin to work in that spirit and in course of time all these angularities of the majority and minority communities, the Hindu community and the Muslim community–because even as regards Muslims you have Pathans, Punjabis, Shias, Sunnis and so on and among the Hindus you have Brahmins, Vashnavas, Khatris, also Bengalees, Madrasis and so on will vanish. Indeed if you ask me this has been the biggest hindrance in the way of India to attain freedom and independence and but for this we would have been free peoples long ago. No power can hold another nation, and specially a nation of 400 million souls in subjection; nobody could have conquered you, and even if it had happened nobody could have continued its hold on you for any length of time but for this. Therefore, we must learn a lesson from this. You are free; you are free to go to your temples, you are free to go to your mosques or to any other place of worship in this State of Pakistan. You may belong to any religion or castes or creed–that has nothing to do with the business of the State. As you know, history shows that in England conditions, some time ago were much worse than those prevailing in India today. The roman Catholics and the Protestants persecuted each other. Even now there are some States in existence where there are discriminations made and bars imposed against a particular class. Thank God, we are not starting in those days. We are starting in the days when there is no discrimination, no distinction between one community and another, no discrimination between one caste or creed and another. We are starting with this fundamental principle that we are all citizens and equal citizens of one State. The people of England in course of time had to face the realities of the situation and had to discharge the responsibilities and burdens placed upon them by the government of their country and they went through that fire step by step. Today, you might say with justice that Roman Catholics and Protestants do not exist; what exists now is that every man is a citizen, an equal citizen of Great Britain and they are all members of the Nation. Now, I think we should keep that in front of us as our ideal and you will find that in course of time Hindus would cease to be Hindus and Muslims would cease to be Muslims, not in the religious sense because that is the personal faith of each individual, but in the political sense as citizens of the State.

Well, gentlemen, I do not wish to take up any more of your time and thank you again for the honour you have done to me. I shall always be guided by the principles of justice and fair play without any, as is put in the political language, prejudice or ill-will, in other words, partiality or favoritism. My guiding principle will be justice and complete impartiality, and I am sure that with your support and co-operation. I can look forward to Pakistan becoming one of the greatest nations of the world.

Source: *Jinnah: Speeches and Statements 1947-1948*, Oxford University Press, Karachi; 2000, pp. 25–9.

Appendix 25

Maulana Hasrat Mohani's Ghazal on Tilak

After Tilak's arrest Maulana Hasrat Mohani wrote a whole ghazal in his praise, which is as follows:

اے تلک اے افتخارِ جذبۂ حبِّ وطن   حق شناس و حق پسند و حق یقین و حق سخن

تجھ سے قائم ہے بنا آزادیِ بے باک کی   تجھ سے روشن اہل اخلاص و وفا کی انجمن

سب سے پہلے تو نے کی برداشت اے فرزندِ ہند   خدمتِ ہندوستان میں کلفتِ قیدِ محن

ذاتِ تیری رہنمائے راہِ آزادی ہوئی   تھے گرفتارِ غلامی ورنہ یارانِ وطن

تو نے خودداری کا پھونکا اے تلک ایسا فسوں   یک قلم جس سے خوشامد کی مٹی رسمِ کہن

نازِ تیری پیروی پر حسرتِ آزاد کو   اے تجھے قائم رکھے تادیر ربّ ذوالمنن

O Tilak, O pride of patriotism
The knower, the follower, the believer, and articulator of righteousness
The foundation of openly expressed Freedom rests on you
The assembly of Sincerity and Loyalty is illuminated by you
You were the first to bear O Son of India
Imprisonment in the Service of India
Your being became the beacon light of freedom
Otherwise our friends were shackled in slavery
You have cast such a spell of self respect
With one stroke, it cancelled all rituals of flattery
The free Hasrat prides himself on following you
May the Great God keep you for long

Source: Khalid Hasan Qadiri, *Hasrat Mohani*, Idarah-i-Adabiyat-i-Delhi, Delhi, 1985, p. 150.

Appendix 26

Jinnah and the Muslims of India
By A.G. Noorani

The resolution adopted by the session of the All-India Muslim League at Lahore on 23 March 1940, demanding the partition of India on the basis of religion, is one of the most consequential documents in modern history. It led to the establishment of Pakistan on 14 August 1947. Yet, it is also one of the least understood documents ever. It was either lauded or condemned but never analysed. Within Pakistan debate ranged over the issues whether it envisaged one state or two, the partition of Punjab and Bengal and federal structure at the Centre.

The Congress was too indignant at the proposal to analyse it carefully. Mohandas Karamchand Gandhi missed a fine opportunity of questioning Mohammed Ali Jinnah on its terms and implications when they met in Jinnah House at Mount Pleasant Road in Bombay from 9 to 27 September 1944. He asked questions like 'What is your definition of "minorities"?' and some specific ones which Jinnah evaded or brushed aside ('does not arise by way of clarification').

Gandhi did not persist with the queries he had raised in his letter of 15 September. But on one important point Jinnah gave an answer on 17 September whose significance escaped attention. Gandhi had referred to para 2 of the Resolution which proposed 'adequate, effective and mandatory safeguards' for minorities in both states. Jinnah replied that safeguards 'are a matter for negotiation and settlement which the minorities in the respective States, viz. Pakistan and Hindustan' — not between the two States as an integral part of the agreement embodying the terms for the settlement of the communal question on the basis of partition of India, a surgery which Jinnah claimed would cure the disease.[1]

Neither the British government's statement of 3 June 1947, the Partition Plan which, both, the League and the Indian National Congress accepted, nor the Indian Independence Act, 1947, which they had vetted, contained even a perfunctory reference to the minorities. They were confined to the consequences of the partition — the princely states, assets and liabilities, treaties, etc. The gravest consequence — the presence of minorities in both states — was ignored. Surgery was not necessary.

No one was more aware of this than Jinnah, the record shows that before as well as after the establishment of Pakistan that awareness did into elude him. He was a lawyer with a keen understanding of political realities. 'It does not require political wisdom to realize that all safeguards and settlements would be a scrap of paper, unless they are backed by power. Politics means power and not relying on cries of justice or fair play or goodwill.' Jinnah told the historic Lucknow session of the League on 15 October 1937. To the Muslim

University Union at Aligarh he elaborated, in a speech at the Strachey Hall on 5 February 1938: 'The only hope for minorities is to organize themselves and secure a definite share in power to safeguard their rights and interests. Without such power no Constitution can work successfully in India'.[2]

In this, Jinnah was only too right. Constitutional protection alone is no solution; power or empowerment is necessary. He sought a coalition based sharing of power with the Congress but was rebuffed.[3]

Unfortunately partition led to protectionism in both states. Thus a close analysis of the Lahore Resolution is indispensable to an understanding of Jinnah's dilemmas and the situation he faced in 1947; as, indeed, did the minorities. It had five paras. The first two were preambular; the Government of India Act, 1935 was rejected but no 'revised plan' would be acceptable unless it was 'framed' with the consent of the Muslims.

Para 3, popularly cited as para 1, said that no 'constitutional plan' would be acceptable to them unless it was based on the 'basic principle' of the partition which it defined. While para 4 on the safeguards was bandied about as a sop to the minorities, completely ignored was para 5. It authorized the Working Committee 'to frame a scheme of Constitution in accordance with these basic principles, providing for the assumption finally by the respective regions of all power such as defence, external affairs, communication, customs, and such other matters as may be necessary.' Dr B.R. Ambedkar was one of the very few to ask 'what does the word "finally" which occurs in the last part of the Lahore Resolution mean?'[4] But neither he nor Gandhi nor any one else asked the League to produce the 'scheme' it had promised in the para. One man who was aware of the linkage between the three operative paras was Sir Abdullah Haroon. His committee, set up by the League, drew up a report which harmonized the principle of partition with the effectiveness of the safeguards. Jinnah repudiated the entire exercise.

Sir Sikandar Hayat Khan, author of an earlier draft which was drastically and unwisely pruned a day before the resolution was passed, boldly repudiated the Lahore Resolution in a famous speech to the Punjab Legislative Assembly on 11 March 1941. 'The resolution which I drafted was radically amended by the Working Committee and there is a wide divergence in the resolution I drafted and the one that was finally passed.'[5] What he had in mind was an agency at the centre, set up by mutual consent and with liberty to secede from it. Partition and safeguards ensuring empowerment would be linked in such a scheme Jinnah offered precisely such a proposal to the Cabinet Mission on 12 May 1946 and went on to accept its plan of 16 May 1946. Both were based on sharing power. The Congress had other plans. Partition followed a partition that was delinked altogether from minority safeguards. It was a partition of the kind none had seen even in a wild nightmare.

That disconnect between partition and protection reflected a transformation in Jinnah's splendid record as a champion of the rights of minorities to one who espoused the cause of provinces in which Muslims were in a majority, even to the neglect of safeguards for Muslim minorities. That record bears recalling. It is most instructive in revealing the political compulsions which shaped the course of a man of sturdy independence, sterling integrity and keen realism like Jinnah.

Theories do not reckon with the record and lapse into denigration or adulation. Marguerite Dove deserves credit for highlighting Jinnah's role and self-perception as a mediator between Indian nationalism and Muslim opinion and interests.[6] He asked the All-Parties National Convention on the Nehru Report on 22 December 1928, 'would you be content if I were to say, I am with you? Do you want or do you not want the Muslim India to go along with you?'[7] The jibe about a 'nationalist' who turned 'communalist' is for the ignorant and malicious, Jinnah bore in mind both the interests at all times; the country as well as the community's. They did not conflict.

He questioned the credentials of the 35 Muslims, led by the Aga Khan who waited on a deputation to the viceroy, Lord Minto, on 1 October 1906 in a letter which *The Times of India* did not publish but the *Gujrati* of Bombay did on 7 October. On 27 December 1906 at the Congress' session in Calcutta he praised it for its stand against the Privy Council's ruling on Waqf-alal-aulad (which he succeeded in overriding by Legislation). The next day he said that 'there should be no reservation for any class or community'.[8]

The Muslim League was established at Dacca on 31 December 1906. The Indian Musalman Association was launched to counter it at Calcutta on 8 January 1907. Nawab Syed Mohammed was its president. Jinnah was one of its three vice-presidents.[9] Jinnah was persuaded to join the League only on 10 October 1913. In the Congress, meanwhile, he moved a resolution against extension of separate communal electorates to local bodies but was careful to stress that those were his personal views. 'I do not represent the Muhammedan Community here nor have I any mandate from the Muhammedan Community.'[10]

His outlook was revealed in a moving letter he wrote in January 1910. Hindus and Muslims should 'combine in one harmonious union for the common good, where we have to live together in every district, town and hamlet; where our daily life is interwoven with each other in every square mile of one common country.'[11]

It was in this spirit that the League led by Jinnah, and the Congress led by his friend Bal Gangadhar Tilak agreed on a scheme of reforms at a joint conference of the Congress and the League in Calcutta on 18 November 1916. Both parties held their annual sessions at Lucknow on 30–31 December 1916 and endorsed it; hence, the Lucknow Pact—the Congress accepted separate electorates as well as larger number of seats to the delight of Muslims in provinces where they were in a minority but Jinnah had to scale down Muslim representation in the Punjab and Bengal with lasting consequences. Thirty years later in 1946, despite a convincing victory at the polls, the Nawab of Mamdot could not command a majority in the Punjab assembly.

Under the Congress–League scheme Muslims got over-representation in the provincial legislatures in Bihar, Bombay, Madras and the Central Provinces. Being aware of the dominant position of the Muslims in UP, they were given 30 per cent of the seats there. The price paid for these concessions was that the principle of weightage for the minority community was also applied to Bengal and the Punjab, reducing Muslim representation in the Provincial Legislative Councils from 55 per cent to 50 per cent in the Punjab and to 40 per cent in Bengal.

The Lucknow Pact signified the increasing eagerness of the Congress to win Muslim co-operation in the nationalist movement. The Hindus of UP and the Punjab had misgivings regarding the pact as they felt that their interests had been jeopardized to win Muslim co-operation. On the Muslim side, the Punjab and Bengal were the most vociferous provinces in their condemnation of the Pact.[12]

Prof. Ishtiaq Husain Qureshi pointed out that 'weightage in the minority provinces were not of much use' to the Muslims. They remained a minority, 'whereas the loss of majorities in two major provinces resulted in serious handicaps. Its full effect was felt after the elections of 1937 and 1945, when the Muslim League encountered grave difficulties in forming ministries in the Punjab and Bengal.'[13]

Jinnah faced a genuine problem besides the community's views—separate electorates were meant for a minority, not a majority. But a backward majority felt insecure in voting in joint electorates. When Sir Fazl-i-Husain opposed Jinnah's active entry into Punjab politics in 1936 he complained 'in the case of the Punjab the Muslim majority in the Provincial Assembly is nominal, and it is almost impossible to secure a Muslim majority through a separate control of elections.'[14] Hence, his preference for the secular, if Muslim dominated, Unionist Party.

This is what Jinnah said as a witness appearing before the Joint Select Committee appointed by Parliament on the Government of India Bill, 1919, in reply to questions No. 3808:

> The position of Bengal was this: In Bengal the Muslims are in a majority, and the argument was advanced that any section or any community which is in the majority cannot claim a separate electorate: separate electorate is to protect the minority. But the counter-argument was perfectly true that numerically we are in a majority but as voters we are in the minority in Bengal, because of poverty and backwardness and so on. It was said: Very well, the fix 40 per cent, because if you are really put to test you will not get 40 per cent because you will not be qualified as voters. Then we had the advantage in other Provinces.

However to some critics Jinnah sacrificed the interests of Punjab and Bengal to secure a better deal for Muslims in the provinces where they were in a minority.

It is not necessary to trace here the subsequent course of Indian politics from the perspective of Jinnah's efforts for a settlement and the Congress' rebuffs. Marguerite Dove and Uma Kaura had done it with admirable succinctness and documentation.

Jinnah's outlook was optimistic. He said at the League's session on 31 December 1917:

> Do you think that in the first instance it is possible that the Government of this country can become a Hindu Government? Do you think that the Government can be conducted merely by the ballot box? Do you think that because the Hindus are in a majority they have therefore to carry a measure in the Legislative Council and there is an end of it? If 70 million Musalmans do not approve of the measure which is carried by a ballot box, do you think that it could be enforced or administered in this country? Do you think that the Hindu statesmen with their intellect, with their past history, will ever think of enforcing measures by the ballot box when you get Self-Government? Then what is there to fear? Therefore I say to my Musalman friends: Fear not. This is a bogey, which is put before you by your enemies to frighten you, to scare you away from co-operation and unity which are essential for the establishment of Self-Government. This country has not to be governed by the Hindus and, let me submit, it has not to be governed by the Musalmans either, and certainly not by the English. It is to be governed by the people and the sons of this country. I, standing here—believe I am voicing the feeling of whole of India—demand the immediate transfer of a substantial power of the Government of the country.[15]

Over a decade later and despite his bitter experience over the Nehru Report he said in the Central Legislative Assembly on 7 March 1930:

> Seventy millions of Mussalmans should not be afraid of facing the issue squarely and fairly no matter what the Government do and no matter what the Hindus do. You are seventy millions. What is the good of leaning upon the Government? What is the good of your appealing to the Hindus? Do you want concessions? I do not want concessions. What is the good? You are seventy million Mussalmans. Organise yourselves in this country, and you will be a power, and you will be able to dictate not only to the Government, but to the Hindus and to every one else your just rights. Show a manly attitude.[16]

Theorists are welcome to their sport. The record speaks for itself on the Congress' arrogance of power when it formed ministries in the provinces of Bombay, Madras, Central Provinces, UP, Bihar, Orissa, Assam and the NWFP, Jinnah's *crie de coeur* at Aligarh on 5 February 1938 explains the change: 'At that time there was pride in me and I used to beg from the Congress.'[17]

He had to devise an alternative to the federation. The Viceroy, Lord Linlithgow, asked him to propound an alternative. Jinnah proposed partition but with enough qualifications in the Lahore Resolution (the last para and the reference to 'territorial adjustments') to suggest that he was prepared to consider a power-sharing arrangement at the centre. Jinnah's article in *Time and Tide* of London, on 19 January 1940, said: 'A constitution must be evolved that recognizes that there are in India two nations who both must share the governance of their common motherland. In evolving such a Constitution, the Muslims are ready to co-operate with the British Government, the Congress or any other party so that the present enmities may cease and India may make its

APPENDIX 26

place amongst the great countries of the world.' That was power sharing at the centre in a united India, not partition. If Pakistan was proposed only two months later, it could not have been the last unalterable last word. The Lahore Resolution received a wild reaction, however, and Jinnah's offers of compromise in May 1946 were spurned by Gandhi and the Congress.

Jinnah now began exerting every nerve to achieve Pakistan. He cut the umbilical cord between partition and safeguards for minorities and made little secret that they would have to fend for themselves. The speeches were revealing.

28 December 1948: 'The Muslim minorities in the Hindu provinces would put up with their fate, but they would not stand in the way of Muslim majority provinces becoming free.'[18]

10 March 1941: 'The creation of these independent states will be the surest guarantee for the fair treatment of the minorities. When the time for consultation and negotiation comes, the case of Muslims in the minority provinces will certainly not go by default.'[19] A rare, if not solitary, assurance of safeguards defined in the pact on partition.

30 March 1941: 'In order to liberate 7 crores of Muslims where they were in a majority, he was willing to perform the last ceremony of martyrdom if necessary and let two crores of Muslims be smashed.'[20]

1 July 1942: 'The only way for Britain to do justice is to hand over the Muslim homelands to the Musalmans and the Hindu homelands to the Hindus.'[21] This was bad history. Islam came to Malabar in the South before it appeared in the north. Muslim 'homelands' were spread all over India. The 'homelands' theory, although more plausible there, played havoc in Sri Lanka with the notorious Cleghorn minute on Tamil 'homelands' in the north and east. There was a yet graver flaw in Jinnah's scheme. It was majoritarian and left no room for a composite culture or a secular setup. The winner took all—Hindu rule in one part ('Hindu India') Muslim rule in the other ('Muslim India'). There was another and equally consequential flaw, based on the two-nation theory. Sample this speech at Aligarh on 2 November 1942: 'Three-fourths of India go to Hindus and only one-fourth to Muslims.' Where did this leave the minorities in both states? Worse, he added 'You will protect and safeguard our minorities in your zones and we will protect and guard your minorities in ours.'[22] The implications are staggering.

November 1945: 'Let 3/4ths of India belong to Hindus where they can rule as they wish and let Muslims have 1/4th of India where they are in a majority.'[23]

3 April 1946, interview to the BBC: 'If Britain in Gladstone's time could intervene in Armenia in the name of protection of minorities, why should it not be right for us to do so in the case of our minorities in Hindustan, if they are oppressed.'[24] Britain was then the world's strongest power. Even in 1946 Jinnah knew that Pakistan would be militarily weaker than India.

26 November 1946: Exchange of population should be considered.[25]

14 December 1946: 'The differences between Hindus and Muslims are so fundamental that there is nothing that matters in life upon which we agree.'[26]

The hostage theory was not absent from Jinnah's mind. He told Norman Cliff of the *News Chronicle* of London (12 April 1946) that Muslims in India were 'fortunate that there would be a corresponding minority of 25,000,000 Hindus in Pakistan.' After the partition, Weldon James of *Collier's Weekly* reported (25 August 1947) that Jinnah said: 'The minorities are in effect hostages to the requirement of mutual cooperation and good neighborliness between the Governments of Pakistan and the India Union.'

In 1947 the two states did not enter into a treaty on minority rights; but the fate of the hapless minorities depended on the state of Indio-Pak relations.

This was not unforeseen, Jinnah had told the *News Chronicle* of London, on 15 February 1945 that 'the Hindus must trust their minorities to the Pakistan government and we must trust the Hindus with our Muslim minorities.' Trust is a far cry from the 'adequate, effective and mandatory safeguards' proposed in the Lahore resolution.

But trust in good behaviour by their respective states, rather than effective safeguards, were all that the minorities could hope for. At his last press conference in Delhi on 14 July 1947 Jinnah said:

> 'Minorities, to whichever community they may belong, will be safeguarded. Their religion or belief will be secure. There will be no interference of any kind with their freedom of worship. They will have their protection with regard to their religion, faith, their life, their culture. They will be, in all respects, the citizens of Pakistan without any distinction of caste or creed. They will have their rights and privileges and no doubt, along with it goes the obligation of citizenship. Therefore, the minorities have their responsibilities also and they will play their part in the affairs of this State. As long as the minorities are loyal to the State and owe true allegiance and as long as I have any power, they need have no apprehension of any kind.... You cannot have a minority which is disloyal and plays the role of sabotaging the State. That minority, of course, becomes intolerable in any State. I advise Hindus and Muslims and every citizen to be loyal to his State.[27]

On 22 July 1947 the Partition Council met with the Viceroy, Lord Mountbatten, in the Chair. Jinnah and Liaquat Ali Khan represented the future Government of Pakistan, Vallabhbhai Patel, and Rajendra Prasad represented 'the future Government of India.' Baldev Singh represented the Sikhs. A Joint Communiqué recorded:

> Both the Congress and the Muslim League have given assurances of fair and equitable treatment to the minorities after the transfer of power. The two future governments re-affirm these assurances. It is their intention to safeguard the legitimate interests of all citizens irrespective of religion, caste, or sex. In the exercise of their normal civic rights, all citizens will be regarded as equal, and both the governments will assure to all people within their territories the exercise of liberties such as freedom of speech, the right to form associations, the right to worship in their own way, and the protection of their language and culture. Both the governments

further undertake that there shall be no discrimination against those who before 15 August may have been political opponents.[28]

This fell far short of a formal agreement.

The Muslim League's members in India now thoroughly demoralized, sought Jinnah's counsel before he left for Karachi. Mohammed Raza Khan, a prominent Leaguer from Madras ruefully recorded in his memories *What Price Freedom* (1969):

> About the end of July 1947, the Muslim members of the Central Legislative Assembly met Mr Jinnah who was also the leader of the Muslim League Party in the Assembly. It was for the last time that they met him, for he was then arranging to leave for Karachi. It was their farewell meeting. Many members expressed concern about the future of the Muslims in India. When they sought his advice about their future, and that of the Muslim League, he refrained from saying anything specific. He, however, told them they had enough experience under his leadership, and they would have to evolve their own policy and programme. They had to decide things for themselves in the new set-up, and in the changed circumstances. But he made it clear, in no uncertain terms, that they should be loyal to India, and that they should not seek to ride two horses. It has, therefore, to be said in clearest terms that Mr Jinnah did not give any positive directions or instructions to Indian Muslims as to their future.[29]

The most revealing encounter was between Jinnah and a delegation of the Coorg Muslims at 10 Aurangzeb Road, New Delhi on 25 July. He said:

> Muslims in India have nothing to be afraid of. They will still be several crores in number. They have made many sacrifices along with the Muslims of the majority provinces. It is as a result of the sacrifices made by all of them in India that we have been able to achieve Pakistan. While the Mussalmans of the majority provinces will be in a position to wield authority and power and mould their destinies according to their genius, the Mussalmans in India have yet to go through a number of ordeals, sufferings, and sacrifices. Their future will remain dark for some years to come and thick clouds will be hanging over them. They only way out for them will be to become much more active, much more courageous, and work harder than ever before. Trusting in God they should always be up and doing and go forward undeterred by the discouraging circumstances around them.
>
> What they need first is the correct leadership. If they could find men who are possessed of high ideals and sterling character and men who could understand their difficulties and men who are above board, it will be some consolation to start with. What you have to do is to maintain your identity and your individuality in the first instance. You can adapt yourselves to the changing circumstances and environment, without sacrificing your identity and individuality... You must also avoid occasions of conflict with the majority community and show by dint of your merit and intellectual capacity that you cannot be ignored under any circumstances.
>
> As regards your loyalty, you cannot but be loyal to your country. Just as I want every Hindu in Pakistan to be loyal to Pakistan, so do I want every Muslim in India to be loyal to India. There is no other alternative.

You can be useful citizens of your country in two ways by becoming (i) educationally forward and (ii) economically sound, and thereby making yourselves indispensable to the country. To achieve this you have to devote much of your attention to the education of your young men and see that they are well equipped. You should prepare them for technical and professional careers... While you make progress educationally, you should at the same time continue your business activities so that you are economically strong. Without this you will not be able to keep pace with the march of events... Worse coming to worst, you will have a homeland in Pakistan which will give you a shelter whenever you need it. What is more, there will be adjustments between the two countries and there will be territorial safeguards for the protection of minorities on either side. All that you have got to do so is to find the correct leadership in India, which will guide you and take you through our ordeals smoothly without involving you in a conflict with the powers that be and provide opportunities for you to develop educationally and economically. ... So long as I am alive, I shall watch with great interest, care, and anxiety your struggles in India, your interests, and your future. I shall pray that God may come to our succour in times of our difficulties and be with you to lead you to prosperity and happiness. Your sacrifices in the making of Pakistan are great. How can we ever forget them or forget you? You and your sacrifices will always be in my thoughts and feeling. May God be with you. Goodbye![30]

That was inspiring but not particularly helpful.

Jinnah's historic speech on 11 August 1947 at the inauguration of Pakistan's constituent assembly as its president, is recalled still. It was delivered extempore and reflected sincerity and spontaneity. The fundamentals he propounded are of abiding relevance. He advised tolerance and said:

We should begin to work in that spirit and in course of time all these angularities of the majority and minority communities, the Hindu community and the Muslim community—because even as regards Muslims you have Pathans, Punjabis, Shias, Sunnis and so on and among the Hindus you have Brahmins, Vashnavas, Kharis, also Bengalees, Madrasis, and so on—will vanish. No power can hold another nation, and specially a nation of 400 million souls in subjection; ... You may belong to any religion or caste or creed—that has nothing to do with the business of the state... We are starting in the days when there is no discrimination, no distinction between one community and another, no discrimination between one caste or creed and another. We are starting with this fundamental principle that we are all citizens and equal citizens of one State. I think we should keep that in front of us as our ideal and you will find that in course of time Hindus would cease to be Hindus and Muslims would cease to be Muslims, not in the religious sense because that is the personal faith of each individual, but the political sense as citizens of the State.[31]

While this speech, notable for renunciation of the two-nation theory ('a nation of 400 million') came too late to provide redress, its significance as an enunciation of a noble ideal cannot be underestimated.

It is not necessary to recount here the fate that befell the minorities in both countries after the partition.[32] Jinnah's anguish was sincere and deep. He was pained and genuinely surprised at the situation that confronted him. His interview to Duncan Hooper of Reuters on 25 October 1947 reflected his dismay at the League's decline in India. It bears quotation, in extenso:

> It is also very unfortunate that the Muslims in Hindustan are told threateningly that they must abjure the leadership of the League and declare their 'folly' in having supported Pakistan and in believing in this 'fantastic two-nation theory.' Also that certain tests and standards of loyalty are demanded from them.... As for the two-nation theory, it is not a theory but a fact ... To the Muslim minority and their leaders left in India, I have already conferred advice that they must reorganize themselves under their own chosen leadership as they have a very big part to play in safeguarding the rights and interests of many millions. They have already professed under my advice their loyalty to the Government of India and made their position clear on the very first day when they attended the Indian Dominion Constituent Assembly. In spite of this, insidious propaganda is going on that they have been let down by the Muslim League and Pakistan is indifferent to what may happen to them. The Muslim minority in India have played a magnificent part in the achievement and establishment of Pakistan. They were fully alive to the consequences that they would have to remain in Hindustan as minorities but not at the cost of their self-respect and honour. Nobody visualized that a powerful section in India was bent upon the ruthless extermination of Muslims and had prepared a well organized plan to achieve that and .... I, therefore, while deeply and fully sympathizing with their sufferings, urge upon Muslims in India to bear their trial with courage and fortitude and not get panicky and play into the hands of our enemies by hasty decisions or actions. They should not in their adversity be led away by mischievous propaganda of interested parties and hold the Muslim League and its leadership responsible for all their tribulation. They must hold on to their posts, and Pakistan, I can assure them, will not be a mere spectator of their sufferings. We are deeply concerned with their welfare and future, and we shall do everything in our power to avert the danger that they are facing. I sincerely hope that with the cooperation of the Indian Dominion we shall be able to secure a fair deal for them.[33]

But he made no effort whatever to seek India's 'cooperation' for a joint policy towards the minorities in India and Pakistan. On the contrary he scotched a move by H.S. Suhrawardy in that direction. That was but one of the three fateful decisions Jinnah took which harmed the interests of Indian Muslims instead of improving their lot. It was bad enough to nominate Chaudhry Khaliquzzaman as leader of the League's Party in the Constituent Assembly of India in preference to the highly respected and sternly independent Nawab Mohammed Ismail. It was worse to reproach the pliant Chaudhry Khaliquzzaman for not toeing Pakistan's line on Kashmir. Pakistan's Foreign Minister, Zafrullah Khan, had, in a speech at the United Nations, spoken of 'the slaughter of Muslims.' Chaudhry Khaliquzzaman issued a statement in reply on 20 September 1947. He was being cruelly taunted in India for his past. When he met Jinnah on 5 October 1947 he was taken to task for the statement.

> Mr Jinnah came with my rejoinder to Sir Zafrullah Khan's statement in his hand and read it to me, expressing surprise that it had been broadcast from India for three days.

I reminded him that it was the statement of the Leader of the Opposition in the Indian Constituent Assembly and India had attached great importance to it. Thereupon he said, 'It has hurt us very much!' I asked him how anything said by a Muslim citizen of India could bind down the Government of Pakistan or have any effect on it. Nevertheless as he was dissatisfied with my answer, I said I would not go back to India but would send in my resignation, to enable someone else who might have his confidence to replace me and serve the Indian Muslim. Thereafter Shaheed Suhrawardy gave him the document which he had shown me at Delhi, to go thorough it. Mr Jinnah looked at it and returned it to Shaheed without any comment....

What pained me most in the Quaid-i-Azam's reception of me was the fact that he had been mainly responsible for putting the burden of the leadership of Indian Muslims on my shoulders, but at the time of my interview with him, which was the last in my life, he did not realize my responsibilities towards the Indian Muslim, who were facing a situation never before experienced in their history of a thousand years.[34]

He soon left India for Pakistan as did other League leaders like Hussain Imam and Z.H. Lari.

Khaliquzzaman's reference to the document which Huseyn Shaheed Suhrawardy gave to Jinnah and which Jinnah returned 'Without any comment' had a sad aftermath. Khaliquzzaman revealed:

Shaheed Suhrawardy came to see me one day at Rafi Qidwai's house and showed me a document concerning the Muslim minority in India and suggesting means for their protection. On the very first page of this document there was remark in the handwriting of Gandhiji, "It can be abridged. The question is whether Quaid-i-Azam would abide by it." After examining the document I asked Shaheed whether it had been approved by Mr Jinnah. He asked me to come with him to see Gandhiji to discuss the matter. I said I had talked with him and I did not see any point in meeting him again.[35]

Suhrawardy, undeterred by Jinnah's indifference on 5 October, wrote to him on 8 October setting out detailed suggestions for improving the lot of the minorities. A revealing correspondence ensued which came to light only in 2001 on the publication of *Jinnah Papers*.[36] Its core was a common policy towards the minorities, jointly implemented by both governments. One has only to read some of the suggestions to realize that they would have provided substantial redress. They read:

That it is not the intention of either of the Dominions to go to war and that both the Dominions renounce war for all time as a method of settlings disputes.... A declaration of guarantee to minorities of protection of life, property, etc. ... Representatives of both the Dominions (who may be called Peace Commissioners with diplomatic privileges) will be stationed in various parts of the Dominions and will do all they can to promote peace and harmony between the communities, acquaint themselves with the difficulties and complaints of the majority and minority communities, keep themselves informed of incidents and remove all causes of suspicion and mistrust. They shall be assured safety of their persons and facilities to move whosoever they deem it necessary to proceed for the discharge of their duties. In the services, there should be a mixture of Hindu and Muslim officers and steps should be taken for this purpose. Representatives of minorities should be included in the Ministries. ... The houses and properties of refugees are being dealt with in different manners in the two Dominions. There should be a common policy.

Annexed to the letter was a draft declaration.

Gandhi wrote to Jinnah on 11 October 1947 after he heard Suhrawardy's report on his talks with Jinnah. He suggested 'In paragraph 2(4) of his letter dated the 8th October to you, I would add "and will submit to a tribunal of permanent arbitration selected from Indians alone (i.e., from the members of the two Dominions)." In paragraph 2(8) or in any other suitable place, I would like the following idea to be brought out: "Each State will induce the refugees to return and occupy their respective homes".'

Apparently a misunderstanding crept up. Suhrawardy had told Jinnah, when they met on 8 October that Gandhi had made 'endorsements in pencil' on his draft suggestions. Jinnah wrote to Suhrawardy on 16 October asking for that document, which was an exchange between two other persons. A day earlier Suhrawardy had written to Jinnah conveying Gandhi's 'regret at the interpretation of the endorsement which in any event was his reaction but was not meant as a message to you' Gandhi had however accepted Suhrawardy's draft with two changes. So had Nehru, who mattered more as prime minister. Liaquat Ali Khan also agreed. 'You are the only one who can save the situation,' Suhrawardy pleaded with Jinnah.[37] To Jinnah's request he replied on 17 October to say that the first draft with the pencilled comments had been destroyed. In any case Jinnah had the finalized text which Gandhi 'had endorsed'. Jinnah's rejoined on 18 October that Gandhi's letter to him of 11 October seemed to refer an earlier draft. But that hardly mattered. What mattered was the final draft endorsed by Gandhi and Nehru. Jinnah could have suggested changes. He ignored the draft. He insinuated that the earlier draft was destroyed deliberately ('in such a hurry'). Given the stakes—the interest of a minority whose cause he had fought for all his life, it is a pity that Jinnah's distrust beclouded his vision.

Suhrawardy wrote to him, once again, on 28 October from Delhi, to point out that they were Gandhi's 'immediate reactions and were not meant as a message to you ... The final suggestions are now before you, and wait your approval or reactions ... I beg this of you with folded hands. Please do not leave us in the lurch ... we only want you to cooperate, with the Indian Union so that the minorities conditions improve.'[38]

Far worse followed when the council of the All-India Muslim League met in Karachi on 14 and 15 December 1947 for its last session to split up the Party, Jinnah insisted, against the opposition of the Leaguers from India, that the Muslim League re-establish itself in India. Jinnah said: 'There must be a Muslim League in Hindustan. If you are thinking of anything else, you are finished. If you want to wind up the League you can do so; but I think it would be a great mistake. I know there is an attempt. Maulana Abdul Kalam Azad and others are trying to break the identity of Muslims in India. Do not allow it. Do not do it.'

Hussain Imam then moved his amendment: 'In the resolution, "... in place of the All-India Muslim League, there shall be separate League organizations for Pakistan and the Indian Union," the word "shall" should be replaced by "may".' He said, 'People here do not know the difficulties the Muslims are facing in India. They should be left free to decide their future according to the circumstances.' No one supported his amendment.

Jinnah said, 'I sympathize with Mr Hussain Imam. He has not read the resolution properly. You should constitute the Muslim League in India. If you do not, you would go back to 1906. You are forty million; you can have a leader—if not one, then two or more. We cannot give directives to you. When you are strong and Pakistan is developed, the settlement will come.'

Speaking next, Mr Suhrawardy added:

> I oppose this resolution. I am amongst those who had proposed some time ago that the League should be split. So, some might be surprised at my opposition. But before we split, my concern is to do something practical about the protection of minorities. I say when our objective is achieved, then why should we not organize ourselves in such a manner that the minorities are given the opportunity, on a national basis, to join us in the same organization? If you do that in Pakistan, it would help us in the Indian Union. If you form a national body here it would strengthen the hands of Nehru and Gandhi. The AICC passed a very good resolution. We should also have passed a similar resolution.

Abdur Rab Nishtar said, 'Our two friends want to finish the League. I say if the League exists, Islam exists, Mussalmans exist. We shall never allow the League to be wound up. The protection of minorities in India depends on the strength of Pakistan. We shall do all to protect them.'

Liaquat Ali Khan supported Sardar Abdul Rab Nishtar. The resolution was passed with an overwhelming majority. Some ten members, including Suhrawardy and Mian Iftikharuddin, voted against it.

Liaquat Ali Khan and Mohammed Ismail, president of the Madras Provincial Muslim League, were elected as convenors for the Pakistan Muslim League and the Indian Muslim league, respectively. It was decided to hold their sessions shortly at Karachi and Madras.[39]

Mohammed Ismail was not even a member of the League's Working Committee. Jinnah and his colleagues did not heed the interests of Indian Muslims voiced by their representatives. It was the state interests of Pakistan that moved them. Even those interests should have prompted a positive response to Suhrawardy's draft. Sadly, rhetoric apart, Jinnah did nothing to protect the interests of Indian Muslims.

The safeguards envisaged in the Lahore Resolution were not stipulated or negotiated with India at the time of the partition. The Lahore Resolution was torn apart at the very moment of its fulfilment. As the record shows, it followed inexorably from a conscious separation of its two vital paragraphs in 1940 no sooner the resolution was adopted. A promising draft declaration as basis for an Indo-Pak accord was ignored. Khaliquzzaman was reproached for not following Pakistan's line and the Muslim League was foisted on Indian Muslims against the wishes of the Leaguers from India.

Previously published in *Criterion*, Volume III, No. 4, October–December 2008.

Notes

1. Vide *Jinnah–Gandhi Talks*, S. Shamsul Hasan, Central Office, All-India Muslim League, Daryaganj, Delhi, 1944, pp. 18 and 24.
2. Jamiluddin Ahmad, *Speeches and Writings of Mr Jinnah*, Shaikh Mohammad Ashraf, Lahore, Vol. 1, pp. 30 and 43, respectively.
3. Uma Kaura, *Muslims and Indian Nationalism*, Manohar, Delhi, 1977; Marguerite Dove, *Fortified Future: The Conflict over Congress Ministries in British India*, Chanakya Publications, Delhi, 1987, an excellent but neglected work.
4. B.R. Ambedkar, *Pakistan or the Partition of India*, Thacker & Co. Ltd., Bombay, 1946, p. 411.
5. V.P. Menon, *The Transfer of Power in India*, Orient Longman Ltd., India, 1957, p. 444.
6. Dove, p. 398.
7. Syed Sharifuddin Pirzada, *The Collected Works of Quaid-i-Azam Mohammad Ali Jinnah*, Vol. III, p. 321.
8. Pirzada, Vol. I, pp. 1 and 4.
9. Rafiq Zakaria, *Rise of Muslims in Indian Politics: An Analysis of Developments from 1885 to 1906*, Bombay, Somaiya Publications, 1970, p.111.
10. Pirzada, Vol. I, p. 17.
11. Ibid., p. 15.
12. Kaura, pp. 20–1.
13. Ishtiaq Hussain Qureshi, *The Struggle for Pakistan*, University of Karachi, Karachi, 1969, p. 47.
14. Azim Husain, *Fazl-i-Hussain: A Political Biography*, Longmans, Green & Co. 1946, p. 308.
15. Pirzada, Vol. I, p. 252.
16. Pirzada, Vol. III, p. 439.
17. Jamiluddin Ahmad, Vol. I, p. 39.
18. Jamiluddin Ahmad, Vol. I, p. 216.
19. Ibid., p. 242.
20. Ibid., p. 246.
21. Ibid., p. 388.
22. Ibid., p. 441.
23. Ahmad, p. 256.
24. Ibid., p. 286.

25. Ibid., p. 371.
26. Ibid., p. 389.
27. *Jinnah: Speeches and Statements 1947–1948*, Oxford University Press, Karachi, p. 13.
28. A.G. Noorani, *Muslims of India: A Documentary Record 1947–2000*, Oxford University Press, New Delhi, 2003, p. 35.
29. Raza Mohammed Khan, *What Price Freedom*, 1969, pp. 321–2.
30. *Jinnah Papers*, First Series Vol. III, pp. 28–9.
31. *Jinnah: Speeches and Statements 1947-48*, pp. 28–9.
32. Vide an excellent account in Vazira Fazila-Yaqoobali Zamindar, *The Long Partition and the Making of Modern South Asia: Refugees, Boundaries and Histories*; Oxford University Press, Karachi, 2008.
33. *Selected Speeches and Statements of the Quaid-i-Azam Mohammad Ali Jinnah*, Research Society of Pakistan, Lahore, pp. 439–41.
34. Chaudhry Khaliquzzaman, *Pathway to Pakistan*, Longmans, Pakistan Branch, 1961, pp. 410–14.
35. Ibid., pp. 409–10.
36. *Jinnah Papers, 1 October–31 December 1947*, First series, Vol. VI, Government of Pakistan, pp. 689–738.
37. Ibid., p. 712.
38. Ibid., p. 716.
39. Pirzada, *Foundations of Pakistan, All-India Muslim League Documents 1906-1947*, Vol. II, pp. 570–6.

Appendix 27

The Haroon Report
By A.G. Noorani

The Haroon Report is the most neglected document in all the discourse on the Pakistan movement, but is second in significance only to the Lahore Resolution which it was intended to supplement. Its tragic fate reflects the course which events took. It still bears a profound relevance to the relations between India and Pakistan and to the state of the minorities in both countries. The report touched the very core of the problem as it existed in 1940.

Only the political skills of Mohammed Ali Jinnah could have managed the contradictions between the claims of the Muslim-majority provinces of British India and those of Muslims in other provinces. He performed the feat to emerge as the Quaid-i-Azam of the Muslims of the entire subcontinent. Compromises had to be made. Punjab was not happy with the Lucknow Pact of 1916, for instance.

Imminence of independence made the dilemma acute. Secession ensured the independence of the Muslim-majority provinces from an all-India federation. Their separation spelt problems for Muslims minorities elsewhere. Ayesha Jalal holds:

> There were contradictions between Muslim interests in majority provinces, and between an apparently separatist demand for autonomous Muslim states and the need for a centre capable of ensuring the interests of Muslims in the rest of India. At no point was Jinnah able to reconcile these contradictions. He came away from Lahore not with a coherent demand which squared the circle of these difficulties, but simply with the right to negotiate for Muslims on a completely new basis.[1]

Ayesha Jalal's view is shared by many. The Haroon Report resolved the dilemma.

Circumstances forced Jinnah to mould his strategy but he was always prepared to negotiate. The Congress set its face against it. It never propounded an alternative which the Muslim League could reasonably be expected even to consider. The last paragraph of the League's Lahore Resolution of 23 March 1940 on the partition of India was overlooked by politicians on both sides. 'This session further authorizes the Working Committee to frame a scheme of constitution in accordance with these basic principles, providing for the assumption finally by the respective regions of all powers such as defence, external affairs, communications, customs, and such other matters as may be necessary.' That 'scheme of constitution' was never framed, nor did the Congress ever demand that it be produced. The word 'finally' clearly signified an interim centre during the transitional period. In December 1940, the Haroon

Report addressed both these points. Its background and its aftermath provide lessons for today.

In 1938, Sir Abdullah Haroon was not only chairman of the reception committee of the Sindh Provincial Muslim League conference at Karachi but was the brains behind the resolution on partition moved by Shaikh Abdul Majid Sindhi. It envisaged 'the federation of Muslim States and the federation of non-Muslim States'. Jinnah disapproved of it. With his tacit consent, Haroon's draft was passed as modified on 9 October. It mentioned 'two nations' but merely asked the League 'to review and revise the entire question of what should be a suitable Constitution of India' and 'to devise a scheme of Constitution under which Muslims may attain independence'.[2] In 1965 Shaikh Abdul Majid said in a press interview that he was prepared for a centre with limited powers including safeguards for minorities.

Sir Abdullah's ardour was not dampened. He wrote to the Aga Khan on 7 November 1938, 'We are seriously considering the possibility of having a separate federation of Muslims States and Provinces'.[3]

The League Council took a fateful step. On 4 December 1938 it set up the Foreign Committee with Sir Abdullah as chairman. Its objective was propagation of the League's policies and programme in India and abroad. Later in the month the League's 26th session at Patna authorized the president 'to adopt such a course as may be necessary with a view to exploring the possibility of a suitable alternative' to the federation set up by the Government of India Act, 1935.

But if not the Act, 'precisely what alternative did Jinnah propose,' the viceroy, Lord Linlithgow, kept asking. Lord Linlithgow reported to the secretary of state, Lord Zetland, on 28 February 1939, regarding his meeting with Jinnah: 'a couple of days ago...I asked him what suggestions he had to make, to which he replied that, he had in his mind the manipulation of territorial votes and the adjustments of territorial divisions as to bring it about. He blushed a little as I pressed the implication of these suggestions upon him, but in the end maintained that at any rate his project for the carving up of this country was a better one than Sikandar's'.[4] In plain words, a sharing of power on the basis of equality.

The League's Working Committee set up another committee when it met in Castle Mustafa at Meerut on 26 March 1939. Recalling the Patna resolution, it said: 'the President with the concurrence of the Working Committee hereby appoints a Committee of the following gentlemen to examine various schemes already propounded by those who are fully versed in the Constitutional developments of India and other countries and those may be submitted hereafter to the President and report to the Committee their conclusions at an early date'.[5] The members were Jinnah, as president, Sir Sikandar Hayat Khan, Nawab Mohammed Ismail Khan, Sir Abdullah Haroon, Khawaja Nazimuddin, and three others. Liaquat Ali Khan was appointed its convenor. Only the day before, on 25 March 1939, when Liaquat Ali Khan spoke of 'dividing the country in a suitable manner' he added 'If this is done, a limited and specific Federation would not only be easy but desirable.'

By then many proposals were afloat 'including that of dividing the country' but Jinnah made plain to the League's Council on 8 April 1939 that the committee was not pledged to any but was examining all of them 'to produce a scheme which...would be in the best interests of the Muslims of India'.[6] One which caught the fancy was by Dr Syed Abdul Latif of the Osmania University in Hyderabad. He wrote two monographs: *The Cultural Future of India* (1938) and the *Muslim Problem in India* (1939). He proposed 'cultural zones' to achieve which transfer of population may be necessary and a centre.

Sir Abdullah sought to stir a discussion and invited Dr Syed Abdul Latif to meet the Foreign Committee on 29 January 1939 when he was asked 'to prepare a scheme'. He wrote a foreword to the 1939 paper and donated Rs2,000 for its printing and circulation. No shrinking violet, Latif released his scheme to the press. Haroon had written to Jinnah on 22 April 1939 that Latif's scheme 'evoked lot of criticism in the press in the North'. Apparently the Foreign and Constitutional committees coordinated their work but as Aqeel-uz-Zafar Khan wrote in *Dawn* on 23 March 1989 the task of framing the constitutional proposals was mostly performed by the Foreign Committee. On 15 April 1939 Haroon intimated Liaquat Ali Khan regarding the holding of the meeting of the sub-committee at Lahore and requested him to issue a 'Press note to the public to the effect that any one desiring to send any scheme may do so till such and such date.' Liaquat Ali Khan issued a circular letter to the Provincial Leagues on 7 July and again a reminder on 19 August urging them to send the views and suggestions of the Provincial Leagues on the 'schemes for the constitutional development of India as an alternative to the Government of India Act.' On 27 July, Haroon wrote to Liaquat Ali Khan and stressed that he should 'impress the authors to send schemes as early as possible,' to be considered by the sub-committee in October 1939. This shows that his work had the sanction of the Muslim League.

He felt that time was running out and urged Jinnah on 17 July 1939 that 'the Constitution sub-Committee must finish its work by October so that a definite goal is placed before the people.... The Lahore Session of the League ought to be a great success.' Ayesha Jalal reveals that in an unpublished draft of the Working Committee's resolution of 22 October 1939 immediate independence for India was demanded on the basis of 'Constitution of a Confederation of free states' in which the 'rights and interests of all communities shall be adequately safeguarded'.[7] Jinnah's article in *Time and Tide* (London) on 19 January 1940 said 'there are in India two nations who both must share the government of their common motherland...so that...India may take its place among the great nations of the world.' This was a mere two months before the Lahore Resolution. Events moved briskly to a finale.

On 1 February 1940 the Foreign Committee met the authors of the various schemes, which were 'submitted to the League,' under Sir Abdullah's presidentship. He wrote to Liaquat Ali Khan the next day with a request to place the letter before Jinnah. It is truly a historic document. It propounded 5 points:

> (a) The Muslims of India, who constitute ninety millions of people, are a separate Nation entitled to the same right of self-determination which has been conceded in respect of other Nations; (b) The Muslims of India shall in no case agree to be reduced to a position of minority on the basis of extraneous and foreign considerations, or for the sake of any political conveniences or expediencies; (c) That in order to make the Muslims right of self-determination really effective, the Muslims shall have separate National Home in the shape of an autonomous state; (d) That the Muslims living in the rest of India shall be treated as the Nationals of the aforesaid Muslim state and their rights and privileges shall be fully safeguarded; (e) That any scheme of Indian Reforms, interfering with these basic principles, shall be stoutly resisted by the Indian Muslim nation, till it has achieved the aforesaid objectives.[8]

Two days later, on 4 February the League's Working Committee propounded its 5 points to guide the Constitution Committee.

> The following broad outlines were agreed: (1) Mussalmans are not a minority in the ordinary sense of the word. They are a nation. (2) British system of democratic parliamentary system is not suitable to the genius and conditions of the people of India. (3) Those zones, which are composed of majority of Mussalmans in the physical map of India, should be constituted into independent Dominions in direct relationship with Great Britain. (4) In those zones where Muslims are in minority, their interests and those of other minorities must be adequately and effectively safeguarded and similar safeguards shall be provided for the Hindus and other minorities in the Muslim zones. (5) The various units in each zone shall form component parts of Federation in that zone as autonomous units.[9]

When Jinnah met the viceroy on 13 March he warned him that 'if we could not improve on our present solution for the problem of India's constitutional development, he and his friends would have no option but to fall back on some from of partition.'

The League's historic session was held at Lahore on 21–24 March 1940. It appointed a committee to draft the main resolution on 22 March. It discussed a preliminary draft based on Sir Sikandar's draft and the 5 points of 4 February. He had proposed:

> (e) That the regions may, in turn, delegate to a Central Agency, which for the convenience may be designated the Grand Council of the United Dominions of India, and on such terms as may be agreed upon, provided that such functions shall be administered through Committee on which all regions (dominions) and interests will be duly represented and their actual administration will be entrusted to the Units. (f) That no decision of this Central Agency will be effective or operative unless it is carried by at least a two-thirds majority. (g) That in the absence of agreement with regard to the constitution, functions, and scope of the Grand Council of the United Dominions of India, cited above, the regions (dominions) shall have the right to

refrain from or refuse to participate in the proposed Central structure. (h) That adequate, effective, and mandatory safeguards will be specifically provided in the Centre for minorities in the Units, in the regions and in the Centre, in regard to the religious, cultural, economical, political, administration and other spheres.

This did not affect sovereignty. It only provided for coordination.[10] The Subjects Committee dropped these provisions for a centre. They do not figure in the Lahore Resolution as adopted by the session. Jinnah obviously did not wish to commit himself to any central agency ahead of negotiations.

This explains Sikandar's speech in the Punjab assembly on 11 March 1941:

> I have no hesitation in admitting that I was responsible for drafting the original Resolution. But let me make it clear that the Resolution which I drafted was radically amended by the Working Committee, and there is a wide divergence between the Resolution I drafted and the one that was finally passed. The main difference between the two Resolutions is that the latter part of my resolution, which related to the Centre and coordination of the activities of the various units, was eliminated.

He, however, continued to remain a Leaguer.[11] Ayesha Jalal holds:

> By apparently repudiating the need for any centre, and keeping quiet about its shape, Jinnah calculated that when eventually the time came to discuss an all-India federation, the British and Congress alike would be forced to negotiate with organized Muslim opinion, and would be ready to make substantial concessions to create or retain that centre. The Lahore resolution should therefore be seen as a bargaining counter, which had the merit of being acceptable (on the face of it) to the majority province Muslims, and of being totally unacceptable to the Congress and in the last resort to the British also. This in turn, provided the best insurance that the League would not be given what it now apparently was asking for, but which Jinnah in fact did not really want.[12]

Sadly, Jinnah never reckoned with the reality that the Congress would prefer the partition of India, together with partition of Punjab and Bengal to a union in which it would share power with him. Nehru said as much in his prison diary on 31 December 1943: 'It is better to have Pakistan or almost anything if only to keep Jinnah far away....' and reported to the Cabinet Mission in private on 19 June 1946 that Jinnah had no 'real place in the country'.[13] Jinnah evidently did not contemplate this possibility. The Haroon Report's best parts would have helped retrieve the situation.

But Jinnah had another formidable sceptic to deal with, the Nawab of Chhatari, who wrote to Jinnah on 16 October 1940 'even the Lahore resolution will not solve the problem because the Muslims in the minority provinces will suffer in any case.' Jinnah assured him on 22 October 'the resolution made it quite clear that we cannot leave the Muslims in the Hindu provinces to their fate' and asked him to come out 'with a definite scheme of his own' which he promised to consider before making a final decision in this regard.[14] Chaudhry

Khaliquzzaman was also restive despite his support to the Lahore resolution.[15]

Soon thereafter, Syed Abdul Latif went to town. He sent a letter to Haroon with a copy to Jinnah on 23 April containing his scheme for the consideration of the Constitution Committee. Basically he proposed a centre, transfer of population, and the rest. He wrote to Jinnah again on 30 May proposing a confederation—as if the Lahore Resolution had not been passed. All this was for the benefit, he wrote, of 'Sir Abdullah Haroon's Committee'. He was simultaneously urging the Congress' leaders to accept his ideas.[16] He sent Jinnah an amendment on 30 May which, he claimed, sought to 'implement the Lahore resolution' and 'yet preserve the unity of India'.[17]

The Constitution Committee set up in March 1939 apparently went into hibernation. The Foreign Committee did all the running, a fact well known to Jinnah and Liaquat. In November this committee met again after a break of nine months, Jinnah was very patient with Dr Syed Abdul Latif. He wrote to him on 12 October, 'Your scheme is fundamentally different from the basic principles laid down in the Lahore Resolution of the All-India Muslim League, last March.' This, Latif refused to appreciate 'although I tried to explain to you in our talk on 27 of September'.[18]

Finally on 23 December 1940, Haroon submitted his report to Jinnah as 'Chairman, Foreign Sub-Committee' of the League. Clearly Latif swayed the committee on many points. Unfortunately it went beyond the Lahore Resolution to include the princely states with special mention of Hyderabad, predictably. Transfer of population was not overlooked.

Latif's hare-brained ideas marred the report but it contained a precious nugget in paragraph 16 which read:

> The Lahore Resolution of the League does not look forward to the proposed regional states assuming immediately as they are formed, powers of defence, external affairs, customs etc. This argues that there should be a transitional stage during which these powers should be exercised by some agency common to them all. Such a common coordinating agency would be necessary even independent of the above consideration, for under the third principle of the resolution, it will be impossible to implement effectively the provision of safeguards for minorities without some organic relationship subsisting between the states under the Hindu influence. A federation is not to the taste of the Muslims, because they fear that the Hindus will, on the strength of their majority, dominate the Muslims. But since some common arrangement is essential to the fulfilment of the provisions of the resolution, an agreed formula has to be devised whereby the Muslims shall have the control at the Centre on terms of perfect equality with the Non-Muslims.[19]

This agency would have solved Jinnah's dilemma of old. On relations between the two parts of India the report said that 'the subjects to be assigned to this central machinery shall be (a) External relation, (b) Defence, (c) Communications, (d) Customs, (e) Safeguards for minorities and voluntary intermigration etc., subject to the following provision in respect of defence and intermigration.' It went too far and cast an unfortunate gloss on paragraph 16. Each state would have its own army but, 'the Navy will be entirely under the Centre.' The reference to 'intermigration' reveals Latif's hand.

There is every reason to believe that Jinnah, the hard-headed lawyer, would have separated the wheat from the chaff and used the nugget in paragraph 16 of the report constructively—if only it had been kept under warps so as not to tie his hands. It was to be discussed by the Working Committee on 22 February 1941. On 18 February *The Statesman* reported the contents—an obvious leak by a scheming member. The meeting was postponed.

A member, Prof. Mohammed Afzal Hussain Qadri complained that the report was not 'actually completed.' But the unkindest cut came from Latif. He wrote testily to Sir Abdullah Haroon on 8 March insinuating that the report was leaked from people in Delhi and opted out of the committee. He now quibbled over the report's findings which he had found 'in order' on 20 February. Worse still, he criticized 'the cry for Pakistan as envisaged in the Lahore Resolution.' This was rank ingratitude to a man who had helped him as Sir Abdullah did all along.[20]

Latif sent a copy to Jinnah who gave him his desserts on 15 March 1941. But the snub was accompanied by a gross injustice. 'The Muslim League has appointed no such Committee as you keep harping upon'.[21] The record shows that this was simply not true. The Foreign Committee had acted with his full knowledge. Jinnah's exasperation was understandable. The next League session was due to be held in Madras in April, where the Lahore Resolution was to be incorporated into the League's constitution. The embarrassment of a committee of the League pouring cold water on some of its formulations was palpable. Jinnah, true to form, perfumed a surgical operation. He was later to call Latif 'a busy body' not unjustly. Significantly his relations with Sir Abdullah Haroon remained close till his death on 27 April 1942.

Jinnah told the Lucknow session of the League in October 1937 'all safeguards and settlements would be a scrap of paper, unless they are backed by power.' He said at the Aligarh Muslim Union of 5 February 1938: 'The only hope for minorities is to organize themselves and secure a definite share in power to safeguard their rights and interests. Without such power no Constitution can work successfully in India.'[22]

Sir Abdullah also realized that the Lahore Resolution's paragraph on the minorities would be of no avail unless the last paragraph was fleshed out to provide what Coupland called an agency centre in which Muslim would have a voice; two sovereign states linked by such an agency assuring minority rights.

Note the tell-tale signs. The Cripps Mission (1942) file (802) in the Quaid-i-Azam Papers contains his correspondence with Cripps 'regarding the creation of a new Indian Union.' It is 'embargoed.'[23]

Jinnah played with his cards close to the chest. 'If you start asking for 16 annas in a rupee there is room for bargaining'—hence the omission of

Sikandar Hayat's agency from the resolution. The League's convention of legislators passed a resolution on 9 April 1946 removing all ambiguities from the Lahore Resolution. When the Cabinet Mission invited written proposals from both sides, Jinnah had only to send across this resolution. Instead, he sent altogether different proposals on 12 May 1946. Overlooked by supporters and critics, it envisaged a confederation tighter than paragraph 16 of the Haroon Report. He accepted the Mission's Plan of 16 May for a federation. Jinnah had told the Mission on 25 April he would accept a union based on groups of provinces if the Congress did the same. It sabotaged the Mission's Plan leaving Jinnah no option but to press for Pakistan in 1947. Fundamentally it did not wish to share power with the League.[24]

We have travelled a long way since. But even in the altered situation India and Pakistan can reflect on that precious nugget in paragraph 16 of the Haroon Report and apply its logic to the realities of 2008. Its core lesson is Indo-Pak cooperation on an institutional basis as sovereign states as equals. This was the core of the concerns which Jinnah articulated seventy years ago, in 1939.

Previously published in *Criterion*, Vol. III, No. 4, October–December 2008, pp. 64–75.

Notes

1. Ayesha Jalal, *The Sole Spokesman*, Cambridge University Press, 1985, pp. 59–60.
2. Jamiluddin Ahmad (ed.), *Historic Documents of the Muslim Freedom Movement*, Publishers United Ltd., Lahore, 1970, p. 257; vide also R.J. Moore, *Endgames of Empire*, Oxford University Press, 1988, p. 113.
3. Vide also Daulat Haroon Hidayatullah, *Haji Sir Abdullah Haroon*, Oxford University Press, Karachi, 2006.
4. Mushirul Hasan (ed.), *Documents on the Movement for Independence of India: 1939 (Part 2)*, Indian Council on Historical Research, Oxford University Press, 2008, p. 1760.
5. Ahmad, p. 347.
6. Khalid B. Sayeed, *Pakistan; The Formative Phase 1857–1948*, Oxford University Press, 1968, p. 108.
7. Jalal, p. 576, n. 48.
8. For the text vide Muhammad Aslam Malik, *The Making of the Pakistan Resolution*, Oxford University Press, Karachi, 2001, pp. 224–5. This is an excellent survey of those events, based on archival material. It is the best account on the work of the committees.
9. Ibid., p. 226.
10. Ibid., pp. 228–9 for the full text.
11. V.P. Menon, *The Transfer of Power in India, 1757*, pp. 443–58 for the text.
12. Jalal, p. 57.

13. S. Gopal (ed.), *Selected Works of Jawaharlal Nehru*, First Series, Vol. 13, Orient Longman, New Delhi, 1976, p. 324.
14. Malik, pp. 199–200. This is based on *Quad-i-Azam Papers*, File 242, pp. 33–5. The texts merit close study.
15. Malik, p. 199.
16. Z.H. Zaidi (ed.), *Jinnah Papers: Pakistan: The Goal Defined (1 January–31 August 1940)*, Third Series, Vol. XV, Government of Pakistan, 2007, pp. 287–95.
17. Ibid., p. 373.
18. Nawab Nazir Yar Jang Bahadur (ed.), *The Pakistan Issue*, Sh. Muhammed Ashraf, 1943, p. 62. A collection of Latif's correspondence with Jinnah and the Congress leaders.
19. Ibid., pp. 73–92 for the text.
20. Ibid., pp. 92 and 96–9.
21. Ibid., p. 100.
22. Jamiluddin Ahmad (ed.), *Speeches and Writings of Mr Jinnah*, Vol. I, pp. 30 and 43 respectively.
23. R.J. Moore, *Escape from Empire*, Oxford University Press, 1983, p. 54, bn. 117.
24. Nicholas Mansergh (ed.), *The Transfer of Power 1942–47*, HMSO, Vol. VII covers the Cabinet Mission.

Index

A

Abdullah, Sheikh Mohammed, 244
Abell, George, 171, 195, 228
Ahmad, Sahibzada Khurshid, 247, 248
Ahmed, Dr Z.A., 154
Ahmedabad, 12, 59, 60, 144
Ahmediyas, 73
Ahmednagar, 7, 126
AICC, *see* All-India Congress Committee
AIML Council, *see* All-India Muslim League
Akhand Bharat, 263
Akola Station, 48
Albuquerque Road, 200
Alexander, A.V., 177, 200, 205, 206, 220
Ali Brothers, 39, 45, 48, 62
Ali, Asaf, 61, 114, 115, 122, 126, 127, 158, 230, 231
Ali, Maulana Mohammed, 9, 46, 47, 51
Ali, Maulana Shaukat, 48, 49, 50
Ali, Sir Ameer, 69
Allahabad, 9, 10, 18, 119
Allies, 121, 123
All-India Congress Committee (AICC), 14, 15, 113, 119, 123, 124, 212, 219
All-India Khilafat: Conference, 48; Committee, 49
All-India Muslim League Legislators Convention, 181
All-India Muslim League Working Committee, 145, 155, 156, 179, 192, 222, 226
All-India Muslim League, 9, 12, 14, 15, 17, 18, 19, 22, 24, 26, 35, 40, 41, 43, 51, 61, 62, 66, 82, 85, 87, 95, 97, 98, 99, 100, 101, 102, 103, 104, 105, 106, 107, 110, 112, 113, 114, 119, 120, 127, 128, 132, 134; Council, 157, 219, 158, 162, 163, 165, 166, 167, 168, 169, 171, 172, 175, 176, 180, 181, 183, 184, 185, 186, 187, 189, 191, 194, 195, 199, 201, 202, 206, 208, 211, 212, 214, 215, 220, 222, 223, 224, 225, 226, 229, 230, 235, 236, 237, 238, 239, 240, 242, 245, 245, 251, 256, 257, 258, 259, 260, 267, 270; office-bearers, 141, 143, 146, 147, 149, 153
All-India Students' Conference, 96
All-India Students' Federation, 98, 107
All-Parties' Conference, 98
All-Parties' National Convention, 87, 89
Ambala Division, 103, 157, 165, 170
Ambedkar, B.R., 128, 152, 159, 161, 162, 169, 175, 188, 236
Americans, 246
Amritsar, 176
Amritsar, 34, 36; Congress, 6, 129
Analysis, 190
Ansari, Dr M.A., 61, 82, 86, 93, 94, 95, 116
Apollo Street, 29, 30
Arabian Imperialism, 165
Ashoutosh Hall, 96
Ashraf, K.M., 113, 246
Assam, 157, 172, 176, 177, 178, 183, 185, 186, 189, 191, 201, 203, 211, 218, 227, 234, 238, 239, 269
Associated Press of India, 204, 224, 258
Attlee, Clement, 167, 177, 178, 182, 222, 223, 226, 241, 242, 243, 251
Austria, 260
Autobiography, 109
Avatars, 135
Axis Powers, 120, 121
Azad, 239
Azad, Maulana Abul Kalam, 14, 30, 44, 86, 101, 102, 116, 122, 124, 126, 127, 158, 161, 162, 163, 181, 186, 187, 189, 192, 195, 226, 229, 230, 231, 262, 264, 265
Azim, Anwar-ul, 80

INDEX

B

Bacon, xv
Baloch, 265
Baluchistan, 165, 176, 177, 178, 183, 191, 218, 243
Bangladesh, 263
Banker, S.G., 27
Banker, Shankarlal, 1
Bannerjee, Surendranath, 2, 15, 21
Bapat, Sadashiv Vaman, 13
Baptista, Joseph, 3, 7, 10, 50
Baptista, Uncle, 7
Bapu, 117, 120, 121, 202, *see also* Gandhi
Bardoloi, 122
Barnes, Leonard, 167
Basu, Bhuperdranath, 71
Batchelor, Sir Stanley, 8
Battle of Plassey, 268
Bawany, Yahya Hasim, 81, 82
BBC, 155
Belgaum, 7
Belisarius, 269
Bengal Provincial Congress Committee, 106
Bengal Provincial Khilafat Movement, 51
Bengal Provincial Muslim League, 251
Bengal, 18, 19, 21, 51, 116, 133, 151, 157, 158, 160, 165, 166, 169, 171, 172, 173, 176, 189, 195, 204, 218, 221, 223, 226, 234, 238, 240, 242; assembly, 259, 260, 267, 269; East 243, 245, 251, 252, 253, 254, 255, 256, 257, 258
Bengali, 265
Besant, Annie, 8, 10, 13, 33, 34, 35, 37, 43, 51, 60, 82, 177, 178, 183
Bevan, Aneurin, 167
Bhagwandas, Vibhakar, 30
Bhagwat Gita, 37
Bhangi Colony, 200
Bharat Jyoti, xvii
Bhargava, Gopichand, 188
Bhargava, Thakurdas, 188
Bhasin, Prem, 152
Bihar, 19, 107, 130, 157, 230, 264
Bikaner, 175
Bill of Rights, 39
Birla, G.D., 167, 200, 216
Bogra, Mohammed Ali, 255
Bolsheviks, 76

Bomanji, S.R., 24, 44
Bombay Bar Association, 5
Bombay Chronicle, 1, 26, 31, 32, 59, 83, 85, 94, 110
Bombay Committee of Lawyers for Civil Liberties, 33
Bombay High Court, 3, 4, 6
Bombay Municipal Corporation, 2
Bombay Presidency Provincial Conference, 6
Bombay Provincial Muslim League, 4, 88
Bombay Students' Brotherhood, 84
Bombay University Gardens, 3
Bombay, 1, 2; government of, 7, 8, 9, 10; provincial congress, 12, 14, 19, 22, 23, 24, 27, 29, 30, 31, 32, 33, 34, 43, 52, 57, 60, 64, 65, 69, 75, 76, 78, 89, 92, 115, 156, 168, 186, 212, 234, 245, 254
Bond Street, 110
Bose, Sarat, 252, 253, 254, 255, 256, 257, 258, 259, 260
Bose, Subhas Chandra, 118, 123, 162
Bose, Sugata, 259
Boundary commission, 234, 267
Brain Trust, 173
Brelvi, Syed Abdullah, 94, 95, 110
British, xiv; Cabinet, 84, 91; Empire, 20, 46, 120; government, 104, 119, 121, 124, 125, 127, 128, 141, 153, 111; imperialism, 113, 131, 132, 143, 165, 169, 170, 175, 176, 189, 191, 212, 216, 219, 220, 235, 236, 241, 243, 255, 263; India, 38, 181; objections, 16, 17; parliament, 76, 78, 81; Parliamentary Delegation, 170; policies, 41; Raj, 22; rule, 1
Burdwan Division, 171, 172, 223, 228, 239
Burke, Edward, 247
Burma, 76, 178
Burrows, Frederick, 184, 251, 253

C

Cabinet Mission, 177, 178, 180, 181, 182, 183, 184, 186, 187, 188, 190, 192, 193, 195, 200, 201, 202, 203, 205, 206, 207, 214, 216, 219, 220, 235, 236, 241,

INDEX

270; Plan, xiii, 114, 157, 161, 174, 175, 178, 183, 188, 189, 190, 191, 192, 199, 204, 206, 208, 209, 211, 212, 213, 214, 215, 216, 218, 219, 222, 226, 227, 228, 229, 236, 237, 252, 268
Calcutta (Kolkata), xvi, 2, 9, 20, 35, 39, 82; AICC, 117, 169, 171, 177, 185, 213, 215, 239, 251, 252, 254; special congress, 83, 87, 89; University, 96, 103, 109
Cambridge, 114
Canada, 91, 100
Caroe, Sir Olaf, 173
Casey, Richard G., 133, 160, 172
Caste Disabilities Removal Act, 71
Castle Mustafa, 145
Central Agency, 146
Central Assembly, 73, 79, 100
Central Legislative Assembly, 67, 68, 72
Central Legislature, 92
Central Provinces, 19
Ceylon, 178
Chagla, M.C., xvii, 4, 5, 8, 33, 88
Chand, Lala Dhuni, 61
Chaudhri, Nirad C., 117, 118, 127, 165
Chelmsford, Lord, 19, 23, 24, 76
Chhatari, Nawab of, 147
China Bagh, 1, 26, 31
China, 121
Chintamani C.Y., 13
Chittagong, 176
Chundrigar, I.I., 156
Churchill, Winston, xv
Civil Disobedience, xvi, 35, 60; committee, 83, 250
Clarke, Professor, 199
Cleghorn Minute, 144, 154
Cliff, Norman, 154, 253
Coalition Government, 195, 201; of Bengal, 258
Cocke, Sir Hugh, 74
Collected Works of Mahatma Gandhi, The, 190, 230
Colliers, 155
Commonwealth, 255
Communist Party of India (CPI), 113, 246
Congress–BJP Duo, The, 152
Congress Civil Disobedience Enquiry Committee, 82

Congress Drafting Committee, 175
Congress Election Manifesto, 170
Congress Parliamentary Sub-Committee, 101
Congress Party 101, 102
Congress *see* Indian National Congress
Congress Subject Committee, 40, 49, 50, 147
Congress Working Committee, 101, 106, 118, 119, 120, 122, 123, 124, 125, 126, 141, 146, 148, 187, 192, 200, 201, 203, 204, 217, 218, 223, 225, 230, 236
Congress-Muslim League: Accord, 14, 170; *entente*, 34; Pact, 224, 269; Scheme, 11, 19
Conservative government, 132
Constituent Assembly, 169, 176, 184, 188, 189, 190, 191, 192, 201, 204, 207, 208, 211, 216, 218, 219, 229, 239, 256
Constituent Assembly, 186
Constitution Committee, 147
Constitutional Problem, 174
Copt Christians, 91
Cosgrave, 76
Coupland, Sir Reginald, 91, 100, 157, 171, 174, 187
Criminal Procedure Code, 7
Cripps Mission, 119, 157, 158, 169
Cripps Scheme, 168
Cripps, Stafford, xiii, 119, 122, 157, 167, 168, 169, 173, 174, 177, 178, 179, 180, 181, 182, 187, 190, 191, 193, 195, 199, 200, 202, 203, 204, 206, 208, 209, 211, 220, 243, 270
Criterion, xviii
Croft, Sir William, 173
Crossman, Richard, 167
Cunningham, Governor, 171
Currimbhoy, Sir Fazalbhoy, 28
Czar, 57, 58

D

Dacca/Dhaka, 9, 176
Daily Telegraph, The, 143, 206
Dalvi, D.G., 84, 85
Dandavate, Madhu, 126
Darjeeling, 176, 239
Das, Biswanath, 122

Das, C.R., 21, 34, 38, 45, 49, 51, 52, 120, 124, 126, 128
Daulatram, Shri Jairamdas, 122
Daultana, Mian Mumtaz, 157
Davar, Dinshaw D., 3, 4, 5
Dawal Singh College, 95
Dawn, xvi, 225, 239, 267
Dehlavi, 266
Delhi, 23; Conference, 25, 65, 67, 68, 69, 83, 85; Proposal, 87, 93, 94, 134, 154, 167, 241, 244, 247, 248, 249, 267
Democracy in Plural Societies, 145, 194
Deo, Acharya Narendra, 122
Deo, Shankarrao, 122, 224, 225, 226, 243
Desai, Bhulabhai, 122
Desai, Mahadev, 124
Desai, V.A., 30
Dicey, A.V., 166
Dillard, James E., 105, 106
Dinajpur, 239
Direct Action, 84, 85
Divatia, Harsiddhbhai, 52
Division of Provinces: Group A, 183, 185, 193; Group B, 183, 185, 186, 189, 191, 193; Group C, 183, 184, 185, 186, 191, 193
Dominion Status, 64, 80, 168,
Duma, 57, 58
Durham, Lord, 100
Dwarkadas, Jamnadas, 24, 27, 29, 30, 31, 43, 44
Dwarkadas, Kanji, 1, 5, 44, 242

E

Edge, Sir John, 69
Edwards, Donald, 155
Egypt, 109
Elphinstone Gardens, 27
England, 10, 22, 84, 111, 162
Erulker, Dr, 30
Europe, 114, 144
Executive Council, 80
Extremists, 2, 3, 8, 51

F

Faiz, Faiz Ahmed, xiii
Faridpur, 63
Fatwa, 83
Filkins, 167
First World War, 105
Fischer, Louis, 161
Foreign Committee, 145, 147
Fourteen Points, 98, 112
Free Press Journal, xvii

G

Gadgil, Prof. D.R., 186, 187
Gandhi, Mohandas Karamchand, xiv, xvi, 8, 15, 17, 23, 26, 35, 36, 38, 39, 40, 41, 42, 43, 44, 45, 46, 48, 49; resolution, 50, 51, 52, 53, 57, 58, 59, 60, 61, 65, 82, 84, 86, 89, 95, 104, 111, 115, 116, 117, 118, 120, 121, 122, 123, 124, 125, 126, 127, 128, 129, 130, 131, 133, 134, 141, 144, 158, 159, 160, 161, 162, 180, 182, 189, 190, 191, 194, 199, 201, 202, 203, 204, 205, 206, 208, 209, 211, 213, 214, 215, 216, 218, 229, 231, 235, 236, 237, 240, 241, 246, 247, 253, 254, 255, 256, 258, 259, 260, 262
Gandhi–Nehru, 160
Ganga–Yamuna, 268
Gaur, Dr Hari Singh, 68
Geeta-Rahasya, 6
Germany, 58, 120, 123
Ghalib, xv
Ghosh, Prafulla Chandra, 122
Ghosh, Sudhir, 199, 200, 201, 202, 216
Gibbon, 269
Girgaum, 1, 22
Gokhale Memorial Hall, 159
Gokhale, Gopal Krishna, 8, 13, 18, 32, 57, 59, 81, 84, 96, 105
Gokuldas Market Hall, 52
Gopal, Sarvepalli, 110, 115, 117, 119
Gore, Ormsby, 77
Government of India Act of 1919, 36
Government of India Act of 1935, 91
Government of India Records, 214
Government of India, 145
Grand Council of the United Dominions of India, 146
Great Mutiny, 268
Griffith, Arthur, 84
Guider, I.A., 7
Gujrati, 9
Gurdaspur, 176

H

Haig, Harry Graham, 81
Hans Raj, Rai Saheb, 61, 67
Haq, Fazlul, 34
Haque, Mazhar-ul, 10
Harijan, 104, 117, 190
Haroon, Sir Abdullah, 145
Harun-or-Rashid, 260
Hasan, Mushirul, 86, 87
Hasan, Syed Wazir, 9, 34
Hashim, Abul, 251, 253, 254, 255, 256
Hayat, Shaukat, 157
Herald, xvi
Hifzurrahman, Maulana, 230
Hindu Child Marriage Bill, 69
Hindu Mahasabha, 87, 88, 92, 106, 108, 109, 221, 230
Hindu Sabhas, 154
Hindu: college, 85; communalists, 154; community, 2, 51; Congress, 142; federation, 168; government, 20; majority, 132, 135, 157, 173, 167; nationalists, 14; of Bengal, 260, 262, 264, 265, 267; Raj, 153; rights, 103, 105; Sanatani, 135, 141, 143, 147, 149, 151, 152; territory, 170, 238, 239, 244, 246, 247, 252, 253, 254, 255, 256, 257, 258
Hindu-Muslim: unity, 6, 109, 115, 131; cooperation, 17; strife, 107; question, 116, 141, 142; accommodation, 157, 185, 230; backlash, 246; problem, 263; India, 268
Hindustan, 178, 245, 253, 264, 265
Hindutva, 143
His Majesty's Government (HMG), 171, 227, 229, 254, 255
Hitler, 118
Hodson, H.V., 156, 157
Home Rule day, 26
Home Rule League: *see* Indian Home Rule League
Home Rule party, 24
Home Rulers, 30
Horniman, B.G, 1, 24, 27, 28, 29, 30, 31
House of Commons, 82, 222
Hussain, Syed, 28

I

Iftikharuddin, Mian, 113
Imperial Hotel, 245, 267
Imperial Legislative Council, 9, 10, 26, 34, 71, 81
Independents, 63, 66
India: A Restatement, 174
India: academia in, xiii; unsung heroes of, xv; nationalism, 104
Indian Association Room, 15
Indian Constitutional Reforms, 72
Indian Diary, 8
Indian Express Group, xviii
Indian Home Rule League, 6, 8, 10, 22, 24, 26, 35, 43, 49, 52, 53, 57, 81
Indian Mussalman Association, 9
Indian National Congress: 22nd session, xiv; annual session, 59; Calcutta session, 21; 34, 35, 36, 37, 38, 39, 40, 42; Muslims 169, 231, 170, 171, 173, 174, 175, 179, 180, 181, 183, 185, 189, 190, 191, 192, 193, 194, 195, 199, 200, 202, 204, 205, 206, 208, 211, 213, 214, 215, 219, 220, 222, 223, 224, 225, 226, 227, 228, 229, 230, 234, 235, 236, 237, 238, 239, 240, 241, 242, 243, 245, 255, 257, 258, 260, 265, 266, 270; Nagpur session, 44, 45, 46, 49, 50, 51, 52, 53, 57; non-cooperation 110, 111, 112, 113, 114, 118, 119, 121, 122, 124, 125, 126, 127, 128, 130, 131, 132, 133, 134, 135, 142, 143, 145, 152, 154, 158, 161, 162, 165, 167, 168; session at Calcutta and Nagpur, xvi, 2, 6, 10, 3, 5, 8, 9, 10, 12, 14, 15, 16, 19, 20; working committee, 60, 61, 62, 63, 65, 66, 78, 82, 85, 86, 87, 88, 91, 92, 98, 100, 101, 103, 104, 105, 107, 108, 109
Indian Penal Code, 5
Innis, Roy, 245, 246
Iqbal, Allama, 94, 134, 165, 231
Iran, 109
Iraq, 120
Ireland, 12, 76, 84
Irish nationalists, 82
Irwin Road, 200
Irwin, Viceroy Lord, 65
Islam, 109, 153, 154, 165
Islington, Lord, 78

Ismail, Mirza, 131
Ismail, Nawab, 156
Ismaili College, 73
Ismay, Lord, 237
Ispahani, 172
Italy, 120
Iyengar, S. Kasturi Ranga, 83

J

Jagat Narain resolution, 119
Jalal, Ayesha, 156, 157
Jallianwala Bagh, 34
Jalpaiguri, 176
Jamiat-ul-Ulema, 83
Jamiat-ul-Ulema-i-Hind, 230
Jammu and Kashmir, 73
Janata, 126, 152
Janpath, 245, 267
Japan, 118
Japan, 120, 121, 123, 124, 125, 127
Jayakar, M.R., 3, 13, 39, 43, 44, 45, 52, 59, 60, 63, 64, 81, 84, 87, 90, 129, 162, 220, 221, 222, 241
Jeejeebhoy, Sir Jamsetjee, 28, 29
Jehangir, Cowasji, 60
Jenkins, Evan, 166
Jenkins, Sir Lawrence, 69
Jessore districts, 176
Jinnah, Quaid-i-Azam Mohammad Ali, xiv, xvi, xvii, xviii, 1, 2, 3, 4, 5, 6, 7, 8, 9, 10, 15, 18, 19, 20, 21, 22, 23, 24, 25, 26, 27, 28, 29, 30, 31, 32, 33, 34, 35, 38, 40, 42, 44, 45, 46, 47, 48, 49, 50, 51, 52, 53, 57, 59, 60, 61, 62, 64, 65, 66, 67, 68, 69, 71, 72, 74, 76, 77, 79, 82, 83, 97, 98, 99, 100, 102, 104, 109, 110, 111, 112, 113, 114, 115, 116, 117, 126, 127, 128, 131, 133, 134, 141, 142, 143, 144, 145, 146, 147, 148, 152, 154, 155, 156, 157, 158, 159, 160, 161, 162, 163, 165, 166, 167, 168, 169, 170, 171, 172, 173, 174, 175, 176, 178, 179, 180, 181, 182, 185, 186, 192, 202, 205, 206, 208, 209, 211, 212, 213, 215, 216, 219, 220, 223, 224, 228, 229, 231, 234, 235, 236, 237, 238, 240, 242, 243, 244, 245, 246, 247, 250, 251, 252, 258, 262, 266, 267, 268, 269, 270
Jinnah, Ruttie, xvi, 28, 30, 39, 48, 86

Jinnah-Nehru correspondence, 116
Jinnah-Rajendra Prasad Pact, 18, 103
Joint Parliamentary Committee (JPC), 72, 93
Jowitt, Lord Chancellor, 216

K

Kaisar Bagh, 15
Kalbadevi, 1
Kamdar, Mrs Ramibai, 30
Kanpur, 155
Kantawala, R.M., 33
Karachi, 39, 185, 222, 243, 247, 266
Kaura, Uma, 18
Kaysen, Carl, 246
Kelkar, N.C, 1, 10, 24, 45
Kennan, George F., xvii
Kennedy, John F., 246
Ker, James Campbell, 35
Kerala, 154
Kesari Mahratta Library, xviii
Kesari, 45
Ketkar, Kumar, xviii
Khaddar, 129
Khadi, 64
Khadilkar, 1
Khaliquzzaman, Chaudhry, 101, 102, 108, 147, 171, 172, 262, 163
Khan Saheb, Dr, 194
Khan, Aga, 9; palace, 171
Khan, Aurangzeb, 171
Khan, Hakim Ajmal, 82, 83, 86
Khan, Khan Abdul Ghaffar, 240
Khan, Liaquat Ali, 92, 146, 163, 167, 168, 172, 216, 220, 224, 225, 226, 240, 252
Khan, Nawab Mohammad Ismail, 146, 173
Khan, Sir Sayyed Ahmed, 2, 134
Khan, Sir Sikandar Hayat, 141, 146, 148, 168, 173, 234
Khan, Sir Zulfiqar Ali Khan, 79
Khaparde, G.S., 1, 51, 53, 129, 130
Khare, I.G., 30
Kher, B.G., 115
Khilafat, 14, 17, 39, 41, 42, 48, 49, 50; Committee, 134; day, 48; Movement, 51, 60, 62, 83, 133, 160
Khulna, 239

INDEX

King's Commission, 25
Kitchlew, Saifuddin, 61
Kripalani, Acharya, 125
Kripalani, J.B., 106, 122, 220, 221, 222, 230
Kunzru, Hridayanth, 15
Kuwajimi, Prof. Sho, 194

L

Labour government, 132, 167, 242
Labour Party, 184
Lahore Resolution, 128, 134, 147, 148, 149, 153, 156, 157, 158, 166, 169, 212, 266,
Lahore, 61, 67, 95, 111, 168
Lalaji, 66
Lam, B.D., 32
Laski, Harold, 167
Legal Aspects of the Grouping Question, 206
Legislative Assembly, 66
Legislative Council, 58
Lele, P.R., 186
Lex Loci Act XXI, 71
Liberal government, 132
Liberals, xiv, 22, 63, 87, 130
Life of Tilak, 45
Lijphart, Arend, 144
Linlithgow, Viceroy, 123, 145
Lloyd, Lord, 76
Loksatta, xviii
London, 9, 22, 76, 92, 93, 111, 129, 132, 133, 155, 176, 189, 216, 236, 243, 258
Lowndes, Sir George, 4
Lucknow Pact, xvi, 3, 6, 13, 14, 15, 17, 19, 20, 21, 51, 52, 87, 98, 100, 143, 145, 186
Lucknow, 15, 16, 95, 96
Ludhiana Government College, 270
Ludhianvi, Sahir, 270

M

Madras, 19, 51, 112, 120, 264
Maharashtra, 6, 51
Mahmud, Syed, 230
Mahmudabad, 14; Raja of, 15
Malabar Hill, 168

Malaviya, Pandit Madan Mohan, 3, 10, 13, 14, 152
Mamdot, Nawab of, 19
Manchester Guardian, The, 111
Mandalay, 6, 7, 13
Mandvi, 1
Mangla Ben, xv
Mappilas, 154
Maratha, 14
Marathi, 3, 7, 13
Martin, Freda, 173
Mathews, P.M., xviii
Mauzun, Raja Ram Narain Mauzun, 268
Mazumdar, Ambika Charan, 15
Meerut, 145, 173
Meherally, Yusuf, xvii
Mehta, Jamnadas, 75
Mehta, Pherozeshah, 3, 8
Mehta, Pranjivan, 23
Memorandum of Nineteen, 10
Menon, Krishna, 167
Menon, V.P., 166, 171, 175, 176, 181, 189, 229
Mesopotamia, 40
Middle East, 160
Midnapore, 239
Mieville, Eric, 227, 252, 253
Miller, Prof. Roland, 154
Minto, Viceroy Lord, 9
Mira Ben, 123
Mitha, Suleman Cassim, 28
Moderates, 2, 3, 44, 49, 51
Mohajirs, 268
Mohammed, Nawab Syed, 9
Mohammedan Community, 9
Mohammedans, 12, 13, 14, 16, 43, 50, 71, 72
Mohani, Maulana Hasrat, 2, 245
Montagu Reforms Act, 45
Montagu, Edwin S., 8, 11, 19, 20, 23, 34, 36, 37, 49, 76, 77
Monteath, Sir David, 173
Montford: Declaration, 169; Reforms, 6; Report, 33, 34, 35, 36
Mookerjee, Shyama Prasad, 252, 253, 254
Moon, Penderel, 173, 234
Moonje, Dr B.S., 51, 230
Moore, Prof. R.J., 157, 167, 208
Moraes, Frank, 244

462 INDEX

Morarji, Ratansey D., 31
Morgan, Prof., 12
Morning Herald, 254
Morning News, 239
Mosley, Leonard, 214
Mountbatten, Viceroy Lord Louis, 114, 209, 226, 227, 228, 235, 237, 238, 240, 241, 243; Plan, 244, 245, 251, 252, 253, 254, 255, 258, 259
Muhammad ibn Qasim, 154
Mujibabadi, Akbar Shah, 134
Mukherjee, Shyama Prasad, 96, 221
Mulji Jetha Cloth Market, 1
Multan, 176
Mumbai, xv, xviii, 2
Munshi, K.M., 26, 27, 31, 32, 44, 51, 52, 123, 187, 188, 246
Murshed, S. Iftikhar, xviii
Murshidabad, 176
Muslim League Constitution Committee, 62
Muslim League Reforms Committee, 15
Muslim League, *see* All-India Muslim League
Muslim Students Federation, 98
Muslim University at Aligarh, 107, 108
Muslim University Union, 131
Muslim: community, 12, 132, 52, 78; constituencies, 103, 105; constituencies, 194, 195, 223; extremists, 111, 142, 143; federation, 168, 169, 172, 175, 176, 177, 180, 181, 182, 185, 186; majority, 144, 147, 148, 149, 150; minority provinces, 166, 167; nationalists, 229, 230, 237, 239, 244, 245, 246, 247, 248, 253, 254, 255, 256, 257, 260, 262, 263, 264, 265, 266, 267, 268; of India, 109
Muslims Mass Contacts Movement, 106
Muslims, Nationalism and the Partition: 1946 Provincial elections in India, 194,
Mussalman community, 12
Mussalman Criminal Law, 71
Mussalman Wakf Validating Act, 9
Mussalmans, 16, 18, 20, 21, 40, 41, 71, 97, 98, 104, 116, 131, 132, 153, 212
Mysore Resolution, 117, 226

N

Nadia, 176
Nadvi, Maulana Syed Suleman, 154
Nagpur, xvi; Congress, 6, 35, 49, 51, 82, 83, 86; session, 116, 135, 144
Naidu, Sarojini, 109, 112, 122, 126, 143
Naoroji, Dadabhai, 2, 15, 32
Naqvi, M.B., 262
Narayan, Jayaprakash, xv, 152
Nathwani, N.P., 33
National Congress, *see* Indian National Congress
National Union of Railwaymen, 184
Nationalist Party, 152
Nazi: invasion, xv, 118
Nazimuddin, Khwaja, 146, 172, 252
Nehru Report, xvi, 86, 88, 89, 95, 133
Nehru, Jawaharlal, 8, 52, 61, 62, 66, 95, 98, 103, 104, 106, 107, 108, 109, 110, 111, 112, 113, 114, 115, 116, 117, 118, 121, 122, 123, 124, 125, 126, 127, 133, 141, 143, 154, 158, 160, 162, 167, 168, 169, 170, 175, 180, 189, 190, 194, 199, 211, 212, 213, 215, 216, 220, 221, 222, 225, 237, 240, 243, 244, 246, 247, 248, 250, 270
Nehru, Motilal, 10, 13, 18, 34, 36, 45, 52, 62, 65, 66, 68, 82, 83, 86, 87, 88, 105, 222, 226, 230, 231, 253, 259, 262
Neogy, K.C., 252
New Delhi, 155, 182, 185, 189, 223, 245, 251, 258, 267
New India, 12
News Chronicle, 154, 253
Next Step in India, The, 175
Non-Cooperation, xiv, 6, 35, 39, 45, 49, 59, 129, 133, 144, 230
North-West Frontier Province (NWFP), 107, 165, 176, 177, 178, 183, 189, 191, 194, 195, 211, 218, 235, 238, 239, 243, 248
Note for the Cabinet Mission, 205
Nuffield College, 174

O

Objectives Resolution, 222
Office Note on the Legal Aspects of the Grouping Question, 207

INDEX

Old Delhi, 268
Orissa, 245
Osaka University of Foreign Affairs, 194
Owen, Hugh F., 3, 8, 13, 14, 17
Oxford, 174

P

Pakistan and the Punjab, 176
Pakistan Economist, 262
Pakistan or the Partition of India, 152
Pakistan: academia in, xiii; Constituent Assembly, 262, 263, 264, 265, 266, 267, 268, 269, 270; Resolution, 99, 155, 113, 114, 128, 143, 149, 151, 153, 154, 156, 157, 158, 163, 167, 169, 170, 171, 172, 173, 175, 176, 177, 179, 180, 181, 185, 188, 192, 211, 213, 218, 219, 226, 234, 235, 236, 237, 238, 239, 242, 243, 244, 245, 248, 249, 252, 253, 254, 260
Pal, Bipin Chandra, 21, 40, 50
Palestine, 109
Pall, B.C., 134
Pandit, R.S., 122
Pandit, Vijaya Lakshmi, 222
Panikkar, K.M., 175, 176, 208
Pant, Govind Ballabh, 101, 122, 222
Parikh, G.G., xv
Parliamentary Committee, 110
Parnellites, 82
Parsis, 4
Patel Brothers, 65
Patel, Maniben, 200
Patel, Vallabhbhai, 74, 75, 82, 83, 113, 122, 123, 125, 161, 175, 181, 187, 188, 189, 199, 200, 201, 202, 203, 206, 209, 227, 228, 231, 237, 240, 242, 243, 244, 245, 248, 252, 262
Patel, Vithalbhai, 65
Pathan, 151, 265
Pathway to Pakistan, 262
Patna: resolution, 145, 240, 256
Patwardhan, Achyut, 122
Pearl Harbour, 118
People's Jinnah Hall, 23; Memorial Hall, 33
Peshawar, 185, 195

Pethick-Lawrence, Lord, 161, 169, 176, 177, 180, 181, 187, 200, 204, 205, 206, 208, 211, 216, 220, 227
Petit, Dinshaw, 60
Pius IX, 159
Plan A *see* Scheme A
Plan B *see* Scheme B
Poona (Pune), xviii, 2, 6, 7, 159
Prasad, Mahadeva, 35
Prasad, Narsingh, 30
Prasad, Rajendra, 92, 103, 122, 123, 125, 185, 201, 248
Press Act, 20
Prince of Wales, 60
Princeton, 245
Privy Council, 4, 68
Provincial Legislative Council, 19
Punjab Legislative Assembly, 148
Punjab Pradesh Congress Committee, 113
Punjab, 18; Assembly, 19, 39, 41, 42; atrocities, 49, 60, 83; Muslims League, 91, 106, 141, 150, 151, 157, 158, 165, 169, 173, 176; western, 177 178, 183, 191, 218, 223, 226, 234, 238, 240, 242, 243, 245, 248, 253, 267, 269
Punjabi, 265
Puranas, 135
Pyarelal, 199, 202, 240

Q

Qaiyum, Nawab Sir Sahibzada Abdul, 79, 80
Qizilbash, Sir Muzaffar Ali, 185
Quaid-i-Azam Papers, 156, 157
Quaid-i-Azam *see* Jinnah, Quaid-i-Azam Mohammad Ali Jinnah
Queensway, 245
Quetta, 185
Quit India: Movement, xv; Resolution, 114, 115, 118, 123, 126, 128, 158, 241
Quran, 69, 71, 109
Qureshi, Ishtiaq Husain, 19, 50, 267

R

Radcliffe Commission, 234
Radcliffe, 185
Rahimtoola, Ibrahim, 10

Rai, Lala Lajpat, 40, 45, 50, 51, 65, 67, 133, 151, 152, 165
Raisina Hill, 185
Rajagopalachari, C. (aka Rajaji), 34, 45, 50, 51, 52, 53, 60, 65, 66, 67, 82, 87, 88, 92, 120, 127, 128
Rajaji Formula, 236
Rajaji resolution, 122
Rajshahi division, 176
Ranade, Gandhi, and Jinnah, 159
Randhawa, M.S., 247, 248
Rangoon, 121
Rao, B. Shiva., 130, 219
Rau, Sir B.N., 175, 176, 219
Rawalpindi, 176, 185
Reading Road, 200
Reading, Lord, 59, 60, 76
Rediscovery of Achyut Patwardhan, 126
Reed, Sir Stanley, 27
Reform Committee, 15
Reforms Act, 35
Rehman, Fazlur, 254, 255
Reid, Colin, 206
Report on Indian Constitutional Reform, 20
Resolution II, 24
Robertson, L., 24
Round Table Conference, xvi, 60, 61, 80, 88, 91, 95, 99, 111, 133
Rowlatt, 18, 41, 48
Roy, Binoy Kumar, 253, 254
Roy, Kiran Shankar, 251, 252, 255
Russia, 57, 58, 121

S

Saadulla, 172
Sabarmati, 65
Sabha, Gurjar, 8
Sajjad, Maulana Muhsin, 230
Salt Satyagraha Movement, 125
Sapru, Tej Bahadur, 10, 13, 18, 65, 68, 130, 131, 229
Sarabhai, Ambala, 60
Sardar Griha, 1
Sarvakar, N.D., 31
Satyamurti, Shri, 122, 126
Satyapal, 61
Savarkar, V.D., 141, 143, 230
Savile Row, 110

Scheme A, 177, 179, 180
Scheme B, 177, 178, 179, 206, 240
Seditions Meetings Act, 20
Seervai, 236
Session Court, 3
Setalvad, Sir Chimanlal, 51, 130, 266
Shafi, Sir Mohammad, 91
Shah Nawaz, Mian Mohammad, 80
Shah, J.C., 33
Shah, K.T., 110
Shah, Lallubhai, 8
Shah, Sonal, xv
Shantaram Chawl, xviii, 1, 22, 23, 26, 29, 30, 67, 81
Shariat, 83
Sheth, Mowji Govindji, 28, 30
Siddiqi, A.R., 266, 267, 268
Siddiqi, Zuhair, 262
Sikandar, 145
Sikh delegates, 87, 108, 149, 185, 188, 191, 218, 238
Simla, 9, 25, 181, 182; Conference, 236
Simon Commission, xvii, 65, 66, 67
Sindh, 1, 151, 154, 165, 176, 177, 178, 183, 191; legislature, 239, 243, 265
Singh, Baldev, 216
Singh, Bhagat, 69, 75, 76
Sinha, Prakash Kumar, xviii
Sinha, Sachidanand, 131
Sinn Fein, 83, 84
Sirajuddaulah, 268
Slade, Madeleine (Miraben), 119
Sobani, Omar, 1, 27, 43
Socialist Republic of Bengal, 254
South India, 153, 154
Soviet Union, 118
Special Marriage Bill, 71
Sri Lanka, 144, 154
Srinagar, 73
Stalinist, 2, 23
Star Chamber Legislation, 34
Star of India, 239
Statesman, The, 148
Subedar, 29
Subh Azadi (Dawn of Freedom), xiii
Suhrawardy, Huseyn Shaheed, 251, 252, 253, 254, 255, 258, 259, 260
Suhrawardy-Bose-Roy formula, 260
Surat, 2, 5; Congress, 6
Swaraj, 14, 45, 60, 61, 64, 79

INDEX

Swarajists, 65, 66, 87
Swarajya Sabha, 39, 44, 63, 83
Sydenham, Lord, 22
Sylhet District, 157, 176, 177, 178

T

Tagore, Rabindranath, 21
Tairsee, 27
Taj Mahal Hotel, 14
Tamil, 144, 154
Tara village, xv
Telang, P.K., 28
Thakurdas, Purshotamdas, 60, 86
Third World, 144
Tilak, Lokmanya Bal Gangadhar, xiv, xvi, xviii, 1, 2, 3, 4, 5, 6, 7, 8, 9, 11, 13, 14, 15, 16, 18, 21, 22, 23, 24, 34, 35, 36, 37, 38, 39, 45, 52, 84, 98, 105, 129, 133, 144, 162, 173, 186, 240, 242, 247, 269
Time and Time, 155
Times of India, The, 27, 42, 48, 59, 86, 118
Tithal, 115
Town Hall, 26, 27, 28, 29, 30, 33
Trade Disputes Bill, 69
Transfer of Power in India, 229
Transfer of Power, The, 200, 227, 245
Treasury Bench, 76, 80
Tribune, The, 151
Trotsky, 241
Tulzapurkar, V.D., 33
Turkey, 109
Two-Nation Theory, 99, 100, 106, 112, 143, 153, 158, 235, 246, 250
Tyabji, Abbas, 34
Tyabji, Justice Badruddin, 3

U

Ulema, 83
Umar, Caliph, 154
Unionists, 176, 185
United Provinces (UP), 8; Legislature Council, 13, 16, 18, 101, 102
United States, 118, 246
Upanishad, 135
Urdu, 263, 268
USSR, 255

Uttar Pradesh (UP), 87, 103, 107, 130, 154, 157, 167, 171, 245, 265

V

Varnashrama Dharma, 135
Vedas, 135
Viceregal Lodge, 181
Viceroy, 4, 23, 60, 61
Viceroy's Executive Council, 23
Viceroy's Imperial Legislative Council, 9
Viceroy's Study Group, *see* Brain Trust
Vismi Sadi, 82

W

Wacha, Sir Dinshaw Edulji, 10, 28
Wakf bill, 9
Wavell, Viceroy Lord Archibald, 113, 160, 176, 202, 204, 205, 206, 208, 214, 215
Wavell: The Viceroy's Journal, 200, 204
Weldon, James, 155
Wells, Ian Bryant, 76, 111
White Paper Scheme, 93
Willingdon Crescent, 200
Willingdon, Lord, 1, 23, 24, 27, 29, 32, 33, 49, 76, 81
Wint, Guy, 173, 175
Wyatt, Major Woodrow, 170, 171, 182
Wylie, Francis, 131
Yakub, Sir Mohammad, 92
Young India, 129, 134, 135
Yusuf Meherally Centre, xv

Z

Zamindar, Vazira Fazila-Yacoobali, 247
Zetland, Lord, 145